Philosophy

Asking Questions—Seeking Answers

Philosophy

Asking Questions—Seeking Answers

SECOND EDITION

STEPHEN STICH
RUTGERS UNIVERSITY

TOM DONALDSON
SIMON FRASER UNIVERSITY

OXFORD
UNIVERSITY PRESS

Oxford University Press is a department of the University of Oxford.
It furthers the University's objective of excellence in research, scholarship,
and education by publishing worldwide. Oxford is a registered trade mark
of Oxford University Press in the UK and in certain other countries.

Published in the United States of America by Oxford University Press
198 Madison Avenue, New York, NY 10016, United States of America.

© 2024 by Oxford University Press

For titles covered by Section 112 of the US Higher Education Opportunity
Act, please visit www.oup.com/us/he for the latest information about
pricing and alternate formats.

All rights reserved. No part of this publication may be reproduced,
stored in a retrieval system, or transmitted, in any form or by any means,
without the prior permission in writing of Oxford University Press,
or as expressly permitted by law, by license, or under terms agreed with
the appropriate reprographics rights organization. Inquiries concerning
reproduction outside the scope of the above should be sent to the Rights
Department, Oxford University Press, at the address above.

You must not circulate this work in any other form
and you must impose this same condition on any acquirer

Library of Congress Cataloging-in-Publication Data

Names: Stich, Stephen P., author. | Donaldson, Tom (Philosopher) author.
Title: Philosophy: Asking Questions Seeking Answers / Stephen Stich,
   Rutgers University; Tom Donaldson, Simon Fraser University.
Description: [2e]. | New York : Oxford University Press, [2025] | Includes
   index. | Summary: "Philosophy: Asking Questions Seeking Answers is a
   brief and accessible guide designed for students with no prior knowledge
   of the subject. Written by renowned scholars Stephen Stich and Tom
   Donaldson, it focuses on the key issues in Western philosophy,
   presenting balanced coverage of each issue and challenging students to
   make up their own minds. Comprehensive enough to be used on its own,
   Philosophy can also be used as a supplement to any introductory
   anthology"—Provided by publisher.
Identifiers: LCCN 2023043712 (print) | LCCN 2023043713 (ebook) | ISBN
   9780197768013 (paperback) | ISBN 9780197768020 (epub) | ISBN
   9780197768037 (ebook)
Subjects: LCSH: Philosophy—Introductions.
Classification: LCC BD21 .S773 2025 (print) | LCC BD21 (ebook) | DDC
   100—dc23/eng/20231205
LC record available at https://lccn.loc.gov/2023043712
LC ebook record available at https://lccn.loc.gov/2023043713

Printed by Sheridan Books, Inc., United States of America

CONTENTS

Preface xiii

CHAPTER 1   **What Is Philosophy?   1**
    1.1 Philosophy Is Everywhere   1
    1.2 What Is a Philosophical Question?   2
    1.3 The Philosophical Method   4
    1.4 Philosophy and Science   5
    1.5 Why Bother?   6
    Discussion Question   6
    Notes   6

CHAPTER 2   **What Are Arguments, and How Should We Evaluate Them?   9**
    Introduction   9
    2.1 Premises and Conclusions   10
    2.2 Evaluating Arguments   13
    2.3 Deductive Validity   14
    2.4 Induction and Abduction   15
    2.5 Multistep Arguments   18
    2.6 Evaluating Multistep Arguments   20
    2.7 Some Arguments to Evaluate   23
    2.8 Answers to Problems   25
    What to Look at Next   28
    Glossary   29
    Notes   30

CHAPTER 3 Does God Exist? 31

Introduction 31
3.1 The First Cause Argument 33
3.2 Some Questions About the First Cause Argument 37
3.3 Leibniz's Cosmological Argument 38
3.4 The Design Argument 41
3.5 Criticisms of the Design Argument 44
3.6 Anselm's Ontological Argument 48
3.7 What, if Anything, is Wrong with Anselm's Ontological Argument? 52
3.8 A Pragmatic Case for Theism? 53
Conclusion 55
Glossary 56
Comprehension Questions 57
Discussion Questions 58
What to Look at Next 60
Notes 61

CHAPTER 4 Why Does God Leave Us to Suffer? 63

Introduction 63
4.1 Three Logical Puzzles for Theists 64
4.2 Introducing the Problem of Evil 66
4.3 Three Inadequate Responses 68
4.4 Rethinking the Nature of God 70
4.5 Theodicy 71
4.6 Skeptical Theism 74
Conclusion 75
Glossary 76
Comprehension Questions 77
Discussion Questions 77
What to Look at Next 79
Notes 79

CHAPTER 5 Can We Be Completely Certain of Anything? 81

Introduction 81
5.1 Descartes's Project 81
5.2 Certainty Is Hard to Find 83
5.3 Achieving Certainty 87
5.4 Clear and Distinct Perception 89
5.5 Descartes's Theism, and His Solution to the Evil Demon Problem 90

5.6 The Cartesian Circle   92
5.7 Descartes's Legacy   93
Conclusion   95
Glossary   95
Comprehension Questions   96
Discussion Questions   97
What to Look at Next   98
Notes   99

CHAPTER 6   **Can We Trust Our Senses?   101**
6.1 Rationalism and Empiricism   101
6.2 Indirect Realism   102
6.3 Primary and Secondary Qualities   105
6.4 Do Material Objects Really Exist?   109
6.5 Berkeley's Idealism   110
6.6 Direct Realism   116
Conclusion   117
Glossary   118
Comprehension Questions   120
Discussion Questions   121
What to Look at Next   122
Notes   123

CHAPTER 7   **Will the Sun Rise Tomorrow?   125**
Introduction   125
7.1 Making Predictions   126
7.2 Hume's Problem   128
7.3 Karl Popper   131
7.4 Peter Strawson   134
7.5 Epistemically Basic Beliefs   136
7.6 Beyond Enumerative Induction   138
Glossary   140
Comprehension Questions   140
Discussion Questions   141
What to Look at Next   142
Notes   143

CHAPTER 8   **What Is Knowledge?   145**
Introduction   145
8.1 Three Kinds of Knowledge   145
8.2 Analyzing Propositional Knowledge:
     The Easy Part—Belief and Truth   146

8.3 Analyzing Propositional Knowledge: The Hard
Part—Justification   147
8.4 Foundationalism   149
8.5 Coherentism   152
8.6 Internalism and Externalism   154
8.7 Fallibilism and Skepticism   156
8.8 Gettier Cases—A Challenge to the Justified True
Belief Account of Knowledge   158
Glossary   159
Comprehension Questions   161
Discussion Questions   162
What to Look at Next   163
Notes   164

CHAPTER 9   **Do We Have Free Will?   165**
9.1 What Is Determinism?   165
9.2 Incompatibilism   167
9.3 Compatibilism   170
9.4 Libertarianism   174
Glossary   178
Comprehension Questions   178
Discussion Questions   179
What to Look at Next   180
Notes   181

CHAPTER 10   **Race   183**
Introduction   183
10.1 Racialism   184
10.2 Nonracialist Meanings of "Race"   187
Summary   193
Glossary   194
Comprehension Questions   195
Discussion Questions   196
What to Look at Next   197
Notes   198

CHAPTER 11   **How Is Your Mind Related to Your Body?   201**
Introduction   201
11.1 Cartesian Dualism   204
11.2 Philosophical Behaviorism   209
11.3 The Mind-Brain Identity Theory   215
11.4 Functionalism   219

11.5 Physicalism, Zombies, and a Revival
of Dualism   225
Glossary   227
Comprehension Questions   231
Discussion Questions   232
What to Look at Next   233
Notes   235

CHAPTER 12   **Will You Be the Same Person in Ten Years?
Could You Survive Death?   239**
12.1 The Philosophical Issue and Its Practical
Importance   239
12.2 The Soul Theory   243
12.3 Problems for Soul Theory   245
12.4 Memory Theories   247
12.5 Personal Identity and the Brain   259
Glossary   262
Comprehension Questions   264
Discussion Questions   265
What to Look at Next   267
Notes   268

CHAPTER 13   **Are There Objective Truths About Right
and Wrong?   269**
Introduction   269
13.1 Objective Truth   270
13.2 The Divine Command Theory   272
13.3 Cultural Relativism   276
13.4 Subjectivism and Expressivism   280
13.5 The Qualified Attitude Theory   283
Conclusion   285
Glossary   286
Comprehension Questions   289
Discussion Questions   290
What to Look at Next   292
Notes   293

CHAPTER 14   **What Really Matters?   295**
Introduction   295
14.1 Hedonism   296
14.2 Sartre   300
14.3 Susan Wolf on Meaningfulness   305

Conclusion 309
Glossary 310
Comprehension Questions 312
Discussion Questions 312
What to Look at Next 313
Notes 314

CHAPTER 15 **What Should We Do? (Part I) 317**
15.1 Act Consequentialism and Act Utilitarianism 317
15.2 Objections to Act Utilitarianism 322
15.3 Rule Consequentialism and Rule Utilitarianism 325
15.4 Kant's Universalization Test 328
15.5 Kant's Humanity Formula 331
15.6 Comparing Kantianism and Consequentialism 333
Glossary 334
Comprehension Questions 336
Discussion Questions 337
What to Look at Next 338
Notes 339

CHAPTER 16 **What Should We Do? (Part II) 341**
Introduction 341
16.1 Is It Morally Wrong to Go to the Opera While People Are Starving? 342
16.2 Vegetarianism 347
16.3 Is Abortion Morally Wrong? 352
Glossary 359
Comprehension Questions 360
Discussion Questions 361
What to Look at Next 363
Notes 364

CHAPTER 17 **Why Democracy? 367**
Introduction 367
17.1 What Is Democracy? 369
17.2 The Basic Argument Against Democracy 371
17.3 A Modest Defense of Democracy 373
17.4 Are Democratic Countries Well Run? 376
17.5 Noninstrumental Defenses of Democracy 378
Conclusion 379
Glossary 380

Comprehension Questions 381
Discussion Questions 382
What to Look at Next 382
Appendix: A General Knowledge Quiz 383
Notes 385

Appendix A: Reading and Writing Tips 387
   Seven Tips on Reading Philosophy 387
   Eighteen Tips for Writing Philosophy Papers 389

Appendix B: The Truth About Philosophy Majors 395
   Careers 395
   Salaries 399
   Meaning 401
   Notes 401
   Resources 402

Glossary 403
Credits 423
Index 425

PREFACE

Who is this book for?

If you know little or nothing about philosophy, and you want to learn, this is the book for you. We will introduce some of the biggest questions in the subject. However, we keep it simple, and we start at the beginning.

Which philosophical topics do you cover?

You should check out our table of contents for a detailed answer, but briefly:

- Chapter 1 talks about what philosophy is.
- Chapter 2 gives you some tips on how to analyze arguments.
- Chapters 3 and 4 are about God.
- Chapters 5, 6, 7, and 8 are about epistemology: a branch of philosophy traditionally defined as the theory of knowledge.
- Chapters 9, 10, 11, and 12 are about what kind of a thing *you* are. Are you a purely physical thing, or do you have a nonphysical component—a mind or soul? Do you have free will? Could you survive death? What is race?
- Chapters 13, 14, 15 and 16 are about ethics.
- Chapter 17 is about the case for (and against!) democracy.

That's a lot to cover in a small book.

Well, yes, but we have to admit that there are many philosophical topics not covered in this book. There's not much about the history of philosophy, the philosophy of science, or the philosophy of art.

And the book is incomplete in another way. Both of us were trained in the Western philosophical tradition. This is a tradition that originated in Europe and has been strongly influenced by the Abrahamic religions—Judaism, Christianity, and Islam. This book is really about Western philosophy. If you want to learn about other philosophical traditions, you should consider picking up one or more of these books:

- Bryan W. Van Norden: *Introduction to Classical Chinese Philosophy*
- Mark Siderits: *Buddhism as Philosophy: An Introduction*
- J. N. Mohanty: *Classical Indian Philosophy*
- Lee M. Brown: *African Philosophy: New and Traditional Perspectives*
- Kwasi Wiredu: *A Companion to African Philosophy*
- Susana Nuccetelli, Ofelia Schutte, and Otávio Bueno: *A Companion to Latin American Philosophy*
- Eliot Deutsch and Ron Bontekoe: *A Companion to World Philosophies*

Can I skip the chapters that don't interest me?

The chapters of this book are largely independent. You can read them in any order, and you can omit chapters that don't interest you.

This stuff is interesting. What I else should look at?

We make recommendations for further reading at the end of each chapter. We recommend some movies too. And you might like to go to this book's website (www.oup.com/us/stich) for links to podcasts, videos, and so on.

How did you come to write this book?

Some books take a long time to create. This one has taken a very long time. The story of how this book came to be begins when the older of the two authors, Stephen Stich, was assigned to teach the Introduction to Philosophy lecture course shortly after he began his teaching career at the University of Michigan, fifty-five years ago. It was a daunting assignment since Stich had never taken an Introduction to Philosophy course as an undergraduate. Nor had he ever taken a big lecture course in philosophy. The Michigan Intro course was very big—almost 400 students taught in a huge lecture hall with both a main floor and a balcony. After checking out the lecture hall, Stich was terrified. He spent an entire summer doing nothing but preparing notes for Intro to Philosophy lectures. His goal was to present students with the best case to be made for both sides on a range of hotly debated issues that are central to Western philosophy.

When Stich stepped out onto the stage on the first day of class, microphone in hand, he was petrified. But about ten minutes into the lecture, he paused to take a sip of water and thought to himself, "Hey, this is fun!" He's been teaching an Introduction to Philosophy course almost every year since 1968, and it is still fun. Every year, the course evolves a bit, expanding material that went well in the previous few years and dropping material that didn't. What doesn't change is the goal of focusing on central issues in Western philosophy, presenting the best case for both sides of every issue considered, and challenging students to make up their own minds.

In 2010, Tom Donaldson, then a PhD student at Rutgers University, was a teaching assistant (TA) in Stich's course. At one of the weekly meetings with the course TAs, Stich noted that the course notes, which had migrated to PowerPoint slides over the years, might be the basis for a course textbook, but he doubted he would ever have enough time to write the book on his own. Donaldson said he would be interested in working on that project. And that's when the work on this book began in earnest.

We met with Robert Miller, our terrific editor at Oxford University Press, and planned to have the volume completed in about two years. But lots of stuff slowed us down. Donaldson spent two years as a Junior Fellow at Harvard, and then launched his teaching career at Stanford. Stich was organizing large international research teams to study how philosophical concepts varied across cultures. Chapters were written, critiqued, and rewritten. Two years stretched to eight. Throughout this long process, our goal has remained the same: to write a book that would offer students a lively and sophisticated introduction to some of the most important issues in Western philosophy, presenting both sides and encouraging students to make up their own minds about which side has the stronger case.

Is there anyone that you want to thank?

Lots of people have helped. Robert Miller, Jeff Marshall and the staff at Oxford University Press have been a constant source of good advice, encouragement, and patience. Robert also arranged for earlier drafts to be critiqued by more than a dozen colleagues who teach the Introduction to Philosophy course at a wide range of colleges and universities. Since their reports were anonymous, we can't thank these colleagues by name, but their invaluable feedback has led to many improvements in the book.

Our greatest debt is to the thousands of undergraduate students who have taken Stich's Introduction to Philosophy course over the last fifty-five years and to the dozens of graduate students who were teaching assistants in the course. They offered, and continue to offer, the best feedback on how to make the problems of philosophy clear, engaging, and fun. Four recent teaching assistants, Christopher Hauser, Olivia Odoffin, David Rose, and Michael Schapira, deserve special thanks since they used an earlier version of the material in this book and gave us a steady stream of useful suggestions on how to make the book better.

We would also like to thank Tae Shin Lee for his advice on Chapter 1, Jorah Dannenberg for his help with Chapter 15, Tessa Donaldson for her advice on Chapter 3, and Meena Krishnamurthy for helping us find the right quotation from Martin Luther King Jr. Jennifer Wang and Thomas Icard gave us helpful comments on many parts of the book.

Stephen Stich
Tom Donaldson

Oxford Learning Link

Oxford Learning Link delivers a wealth of engaging digital learning tools and resources to help both instructors and students get the most of their Oxford University Press title. Instructors can view instructor resources at www.oup.com/he/stich-donaldson2e.

Instructors

This title can be integrated directly into learning management systems. To find out more about integration, or if you have any questions about the course content, please contact your OUP representative at (800) 280-0280 or http://learninglink.oup.com/support

Oxford Learning Link for *Philosophy: Asking Questions, Seeking Answers* includes the following resources.

Instructor Resources

- Test Bank—test questions in multiple choice, short answer, and essay formats
- Instructor's Manual—includes chapter summaries, section summaries, and key terms with definitions
- Lecture PowerPoints—presentations for course instruction, enabling instructors and/or lecturers to spend less time preparing class materials and more time with students
- Figure PowerPoints—with high-resolution images from the text
- Chapter Quizzes
- Flashcards

THE TIMELINE OF WESTERN PHILOSOPHY

Philosophers Discussed in This Volume	Some Important Historical Figures & Events
THE ANCIENT PERIOD	
Socrates (c. 470–399 BCE)	Athenians defeat Persians at Marathon (490 BCE)
Democritus (c. 460–370 BCE)	
Plato (c. 428–348 BCE)	Alexander the Great (356–323 BCE)
Aristotle (384–322 BCE)	Julius Caesar (100–44 BCE)
Epicurus (341–270 BCE)	Jesus Christ (c. 4 BCE–30/33 CE)
	Romans destroy the temple in Jerusalem (70 CE)
THE MIDDLE AGES	
Augustine of Hippo (St. Augustine) (354–430)	Fall of the Roman Empire (476)
	Muhammad (571–632)
Anselm (c. 1033–1109)	Norman conquest of England (1066)
Thomas Aquinas (1225–1274)	The Black Death (1346–1353)
FROM THE RENAISSANCE TO THE PRESENT	
René Descartes (1596–1650)	Leonardo da Vinci (1452–1519)
Princess Elisabeth of Bohemia (1618–1680)	Nicolaus Copernicus (1473–1543)
Blaise Pascal (1623–1662)	Christopher Columbus "discovers" America (1492)
John Locke (1632–1704)	
Gottfried Wilhelm Leibniz (1646–1716)	William Shakespeare (1564–1616)
George Berkeley (1685–1753)	Galileo Galilei (1564–1642)
Voltaire (1694–1778)	Rembrandt van Rijn (1606–1669)
Thomas Reid (1710–1796)	Isaac Newton (1642–1727)
David Hume (1711–1776)	Napoleon Bonaparte (1769–1821)
Immanuel Kant (1724–1804)	Ludwig van Beethoven (1770–1827)
William Paley (1743–1805)	American Revolution (1775–1783)
Jeremy Bentham (1748–1832)	French Revolution (1789–1791)
John Stuart Mill (1806–1873)	Charles Darwin (1809–1882)
William James (1842–1910)	Karl Marx (1818–1883)
Bertrand Russell (1872–1970)	Queen Victoria (1819–1901)
G. E. Moore (1873–1958)	Friedrich Nietzsche (1844–1900)
Martin Heidegger (1889–1976)	Sigmund Freud (1856–1939)
Gilbert Ryle (1900–1976)	American Civil War (1861–1865)
Karl Popper (1902–1994)	Franklin Delano Roosevelt (1882–1945)
Jean-Paul Sartre (1905–1980)	Ludwig Wittgenstein (1889–1951)
A. J. Ayer (1910–1989)	Mao Zedong (1893–1976)
Elizabeth Anscombe (1919–2001)	World War I (1914–1918)
Peter Strawson (1919–2006)	Martin Luther King Jr. (1929–1968)
Alvin Plantinga (1932–)	World War II (1939–1945)
Derek Parfit (1942–2017)	Atomic bomb dropped on Hiroshima (1945)
Peter Singer (1946–)	Apollo 11 commander Neil Armstrong walks on the Moon (1969)
Susan Wolf (1952–)	
Kwame Anthony Appiah (1954–)	Terrorist attack destroys World Trade Center (2001)

Philosophy

Asking Questions—Seeking Answers

The *Death of Socrates*, painted by Jacques-Louis David in 1787. Socrates, though he is about to die, is still teaching. Plato sits at the foot of the bed.

CHAPTER 1

What Is Philosophy?

1.1 Philosophy Is Everywhere

Many people think that philosophy is an esoteric subject. Admittedly, professional philosophers in universities do sometimes devote themselves to abstruse questions. We have colleagues who've devoted many years to figuring out exactly how "a" and "the" differ in meaning, and we have friends who stay up late at night discussing whether God could change the laws of logic.

But in fact, philosophical questions often come up in everyday life. Think about the familiar question of whether it is okay to buy and eat meat. This is a philosophical question, and it quickly leads to others. As we'll see in chapter 16, some vegetarians argue that you should not buy meat because it is wrong to inflict pain on animals. Meat-eaters might reply that it is okay to buy meat from humane farms, or that it is okay to buy the meat of animals incapable of experiencing pain—oysters, for example.

Let's think about that last claim for a moment. How can we tell whether oysters experience pain? You might think that we can figure out whether oysters experience pain by investigating their nervous systems. But to do this, we'd have to understand the relation between conscious mental states (e.g., pain) and the nervous system—and this is a notoriously difficult philosophical problem. We'll discuss the topic in chapter 11.

Some Christians argue that it is okay to eat meat on the basis of certain passages from the book of Genesis, including this one:

> God blessed Noah and his sons, and said to them, "Be fruitful and multiply, and fill the Earth. The fear and dread of you shall rest on every animal of the Earth, and on every bird of the air, on everything that creeps on the ground, and on all the fish of the sea; into your hand they are delivered. Every moving thing that lives shall be food for you; and just as I gave you the green plants, I give you everything."[1]

Of course, this argument won't convince vegetarians who aren't Jewish or Christian, and even some Jews and Christians question this approach to scripture.

In a few minutes of conversation, we've already come across some deep and important philosophical questions:

- Is it okay to eat meat?
- How is consciousness related to the nervous system?
- Does God exist?
- Is the Bible a good source of information about God's wishes?

These are not esoteric questions. You may not think about such questions every day, but everyone has to confront philosophical questions from time to time.

1.2 What Is a Philosophical Question?

It might strike you that the philosophical questions in the list that we present have little in common. Why are all these classified as *philosophical* questions? What *is* a philosophical question?

According to a popular story, when G. E. Moore (a prominent British philosopher of the early twentieth century) was asked what philosophy is, he simply pointed to his bookshelf and said that philosophy is "what all these books are about." We sympathize: it is far from easy to say what all the different philosophical questions have in common. But we will try to give you a more informative answer than Moore.

Part of the answer, we think, is that much of philosophy concerns "normative" questions—that is, questions about right and wrong, good and bad. This includes questions about how we should live ("Is it okay to eat meat?"), what constitutes good reasoning ("What are the limitations of the scientific method?"), and how society should be structured ("Should it be compulsory to vote?").

A list of philosophical questions

- Is it possible to travel backward in time?
- Is it good to be patriotic? What are the differences, if any, between patriotism and nationalism?
- Why does God permit so much suffering?
- What is the difference between knowledge and opinion?
- What is the scientific method? Can we use the scientific method in ethics?
- Could a digital computer have consciousness?
- God is sometimes said to be "all powerful," but what does that mean?
- How can we distinguish true experts from charlatans?
- Do you have a nonphysical soul, which will persist after your death?
- Do you have free will?
- What is art?
- When, if ever, is it okay to lie?
- Can we know anything for certain?
- In social science, to what extent should we assume that people make choices rationally?
- What limits are there, if any, to the right to free speech?
- Is it good to have faith? If so, what is faith?
- Who should be allowed to vote in elections?
- What are numbers?

Another part of the answer is that philosophers spend a lot of time questioning our most basic assumptions. For example, it is a central principle of Christian thought that God exists and that the Bible is a good source of information about him. Philosophers question these assumptions.

This last choice of example is perhaps misleading because it might suggest that philosophy is an antireligious activity. In fact, it is not only religious assumptions that are challenged by philosophers. Philosophers also scrutinize the basic assumptions of science, politics, art ... everything. Which may explain why philosophy has sometimes been regarded as a subversive activity. Indeed, the ancient Greek thinker Socrates (c. 470–399 BCE), who is sometimes regarded as the founder of the Western philosophical tradition, was condemned to death for "corrupting the youth." In a Socratic spirit, we hope that this book will corrupt you.

1.3 The Philosophical Method

Philosophers attempt to state their views *clearly* and *precisely*, and they give explicit *arguments* for their claims.

We should explain what we mean when we say that philosophers attempt to state their views clearly and precisely. In 1948, philosophers Frederick Copleston and Bertrand Russell debated the existence of God. Their discussion began like this:

> COPLESTON: As we are going to discuss the existence of God, it might perhaps be as well to come to some provisional agreement as to what we understand by the term "God." I presume that we mean a supreme personal Being—distinct from the world and Creator of the world. Would you agree—provisionally at least—to accept this statement as the meaning of the term "God"?
> RUSSELL: Yes, I accept this definition.
> COPLESTON: Well, my position is the affirmative position that such a Being actually exists, and that His existence can be proved philosophically. Perhaps you would tell me if your position is that of agnosticism or of atheism. I mean, would you say that the non-existence of God can be proved?
> RUSSELL: No, I should not say that: my position is agnostic.[2]

Notice that the two philosophers aren't content just to say that Copleston believes God exists while Russell doesn't. They articulate their disagreement more precisely than that. They agree on what they mean by "God," and they clarify that Copleston believes God's existence "can be proved philosophically" while Russell's position is agnostic—that is, Russell doesn't believe God exists, but he doesn't think that God's nonexistence can be proven.[3]

What do we mean when we say that philosophers attempt to give explicit arguments for their claims? We will talk about arguments and how to evaluate them in chapter 2. For now, suffice it to say that philosophers don't like to defend their views merely by appeal to authority or tradition. As we've said, one of the goals of philosophy is to scrutinize received wisdoms; it defeats the point of the exercise to assume that the existing authorities have figured it all out already.

This is not to say that appeals to authority are always fallacious. On the contrary, it is often perfectly appropriate to gather information from experts. Our point is that, in a philosophical context, our goal is to present arguments for our views without simply leaning upon existing authorities.

For example, suppose that you're thinking about how the state should be structured. You might find it helpful to read through classics like *The Federalist Papers*; however, in philosophical work, you're expected to present arguments for your claims. "Hamilton said so" or "Madison said so" won't cut it.

It is perhaps for this reason that philosophers don't usually get involved in the interpretation of sacred texts. This is part of what separates philosophy from theology and religious studies.

1.4 Philosophy and Science

It is sometimes suggested that philosophy is not needed anymore because science has taken over. Stephen Hawking and Leonard Mlodinow don't mince their words:

> How does the universe behave? What is the nature of reality? Where did all this come from? Did the universe need a creator? ... Traditionally these are questions for philosophy, but philosophy is dead. Philosophy has not kept up with modern developments in science, particularly physics. Scientists have become the bearers of the torch of discovery in our quest for knowledge.[4]

Hawking and Mlodinow are right about one thing: it is important when thinking about philosophical questions to keep up-to-date with relevant work in the sciences. It would be a big mistake, for example, to write about which animals can experience pain without drawing upon the work of psychologists, zoologists, neuroscientists, and so on. But it won't surprise you to learn that we reject Hawking's claim that philosophy is dead. Our reason is simple: there are many philosophical questions currently unaddressed in the scientific literature. No matter how much time you spend reading zoology and neuroscience journals, you won't find an answer to the question of whether it's morally okay to eat fish. Psychology and computer science journals won't tell you whether it's possible for a digital computer to be conscious. Psychology journals contain important discoveries about human decision-making, but the question of whether we have free will is left unanswered.

In saying this, we don't mean to imply that philosophical questions can't ultimately be answered using scientific methods. Many philosophers have made it their goal to find ways of applying scientific methods in new domains, and we applaud these efforts. All we're saying is, again, that many philosophical questions are *currently* outside the scope of the sciences as they are usually delimited.

1.5 Why Bother?

Students in their first philosophy class (especially those for whom the class is compulsory!) often ask why they should bother with philosophy. Our answer is that philosophy is inevitable. We all have to think about how to live, and so we are forced to think about normative questions at one time or another. What's more, we now live in pluralist societies; that is, we live with people whose worldviews differ greatly from our own. When we meet such people and try to understand our differences, we are forced to discuss our basic assumptions—and this is philosophy.

So even though philosophical questions don't come up every day, we're all forced to confront them sometimes. We hope this book helps you to think about philosophical questions and to reach your own conclusions.

And even if you *aren't* able to reach your own conclusions, we think you can benefit from the time spent thinking the issues through. In such cases, philosophy shows you something important about the limitations of your knowledge. What's more, even if you can't find the right answer to a philosophical question, you may still be able to achieve a deeper understanding of other people's views about the topic. And the better we understand each other's views, the better we understand each other.

Discussion Question

1. Look at the list of philosophical questions with a friend. Do the two of you disagree about the answer to a question? If you find a disagreement, can you articulate it precisely? Then, how well can you give an argument supporting your view?

Notes

1. Gen. 9:1–3 (NRSV).
2. You may be able to find parts of this discussion online. For a full transcript, look in Bertrand Russell, *Why I Am Not a Christian* (London: Routledge, 2004), 125–152.

3. Russell and Copleston could perhaps have been still more precise about their disagreement. Their claim that God is "supreme" is, we think, slightly obscure. We suspect that when Copleston says that God is "supreme," he meant that God is all-powerful, all-knowing, and perfectly morally good—but it's hard to be completely sure.
4. Stephen Hawking and Leonard Mlodinow, *The Grand Design* (New York: Bantam Books, 2010), 1.

CHAPTER 2
....

What Are Arguments, and How Should We Evaluate Them?

Introduction

You probably know people who have profoundly different worldviews from you and profoundly different views about how to lead a good life. Perhaps you disagree about whether there is a god, whether it's okay to eat meat, or whether morality is objective. Philosophy is a conversation about questions like these—a conversation between people with very different personal convictions. In philosophy, evocations of personal feelings are usually of little value because people's feelings about philosophical questions differ so greatly. Appeals to authority and tradition are not much better: one person's revered authority is another person's discredited blowhard.

So what is to be done? The short answer is that philosophers present arguments for their views.

Sometimes the word "argument" is used to mean *dispute* or *debate* or *quarrel*. That's not what we mean. An **argument**, in our sense, is an attempt to justify some conclusion by rational means. Here is an example:

> The quality of government in a country correlates positively with voter turnout: the greater the voter turnout, the better the government. Therefore, low voter turnout causes bad government. So if you're eligible and you fail to vote, you make the government worse. What's more, democracy can only persist if enough people turn out

to vote; therefore, if you're eligible to vote and you don't do so, you imperil democracy itself. It follows that if you're eligible to vote, it's morally wrong for you not to do so.

The **conclusion** of this argument is that if a person is eligible to vote, then it's morally wrong for that person not to do so. If you are unconvinced, you should be able to articulate *where* exactly you think the argument fails. And perhaps you should back up your claims by presenting arguments of your own . . . and so the conversation that is philosophy continues.

In this chapter, we discuss the structure of arguments, and we talk about how to evaluate arguments. It will help to use simple examples; indeed, some of our examples may seem rather goofy. But please don't be put off: there's nothing goofy about the techniques we describe in this chapter. We're describing the methods of the world's foremost philosophers.

2.1 Premises and Conclusions

Here is the simplest argument you'll find in this book:

> No elephant is a reptile. Jumbo is an elephant. Therefore, Jumbo is not a reptile.

The conclusion of this argument is that Jumbo is not a reptile. The other two statements are **premises**—these are statements that the writer assumes while making the case for the conclusion. The premises are the starting points of the argument. Sometimes it's helpful to write an argument in this form, with a horizontal line separating the premises from the conclusion:

> No elephant is a reptile.
>
> Jumbo is an elephant.
> ___
> Jumbo is not a reptile.

The advantage of presenting arguments this way is that it makes explicit what the conclusion of the argument is and what the premises are.

Here is another example:

> Fido didn't come in through the cat flap: it's tiny, and Fido is a large dog.

In this case, the writer assumes that the cat flap is tiny and that Fido is a large dog; these are the premises. The writer infers that Fido could not have come in through the cat flap; this is the conclusion.

The cat flap is tiny.
Fido is a large dog.
Fido didn't come in through the cat flap.

Sometimes a writer will add extraneous comments to an argument:

> One of you ate the cookies, for Pete's sake! Since you all deny it—which is infuriating—one of you must be lying. (Why do we have to do this every week?)

The argument in this passage is this:

> One of you ate the cookies.
> Each of you denies having eaten the cookies.
> One of you is lying.

"For Pete's sake," "which is infuriating," and "Why do we have to do this every week?" are not parts of the argument; they are mere asides.

Sometimes a writer will explicitly identify the conclusion and premises. Very often, however, it takes some effort on the part of the reader to find them. There are certain giveaway words and phrases often used to mark the conclusion of an argument. For example:

therefore	hence
consequently	so
in conclusion	thus
it follows that	necessarily
then	we infer that
implies that	

Consider, for example, this argument:

> If taxes are not increased, the budget deficit will become very large. We should not let the budget get out of control. Thus, taxes should be raised.

The word "thus" indicates that "taxes should be raised" is the conclusion. The other two sentences are premises.

Another way of marking the conclusion of an argument is to use the verb "must." For example:

> Jonathan *must* be home because his car is in the driveway.

The conclusion of this short argument is that Jonathan is home; the premise is that Jonathan's car is in the driveway.

There are also certain giveaway words and phrases in English that a writer can use to indicate that some statement is a premise:

I suppose that	it is assumed that
since	because
for	as
on the grounds that	for the following reason
follows from the fact that	given that
may be inferred from the fact that	

Consider, for example, this argument:

> Alan must have burnt the bagel because there is smoke in the kitchen.

The word "because" indicates that "there is smoke in the kitchen" is a premise. "Alan burnt the bagel" is the conclusion.

Sometimes a writer will not use giveaway expressions. For example:

> John stole the laptop. It was either John or Ashni, and Ashni would never steal.

There are no giveaway words here, so we just have to apply common sense to figure out what the conclusion of the argument is and what the premises are.

> It was either John or Ashni who stole the laptop.
> <u>Ashni would never steal.</u>
> John stole the laptop.

Look at the arguments that follow. In each case, identify the premises and the conclusion:

(a) Tom was at the party, for sure. He must have been drinking because *everybody* at the party was drinking.
(b) Everyone who lives in Snooty Towers is stuck up. Mehdi lives in Snooty Towers. Therefore, Mehdi is a snob.
(c) You should stop dating James. He swears at strangers in the street; he never leaves a tip when he goes to a restaurant; and his breath smells.
(d) The walking stick won't be very useful to Li Na: the stick is rather short, and she is very tall.
(e) A long holiday would be better for both of us, so we should go for it!

2.2 Evaluating Arguments

When evaluating an argument, it is important to think about two questions. First: Are the premises of this argument true? Second: Assuming that the premises are true, to what extent do they support the conclusion? Here is an example:

Diet soda drinkers are more likely to be obese than people who do not drink diet soda.

Drinking diet soda causes obesity.

There is some evidence that the premise of this argument is true, at least in the United States.[1] Nevertheless, we don't think that this is a good argument. As the cliché goes, "correlation doesn't imply causation": even if it is true that there is a correlation between diet soda drinking and obesity, it doesn't follow that drinking diet soda causes obesity. After all, it might be the other way around: perhaps the correlation exists because people who put on weight respond by drinking diet soda.

In saying that this is a bad argument, we are not denying the truth of its conclusion. Some public health experts have argued that drinking diet soda causes obesity, and we do not dispute their claim. We claim only that this argument, as it stands, does little to support their position. This illustrates an important point: a bad argument can nevertheless have a true conclusion. Don't confuse the question "Is this a good argument?" with the question "Do you agree with this writer's conclusions?"

Have a look at the following arguments. In each case, consider the two crucial questions: *Are the premises of this argument true?* and *Do the premises of the argument, if true, support the conclusion?*

(f) Any person born in the United States is eligible for US citizenship.
Tom Cruise is a US citizen.
Tom Cruise was born in the United States.

(g) Every octopus is a cephalopod.
No cephalopod has a spine.
No octopus has a spine.

(h) Extraterrestrial life has never been observed.
There is no extraterrestrial life in our galaxy.

Aristotle (384–322 BCE) made seminal contributions to the theory of logic.

2.3 Deductive Validity

Here is another argument for you to evaluate. Think about it before reading on:

> The population of Kenya is less than 70 million.
> The population of Nigeria is more than 150 million.
> The population of Nigeria is more than the population of Kenya.

Even if you don't know whether the premises of this argument are true, you should be able to see that *if* the premises are true, *then* the conclusion must be true as well. If the premises are true, this guarantees the truth of the conclusion. The argument is, to use the jargon, **deductively valid** (or just "valid" for short).

Here are some more examples:

> Lou owns a dog, and he owns a cat.
> Lou owns a dog.

> Everyone at the party is married.
> John is at the party.
> John is married.

> Ashni is married to Jo.
> Jo is married to Ashni.

In every case, it is guaranteed that *if* the premises are true, the conclusion must be true as well.

This is an argument that is *not* valid:

> Desiree eats sushi for lunch every day.
> Desiree likes the taste of sushi.

This argument is not valid because the truth of the premise doesn't *guarantee* the truth of the conclusion. Even if it's true that Desiree eats sushi for lunch every day, it might nevertheless be false that she likes the taste of sushi—perhaps she only eats sushi because her doctor advised it.

An argument is said to be "sound" if it is valid *and* has true premises.

Take a look at these arguments. Which are valid?

(i) Mei is either at the store or at home.
   Mei is not at home.
   Mei is at the store.

(j) Tiki is a bird.
   Tiki can fly.

(k) Everyone who can run 100 meters in less than eleven seconds is on the team.
   Ella is on the team.
   Ella can run 100 meters in less than eleven seconds.

2.4 Induction and Abduction

Deductively valid arguments are important, especially in mathematics. But arguments that are not valid can be very persuasive too.

Suppose that you are a zoologist studying a newly discovered type of bird (the "snocker bird," let's say). You do this by making observations of some sample of snocker birds and drawing conclusions about snocker birds in general. For example, you might argue the following:

<u>All the snocker birds in my sample have green heads.</u>
All snocker birds have green heads.

Is this argument convincing? This depends on the sample. If your argument is to be convincing, you need a large enough sample: it is not enough to observe only two or three snocker birds. Your sample must also be *varied*. In other words, you should observe both male and female snocker birds; you should observe snocker birds of different ages; you should observe snocker birds from different places and at different times of the year; and so on. Assuming that your sample is sufficiently large and varied, however, the argument is persuasive.

Even so, the argument about the snocker birds isn't deductively valid. Even if you studied a large and varied sample of snocker birds, all of which were observed to have green heads, it remains possible (though perhaps unlikely) that some snocker birds outside the sample do not have green heads. This illustrates the point that not all persuasive arguments are deductively valid.

The argument about the snocker birds is an example of **enumerative induction** (or induction for short). In an inductive argument, you start by identifying some pattern in cases that have been studied; you suggest on this basis that the pattern will extend to other cases as well.

Here are some further examples:

<u>Every cake I have bought from Tina's Café has been stale.</u>
Most of the cakes sold at Tina's Café are stale.

<u>So far, no emperor penguin has been seen to lay more than one egg in a year.</u>
Emperor penguins lay no more than one egg in a year.

I've met several of John's friends, and they have all been soccer enthusiasts.
<u>Sean is John's friend.</u>
Sean is a soccer enthusiast.

Every dog I have owned has been badly behaved.

The next dog I own will be badly behaved.

We will further discuss enumerative induction in chapter 7. In that chapter, we focus on cases in which induction is used to make a prediction based on past observations. For example, in New York City, every year so far it has been true that on average it is hotter in July than in February. And so, by induction, we anticipate that next year in New York, July will be on average hotter than February.

Now let's talk about **abduction**. When one gives an abductive argument, one starts with a number of observations, and one puts forward an explanation for the observations. If one judges that the proffered explanation is a good explanation and better than any available alternatives, one cautiously infers that the explanation is correct.

Let's look at an example. Suppose that you wake up one morning and find, to your surprise, that on the kitchen table there is a used bowl, an open carton of milk, and an open box of cereal. It occurs to you that this might be because your roommate overslept, had breakfast, and then rushed out of the house, not having enough time to clean up.

If this strikes you as more credible than any other explanation, you are likely to conclude that your explanation is correct:

There is a used bowl, an open carton of milk, and an open box of cereal on the kitchen table.

My roommate overslept.

This sort of argument is often called **inference to the best explanation**, for obvious reasons.

Many philosophers believe that scientific theories are commonly supported by abduction. Newton's theory of gravitation is a plausible example. Newton started with a collection of observations: observations of the motions of cannonballs, the planets, the Moon, the tides, and so on. He found that he could explain all of these observations using his theory of gravitation. Since this was better than any other explanation available at the time, the theory was accepted.

(l) Give two more examples of enumerative induction.

(m) Give one more example of abduction.

(n) Give another example of the use of abduction in the sciences.

2.5 Multistep Arguments

Have a look at these two arguments:

All frogs are amphibians.
Fernando is a frog.
Fernando is an amphibian.

Fernando is an amphibian.
All amphibians are vertebrates.
Fernando is a vertebrate.

Notice that the conclusion of the left-hand argument is the same as one of the premises of the right-hand argument. You might want to join these two arguments together to make one longer argument.

Multistep arguments like this are hard to present clearly. One way is to number the statements and use marginal comments to explain how the statements are related:

(1) All frogs are amphibians.   (Premise)
(2) Fernando is a frog.   (Premise)
(3) Fernando is an amphibian.   (From 1, 2)
(4) All amphibians are vertebrates.   (Premise)
(5) Fernando is a vertebrate.   (From 3, 4)

Here is another multistep argument:

If it was the taxi driver who murdered the drummer, there would have been blood on the seats of the taxi. But there was no blood in the taxi. It was either the taxi driver or the roadie who murdered the drummer. Since it can't have been the taxi driver, it must have been the roadie.

It is clear that the final conclusion of this argument is that the roadie murdered the drummer. The writer reaches this conclusion by saying that the murderer was either the taxi driver or the roadie, but that it wasn't the taxi driver:

It was either the taxi driver or the roadie who murdered the drummer.
The taxi driver didn't murder the drummer.
The roadie murdered the drummer.

The writer backs up the second premise of this argument with another argument:

If it was the taxi driver who murdered the drummer, there would have been blood on the seats of the taxi.
There was no blood in the taxi.
The taxi driver did not murder the drummer.

Putting the two parts of the argument together, we get:

(1) If it was the taxi driver who murdered the drummer, there would have been blood on the seats of the taxi. (Premise)
(2) There was no blood in the taxi. (Premise)
(3) The taxi driver didn't murder the drummer. (From 1, 2)
(4) It was either the taxi driver or the roadie that murdered the drummer. (Premise)
(5) The roadie murdered the drummer. (From 3, 4)

Now let's look at an argument that is more complex and philosophically interesting. You may recognize this passage from the beginning of the chapter. (Note that "voter turnout" is the percentage of eligible voters who cast a ballot in an election.)

> The quality of government in a country correlates positively with voter turnout: the greater the voter turnout, the better the government. Therefore, low voter turnout causes bad government. So if you're eligible, and you fail to vote, you make the government worse. What's more, democracy can only persist if enough people vote; therefore, if you're eligible to vote and you don't do so, you imperil democracy itself. It follows that if you're eligible to vote, it's morally wrong for you not to do so.

The writer's conclusion is "if you're eligible to vote, it's morally wrong for you not to do so." The writer provides two reasons for accepting this conclusion: first, "if you're eligible, and you fail to vote, you make the government worse," and second, "if you're eligible to vote and you don't do so, you imperil democracy itself." So part of the argument is this:

> If you're eligible and you fail to vote, you make the government worse.
> <u>If you're eligible to vote and you don't, you imperil democracy itself.</u>
> If you're eligible to vote, it's morally wrong for you not to do so.

The author backs up the contention that those who choose not to vote "make the government worse" by saying that low voter turnout causes bad government. The author infers this latter claim from the observation that countries with greater voter turnout have better government. The author backs up the contention that those who choose not to vote "imperil democracy itself" by claiming that "democracy can persist only if enough people vote."

Putting all this together, the argument is as follows:

(1) The quality of government in a country correlates positively with voter turnout. (Premise)
(2) Low voter turnout causes bad government. (From 1)
(3) If you're eligible and you fail to vote, you make the government worse. (From 2)
(4) Democracy can only persist if enough people vote. (Premise)
(5) If you're eligible to vote and you don't do so, you imperil democracy itself. (From 4)
(6) If you're eligible to vote, it's morally wrong for you not to do so. (From 3, 5)

Here are some multistep arguments for you to analyze:

(o) All the guys in ΓΔ are rude. John is in ΓΔ, so he's rude too. You shouldn't invite rude people to your parties, so John shouldn't be invited.
(p) Joe is often mean to me, so either he loves me or he hates me. I've done nothing to make him dislike me, so he loves me.
(q) Mr. Singh is at least fifty years old, since he was born in the 1950s. So he must be older than Min.
(r) Four, nine, sixteen, twenty-five, thirty-six, and forty-nine all have an odd number of factors. So *all* square numbers have an odd number of factors. Now 2,401 is square, so it has an odd number of factors.
(s) I only have ten dollars to spend. The starters at The Snail cost more than that, so that's out. I shouldn't take Amie to The Rose either because they don't serve vegetarian food. Those are the only two restaurants open. So we should stay in tonight.

2.6 Evaluating Multistep Arguments

When you evaluate an argument, it's often a good idea to write out the argument as a series of numbered statements first. That way, if you criticize the argument, then you can be precise in your criticism: you can say *exactly* where you think the argument goes wrong. To see how this works, let's look again at the argument about the supposed duty to vote from the last section.

(1) The quality of government in a country   (Premise)
    correlates positively with the voter turnout.
(2) Low voter turnout causes bad government.   (From 1)
(3) If you're eligible and you fail to vote, you   (From 2)
    make the government worse.
(4) Democracy can only persist if enough   (Premise)
    people vote.
(5) If you're eligible to vote and you don't, you   (From 4)
    imperil democracy itself.
(6) If you're eligible to vote, it's morally wrong   (From 3, 5)
    for you not to.

To evaluate the argument, we examine all six statements in turn.

1. To evaluate premise (1) properly, we would need to do some serious empirical research. We have no idea what the result of this research would be, so we don't know whether premise (1) is true.
2. The inference from (1) to (2) is questionable. Suppose for the moment that the quality of government does indeed correlate positively with voter turnout. This *might* be because low voter turnout causes bad government—but this isn't clearly the correct explanation. Perhaps it works the other way around: when government is bad, this causes disillusioned voters to stay at home on the day of the election.
3. The inference from (2) to (3) is also questionable, which you can see by way of analogy. It may well be that, other things being equal, an increase in the number of cars on the road causes an increase in the number of traffic accidents. It doesn't follow that each individual driver causes an increase in the number of traffic accidents.
4. We are inclined to think that (4) is true: if voter turnout were persistently below some threshold in some country, the country could not continue to function as a democracy. However, it is not at all clear how many people are "enough"—that is, it's not clear how many need to vote to ensure democracy continues.
5. We don't think that (5) follows from (4). An eligible voter might reasonably protest, "In my country, it's clear that 'enough' people will vote, even if I do not. So if I choose not to vote, I do not imperil democracy."

6. The inference from (3) and (5) to (6) may seem strong, but we have a caveat to add. Suppose that, on election day, you failed to vote because you were doing some other important thing: perhaps you were putting out a fire or performing surgery. In this case, it seems, you were not obliged to vote. So perhaps the conclusion of the argument ought to be more nuanced: if you're eligible to vote, it's morally wrong for you not to do so, unless you have something more important to do on the day of the election.

Now for a second example:

> I assume that God exists. Then he is all-knowing, and he existed before you were born. Being all-knowing, before you were born God knew *everything* that would happen in your life. He could foresee your every action and every decision. It follows that your whole life was predetermined, and so none of your choices has been genuinely free. Thus, you don't have free will.

We encourage you to have a go at evaluating this argument before looking at our evaluation.

This is our analysis of this argument:

(1) God exists. (Premise)
(2) God is all-knowing. (From 1)
(3) God existed before you were born. (From 1)
(4) Before you were born God knew *everything* that would happen in your life. (From 2, 3)
(5) It follows that your whole life was predetermined. (From 4)
(6) None of your choices has been genuinely free. (From 5)
(7) You don't have free will. (From 6)

Now we can evaluate the argument. Once again, we do this by going through the steps one by one.

1. We won't say much about (1) here. We discuss the existence of God in chapters 3 and 4.
2. It has often been assumed in the past that God is all-knowing if he exists. Nevertheless, we could reject the inference from (1) to

(2). We could endorse a revisionary version of theism, according to which God is not all-knowing.
3. The inference from (1) to (3) is more difficult to reject. It's hard to believe that God exists, but that he only came into existence during your lifetime.
4. An obvious definition of "all-knowing" is this: an omniscient being is a being who knows *everything*. Given this definition, (4) does seem to follow from (2) and (3). But we could reject this inference by insisting on a different definition of "all-knowing." Perhaps to be all-knowing is to know everything *which it is possible to know*. On this definition, it's not so obvious that (4) follows from (2) and (3).
5. If we accept (4) but reject (5), we'll end up with a view on which God knew all our actions in advance, but even so, those actions weren't predetermined. It's difficult to know whether this position is coherent: we'd need to think very carefully about what "predetermine" means to figure this out.
6. As we discuss in chapter 9, some philosophers (**compatibilists**) think that our having free will is compatible with **determinism**. Perhaps we could adopt a similar view, and say that our actions are free despite being predetermined. So the inference from (5) to (6) is not beyond dispute.
7. The inference from (6) to (7) looks solid. If there's a mistake in the argument, it isn't here.

2.7 Some Arguments to Evaluate

(t) Weather forecasts for the coming week or so are more or less accurate, but longer range weather forecasts are untrustworthy. Also, the longer the range of the forecast, the less trustworthy it is. When climate scientists make predictions about global temperatures over the next few decades, they are, in effect, issuing very long-term weather forecasts. So these predictions are not to be taken seriously.

(u) We all know that it is very difficult to lead a completely monogamous life. Even in the case of couples who are devoted to monogamy, so-called cheating is very common. Nevertheless, most people continue to believe that monogamy should be our goal. I think that this is wrong. It is a mistake, I think, to live monogamously. Monogamy is rare in the animal kingdom. What's more, none of the species most closely related to humans are monogamous. This shows that monogamy is unnatural. Our problem is not that we fail to live up to the ideal of monogamy; our problem is that we make this our ideal in the first place.

(v) A given quantity of money is worth more to a poor person than to a rich person. (For example, for a rich person, $1,000 is a weekend in New York; for a poor person, $1,000 is the difference between going hungry and having enough to eat.) This means that if a quantity of money is taken from a rich person and transferred to a poor person, the loss of welfare to the rich person is smaller than the gain in welfare to the poor person. This means that a redistributive system of tax and benefits increases the average welfare level in society. The government's goal should be to increase the average level of welfare in society. And so the government should maintain a redistributive system of tax and benefits.

(w) Even among protagonists of a free market society, there are some who claim that markets are "morally neutral." This allegation constitutes a dangerous concession to the enemies of freedom.... In fact the judgement is comprehensively mistaken. Markets are not morally neutral. They both presuppose and generate virtue.... Moral action presupposes choice. Virtue entails an opportunity for vice foregone.... Thus morality is possible only in conditions of liberty. Without personal autonomy, I can do neither good nor evil. The free market is an essential component of the social structure of liberty, and ipso facto ... an indispensable component of the social structure of virtue.... Markets are thus neither morally negative ... nor even ... morally neutral. They are, on the contrary, resoundingly and constitutively positive in their moral implications and effects ... markets are one of the several indispensable preconditions of liberty, and as such are preconditions to any genuinely moral action. In the medium term, if not in the short term, no market, no freedom, no virtue. QED.[2]

2.8 Answers to Problems

Question (a)
Everyone at the party was drinking.
<u>Tom was at the party.</u>
Tom was drinking.

Question (b)
Everyone who lives in Snooty Towers is stuck up.
<u>Mehdi lives in Snooty Towers.</u>
Mehdi is a snob.

Question (c)
James swears at strangers in the street.
James never leaves a tip when he goes to a restaurant.
<u>James's breath smells.</u>
You should stop dating James.

Question (d)
The walking stick is short.
<u>Li Na is very tall.</u>
The walking stick won't be very useful to Li Na

Question (e)
<u>A long holiday would be better for both of us.</u>
We should have a long holiday.

Question (f)
The first premise of this argument is not *quite* true: there are exceptions to the principle that any person born in the United States is eligible for US citizenship. However, the larger problem with this argument is that the conclusion doesn't follow from the premises.

Question (g)
The premises of this argument are true, and the conclusion does indeed follow from the premises.

Question (h)

We take the premise of this argument to be true. There is room for dispute about the extent to which the premise supports the conclusion. For what it's worth, we don't find the argument very convincing. It doesn't seem unlikely that there are bacteria-like organisms on some distant planet in our galaxy that we are currently unable to observe.

Question (i)

The argument is valid.

Question (j)

The argument is not valid.

Question (k)

The argument is not valid.

Question (o)

(1) All the guys in ΓΔ are rude. (Premise)
(2) John is in ΓΔ. (Premise)
(3) John is rude. (From 1, 2)
(4) You shouldn't invite rude people to your parties. (Premise)
(5) You shouldn't invite John to your party. (From 3, 4)

Question (p)

(1) Joe is often mean to me. (Premise)
(2) Either Joe loves me or Joe hates me. (From 1)
(3) I've done nothing to make Joe dislike me. (Premise)
(4) Joe loves me. (From 2, 3)

Question (q)

(1) Mr. Singh was born in the 1950s. (Premise)
(2) Mr. Singh is at least fifty years old. (From 1)
(3) Mr. Singh is older than Min. (From 2)

Question (r)

(1) Four, nine, sixteen, twenty-five, thirty-six, and forty-nine all have an odd number of factors. (Premise)

(2)	All square numbers have an odd number of factors.	(From 1)
(3)	2,401 is square.	(Premise)
(4)	2,401 has an odd number of factors.	(From 2, 3)

Question (s)

(1)	I only have ten dollars to spend.	(Premise)
(2)	The starters at The Snail cost more than ten dollars.	(Premise)
(3)	I shouldn't take Amie to The Snail.	(From 1, 2)
(4)	The Rose doesn't serve vegetarian dishes.	(Premise)
(5)	I shouldn't take Amie to The Rose.	(From 4)
(6)	The only two restaurants open are The Snail and The Rose.	(Premise)
(7)	We should stay in tonight.	(From 3, 5, 6)

Question (t)

Weather forecasts made more than a week in advance are untrustworthy.

The longer the range of a forecast, the less trustworthy it is.

When climate scientists make predictions about global temperatures over the next few decades, they are in effect issuing very long-term weather forecasts.

Therefore:

Climate scientists' predictions about global temperatures over the next few decades are not to be taken seriously.

Question (u)

(1)	Monogamy is rare in the animal kingdom.	(Premise)
(2)	None of the species most closely related to humans are monogamous.	(Premise)
(3)	It is unnatural to live monogamously.	(From 1, 2)
(4)	It is a mistake to make monogamy our ideal.	(From 3)

Question (v)

(1)	A given quantity of money is worth more to a poor person than to a rich person.	(Premise)

(2) If money is taken from a rich person and transferred to a poor person, the loss of welfare to the rich person is smaller than the gain in welfare to the poor person. (From 1)

(3) A redistributive system of tax and benefits increases the average level of welfare in society. (From 2)

(4) The government's goal should be to increase the average level of welfare in society. (Premise)

(5) The government should maintain a redistributive system of tax and benefits. (From 3, 4)

Question (w)

(1) An action is virtuous only if, in doing that action, the agent forwent the opportunity to do some other, vicious action. (Premise)

(2) Virtuous action is possible only in "conditions of liberty." (From 1)

(3) Only in a market economy are we in conditions of liberty. (Premise)

(4) Virtuous action is possible only in a market economy. (From 2, 3)

(5) Markets presuppose and generate virtue. (From 4)

What to Look at Next

There are many good books available on the analysis and evaluation of arguments. This field is often called "informal logic." Walter Sinnott-Armstrong and Robert Fogelin's *Understanding Arguments: An Introduction to Informal Logic* is excellent; so is Richard Feldman's *Reason and Argument*. Anthony Weston's *A Rulebook for Arguments* is also excellent, though it is more about creating your own arguments than about evaluating the arguments of other people. But we stress that learning to evaluate arguments is rather like learning to swim: reading is not enough; you have to practice. When you come across an argument, think of it as an opportunity to develop your analytical skills. Think as carefully as you can about the internal structure of the argument, and then scrutinize each step in the argument individually.

Glossary

abduction: In an abductive argument, one starts with a number of observations, and one puts forward an explanation for the observations. If one judges that the proffered explanation is a good explanation and better than any available alternatives, one cautiously infers that the explanation is correct. Also called "inference to the best explanation".

argument: Very often, the term "argument" is used to mean *dispute* or *quarrel*. This is not what the term means in this book. In our sense, an argument is an attempt to rationally justify some assertion—what is called the "conclusion" of the argument. Typically, when you make an argument, you take certain things for granted (these are your "premises"), and you attempt to show that if one accepts the premises, one should accept the conclusion too.

compatibilists: Compatibilists believe that determinism is compatible with the claim that we have free will. See chapter 9 for discussion

conclusion: When one makes an argument, one attempts to rationally justify some assertion. This assertion is the conclusion.

deductively valid: When an argument is deductively valid, the truth of the premises *guarantees* the truth of the conclusion: given that the premises are true, the conclusion *must* be true as well.

determinism: According to determinists, given the state of the universe at any one time, the laws of physics fix the whole of the rest of history. So if you could "rewind" history and run it again from exactly the same starting point, history would be exactly repeated. See chapter 9 for discussion.

enumerative induction: In an inductive argument, one starts by identifying some pattern in cases that have been studied; then, one suggests on this basis that the pattern will extend to other cases as well. For example, if you buy a few cakes from Tina's Café and they are all stale, you might infer that most or all the cakes that Tina sells are stale. Also called "induction" for short.

inference to the best explanation: See abduction.

premises: When you make an argument, typically you have to take certain things for granted. These are your premises.

Notes

1. Chee W. Chia et al., "Chronic Low-Calorie Sweetener Use and Risk of Abdominal Obesity among Older Adults: A Cohort Study." *PLOS ONE* 11, no. 11 (2016): e0167241.
2. This is a highly abbreviated version of the opening of David Marsland's "Character, Liberty and Social Structure," in *Economy and Virtue*, ed. Dennis O'Keefe (London: Institute for Economic Affairs, 2004), 101–115.

CHAPTER 3
....

Does God Exist?

Introduction

Suppose your friend claims to be descended from Benjamin Franklin, or says that New Yorkers are on average taller than the residents of Paris, or declares that raccoons (like dogs) can be trained to respond to some English commands. You might well ask your friend for some reason for believing her claim. If your friend replies, "That's just what I believe!" or "I don't need a reason!" or "I don't have to justify my beliefs!" you'd probably think your friend was being unreasonable. Or even a bit crazy. It is natural to think that the same applies to religious beliefs. It would seem to be unreasonable for someone to maintain the belief that God exists without having some reason for holding this belief.

In this chapter, we look at some reasons—or supposed reasons—for believing that God exists. Before we get started, we want to distinguish between **evidential reasons** and **pragmatic reasons** for belief. The jargon is cumbersome, but the distinction is not difficult. We'll explain it with a couple of examples.

Suppose that your friend is about to run a marathon, and she tells you that she thinks she'll finish in under three hours. You're not sure her belief is true, and you ask her to justify it. Here are two things she might say:

(a) I've run ten marathons in the last two years, and all of my times have been comfortably under three hours. The conditions look good for this weekend, and I'm in good form. So I expect to finish in less than three hours as usual.

(b) My big problem when running is lack of confidence. If I start to doubt myself, I run slowly or drop out altogether. So it's important for me to be confident in advance of the race. So I'm telling myself that I'm going to break three hours this time.

In both cases, your friend has given you a justification for her belief, but the two justifications are of very different kinds. In case (a), she has given you *evidence* for her belief that she will finish in less than three hours. In case (b), she's shown you that her belief is likely to be advantageous to her but has not provided evidence for it. In the jargon, (a) is an evidential reason, and (b) is a pragmatic reason.

Here's another example. Suppose that you meet a man with a serious illness. He tells you that he expects to recover fully by the end of the year. Tactlessly, you ask him to justify this belief. Here are two things he might say:

(a) My doctor told me that she's very confident I'll recover fully by December. I know that she's an expert on the topic and that she's totally honest.

(b) It makes me unhappy to think that the illness will last for a long time, so I've chosen to believe that I'll get better soon.

Here, (a) is an evidential reason, and (b) is a pragmatic reason. In case (a), the man is giving you evidence for his belief that he'll recover by December. In case (b), the man has given you no evidence that his belief is true, but he's given you reason to think that he's likely to be better off if he maintains the belief.

Philosophers and theologians have given both evidential arguments and pragmatic arguments for theism. When someone gives an evidential argument for theism, the goal is to give you evidence for the contention that God exists. When someone gives a practical argument for theism, the goal is to show that there may be benefits to being a theist, and that these possible benefits justify theism. We start by looking at some evidential arguments for theism. Then, in section 3.8, we turn to a pragmatic argument.

To avoid any confusion, we will start by saying something about what we mean by **theism** and **atheism**. These terms are easy to define:

a theist is someone who believes God exists; an atheist is someone who believes he doesn't exist.[1] However, in the absence of some explanation of what "God" means, these definitions aren't all that helpful.

If you explore a variety of discussions of theism from different traditions, you will find that different theists have very different views about what God is like. We might say that there are many different versions of theism, corresponding to different conceptions of the divine. In this chapter, we focus on the version of theism that has been most discussed within the Western philosophical tradition. This version of theism includes the following claims:

1. God created the universe from nothing.
2. God is all-powerful (or **omnipotent**, as philosophers and theologians sometimes put it).
3. God is perfectly good.
4. God knows everything (he is **omniscient**, to use the jargon).
5. God deserves our unqualified love and complete obedience.

These claims are central to many—but not all—forms of Judaism, Christianity, and Islam. The Hindu conception of God is rather different. We should stress that, by focusing on this particular version of theism, we do not wish to imply that other versions of theism are less worthy of study.

3.1 The First Cause Argument

The universe has a long history: processes we observe today began hundreds, thousands, or millions of years before any of us were born. Today's egg came from a chicken, which came from another egg, which came from another chicken, and so on backward into the unremembered past. According to many theists, it was God that initiated the whole thing; the whole history of the universe began with a divine act of creation. Atheists, of course, deny this. So it seems reasonable for the theist to challenge the atheist with the following question:

> If God didn't initiate the history of the universe, how did it all get started?

The atheist might respond that the history of the universe has no beginning, that it stretches backward infinitely. Some theists think this is absurd, on the grounds that a completed infinity is impossible (more on this later). Alternatively, the atheist might say the history of the universe *just started*, without any cause. It just happened. The theist might reply that is ridiculous: nothing comes from nothing. (It sounds better in Latin: *ex nihilo, nihil fit*.) So, the theist may continue, the history of the universe must have been initiated by some cause, and it's hard to see what this cause could have been, if not an act of God. That's the basic idea behind the **first cause argument**.

St. Thomas Aquinas (1225–1274) developed a version of the first cause argument.

To get a better handle on the argument, we need to introduce a technical term: "causal chain." A causal chain is a sequence of events, where each event in the sequence (except the first event, if there is one) is caused by the previous event in the sequence. Suppose, for example, that Ashni broke up with John because she found his love letter to Sarah. She found the letter in one of John's drawers while she was searching for her book, which John had left on a train. That's a causal chain, and we can depict the whole thing with a simple diagram, pictured in figure 3.1.

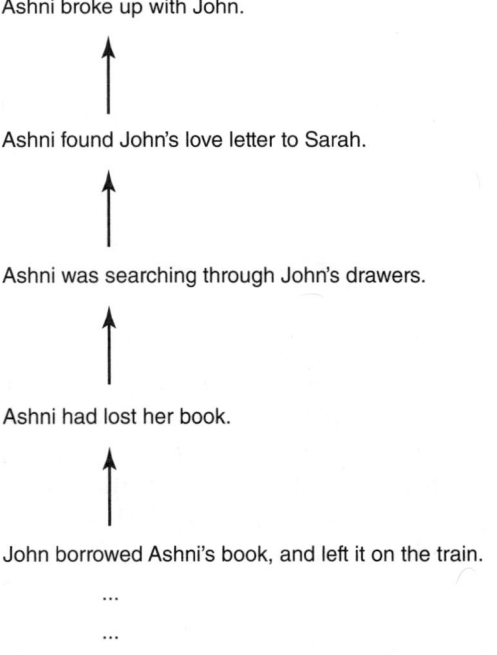

FIGURE 3.1

In practice, it's often difficult to trace a causal chain backward more than a few steps because it's often difficult to find the cause of an event. But suppose we could trace a causal chain backward as far as we wanted—what might we discover? It seems obvious that there can't be any *loops* in a causal chain. That is, it seems that if you start at one event and trace its causal chain backward, you'll never get back to where you started. Causal chains never look like what is pictured in figure 3.2.

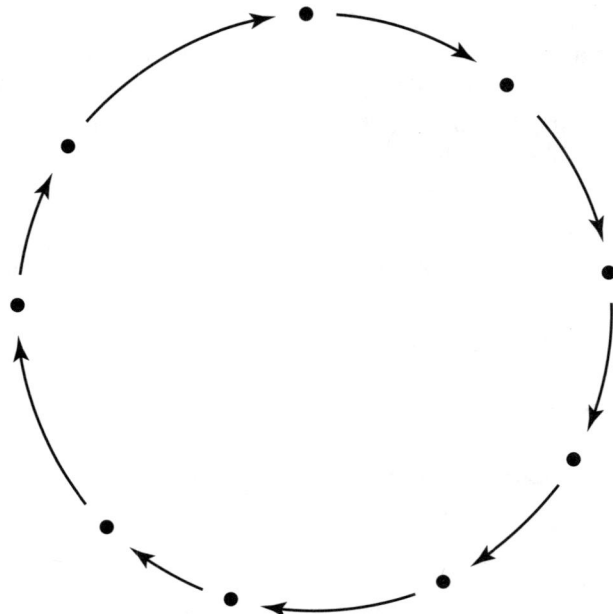

FIGURE 3.2

The cause of an event must occur earlier in time than the event itself. So if a causal chain went in a circle, each event in the circle would have to occur earlier than itself, which is absurd.

Now for another technical term. A **potentially infinite process** is a process that could, in principle, be continued on and on without end. For example, consider the process of counting:

0, 1, 2, 3, 4, 5, ...

In principle, this process need have no end: the numbers just keep on coming. Many philosophers have thought that, while there are *potentially* infinite processes, it is impossible for an infinite sequence of events to be completed. The process of counting, as we said, is potentially infinite. However, a person can't *finish* counting through all the numbers—and not just because death or boredom would prevent one from doing so. This illustrates the more general claim that a completed infinity is impossible; that is, an infinite process can never come to an end. If this is right, then no causal chain can stretch backward infinitely.

Now if it is true that a causal chain can't stretch backward infinitely, and that a causal chain can't have loops in it, then it follows that every causal chain must have a *beginning*. Every causal chain must look something like figure 3.3.

first cause   now

FIGURE 3.3

It's hard to see what this "first cause" could be, other than a divine act of creation. This suggests that if you could trace back any causal chain to its beginning, you would find that it starts with God creating the universe from nothing.

3.2 Some Questions About the First Cause Argument

We think that the first cause argument is not very convincing. Or rather, it is not very convincing as it stands. Here are some questions that a proponent of the argument would have to answer in order to make it convincing.

Q1: Why can't a causal chain extend backward infinitely?

In the fifth century BCE, the ancient Greek atomists (Democritus and Leucippus) claimed that the universe consists of atoms that fly around in otherwise empty space, colliding and bouncing off one another. Sometimes these atoms stick together to make larger objects—like planets, rocks, or organisms. They thought that atoms can be neither created nor destroyed, and so the atoms in the universe today must have existed *forever*. So according to the atomists, the physical universe has no beginning; it has always existed. On this view, there are causal chains that go backward forever: an atom A is moving today because it was struck yesterday by atom B, which was struck the day before that by atom C, which was struck the day before that by atom D, and so on.

We don't see anything incoherent about this atomist worldview—so it seems to us coherent to suppose that the universe has always existed.

Q2: Why must there be just one first cause?

Suppose we agree that no causal chain can have a loop in it and that no causal chain can be infinitely long. Then, we must agree that every causal chain had a beginning—there must be a *first* event in each chain. But it doesn't follow that every causal chain must have the *same* first event.

Aristotle, a Greek philosopher who lived in the fourth century BCE, gave an argument very much like the one we just discussed.[2] He argued that each causal chain must start with an "unmoved mover"—a being that *causes motion* but whose motions are themselves *not caused*. Aristotle wasn't sure that there is only *one* unmoved mover—he thought that there might be several. At one point, he suggested that there were forty-seven! In the absence of an argument against this sort of position, it seems to us, the first cause argument is not complete.

Q3: Even if there is a first cause, why must it be a divine act of creation?

The proponent of the first cause argument assumes that if there is a first cause, it must be God's creation of the universe—but it's not clear this assumption is justified.

According to physicists today, the universe began almost 14 billion years ago in a very hot, very dense state; it expanded very rapidly (an event known as "the Big Bang") until it cooled enough for atoms to form, which eventually combined to form stars and planets. Perhaps the Big Bang was the first cause, and no god was involved.

Q4: Even if the universe has a creator, why assume that the creator still exists and is omnipotent, omniscient, and perfectly good?

It seems to us that the first cause argument doesn't establish that the universe was created by God. However, even granting this conclusion, it hasn't been established that he is omnipotent, omniscient, and perfectly good, or even that he still exists!

So as we said, we think that the first cause argument is not very convincing as it stands: too many questions have been left unanswered. Later writers have attempted to plug the gaps in the argument we've mentioned.

3.3 Leibniz's Cosmological Argument

In the previous section, we found that the atheist has available a number of apparently reasonable answers to the question, "If God didn't initiate the history of the universe, how did it all get started?" For example, the atheist may say that the history of the universe stretches backward infinitely, or that the universe began with the Big Bang and no god was involved.

Even if theists concede that these are adequate responses to the first cause argument, they might still feel that there's something missing from the atheist's worldview: for the atheist has yet to explain fully *why* the universe exists. That is the basic idea behind Leibniz's **cosmological argument**.[3]

The most important premise in Leibniz's argument, called the **principle of sufficient reason**, goes like this:

> Every "Why?" question has an answer, although we may not be able to figure out what it is.
>
> Alternatively: Every fact has an explanation.

Here's an example. Suppose you return one evening to find that your TV is smashed on the floor. You ask your roommate, "Why is the TV smashed up? What happened?" If she says, "There's no reason. The TV is just smashed up; it can't be explained," you'd have a right to be suspicious. You would think there must be *some* explanation for the state of your TV. Of course, there are some "Why?" questions whose answers we don't know. For example, we don't know why Stonehenge was built. But Leibniz would have said that there must *be* some explanation, even if we are unable to find it.

Now consider the question:

> Why does the universe exist?

According to the principle of sufficient reason, this question *must have an answer*. But what could the answer be? Let's look at some options.

One suggestion is that the universe exists because the Big Bang occurred, and the Big Bang caused all subsequent events in the universe. The Big Bang theory wasn't devised until the twentieth century, so Leibniz never discussed it. But we can be pretty sure what he would have said. While he might have agreed that later events in the universe can be explained by asserting they were caused by the Big Bang, he would have added that we still need an answer to the question, "Why did the Big Bang occur?"

Another idea is that each event in the universe is explained by its cause, which is explained by *its* cause, which is explained by *its* cause, and so on, forever—like figure 3.4.

... ⟶ Event 5 ⟶ Event 4 ⟶ Event 3 ⟶ Event 2 ⟶ Event 1

FIGURE 3.4

Leibniz would have agreed, in this case, that we can answer the question, "Why did event 1 occur?" by saying, "It was caused by event 2." And we can answer the question, "Why did event 2 occur?" by saying, "It was caused by event 3." And so on. But even so, Leibniz would have insisted, none of this explains the existence of the *whole sequence*.

More generally, Leibniz thought that we can't explain the existence of the universe itself just by describing events and processes *in* the universe—for these events and processes are part of what needs to be explained. He reasoned that the only way of explaining the existence of the universe itself is by way of something *outside* the universe—specifically, God.

Of course, Leibniz needed an answer to the question, "Why does God exist?" After all, Leibniz claimed that every "Why?" question has an answer, so he had to agree that *this* "Why?" question has an answer.

Leibniz answered "Why does God exist?" by saying that God is a **necessary being** rather than a **contingent being**. These terms deserve some explanation. A contingent being is something that could have not existed. You, for example, are a contingent being, because if your parents had not met you would never have been born. Anything not contingent is necessary. According to Leibniz, God's existence is necessary—and this is enough to answer the question, "Why does God exist?"

We mention two objections to Leibniz's argument.

First, it's not clear that the principle of sufficient reason is true. That is, it's not clear that every "Why?" question has an answer. The philosopher Bertrand Russell (1872–1970) once said, "the universe is just there, and that's all"[4]—and perhaps that's all one should say in response to the question, "Why does the universe exist?" Perhaps this is one "Why?" question that has no answer.[5]

Second, granting the existence of the universe has an explanation, it's not clear that the explanation must involve an omnipotent, perfectly good, omniscient God who still exists. Perhaps the universe was created by a god who subsequently vanished; perhaps it was made by a team of gods (only some of whom are benevolent) . . . and so on. And so Leibniz's argument doesn't seem to establish theism, in our sense of the term.

3.4 The Design Argument

In this section, we discuss the design argument.[6] We think this is a *much* more impressive argument than the first cause argument or Leibniz's cosmological argument. Indeed, we like to think if we lived 200 years ago, we would have been convinced by the design argument. In the middle of the nineteenth century, however, a powerful new objection to the design argument emerged. Unlike the problems that beset the first cause argument and Leibniz's cosmological argument, there is nothing obvious about this new objection. Rather, it grew out of one of the greatest scientific achievements of all time, Charles Darwin's theory of evolution by natural selection. But we are getting ahead of ourselves. Let's start at the beginning and explain how the design argument attempts to establish God's existence.

The **design argument** begins with two facts about the biological world—facts that are obvious to casual inspection and that are confirmed by more careful observation and biological research. The first of these is that many of the parts of plants and animals have a *function*. In vertebrates, including humans, the function of the heart is to pump blood, the function of the eye is to enable vision, and the function of the ovaries is to produce eggs; in mammals, birds, and reptiles, the function of the lungs is to oxygenate the blood; in green plants, the function of chlorophyll is to enable photosynthesis; and in flowering plants, the function of the nectar often found within the flower is to attract insects that pollinate the plants. The list goes on and on. Much research in biology is aimed at discovering the function of parts of organisms whose function is not immediately obvious. For example, not until the late nineteenth century was it discovered that a function of bone marrow is the production of blood cells. The second fact is that the parts of organisms that perform functions are often amazingly well designed. The eye in humans and other mammals is a favorite example. Our eyes have a flexible lens (see figure 3.5) whose shape can be changed by tiny muscles, enabling the eye to focus on objects that are nearby or faraway; they also have an aperture, the iris, that can open and close, letting more light enter the eye in dim surroundings and less light in bright surroundings; and they have an intricate set of exterior muscles that control the direction in which the eye is pointing.

Here, again, the examples known to biologists are almost endless. The joints of the human hand, the structures of the inner ear, the

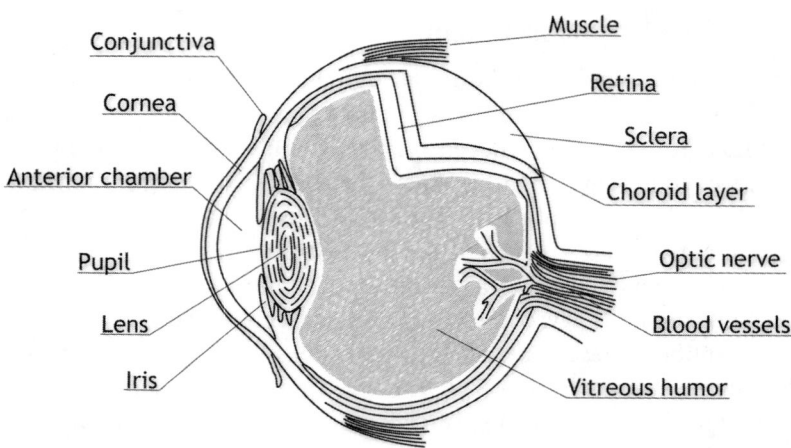

FIGURE 3.5 A cross-section of the human eye

immune system, and the system that regulates the amount of sugar in our blood all are impressively well designed to fulfill their functions. So the first premise of the design argument is that a great many things in the biological part of the natural world have a function, and that they are exceptionally well designed to accomplish their function.

It is important to note that the sort of function and excellent design that can be found everywhere in the biological world is not a common feature of the nonbiological part of the universe. If you come upon a boulder while hiking in the mountains, it would be very odd indeed to ask what its function is or whether it is well designed to carry out that function. In all likelihood, that boulder has no function at all, and it is neither well designed nor poorly designed. It's just there. Much the same can be said of more substantial parts of the nonbiological world. Mars is our closest planetary neighbor, but is it well designed to perform its function? The answer, it seems, is that Mars is neither well designed nor poorly designed to perform its function because it *has* no function.

The next step in the design argument is to ask how the existence of the superb design that is ubiquitous in biological nature can be explained. The answer proposed is that good design requires an intelligent designer, and that the design found in the biological world is so elegant and sophisticated that it must be the product of an exceptionally intelligent designer—a designer with a mind that is far more powerful than the mind of even the most intelligent human. The intelligent designer that must be posited in order to explain the existence of the brilliant design found throughout biological nature is God.

The English philosopher and theologian William Paley (1743–1805) offered a famous analogy to explain the reasoning invoked in the design argument. Suppose you are walking in the country and you happen upon an object on the path. When you pick it up and examine it, you see that it is a watch. Its function is clearly to keep time, and its many internal parts are exceptionally well designed to achieve this function. How can the existence of that watch be explained? One hypothesis is that it is just an accident—that all the intricate pieces of the watch were formed and happened to come together by chance. Another hypothesis is that the watch was designed by a very clever craftsman. Obviously, the second hypothesis is much more plausible than the first; it offers a much better explanation for the existence of the watch. Paley suggests that the watch is analogous to the wonderfully well-designed systems we find in the biological part of the natural world. When we explore the biological world, we find a vast number of quite different biological systems, all of which are better designed than any watch. So if the best explanation for the existence of the watch is that it was designed by an intelligent watchmaker, the best explanation for the existence of the many well-designed biological systems is that they were designed by a being far more intelligent than the best watchmaker in the world. That super-intelligent designer is God.

As Paley's analogy makes clear, the design argument is an example of what philosophers sometimes call an inference to the best explanation, or abduction (discussed in chapter 2). In arguments of this sort, which are commonplace both in science and in everyday life, a number of facts are assembled, and a hypothesis is offered that can explain those facts. If the hypothesis offers the best available explanation of the facts, then it is concluded that the hypothesis is true. Paley suggests a pair of hypotheses that might explain the existence of well-designed systems. First, they are an accident—the result of a number of chance occurrences; second, they are the work of an intelligent designer. Since the first hypothesis is absurdly unlikely, Paley concludes that the second hypothesis is the best one available, and that we should accept the hypothesis as true.

3.5 Criticisms of the Design Argument

Paley was not the first philosopher to propose the design argument. Far from it, in fact. According to the ancient Greek historian Xenophon, a version of the design argument was proposed by Socrates (c. 470–399 BCE), who is widely regarded as the first great Western philosopher. In the middle of the eighteenth century, the Scottish philosopher David Hume (1711–1776), one of the greatest philosophers of all time and who may have been an atheist, offered an extended critique of the design argument. One of the most persuasive points Hume makes is that, even if we put other concerns aside, the design argument does not establish the sort of monotheistic theism that is endorsed by Judaism, Christianity, and Islam. For even if it is true that the design evident in nature requires an intelligent designer, the design argument gives us no reason to think there was only *one* designer. Perhaps the biological world, like many watches, was designed by several very intelligent minds. Or perhaps our world was designed by a rather stupid god, who copied from other, smarter gods. Those smarter gods may have created other, better designed worlds that the dim-witted divinity who designed our world could not match. Perhaps our world was designed by a sequence of gods who gradually learned, by trial and error, to make better worlds. Or perhaps—and this is the most serious challenge—the biological wonders of our world were designed by a brilliant but elderly deity who died a long time ago. The design argument, Hume points out, offers us no reason to reject *that* hypothesis.

We are inclined to think that Hume's rather sarcastic list of alternative hypotheses makes it clear that the design argument is not sufficient to establish the version of theism that we are concerned with in this chapter. Even if it makes a good case for the existence of a highly intelligent and resourceful designer, it gives us no reason to think that the designer is omniscient, or omnipotent, or perfectly morally good. Indeed, it doesn't even give us a reason to think that the designer still exists. However, Hume seemed to regard this as at best a Pyrrhic victory:

> When we argued earlier about the natural attributes of intelligence and design, I needed all my skeptical and metaphysical subtlety to escape your grasp. In many views of the universe and of its parts, particularly its parts, the beauty and fitness of final causes [i.e., aims or functions] strike us with such irresistible force that all objections seem to be (as I think they really are) mere fault-finding and trickery; and then we can't imagine how we could ever give weight to them.[7]

Though the design argument is not sufficient to establish the existence of the God of the Judeo-Christian-Islamic tradition, even Hume, perhaps the most skeptical philosopher of his day, may have been persuaded that it makes a good case for the claim that an intelligence much greater than our own played a central role in the design of the biological world. But then Hume never heard of Darwin . . .

As we noted in our discussion of Paley, the design argument is an instance of inference to the best explanation, or abduction. There are, Paley suggests, two explanations of the extraordinarily good design to be found in the biological world: chance, and a designer with super-human

Charles Darwin (1809–1882) came up with the theory of evolution by natural selection.

intelligence. And if these are the only two options, then the intelligent designer seems far more plausible. But in 1859, Charles Darwin published *The Origin of Species*, a book that revolutionized biology and posed a major challenge to the design argument. For our purposes, what makes Darwin's work important is that it proposed another explanation for the existence of design in the biological world, an explanation that looks to be *better* than the appeal to an intelligent designer.

Darwin's explanation for the existence of excellent design in the biological world can be understood by focusing on two phenomena that played an important role in Darwin's thinking. The first is "artificial selection"—the process that plant and animal breeders use to produce plants and animals that are better suited to their needs. Dairy farmers, for example, want cows that produce lots of milk. But in most herds of dairy cattle, there is considerable variation in how much milk the cows produce. So the dairy farmer selects the best milk producers to be the mothers of the next generation. They are allowed to produce many calves, and the female calves are kept for milk production. Offspring of the cows that do not produce much milk are sent to the slaughterhouse. Gradually, the average milk production of the herd increases. Much the same process has been used by plant breeders to produce sweeter corn, more-drought-resistant wheat, and many other sorts of plants better suited for one or another agricultural purpose. Darwin was well acquainted with this sort of artificial selection, which in his day was widely used to produce many breeds of domestic animals, including dogs and pigeons.

The second phenomenon that led Darwin to his theory of natural selection was emphasized in the writings of Thomas Malthus (1766–1834), an English clergyman who was a pioneer in the study of demography. Malthus noted that human populations tend to grow much more quickly than the food supply, and that this process could not continue for long. Sooner or later, starvation, disease, or war would have to cull the population to the point where there was enough food for those who survived. Though Malthus's focus was on human populations, Darwin realized the same is true for animal populations. They too tend to reproduce much faster than the available resources, and thus starvation, disease, and predation must kill most animals before they can reproduce. But Darwin also saw that this culling process is not random. Organisms that were better able to find food, avoid predators, and resist disease would be more likely to survive and reproduce. Those who were less good at the business of surviving in a hostile environment where resources were scarce would be less likely to leave offspring. This selection process, Darwin noted, is very similar to the selection process of animal and plant breeders. Except in this case, it is *nature*, not a human agent, that is doing the selecting. And what organisms are selected for are not the characteristics that farmers or dog breeders want, but the characteristics that enable them to do a better job of surviving and reproducing. If good vision was important for survival in the environment of a population of animals, then this process of "natural selection" would gradually produce animals that were increasingly well designed for acute vision. If running speed was important for survival, then natural selection would produce organisms that were increasingly well designed to run swiftly. And so on for any other characteristic that would enable an organism to do a better job at surviving and reproducing than other organisms in its population.

The process of natural selection that Darwin described produces organisms whose parts are well designed for seeing, running, fighting, resisting disease, and so on *without* the intervention of an intelligent designer. Though Darwin did not know why organisms in a population tend to differ from one another, we now know that much of that variation is due to random mutations in an organism's genetic structure. And while most mutations tend to be harmful, occasionally a mutation will occur that gives an organism a competitive edge over the other organisms in its population. Natural selection will then tend to make that gene increasingly common in the population. Paley maintained that pure chance—accident, randomness—is an absurdly unlikely explanation for good design. And surely he was right about that. So it is important to see that Darwin's explanation for good design is not a "pure chance" explanation. Yes, there is randomness in the process. Mutations are random. But mutations are only part of the explanation that contemporary Darwinians offer for the existence of superb design in the biological world. The other part is *selection*—the culling process carried out by phenomena like disease, starvation, and predation. The mantra of modern Darwinians is "random mutation and selective retention"—and that process, they argue, offers a much better explanation for the beautiful design we see in the biological world.

The design argument maintains that an intelligent designer is the best explanation for the superb design that abounds in the biological world. Darwin's theory offers another explanation. But is it a *better* explanation? Though this remains a hotly debated issue, most biologists maintain that it is.[8] This is not the place to review all the evidence that they offer, but we will mention one line of argument that has played an important role in the debate from Darwin's time onward. This argument focuses on the many examples of *imperfect* design found in the biological world. The eyes of humans and other mammals provide a striking example. The photo-receptive cells in the human eye (the rods and cones) are located toward the inner surface of the retina. They are connected to nerve cells that carry visual information to the brain. But those nerve cells are located toward the outer surface of the retina—the surface that the light reaches first. Thus, in order to reach the brain, these nerves must pass *through* the retina, which they do at a place called the "optic disc." Since there is a gap in the retina at that point, we all have a blind spot in our visual field.[9] This seems to be a clear example of quite bad design. Were an engineer at the Nikon camera company to produce a camera that had a blind spot in the middle of the image, that engineer would no doubt be fired on the spot. Darwinians have no trouble explaining the many examples of suboptimal design in biology, since natural selection must work with what it has available and exploit the mutations that happen to arise. For defenders of intelligent design, these cases pose a serious challenge because they suggest that, on many occasions, the designer was actually rather stupid.

We won't offer a final verdict on the design argument. Rather, we suggest that you dig more deeply into the contemporary debate and decide for yourself.[10] However, before leaving the design argument, we want to emphasize an important logical point. Even if it is true that Darwin's theory (and the work of many other biologists) has shown that the design argument is untenable, this does *not* show, or even begin to show, that theism is false or that God does not exist. At most, what Darwinian arguments can show is that one important argument *for* theism is not convincing.

3.6 Anselm's Ontological Argument

An eleventh-century monk, Saint Anselm of Canterbury, gave an extremely ingenious argument for theism, which we discuss in this section. The argument is now often called the **ontological argument** (**ontology** is a branch of philosophy concerned with existence). Later philosophers have given similar arguments, which are often also called ontological arguments—but we'll stick to Anselm's original. Anselm's argument is complicated, so we'll need to explain a few points before we get to the argument itself.

First Point: Reductio ad absurdum

Anselm's ontological argument is an argument by **reductio ad absurdum**. In a *reductio* argument, you show that some claim is false by assuming it is true and then deriving a contradiction from that assumption. Here's an example. Suppose that a programmer brags to you about writing a piece of software that plays chess faultlessly. The programmer tells you that the software can be installed on a normal personal computer and that it is guaranteed to win every single game against any opponent, whether it plays as black or white. It will never lose a game, and it will never draw: it will win every single time. The programmer even boasts that several grandmasters have taken on this program and all of them have lost.

It's easy to see that the programmer's claim can't be right. Suppose that what the programmer says is true. Then, it is possible to install the program on two computers and have the two computers play chess against each another. Then, both computers will win the game. But this is absurd, because the rules of chess allow at most one winner.

This is a *reductio* argument. We started off by assuming that what the programmer says is true, and we derived a contradiction from that assumption, thereby showing that the assumption is false. *Reductio* arguments are extremely common in mathematics. For example, the standard proof of the irrationality of the square root of two is a *reductio ad absurdum*.

Second Point: Anselm's definition of God

Anselm in effect defines "God" as the greatest possible being. "Greatest" here doesn't mean "largest"; it means "most perfect." For example, *you* are not God because a being greater than you is possible: a stronger and smarter version of you would be greater. If God exists at all, according to Anselm's definition, he is so great that nothing greater is possible.

It seems that, according to this definition, God must be omnipotent, if he exists at all. For if God exists and is *not* omnipotent, then something greater than God is possible (namely, a being that is like God in every respect except that it is omnipotent). In much the same way, it seems that, given Anselm's definition, if God exists at all he is perfectly good and omniscient.

On the other hand, Anselm's definition doesn't seem to imply that God created the world—you might think this is a fault with the definition. However, when Anselm tells us that this is his definition of the term "God," we cannot sensibly disagree. We might think that Anselm is using the term "God" in an eccentric or unusual way, but Anselm is free to use the word however he likes.

Third Point: The distinction between "existence in the mind" and "existence in reality"

This distinction is best explained with examples. Here are some things that exist in the mind but don't exist in reality:

- unicorns
- Sherlock Holmes
- Middle Earth

Here are some things that exist in reality:

- horses
- the Moon
- Canada

It is generally agreed that God exists in the mind. The big question is whether he exists in reality too.

Fourth Point: Existence and greatness

Here's a key premise in Anselm's argument:

> If God exists in the mind only (and not in reality), then he would be greater if he existed in reality too.

To see that this is plausible, imagine you are approached by a guy from a dating agency. He tells you that (for a fee, of course) he will arrange a *perfect date* for you. He or she will be as good-looking as it is possible to be, charming, smart, funny, and—well, perhaps it's best not to get into too much detail here. You agree and pay the fee. A week later, he sends you a description of the perfect date.

You ask, "When will I actually get to meet the date?" and the guy tells you that the date exists in the mind only, not in reality. It seems that you'd be justified in feeling cheated. You'd say that you paid him to arrange the perfect date for you, and he failed to deliver. It would be a much better date if he or she existed in reality and not just in your mind.

Okay, now we're ready to tackle the argument itself. Since the argument is complicated and somewhat confusing, we label the steps with letters as we go. As we said, it is a *reductio* argument, so we start by assuming that God does *not* exist in reality:

(a) God does not exist in reality.

If we can derive a contradiction from this assumption, we'll have shown that the assumption is false—that is, we will have shown that God *does* exist in reality. Next, we assume:

(b) God does exist in the mind.

This seems uncontroversial. As noted, fictional characters like Sherlock Holmes exist in the mind, and even atheists agree that God "exists" in this sense. Putting (a) and (b), together we infer:

(c) God exists in the mind but not in reality.

We already discussed this next premise:

(d) If God exists in the mind only (and not in reality), then he would be greater if he existed in reality too.

From (c) and (d), we can infer:

(e) If God *did* exist in reality, he would be greater than he is.

We have found that God exists in the mind only. If he existed in reality, he would be greater—just as a date that exists in reality is greater than an otherwise similar date that exists in the mind only. Here's the next premise:

(f) God *could* exist in reality.

There are some things that *could not possibly exist*. For example, it seems that there could not possibly exist a square circle. But—Anselm argued—God is not an impossible being, like a square circle. Even if he doesn't exist, he *could* have existed. The claim that God exists, even if false, is not contradictory, like the claim that a square circle exists. From (e) and (f), we can infer:

(g) God could be greater than he is.

But now remember that "God" is defined as "the greatest possible being," so from (g), we can infer:

(h) The greatest possible being could be still greater.

But this is a contradiction—nothing could be greater than the greatest possible being.

Remember how *reductio* arguments work: by deriving a contradiction from some claim, you show the claim is false. We derived a contradiction from the assumption that God does not exist in reality, and so it seems that we are in a position to infer that he *does* exist in reality after all.

3.7 What, if Anything, is Wrong with Anselm's Ontological Argument?

Ontological arguments like the one we looked at in the previous section have been the subject of philosophical controversy for almost a millennium. Some philosophers are convinced either by Anselm's argument or by one of its more sophisticated descendants. Opponents of these arguments sometimes argue that there must be something wrong with them, by producing *parodies* of the argument.

A contemporary of Anselm, Gaunilo of Marmoutiers, devised the following parody. We define "Utopia" as "the best possible island" and then argue as follows:

(a) Utopia does not exist in reality. (Assumption, for *reductio*)
(b) Utopia does exist in the mind. (Premise)
(c) Utopia exists in the mind but not in reality. (From (a) and (b))
(d) If Utopia exists in the mind only (and not in reality), then it would be greater if it existed in reality too. (Premise)
(e) If Utopia did exist in reality, it would be greater than it is. (From (c) and (d))
(f) Utopia could exist in reality. (Premise)
(g) Utopia could be greater than it is. (From (e) and (f))
(h) The greatest possible island could be still greater. (From (g) and the definition of "Utopia")

Again, we're supposed to recognize that (h) is a contradiction and infer that Utopia does exist in reality after all.

Of course, we all know that Utopia doesn't exist. No matter how great the island of Hawai'i is, it could have been even greater, so it is not the greatest possible island. So Gaunilo's argument has a false conclusion. Gaunilo's thought was that since the Utopia argument is flawed, there must be something wrong with Anselm's ontological argument too (even if it is hard to figure out exactly what that is).

Many philosophers think that parodies like this show that there is *something* wrong with Anselm's original argument. Even if this is right, it's not clear precisely *where* Anselm's argument goes awry. So we'll finish with a pair of questions. If you think Anselm's argument goes wrong somewhere, can you identify a specific error in the argument? And if you think that Anselm's argument is correct, how do you respond to the claim that the parodies discredit the argument?

3.8 A Pragmatic Case for Theism?

We think it's clear that *some* people benefit from believing that God exists. We're not talking about the benefits that supposedly accrue to believers after death: we have in mind the more immediate effects of theism. We'll give you an example. In the following passage from his sermon "God Is Able," Martin Luther King Jr. described an experience he had shortly after the Montgomery bus protest:

> One night . . . after a strenuous day . . . just as I was about to doze off the telephone rang. An angry voice said, "Listen, [slur term], we've taken all we want from you, before next week you'll be sorry you ever came to Montgomery." I hung up, but I couldn't sleep. It seemed that all of my fears had come down on me at once. I had reached the saturation point. I got out of bed and began to walk the floor. Finally I went to the kitchen and heated a pot of coffee. I was ready to give up. With my cup of coffee sitting un-touched before me I tried to think of a way to move out of the picture without appearing a coward. In this state of exhaustion, when my courage had all but gone, I decided to take my problem to God. With my head in my hands, I bowed over the kitchen table and prayed aloud. The words I spoke to God that midnight are still vivid in my memory: "I am here taking a stand for what I believe is right. But now I am afraid. The people are looking

to me for leadership, and if I stand before them without strength and courage, they too will falter. I am at the end of my powers. I have nothing left. I've come to the point where I can't face it alone." At that moment I experienced the presence of the Divine as I had never experienced Him before. It seemed as though I could hear the quiet assurance of an inner voice saying "Stand up for righteousness, stand up for truth, and God will be at your side forever." Almost at once my fears began to go. My uncertainty disappeared. I was ready to face anything. The outer situation remained the same, but God had given me the inner calm to face it. Three nights later . . . our home was bombed. Strangely enough, I accepted the work of the bombing calmly. My experience with God a few nights before had given me the strength to face it.[11]

In this case, King benefited from his religious belief—his theism helped him cope in the face of a threat to his life. And, of course, many millions benefited from what King went on to achieve.

Now the fact that religious belief can provide (to use King's words) "inner peace amid outer storms"[12] perhaps motivates religious belief in some cases. But suppose that someone adopts religious convictions because they give moral support. Would this person's religious convictions then be justified? Some would call this "wishful thinking," and it is often thought that wishful thinking is an intellectual defect or worse.

The English mathematician W. K. Clifford used a story to illustrate the claim that it is wrong to believe with insufficient evidence. The antihero of the story is a man who owned a ferry. The ship was rather old and probably wasn't well-constructed in the first place. So the man began to worry that the ship was not seaworthy. But he knew that the ship would be very expensive to repair, so he stifled his concerns and didn't have the ship inspected or repaired. By the time he sent the ship out to sea on its next voyage, he'd completely convinced himself that the ship was in good condition, and so he felt no concern at all as he watched it pull out of the harbor. But then the ship sank, and all the passengers and crew drowned. Clifford said that the shipowner was responsible for the deaths of the people on the ferry. It was his fault that they all died. He shouldn't have stifled his doubts about the seaworthiness of the ship, Clifford claimed. The man's belief that the ship was in good condition wasn't justified. He should not have believed this without evidence. Clifford used this story to motivate the following conclusion:

> It is wrong always, everywhere, and for anyone, to believe anything upon insufficient evidence.[13]

Many of Clifford's critics have accused him of overgeneralizing. It may be that it was wrong for the shipowner to believe with insufficient evidence, but this doesn't show that it is *always* wrong to believe with insufficient evidence. Indeed, Clifford's critics have devised their own stories, hoping to show that it is *not* always wrong to believe with insufficient evidence. Here's our version:

> Jim is preparing for a job interview. He's very well suited to the job, and his qualifications and references are excellent. There's just one problem: Jim is very shy. He knows from past experience that he is likely to be paralyzed by embarrassment during his interview. There will be long, awkward silences; his sentences won't make sense; he won't be able to look his interviewers in the eye; his knowledge of his field will suddenly disappear. But Jim has an idea. Jim thinks that if he can convince himself in advance that the interview will be a success, this conviction will give him confidence and he won't have his usual problems. He'll be fluent, friendly, and his knowledge of the field will be obvious. So he forces himself to believe that the interview will go well.

Now it doesn't seem to us that Jim acts wrongly in trying to convince himself that the job interview will be a success. We certainly don't think that Jim will, in Clifford's words, "catch a stain which can never be wiped away."[14] This casts doubt on Clifford's claim that it is wrong "always, everywhere, and for anyone, to believe anything upon insufficient evidence."

Where does this leave us? Clifford's ship story seems to establish that it is wrong *in some cases* to believe with insufficient evidence. Jim's job interview story seems to show that it is not *always* wrong to believe with insufficient evidence. It is so far unclear, then, whether it is okay to believe that God exists on the grounds that theism provides "inner peace amid outer storms."

Conclusion

To wrap up this chapter, we present a question. Suppose you have reviewed all the arguments for theism presented in this chapter, and you have concluded that all of these arguments are unsuccessful. Should you then conclude that God does not exist?

We think not, for two reasons. First, in this chapter, we haven't covered *all* the arguments that have been given for theism. So even if the arguments we have considered are no good, it may be that other arguments are persuasive. Second, it would be wrong to conclude that God does not exist before you have evaluated the arguments for atheism. We look at some of these arguments in chapter 4.

Glossary

atheism: Atheism is the claim that God does not exist. Atheists are people who think that theism is false. (See theism).

contingent beings and necessary beings: A contingent being is a thing that could have not existed. For example, you are a contingent being because your parents could have never met, in which case you would not exist. A necessary being is any being that is not contingent.

cosmological argument: Proponents of cosmological arguments think that there must be some explanation for the existence of contingent things or the existence of the universe as a whole or the occurrence of contingent events. They argue that the best or only explanation is that God created the universe and initiated all causal chains. See sections 3.1 to 3.3.

cosmology: The study of the history and future of the universe as a whole. Currently, it is usually regarded as a branch of physics.

design argument: Proponents of design arguments (or teleological arguments) argue that many parts of the biological world appear to be exceptionally well designed; they argue that God must be the designer.

evidential reasons and pragmatic reasons: When you have evidence that a belief is true, that's an *evidential reason* for the belief. When you have evidence that a belief is likely to be beneficial, that's a *pragmatic reason* for the belief. For examples, see the chapter Introduction.

first cause argument: Proponents of the first cause argument claim that God is the "first cause" or "unmoved mover"—that he initiated all the causal processes in the universe. See section 3.1.

necessary being: See contingent beings and necessary beings.

omnipotent: Many theists believe that God is all-powerful. To use the philosophical jargon, the claim is that God is "omnipotent." Often, this is understood to mean that God is capable of doing *anything*. However, see section 4.1 of chapter 4 for some discussion of this point.

omniscient: Many theists believe that God is omniscient—that is, that he knows everything.

ontological argument: Anselm's argument (see section 3.6) and other arguments similar to it are called "ontological arguments."

ontology: This is the study of which things exist. For example, "Do souls exist?" is an ontological question.

potentially infinite process: A potentially infinite process is a process that could in principle be continued indefinitely. For example, the process of counting (1, 2, 3, 4, . . .) is potentially infinite. Some philosophers have claimed it is impossible for an infinite sequence of events ever to be completed.

pragmatic reasons: See evidential reasons and pragmatic reasons.

principle of sufficient reason: There are different versions of the principle of sufficient reason. The simplest version, which we discussed in section 3.3, is this: "Every 'Why?' question has an answer."

reductio ad absurdum: In a proof by *reductio ad absurdum* (or *reductio* for short), one shows that a claim is false by deducing a contradiction from it. For an example, see section 3.6. Sometimes *reductio* arguments are called "proofs by contradiction."

teleological argument: See design argument.

theism: Theism is the claim that God exists. Theists are people who believe that God exists. In this chapter, we have chosen to assume that if God exists at all, the following things are true of him:

1. God created the universe.
2. God is omnipotent.
3. God is perfectly good.
4. God is omniscient.
5. God deserves our unqualified love and complete obedience.

Comprehension Questions

1. Briefly summarize the first cause argument.
2. Briefly describe some objections to the first cause argument.
3. Briefly summarize Leibniz's cosmological argument.
4. Briefly describe some objections to Leibniz's cosmological argument.

5. Give an example of something in the biological world that has a purpose and is well suited to its purpose. (Don't repeat an example from the chapter).
6. Briefly describe the design argument.
7. What were Hume's objections to the design argument?
8. Describe the Darwinian objection to the design argument.
9. Explain how *reductio* arguments work.
10. How did Anselm define "God"?
11. Outline Anselm's ontological argument.
12. Suggest an example of a benefit of theism.
13. How did Clifford argue for his claim that it is "wrong always, everywhere, and for anyone, to believe anything upon insufficient evidence"?

Discussion Questions

1. In 1654, the philosopher and mathematician Blaise Pascal had an intense religious experience, which he described in a document now known as "Memorial." It began:

   From about half past ten at night until about half past midnight,
   FIRE
   GOD of Abraham, GOD of Isaac, GOD of Jacob
   not of the philosophers and of the learned.
   Certitude. Certitude. Feeling. Joy. Peace

   In this passage, Pascal suggests that the God of his personal experience is unlike the "God of the philosophers and of the learned." At the end of this chapter's Introduction, we characterized God as follows:

   - God created the universe from nothing.
   - God is all-powerful (or omnipotent, as philosophers and theologians sometimes put it).
   - God is perfectly good.
   - God knows everything (he is omniscient, to use the jargon).
   - God deserves our unqualified love and complete obedience.

   If you consider yourself a theist: Do you accept these five claims? Are there any other important truths about God we omitted?
   If you consider yourself an atheist: Do you think we accurately characterized the theism of people that you know?

2. Here is another cosmological argument—sometimes called the "Kalām cosmological argument":

   First premise: Everything that begins to exist has a cause.
   Second premise: The universe began to exist.
   Conclusion: The universe has a cause.

   (a) Suppose the premises are true: Must the conclusion be true as well?
   (b) Is the first premise true?
   (c) Is the second premise true?
   (d) If the conclusion is true, does it follow that theism is true?

3. Do you think that the physical universe is a necessary being or a contingent being? Why?

4. (a) In section 3.5, we gave the blind spot in the human eye as an example of a poor design in biology. What is another example?
   (b) Do such examples undermine the claim that organisms were designed by an omniscient and omnipotent God?

5. What is the best objection to Darwin's theory of evolution by natural selection? What is the best reply to this objection available to the Darwinian?

6. Here is another ontological argument, which is based on an argument put forward by Descartes:[15]

(1)	God has all perfections.	(This is the definition of "God")
(2)	Existence is a perfection.	(Premise)
(3)	God has existence (i.e., God exists).	(From 1, 2)

   The term "perfection" requires some explanation. The idea is that a "perfection" is a property that something must have in order to be a perfect being. For example, omnipotence, omniscience, and perfect goodness are "perfections."

   (a) Do you think that (1) is a good definition of "God"?
   (b) Is it plausible that existence is a perfection?
   (c) Does (3) follow from (1) and (2)?
   (d) Can you create a parody of this ontological argument?
   (e) Do you think that the above ontological argument is successful?

7. "If God exists, only those who believe that he exists will make it to heaven. If God doesn't exist, then believing that he exists will do little harm. So there is an enormous potential benefit to believing that God exists, and little potential harm. So on balance it's best to believe that God exists." What do you make of this reasoning? When thinking about your answer, you might like to carry out some research on "Pascal's Wager."

8. Suppose that an atheist gives the following argument:

> Premise: There is no good argument for theism.
> Conclusion: God does not exist.

Suppose for the sake of argument that the premise is true. Does the conclusion follow?

What to Look at Next

- As we said in the chapter's Introduction, there are many different versions of theism. *God: A Very Short Introduction* by John Bowker will introduce you to Jewish, Christian, and Islamic conceptions of God. It also includes a chapter on theism in Indian philosophy.
- In 1948, the Jesuit priest Frederick Copleston and the atheist philosopher Bertrand Russell had a debate on British radio about whether God exists. You may be able to find a recording of this debate online. Alternatively, a transcript has been published in John Hick, ed., *The Existence of God*.
- For a much longer discussion, see *God? A Debate Between a Christian and an Atheist* by William Lane Craig and Walter Sinnott-Armstrong. We recommend in particular William Lane Craig's presentation of the "fine-tuning argument"—an argument for theism that we have not discussed. The argument is in chapter 1.
- You can find a version of David Hume's *Dialogues Concerning Natural Religion* at www.earlymoderntexts.com.
- For scientifically informed discussion of the design argument, see Robert Pennock ed., *Intelligent Design Creationism and Its Critics: Philosophical, Theological, and Scientific Perspectives*. It is a long book. If you're not sure where to start, we recommend looking first at chapter 10, "Molecular Machines: Experimental Support for the Design Inference" by Michael J. Behe, and then at chapter 11, "Born-Again Creationism" by Philip Kitcher.

- Michael Behe's *Darwin's Black Box: The Biochemical Challenge to Evolution* is a highly influential and very readable attack on Darwin's theory of evolution by natural selection.
- Jerry Coyne's *Why Evolution Is True* is a spirited, entertaining, and well-informed defense of Darwinism.
- "The Will to Believe" by William James and "The Ethics of Belief" by W. K. Clifford are easy to find online. You should focus on the first section of Clifford's essay—the later sections are not often read today.
- The most comprehensive examination of the arguments for theism is Graham Oppy's *Arguing about Gods*. But beware—this is not an easy book!
- The book *The Life of Pi* by Yann Martel, and the movie of the same name directed by Ang Lee, deal with the topic that we discuss in section 3.8.

Notes

1. Following tradition, we are using masculine pronouns when talking about God. We do not mean to imply that God is literally male. It seems to us that it would be no less accurate to use feminine or neutral pronouns when discussing God.
2. Another influential version of the first cause argument was proposed by Thomas Aquinas, an important thirteenth-century Christian philosopher and theologian, in his book *Summa Theologica*.
3. Cosmology is a branch of physics. It includes the study of the origin and development of the universe.
4. Bertrand Russell and Frederick Copleston, "Debate on the Existence of God," in *The Existence of God*, ed. John Hick (New York: Macmillan, 1964).
5. Indeterministic processes also provide potential counterexamples to the principle of sufficient reason. See chapter 7.
6. The design argument is sometimes called the **teleological argument**.
7. David Hume, *Dialogues Concerning Natural Religion*, part 10, trans. Jonathan Bennett. The text is available at http://earlymoderntexts.com/assets/pdfs/hume1779.pdf.
8. One of the most trenchant and influential defenders of the Darwinian explanation is the Oxford biologist Richard Dawkins. His book *The Blind Watchmaker* (1986) offers a lively and biologically sophisticated contemporary response to Paley's design argument. In *The God Delusion* (2006), Dawkins argues that God almost certainly does not exist and that belief in God is a delusion.

9. It is easy to find your blind spot on a computer screen. Place a small icon of some sort in the center of your screen, then close your left eye and focus on the icon with your right eye. Now locate the cursor on the icon and gradually move it to the right. A few inches from the icon, the cursor will disappear; keep moving it to the right, and it will reappear. To find your left eye blind spot, close your right eye, focus on the icon, and move the cursor to the left of the icon.
10. A good place to start would be Robert Pennock, ed. *Intelligent Design Creationism and Its Critics: Philosophical, Theological, and Scientific Perspectives* (Cambridge, MA: MIT Press, 2002).
11. From Martin Luther King Jr., "Our God is Able," in *Strength to Love* (1963).
12. Ibid
13. Clifford, W. K. (1877). The Ethics of Belief. In The Ethics of Belief and Other Essays. Amherst, New York: Prometheus Books. pp. 70–97.
14. Ibid
15. Descartes makes this argument in the fifth of his *Meditations on First Philosophy*. You can find a translation of this book at www.earlymoderntexts.com.

CHAPTER 4

Why Does God Leave Us to Suffer?

Introduction

In a TV interview in 2015, the atheist comedian Stephen Fry was asked to imagine that, after death, he finds himself speaking to God. What would he say? Fry replied:

> I'll say, "Bone cancer in children: what's that about? How dare you? How dare you create a world in which there is such misery that's not our fault? It's evil; it's utterly, utterly evil. Why should I respect a capricious, mean-minded, stupid god who creates a world which is so full of injustice and pain?" That's what I would say. . . . Yes, the world is very splendid, but it also has in it insects whose whole lifecycle is to burrow into the eyes of children and make them blind. They eat outwards from the eyes. Why? Why did you do that to us? You could easily have made a creation in which that didn't exist.[1]

Of course, Fry wasn't seriously suggesting that the universe was created by an evil god. Rather, he was arguing that the God of Judaism, Christianity, and Islam doesn't exist at all. This is a version of "the problem of evil," which we discuss in this chapter. But first, we want to look at a number of other, less prominent arguments for **atheism**.

4.1 Three Logical Puzzles for Theists

Let's define the term "super-heavy stone" by stipulating that a super-heavy stone is a stone so heavy that even God cannot move it. Now here's a question for theists: Is God able to produce a super-heavy stone?

At first glance, the answer is simple. The theist believes that God is **omnipotent**, or all-powerful. This means that there is no limit to his power, and hence no limit to what he is able to do. And this implies that God is able to do *anything*—in particular, he must be able to produce a super-heavy stone. We seem now to have established:

(a) If God exists, he is able to produce a super-heavy stone.

But not so fast. Here's another line of thought. If God is omnipotent, he can move any stone, and from this, it apparently follows that super-heavy stones are impossible. And if super-heavy stones are impossible, it seems to follow that even God is not able to make one:

(b) If God exists, he is not able to make a super-heavy stone.

But now, comparing (a) and (b), we see that **theism** has conflicting implications. It follows, then, that theism must be false.

Thomas Aquinas proposed an elegant response to this argument.[2] To solve the problem, Aquinas thought that we need to think carefully about what "omnipotent" means. In our argument for (a), we assumed the following definition:

An omnipotent being is able to perform any action whatever.

Aquinas thought that this is a mistake, on the grounds that even an omnipotent being is unable to make a square circle or a lemon that is not a lemon. Even an omnipotent being, Aquinas thought, is unable to bring about impossible outcomes. Inspired by Aquinas, we might characterize omnipotence in the following way:

An omnipotent being is able to bring about any *possible* outcome.

Even an omnipotent being isn't able to bring about *impossible* outcomes. For example, even an omnipotent being isn't able to produce a square circle.

Now Aquinas thought that, because God is omnipotent, he can move any stone. Aquinas inferred that super-heavy stones are impossible and concluded that even God isn't able to make one. And so Aquinas accepted (b) but not (a).

Here is another puzzle for the theist: Is God able to do something morally wrong? Our first thought might be that if God exists, he is omnipotent and hence able to act immorally:

(c) If God exists, he is able to do something morally wrong.

At the same time, the theist's position is that God is perfectly good, and it would seem that a perfectly good being cannot act immorally. Hence:

(d) If God exists, he is not able to do something morally wrong.

As before, it seems that theism has incompatible implications—and so theism must be false.

We suspect that the theist should respond by again appealing to Aquinas's idea that God is not able to bring about impossible outcomes. We may argue that, because God is perfectly good, it is impossible for God to act immorally. Appealing to our Aquinas-inspired account of omnipotence, we can infer that God is not able to bring it about that God acts immorally. That is, God is not able to do something morally wrong. So we accept (d) but not (c).

We finish this section with one more puzzle for the theist, along the same lines. We quote from Richard Dawkins's popular book *The God Delusion*:

> It has not escaped the notice of logicians that omniscience and omnipotence are mutually incompatible. If God is omniscient, then he must already know how He is going to intervene to change the course of history using his omnipotence. But that means He can't change his mind about his intervention, which means He is not omnipotent.[3]

Here is an example. (The example is directed at Christians and Jews, but similar examples could be used for Islam.) In the book of Genesis, we are told that God promised never again to destroy the Earth with a flood. God is **omniscient** and would not lie, and so God *knew* at the time of his promise he would never again destroy the Earth with a flood. But if God knew *then* that he would never again destroy the Earth with a flood, it is not *now* possible for him to do so. But this apparently implies that God is not currently omnipotent. How do you think the theist should respond to Dawkins's claim that "omniscience and omnipotence are incompatible"?

4.2 Introducing the Problem of Evil

Suppose that you buy a cake and find that it is burnt. You would probably conclude the cake was made by a less-than-perfect baker. A perfect baker, presumably, would make a perfect cake. In the same way, it seems, a perfect God would make a perfect universe—or at least a universe that is as good as it is possible for a universe to be. Many theists believe that our world was made by God and that he is perfect. And some theists have concluded that our universe must be as good as a universe could be.

Gottfried Wilhelm Leibniz (1646–1716) developed a version of this argument in his book *Theodicy*.[4] Leibniz claimed that we live in the best possible universe. Our universe, he thought, is so good that it could not be better. Omitting some of the subtleties, Leibniz's argument went like this. Because he is omniscient, when God created the universe he knew how to make it as good as possible. Because he is omnipotent, he was able to create the best possible universe. Because he is perfectly good, he wouldn't choose to make a suboptimal universe. And so, Leibniz concluded, God must have made the best possible universe.

On the left is Gottfried Leibniz (1646–1716), who thought that we live in the best possible universe. On the right is Voltaire (1694–1778), who ridiculed this idea in his "The Lisbon Earthquake" and *Candide*.

In 1755, about half a century after Leibniz wrote *Theodicy*, there was a powerful earthquake in the Atlantic Ocean; its epicenter was just off the coast of Portugal. The earthquake, along with the tsunami and fires that it caused, destroyed the city of Lisbon, and many thousands of people were killed. The French philosopher Voltaire (1694–1778) wrote a poem about the event[5] in which he mocked Leibniz's suggestion that we live in the best possible universe: surely the universe would have been better if the earthquake had occurred farther out to sea, or had been less violent, or if the people of Lisbon had been warned, or if the earthquake had not occurred at all.

You can see here the beginnings of an argument for atheism. Suppose Leibniz was right that theism implies we live in the best possible universe. And suppose Voltaire was right that we *don't* live in the best possible universe. It then follows that theism is false. Theists sometimes call this "the problem of evil."[6]

It will be helpful to develop the problem in a way that avoids Leibniz's somewhat obscure talk of "possible universes." Here's the first premise of the atheist's argument:

(1) If God exists and is omnipotent, he could have prevented the Lisbon earthquake or ensured that it was less severe.

This seems obvious. If God exists and is omnipotent, he can do anything.[7] Therefore, if God exists, he could have prevented the earthquake or at least done something to mitigate its effects. He could have sent a clear warning to all the people of Lisbon in advance, or he could have performed a miracle to prevent the tsunami from reaching the shore. Next premise:

(2) If God exists and is omniscient, he knew how terrible the Lisbon earthquake would be and how to prevent it or ensure that it was less severe.

Again, this seems obvious. Next:

(3) If God exists and is perfectly good, he would have wanted to prevent the Lisbon earthquake or ensure that it was less severe.

This seems obvious too. Only a less than perfectly good God would have been happy to let many thousands of innocent people, including infants and children, die horrible deaths. Next:

(4) If God exists, then he is omnipotent, omniscient, and perfectly good.

From (1), (2), (3), and (4), the atheist infers:

(5) If God exists, the Lisbon earthquake would have been prevented or been less severe.

And so finally:

(6) Theism is not true.

It's easy to devise variants of this argument by appealing to other horrible events. One might ask why God didn't prevent the Holocaust; why he didn't intervene to stop Leopold II's atrocities in the Congo; or why he didn't protect the Chinese from the 1931 floods, which are thought to have killed more than 1 million people. And it's not only such world-historical traumas that present a challenge to the theist; small tragedies that won't be recorded in the history books are just as problematic. You can probably think of family members or friends who have had to endure apparently purposeless suffering: Why didn't God do more to help?

To deal with the problem of evil, it is not enough for the theist to respond to just one of these arguments. What's needed is a general strategy (or collection of strategies) for responding to arguments that have this form.

4.3 Three Inadequate Responses

We think that theists have found some powerful responses to the problem of evil. We will discuss them in a moment. First, however, we clear away a trio of clearly inadequate responses.

The first inadequate response: suffering isn't real.

We think it's obvious that suffering is real and that there's lots of it! Anybody who watches the news should understand this. The claim that suffering isn't real could only be taken seriously by someone who uses the word "suffering" or "real" in some nonstandard sense—and it only confuses the issue to abuse the dictionary. We might call this style of response "bait-and-switch" (or "B.S." for short) because it involves misleading people by using a word in a nonstandard way.

The second inadequate response: evil is merely a privation of good.

We all know that darkness is the absence of light. Augustine of Hippo (354–430) claimed that, in much the same way, evil is the absence of goodness. Here is an alternative analogy. Consider the following instructions for making a bagel:

Step 1: Make the doughy part of the bagel.
Step 2: Make the hole.
Step 3: Attach the hole to the doughy part to create the bagel.

This is clearly wrong. When making a bagel, the hole isn't an extra thing that needs to be constructed and added once the dough has been made and shaped. The hole is merely an absence (or privation) of dough. Make and shape the dough, and the hole is there automatically, without any further work.

According to Augustine, evil is merely an absence (or privation) of goodness. Just as the baker doesn't need to make a hole in addition to the dough, God didn't make evil in addition to goodness. This may be a welcome conclusion for the theist, but as Augustine understood, the idea that evil is a privation does not on its own solve the problem of evil. Even if it is true that the horrors of the Lisbon earthquake or the Holocaust were privations of goodness, they were still appalling, and it still seems that a good, omnipotent, and omniscient God would have done something to prevent the earthquake or mitigate its effects.

> *The third inadequate response: God's goodness is not human goodness— it is divine goodness. God's goodness cannot be understood using the moral terms we use when evaluating the actions of human beings.*

The idea here is that there are two sorts of goodness: "human goodness" and "divine goodness." When we use the word "good" in everyday life, it's human goodness we are talking about. God's goodness is a less familiar kind of goodness, a kind of goodness we don't fully understand: it is *divine* goodness. This is supposed to cast doubt on premise (3) of the argument:

(3) If God is perfectly good, he would have wanted to prevent the Lisbon earthquake or are least ensured that it was less severe.

Given our lack of understanding of divine goodness, it is claimed, we have no grounds for making this claim about how God would behave.

On its own, we think this response to the problem of evil is inadequate. If a person can have "divine goodness" while refusing to take the opportunity to save innocent children from death, "divine goodness" is not a type of goodness at all—just as fool's gold is not a type of gold. We think, then, that the term "divine goodness" is misleading, and that this response is just more B.S. (i.e., bait-and-switch).

However, this response to the problem of evil does point us in an interesting direction. When presenting the problem of evil, we assumed that if God exists, he is omnipotent, omniscient, and perfectly good. But perhaps, to avoid the problem of evil, the theist should deny this. That is, perhaps the theist should reject premise (4) of the argument.

4.4 Rethinking the Nature of God

Few theists have been willing to deny that God is perfectly good, and it is easy to see why. A central component of most versions of monotheism is the idea that God deserves our unqualified love and obedience. But it is hard to see why this should be if God is not perfectly good. If God were only imperfectly good, it seems that theists should start questioning God's commands—saying things like "I usually do what God asks, but I think he's wrong on this one, and so I've decided not to obey him in this case."

Perhaps a more promising approach for the theist is to deny that God is omniscient. In particular, the theist may argue that certain random events are unforeseeable, even by God. For example, the theist might insist that earthquakes are inherently unpredictable events, and that even God couldn't have foreseen the Lisbon earthquake or its devastating effects. This accounts for his failure to prevent the earthquake or mitigate its effects.

This might be a good response to the "Lisbon earthquake" version of the problem of evil. We don't think, however, that it is a good response to the "Holocaust" version of the argument. The Holocaust *was* predictable in advance, and it seems that an omnipotent and perfectly good God could have foreseen it and acted to prevent it or mitigate its effects. So we think that while denying God's omniscience might help with some versions of the problem of evil, we don't think that this is a complete response to the problem.

Alternatively, the theist may respond to the problem of evil by denying that God is omnipotent. In section 4.1, for example, we saw that

Thomas Aquinas thought God could not perform logically impossible tasks. For example, God cannot create something that is both a lemon and not a lemon. Perhaps the theist should also deny that God can break the laws of physics. The theist may then argue that God did not prevent the Lisbon earthquake or the Holocaust because he couldn't do so, because to prevent the earthquake would have required a violation of physical law.

There is another version of theism (known as **dualism**) according to which God is not omnipotent.[8] Dualists claim that, while God is indeed immensely powerful, there is another powerful agent, an evil agent, who is responsible for creating suffering. While God is sure to be victorious in the end, for the time being the evil agent will continue to cause earthquakes, famines, and so on. The Manichaean religion was "dualist" in this sense, as are some versions of Zoroastrianism. There have also been Christian groups with dualist views. To this day, some Christians think that Satan is responsible for some or all of the suffering in the world—and that God is unable for the moment to prevent Satan from causing suffering. We think that this version of theism is not vulnerable to the problem of evil argument.

4.5 Theodicy

Think about vaccinations. Vaccinations can be unpleasant (especially for people who have a fear of hypodermic needles), but we tolerate the vaccination to secure a larger good (namely, immunity from a disease). This is a simple illustration of a general point: sometimes one is justified in permitting or causing suffering. Sometimes it is okay to allow suffering, or even to cause suffering. The theist may appeal to this point in response to the problem of evil. The theist may insist that God is capable of preventing suffering and chooses not to do so, adding that God is completely justified in doing so. Responses to the problem of evil of this kind are called "theodicies." In this section, we look at three theodicies. The first two we find unpersuasive; the third is much more powerful.

Here is the first **theodicy**. Some think that people who have done wrong consequently deserve to suffer—and that if such people do suffer, it is for the best. The theist, taking up this idea, might say that God in some cases permits suffering because the people involved deserve to suffer. For example, God might allow a thief to suffer on the grounds that the thief deserves it. In effect, God punishes the thief by allowing him to suffer.

We think it's clear that this particular theodicy does not constitute a complete solution to the problem of evil. As Voltaire pointed out in his poem, many of the people who died in the Lisbon earthquake were very young babies, who had surely done nothing to deserve their horrible deaths.

The second theodicy is if anything even less impressive. Many people think that in some cases suffering is good for a person in the long term because it is character building. For example, someone who suffers through illness as a child might become more empathetic as a result, and this might cause that person to lead a better life later on. Or someone might learn by suffering to appreciate the good aspects of their life more fully. Developing this idea, a theist may say that God in some cases permits suffering because he wants us to have good characters.

The most obvious response to this theodicy is simply that in many cases suffering is not character building. Think, for example, of military veterans whose lives are blighted by posttraumatic stress syndrome, or PTSD. Or consider again the babies who died horrible deaths in the Lisbon earthquake—the suffering of these babies was not character building. And there's another problem with this theodicy: it's not clear why an omnipotent God would have to make people suffer to improve their characters. Why could he not just ensure that we are born with optimal characters?

The last theodicy we consider is much more powerful. It begins with the idea that human beings have free will. We talk about what this means more fully in chapter 9, but for now, suffice it to say that free will is the capacity for making our own decisions about what to do and then acting on those decisions. Of course, our free will is limited in many ways—there are limits to what we can choose to do. Nevertheless, many people think that free will is enormously valuable.

The "free will" theodicy works like this. Recognizing its enormous value, God made sure that human beings have free will. Because human beings are free, we are capable of making bad decisions: we can act immorally, or just stupidly. This can lead to suffering. God permits this suffering only because he thinks it is of overriding importance that we have free will.

Here is another way of thinking about it. Try to imagine what would happen if God were to prevent all suffering. To do this, he would need constantly to intervene to prevent people from inflicting suffering on one another. He would have to prevent criminals from harming their victims; he would have to prevent politicians from making poor policy decisions; he would have to intervene in people's conversations to stop them from offending each other; he would have to prevent young people from choosing the wrong career paths; he would have to prevent people from becoming parents before they were ready; and so on. But if God were to constantly interfere in people's lives in this intrusive way, our freedom would be hugely curtailed, if not completely destroyed. He would be guilty of cosmic overparenting. Proponents of the free will theodicy say that God permits suffering because, rightly, he wants us to be free.

J. L. Mackie (1917–1981) presented an ingenious objection to the free will theodicy. Mackie thought that a perfect God could create people who have free will, and are thus capable of acting wrongly, but who also have such good characters that they never, or almost never, do so. An omnipotent, omniscient, and perfectly good God, Mackie thought, would create a world populated by Nelson Mandelas and Mother Teresas and empty of Stalins and Hitlers. If this is right, then the idea that God had to permit a great deal of suffering to ensure that we have free will is mistaken.[9]

Mackie's objection raises deep questions about the nature of free will—a topic to which we'll return in chapter 9. For now, we focus on a more straightforward objection to the free will theodicy: that the free will defense neglects cases of **natural evil**—that is, cases in which suffering is not due to human wrongdoing.[10] Consider, for example, famines caused by drought. God could prevent such famines simply by sending more rain—and this would not in any way interfere with our free will.

Proponents of the free will theodicy may reply that natural evil is less common than it might appear to be. For example, economists have stressed that the causes of famine are as much political as natural. Amartya Sen famously argued, "No famine has ever taken place in the history of the world in a functioning democracy."[11]

The point is a good one—but we continue to think there are some cases of genuine natural evil. Sometimes young children get leukemia; this causes tremendous suffering even if the child has access to the best medical care. Occasionally someone is killed or seriously injured by a lightning bolt. Perhaps the Lisbon earthquake is another example. So it seems to us that the free will theodicy is at best a partial solution to the problem of evil.

4.6 Skeptical Theism

The proponents of the various theodicies we considered in the previous section believe that God is able to prevent much of the suffering in the world, but that he chooses not to do so. They then try to explain God's reasons for permitting suffering. Some theists believe that there is something arrogant about this project. They claim that God's intellectual capacities far outstrip our own, and hence we should not expect to be able to understand his reasons. This line of thought leads to a position known as **skeptical theism**.

An analogy may help. Consider a parent taking his young child to be vaccinated. The vaccination will be painful, and the child may have no comprehension of the purpose of the procedure. Even so, the parent is quite right that it is better for the child to be vaccinated. Or think of a parent telling a young child to do math homework. The child protests, "It's boring and there's no point—we all have calculators on our smartphones now anyway!" Again, the parent is quite right that the child should trudge through the math homework, even if the child doesn't understand why. According to skeptical theists, our situation is like that of the children in these examples. God permits our suffering, and he is right to do so, but we are unable to understand his reasons.

Some skeptical theists stress our ignorance of the pattern of cause-and-effect in history. It is often argued that events in history that are bad in themselves nevertheless have good consequences: wars lead to technological advances; the Black Death was a partial cause of the Renaissance; and so on. The skeptical theist may suggest that the Lisbon earthquake had good consequences too—though we may be unable to identify them. Just as a child being vaccinated doesn't understand the beneficial effect of vaccination, so we don't understand the beneficial effects of the Lisbon earthquake.

Other skeptical theists stress our ignorance of value. Dogs can't see the value in great paintings or symphonies: there is a sort of value invisible to dogs. The skeptical theist may suggest that, in much the same way, certain sorts of value are invisible to us. Perhaps some of the consequences of the Lisbon earthquake were very good, but we are unable to see this.

Many people find these ideas extremely implausible. It is tempting to reply, *"Of course it would have been better to prevent the Lisbon earthquake, you monster!"* Nevertheless, skeptical theism has many supporters. Part of its appeal is that skeptical theism can be used in response to *all* versions of the problem of evil argument. God had his reasons for not preventing Leopold II's atrocities in the Congo, though we may never understand those reasons. God was justified in not preventing the 1931 floods in China, though his justification is hidden from us. And so on.

It is a consequence of this position that we are profoundly ignorant about good and bad. It seems *obvious* to us that it would have been better if the Holocaust had been prevented. If the skeptical theist denies this, however, it implies that our ordinary views about value are profoundly mistaken. And we are left with troubling questions, which seem impossible to answer: if God was right not to prevent the Holocaust, does this mean that the Holocaust was part of some divine plan? And if so, does it follow that those who attempted to prevent the Holocaust were obstructing God's plan? Such questions leave us with the disorienting sense that our moral compasses are broken. Critics of skeptical theism allege this leads to "moral paralysis."[12]

Here is a slightly different way to see the problem. Many theists believe that we must do what God wants. The first American saint, Elizabeth Ann Seton, put it well when she said, "the first end I propose in our daily work is to do the will of God; secondly, to do it in the manner he wills it; and thirdly to do it because it is his will." But skeptical theism seems to imply that we have very little understanding of God's goals. And how are theists to "do the will of God" when they are so profoundly ignorant about what God wills? Again, we see that skeptical theism threatens to lead to moral paralysis.

Conclusion

Voltaire returned to the problem of evil in his comic novella *Candide*. The eponymous hero of the novella is convinced by his mentor Dr. Pangloss, a Leibnizian and professor of "metaphysico-theologo-cosmonigology," that we live in the best possible universe. Candide is slowly disabused of this doctrine by a series of comically horrible events. Dr. Pangloss is hanged, insisting always that, somehow, "all is for the best." After watching the hanging, Candide is whipped, to music, by the Portuguese inquisition. As he is tortured, he asks himself, *if this is the best possible universe, what are the others like?* Voltaire's novella was banned throughout much of Europe, in part because the authorities understood that Candide's question presents a formidable intellectual challenge to theists.

However, theists have devised some compelling responses to this challenge. It is unclear to us whether one of these responses (or some combination of them) will ultimately prove satisfactory.

Glossary

atheism: Atheism is the claim that God does not exist. Atheists are people who think that God does not exist. (See theism).

dualism: Beware! "Dualism" is a word used in many different ways in philosophy. In this chapter, we use "dualism" as a label for the claim that (a) God is very powerful, but (b) there is another very powerful agent, an evil agent, who is responsible for creating suffering; and (c) God is incapable for the time being of preventing the evil agent from creating suffering.

moral evil vs. natural evil: When a bad state of affairs arises because of human wrongdoing, it is moral evil. Other bad states of affairs are natural evils.

natural evil: See moral evil vs. natural evil.

omnipotent: Many theists believe that God is all-powerful. To use the philosophical jargon, the claim is that God is omnipotent. Often, this is understood to mean that God is capable of doing *anything*. However, see section 4.1 for some discussion of this point.

omniscient: Many theists believe that God is omniscient—that is, that he knows everything.

skeptical theism: Skeptical theists believe that God has reasons for permitting suffering, reasons that we cannot understand.

theism: Theism is the claim that God exists. Theists are people who believe that God exists. In this chapter, we have chosen to start with the assumption that if God exists at all, the following things are true of him:

1. God created the universe.
2. God is omnipotent.
3. God is perfectly good.
4. God is omniscient.
5. God deserves our unqualified love and complete obedience.

theodicy: To give a theodicy is to explain why an omnipotent, omniscient, and perfectly good God might permit suffering. See section 4.5. (Note that the term "theodicy" is used in several different ways by different philosophers.)

Comprehension Questions

1. A theist writes, "God is omnipotent—this means he has the power to create a square circle." Explain why Aquinas would not have accepted this claim.
2. What is omniscience?
3. What is the problem of evil?
4. What is dualism? Explain how a dualist would respond to the problem of evil.
5. What is a theodicy? Describe some theodicies.
6. Explain the free will theodicy.
7. What is natural evil? Give an example. Explain why such cases are problematic for proponents of the free will theodicy.
8. Explain Mackie's objection to the free will theodicy.
9. What is skeptical theism?
10. It has been alleged that skeptical theism leads to "moral paralysis." Explain this objection.

Discussion Questions

1. Suppose we define "mystery box" by saying that a mystery box is a box whose contents are unknown to *everyone,* including God. Now here is a question for the theist: Is God capable of creating a mystery box? On the one hand, the theist thinks God is omnipotent. This seems to imply that God can do *anything,* and so the theist may be forced to conclude God is capable of creating a mystery box. On the other hand, the theist thinks God is omniscient—and this seems to imply that mystery boxes are impossible. Does this show that it is impossible for God to be both omnipotent and omniscient?
2. As we said in section 4.2, there are many different versions of the problem of evil argument. There is a "Lisbon earthquake" version, a "Holocaust" version, and so forth. Which version(s) of the problem are most powerful, and why?

3. Can you think of an event in your life that was very painful at the time but in retrospect was beneficial for you overall? If so, does this show that a perfect God might permit suffering in some cases?
4. Could there exist a person who has genuine free will but is of such excellent moral character that it is impossible for that person to act wrongly?
5. A skeptical theist might respond to the "moral paralysis" objection in the following way:

> I accept that it is difficult for us to do God's will because it is difficult for us to understand God's plans. However, I don't see this as an objectionable feature of my position, because I think that *everyone* should admit that it is in many cases very hard to figure out what one should do. We regularly face *spectacularly complicated* moral choices, which are inevitably very difficult. It is very difficult for human beings to understand their moral obligations. This is a regrettable but unavoidable feature of the human condition. It is no defect of my position that I face up to this.

Is this an adequate response to the "moral paralysis" objection?
6. In this passage, Martin Luther King Jr. sketches a response to the problem of evil:

> This problem, namely, the problem of evil, has always plagued the human mind. Of course much of the evil we experience is caused by our own folly, ignorance and also by the misuse of our God given freedom. Beyond this I can only say that there is and always will be a penumbra of mystery surrounding God. What appears at the moment to be evil may have a purpose that our finite minds are incapable of comprehending. So in spite of the presence of evil and the doubts that lurk in our minds, we shall not surrender the conviction that our God is [powerful].[13]

King's response is a hybrid of two responses we considered in the chapter. What are they? Is King's response adequate?
7. In chapter 1, we considered the idea that some people benefit from believing that God exists and that this justifies their theism. Might one similarly argue that some people benefit from believing that God *doesn't* exist and that this justifies atheism in some cases? If you think the answer is "yes," provide an example.

What to Look at Next

- As we said in chapter 1, there are many different versions of theism. *God: A Very Short Introduction* by John Bowker will introduce you to Jewish, Christian, and Islamic conceptions of God. It also includes a chapter on theism in Indian philosophy.
- Richard Dawkins's *The God Delusion* was a huge bestseller in 2006. In chapter 4, Dawkins presents a novel argument for atheism.
- David Hume's *Dialogues Concerning Natural Religion* is a classic skeptical critique of orthodox forms of theism. You can find (a slightly reworded version of) it at www.earlymoderntexts.com.
- There is a discussion of the problem of evil in *God? A Debate Between a Christian and an Atheist* by William Lane Craig and Walter Sinnott-Armstrong.
- Chapter 9 of J. L. Mackie's *The Miracle of Theism: Arguments for and Against the Existence of God* is a classic presentation of the problem of evil, and it contains a highly influential discussion of the free will theodicy.
- In *The Problem of Pain*, C. S. Lewis (one of the most popular Christian thinkers) discusses the problem of evil in detail.
- *The Problem of Evil*, edited by Marilyn McCord Adams and Robert Merrihew Adams, is a fascinating collection of papers by different philosophers.
- J. L. Schellenberg's landmark book *Divine Hiddenness and Human Reason* presents a further argument against theism.
- Voltaire's novella *Candide* is short and still very funny, despite its age.
- Many of Ingmar Bergmann's movies deal with the problem of evil and the (closely related) problem of divine hiddenness. *The Seventh Seal* is a good place to start.

Notes

1. Henry McDonald, "Stephen Fry Calls God an "Evil, Capricious, Monstrous Maniac," *Guardian*, February 1, 2015, https://www.theguardian.com/culture/2015/feb/01/stephen-fry-god-evil-maniac-irish-tv.
2. See *The Summa Theologica of St. Thomas Aquinas* (London: Burns Oates and Washbourne, 1921), pt. 1, qu. 25, art. 3.
3. Richard Dawkins, *The God Delusion* (New York: Bantam Books, 2006), 101.

4. Gottfried Wilhelm Leibniz, *Theodicy: Essays on the Goodness of God, the Freedom on Man and the Origin of Evil*, trans. E. M. Huggard (La Salle, IL: Open Court, 1985).
5. Voltaire, "The Lisbon Earthquake," in *Candide, or Optimism*, trans. Tobias Smollett (London: Penguin Books, 2005).
6. Voltaire was not the first to see the problem; it dates back at least to the ancient Greek philosopher Epicurus (341–270 BCE).
7. As we saw in section 4.1, this claim probably requires qualification—but the subtleties don't seem relevant here.
8. The term "dualism" has a number of different meanings in philosophy. We encounter one of these different meanings of "dualism" in chapter 11.
9. J. L. Mackie, *The Miracle of Theism* (Oxford: Oxford University Press, 1982).
10. Natural evil is traditionally contrasted with **moral evil**—that is, bad states of affairs that arise due to human wrongdoing.
11. Amartya Sen, *Development as Freedom* (New York: Anchor Books, 1999), 16.
12. We have taken the expression "moral paralysis" from Scott Sehon, "The Problem of Evil: Skeptical Theism Leads to Moral Paralysis," *International Journal for Philosophy of Religion* 67, no. 2 (2010): 67–80.
13. From Martin Luther King Jr., "Our God Is Able," in *Strength to Love, Special Edition* (Minneapolis, MN: Fortress Press, 2016).

CHAPTER 5

Can We Be Completely Certain of Anything?

Introduction

We *think* that the highest mountain in Mexico is the Pico de Orizaba, but we are not completely certain. We might be wrong: it's easy to make mistakes about that sort of thing, after all. And we *think* that a cubic foot is about 30 liters, but again, we're not totally sure. Many of our beliefs are tainted by doubt.

But is there anything that we can be *completely* certain about? Are there perhaps philosophical, or mathematical, or religious, or scientific doctrines that can be known with total certainty? Is it ever rational to be *100 percent, not a shadow of a doubt, bet your life on it* certain?

In his *Meditations on First Philosophy*, René Descartes (1596–1650) set out to find complete certainty. In this chapter, we follow him.

5.1 Descartes's Project

Before the sixteenth century, few things could have appeared more certain than that the Earth is stationary. It seems so obvious. If you go to the top of hill and look around, you can see moving things—streams, clouds, animals, and so on—but the Earth seems to stay still. This naïve argument was reinforced by the best science of the time: astronomers agreed that the Earth is stationary at the center of the universe, while

René Descartes (1596–1650)

the stars, the planets, the Moon, and the Sun move around the Earth, attached to transparent "celestial spheres." Common sense and science were in agreement: the Earth does not move.

This began to change in 1543 with the publication of Nicolaus Copernicus's *On the Revolutions of the Heavenly Spheres*. Copernicus argued that the Sun is stationary at the center of the universe, while the planets (including the Earth) move around it. Copernicus's idea was slow to catch on, but by the early seventeenth century, many scientists were convinced that Copernicus had been right. One of them was René Descartes.

During Descartes's lifetime, new scientific research undermined other medieval doctrines too. It had been generally believed that celestial bodies are perfectly spherical—a claim which Galileo Galilei (1564–1642) refuted by making careful telescopic observations of mountains on the Moon. William Harvey (1578–1657) established that the heart pumps blood in a circuit around the body: out through the arteries, back through the veins. Most physiologists before Harvey had thought that the liver creates blood, which is then pumped outward by the heart to the different parts of the body, where it is used up.

Descartes knew of these developments in the sciences, and he had a hypothesis about why previous generations of scientists had got so many things wrong: they'd developed their theories with too much haste. Scientists in the past, Descartes thought, were guilty of jumping to conclusions. Descartes came up with a stunningly ambitious plan. Thinking that there might be still more errors hidden in contemporary science, Descartes decided to start again—developing scientific theory entirely from scratch. He initiated this vast project in his book *Meditations on First Philosophy*. To avoid mistakes like those of previous scientists, Descartes decided to put aside all pre-existing doctrine and to only accept a claim once he had shown that it was *certainly* true. He sometimes compared himself to a builder constructing a new building from scratch. He wanted the foundations of his building to be unshakably solid.

5.2 Certainty Is Hard to Find

So Descartes wanted to find truths of which he could be certain—truths to form the foundation of his new science. But the more you think about it, the more you realize that certainty—*complete* certainty—is very hard to find.

An example. You probably think that in New York City next year, July will be on average hotter than December. But can you be certain—*completely* certain, beyond all doubt—that some freak weather pattern won't cause there to be snow in the city in the summer, when there would usually be flip-flops and sunscreen? We think not. Weather prediction is a probabilistic business: *near certain* or *very confident* is as good as it gets.

Another example. You probably think that the Notre Dame Cathedral is in Paris. But are you completely certain? Here's a story:

> Last week the Walt Disney Company bought Notre Dame Cathedral for an undisclosed though no doubt colossal sum. The iconic French

building has been carefully disassembled and the pieces are now in transit to the Walt Disney World Resort. Once the pieces arrive in Florida, the cathedral will be rebuilt and used to house musical performances featuring famous Disney characters.

Can you be 100 percent certain that this story is mistaken? We think not. Strange things do happen, and even today, we sometimes don't hear about an important news story until a week or two after the event. We're not claiming that this story is plausible or likely—it isn't. In fact, it's ridiculous. The point is that you can't be *completely 100 percent certain* that the story is false, and so you can't be completely certain the Notre Dame Cathedral is in Paris.

Maybe it's unsurprising that we can't be certain about the future or about distant things like the Notre Dame Cathedral. But it might seem reasonable to think you *can* be certain about what you can see right now. Descartes denied this. He pointed out that we've all been deceived by our senses in the past. He noted that round towers sometimes look square from a distance, and that large statues sometimes look small when they are placed on tall plinths. You may have noticed that, in dim light, colored surfaces sometimes look gray. And when capsaicin—an active ingredient in chili peppers—is rubbed onto the skin, it can give the sensation of heat even when there is no change of temperature.

Now Descartes claimed that it is "unwise to trust completely those who have deceived us even once"; he concluded that we cannot be completely certain what we "see" is real. This was his argument:

Premise 1: Our senses have deceived us in the past.
Premise 2: It is unwise to trust completely those who have deceived us even once.
Conclusion: One should not place absolute confidence in one's senses.

You might reject the second premise of this argument, on the grounds that, while it is true our senses have deceived us in the past, they have only done so in rather special conditions. For example, vision is unreliable when the objects being inspected are faraway, or when we are tired, or when we not paying attention, or when the light is poor. Perhaps it is only in special cases like these that we should not place absolute confidence in our senses. In good conditions, perhaps you *can* be completely certain of what you see. For example, suppose you're wide awake and in good lighting, and you are looking at a banana on a table right in front of you. Can't you be certain that there is a banana before you—or at least that something yellow and crescent-shaped is there?

But Descartes argued that error is possible even in what seem to be perfect conditions. Sometimes we have dreams that are so vivid they perfectly mimic our waking experiences. Even in the best conditions—when you are fully awake, when the lighting is good, and so on—you can't be completely certain that you are not dreaming. And so, Descartes argued, you can't be completely certain of what you're seeing. In summary:

Premise 1: You can never be completely certain that you are not asleep, having a vivid dream.
Premise 2: You can only be completely certain that your perceptions are accurate if you can be completely certain that you are not currently asleep, having a vivid dream.
Conclusion: You can never be completely certain that your perceptions are accurate.

We can reinforce Descartes's point by thinking about hallucinations. The neurologist Oliver Sacks described a strange experience he had after taking the drug Artane:

> I was in the kitchen, putting on a kettle for tea, when I heard a knocking at my front door. It was my friends Jim and Kathy; they would often drop round on a Sunday morning. "Come in, door's open," I called out, and as they settled themselves in the living room, I asked, "How do you like your eggs?" Jim liked them sunny side up, he said. Kathy preferred them over easy. We chatted away while I sizzled their ham and eggs—there were low swinging doors between the kitchen and the living room, so we could hear each other easily. Then, five minutes later, I shouted, "Everything's ready," put their ham and eggs on a tray, walked into the living room—and found it completely empty. No Jim, no Kathy, no sign that they had ever been there. I was so staggered I almost dropped the tray.[1]

This anecdote shows that even in what seem to be perfect conditions, sense perception can mislead. (Though the story has a happy ending—Sacks had three portions of ham and eggs to himself.)

Now you may have good reason for being confident that you are not now hallucinating. Perhaps you have never hallucinated before and have never knowingly consumed a hallucinogen. Even so, it is never beyond *all* doubt that one is hallucinating. In summary:

Premise 1:   You can never be completely certain that you are not currently hallucinating.
Premise 2:   You can only be completely certain your perceptions are accurate if you can be completely certain that you are not currently hallucinating.
Conclusion: You can never be completely certain your perceptions are accurate.

Descartes then raised the suggestion that certainty can be found in mathematics. Consider, for example, the claim that the sum of 7 and 5 is 12, or the claim that there is no largest prime number. Perhaps we can be completely certain these claims are true. After all, these claims can be *proven* mathematically, in an **a priori** way—that is, without appeal to sense perception. At this point, Descartes raised possibly the most famous thought experiment in the whole history of philosophy. We paraphrase Descartes's thought experiment as follows:

> There exists an "**evil demon**" with supernatural powers. The demon is able to manipulate your mind to deceive you: he can induce hallucinations, and he can modify your memories in whatever way he chooses. None of your present experiences are accurate: they're all hallucinations caused by the demon. All of your real memories have been deleted and replaced by false "memories." You're wrong about what your name is, wrong about where you grew up, wrong about what your body looks like, and so on. The demon is also able to scramble your thought processes, so that, for example, your mathematical calculations go wrong. If you try to find the sum 123 and 456, the demon can ensure that you get the wrong answer.

This story might strike you as silly, and perhaps it is. But Descartes was not suggesting that the story is plausible or likely. As with the story about the Notre Dame Cathedral, the suggestion is just that one cannot be *totally certain* that the story is false. Descartes argued that, because you can't be completely sure that the evil demon story is false, you can't be completely sure that your mathematical calculations are correct. And so it seems that complete certainty is impossible, even in mathematics.

Descartes's evil demon thought experiment introduced to philosophy a new form of **skepticism**, a very radical form of skepticism. We are used to the idea that sense perception occasionally misleads us: illusions and hallucinations do occasionally happen. But Descartes challenged his readers to refute the hypothesis that the entire "physical" world is an illusion created by an evil demon. He even suggested that our "rational" thought processes might be disturbed by an evil demon, so things we take to have been mathematically proven are in fact false.

Lilly and Lana Wachowski's 1999 movie *The Matrix* is an echo of Descartes's evil demon story. The central character in the movie is Neo, who realizes that the apparently physical world around him is instead a vast computer simulation. He learns, too, that what he takes to be his physical body is merely a tiny part of this computer simulation. Almost all the people around him, however, are ignorant of the deceit: they don't know that their surroundings are merely simulated. Following Descartes, we can ask: Can you be completely sure that the "physical" world around you is not merely a computer simulation?

5.3 Achieving Certainty

At this point, you might be starting to think that Descartes's project is hopeless. Seeking complete certainty, you might think, is like searching for a perpetual motion machine, a round square, or the fountain of youth. But despite all the skeptical points discussed in the last section, Descartes thought that complete certainty *is* possible: he claimed to be completely, 100 percent certain of his own existence. As he famously said, I think, therefore I exist: *cogito, ergo sum*.

You might object that Descartes couldn't be totally sure that he existed because he had no way to rule out with certainty the hypothesis that his life is just an extended dream or hallucination. But Descartes had a clever reply to this objection: he pointed out that, even if his life is a dream or hallucination, he must nevertheless exist in order to *have* the dream or the hallucination. Nonexistent things can't dream, and they can't hallucinate.

What about the evil demon? Could Descartes rule out the hypothesis that he believes he exists only because this belief has been inserted by a powerful, deceitful demon? Descartes pointed out that an evil demon, however powerful, can only deceive existing things—it's impossible to deceive something that doesn't exist. So even if Descartes is being tricked by a demon, it's nevertheless true that he exists. (This line of thought is sometimes called the "*cogito* argument.")

Additionally, Descartes claimed to know with complete certainty something about what kind of thing he was: he could be completely sure that he was a thinking thing. (It sounds better in Latin: Descartes was completely certain he was a *res cogitans*.) Descartes used the term **thinking** very broadly, so that it covers all conscious mental activity, including

- dreaming,
- feeling pain,
- seeing yellow,
- doing a calculation,
- having an urge to eat chocolate, and
- deciding to sing a song.

Again, you might object that Descartes's thinking is all part of a hallucination or dream—but Descartes might reply that hallucinating and dreaming are themselves sorts of thinking, in this broad sense.

Though this interpretation is slightly controversial, Descartes is often thought to have claimed that you can have certain knowledge about some of your own conscious mental states. To understand this claim, imagine you go to the doctor complaining that you are in horrible pain. The doctor takes a blood sample, carries out some tests, and then says:

> We've identified your illness. It turns out that you're not in pain after all: that's just an illusion caused by your disease. It may *seem* to you that you're in pain, but you're not *really* in pain.

The doctor's claim seems ridiculous: if it *seems* to you that you're in pain, then you *are* in pain. You may not know the cause of your ailment: perhaps the cause of your pain is entirely psychological, and there is no damage to your body. But whatever the cause of the pain, there's no doubt that you *are* in pain. You can be completely certain that you are in pain, or so it seems.

Here's another example. Suppose that you are looking at a red piece of paper. Having read Descartes, you may find yourself doubting that there is really a red piece of paper in front of you: perhaps you are dreaming or hallucinating, or perhaps the experience is caused by an evil demon. Even so, it seems that you can be certain you are having the *experience* of red. The cause of this experience may be obscure to you, but the experience itself cannot be doubted.

It would be a mistake to claim that we all have complete and perfect knowledge of our own conscious mental states. It's possible to misremember one's mental states. For example, you might seem to remember having a headache yesterday when in fact you haven't had a headache for months. Arguably, it's also possible to fail to notice one's conscious mental states. For example, marathon runners, in their determination to win a race, might fail to notice an ache in the ankle. Nonetheless, it is plausible to think that we can know a great deal about our current mental states with the complete certainty that Descartes sought.

5.4 Clear and Distinct Perception

Descartes took himself to have shown that complete certainty is possible. He could be completely certain that he existed and that he was a thinking thing. Perhaps he could also be completely certain about some of his mental states. Generalizing from these examples, Descartes then proposed a method for achieving certain knowledge.

Descartes claimed that when he reflected on the claim "I exist," or the claim "I am a thinking thing," he felt *compelled* to believe. He couldn't help believing that he existed, and he couldn't help believing that he was a thinking thing. Descartes called this inner compulsion **"clear and distinct perception."**[2] He then proposed the following general rule:

> Whenever I clearly and distinctly perceive that something is true, it *is* true and I am entitled to believe it with complete certainty.

"I exist" and "I am a thinking thing" illustrate this general claim. Descartes clearly and distinctly perceived that he existed and that he was a thinking thing. He inferred that he was entitled to believe with complete certainty that he existed and that he was a thinking thing.

Simple mathematical statements plausibly provide another example. When we reflect on the claim that the sum of 2 and 3 is 5, we find it impossible *not* to believe it. We feel compelled to believe that the sum of 2 and 3 is 5. Perhaps this is another example of clear and distinct perception.

It's important to understand that when Descartes talked about clear and distinct perception, he wasn't talking about *sense* perception. He wasn't talking about vision, hearing, touch, smell, or taste. He was talking about the compulsion to believe, which he experienced when reflecting on the claim that he existed and the claim that he was a thinking thing.

Descartes's idea was that he could use this method for his project of rebuilding science from scratch. When developing his new science, he would accept a claim only once it had been established using clear and distinct perception. In that way, he could be totally certain of all of his conclusions, and he wouldn't make mistakes like those of previous generations of scientists.

5.5 Descartes's Theism, and His Solution to the Evil Demon Problem

Descartes's first application of his theory of clear and distinct perception was his attempt to show that God exists. He offered two different proofs of God's existence; we look at the second:[3]

> The mere fact that I find in my thought an idea of something x, and [clearly and distinctly] perceive x to have a certain property, it follows that x really does have that property. Can I not turn this to account in a second argument to prove the existence of God? The idea of God (that is, of a supremely perfect being) is certainly one that I find within me ... and I understand that it belongs to God's nature that he always exists.

As we interpret this argument, it worked like this. First, Descartes claimed that he clearly and distinctly perceived that God is a supremely perfect being. Appealing to his theory of clear and distinct perception, he inferred that God *is* a supremely perfect being. Now it seems clear that God could not be a supremely perfect being if he didn't even exist. And so Descartes inferred that God exists. In summary:

(1) I clearly and distinctly perceive that God is a supremely perfect being. (Premise)
(2) God is a supremely perfect being. (From 1)
(3) God wouldn't be supremely perfect if he didn't exist. (Premise)
(4) God exists. (From 2, 3)

If you've read chapter 3, you'll recognize this as a variant of Anselm's **ontological argument**. Descartes's claim that God is a "supremely perfect being" is an alternative version of Anselm's claim that God is the greatest possible being. Because we've already discussed Anselm's argument, we can be brief in our evaluation of Descartes's version.

Let's look at the steps in the argument. When Descartes claimed that he had a clear and distinct perception that God is a supremely perfect being, what he meant was that, when he reflected on the claim that God is a supremely perfect being, he felt a compulsion to believe. He couldn't help believing that God is a supremely perfect being. We're willing to take Descartes's word for it that he experienced this sort of compulsion, so we accept premise (1). Premise (3) is very plausible. It's hard to believe that something could be supremely perfect and yet non-existent.[4] It seems clear that (4), the conclusion of the argument, follows from (2) and (3). The real nub of the argument, then, is the inference from (1) to (2). Was Descartes right to say that whatever is clearly and distinctly perceived to be true, is true? We return to this question in the next section. For now, we look at how Descartes sought to solve the evil demon problem.

Here is Descartes's evil demon story again:

> There exists an "evil demon" with supernatural powers. The demon is able to manipulate your mind to deceive you: he can induce hallucinations, and he can modify your memories in whatever way he chooses. None of your present experiences are accurate: they're all hallucinations caused by the demon. All of your real memories have been deleted and replaced by false "memories." You're wrong about what your name is, wrong about where you grew up, wrong about what your body looks like, and so on. The demon is also able to scramble your thought processes, so that, for example, your mathematical calculations go wrong. If you try to find the sum 123 and 456, the demon can ensure that you get the wrong answer.

Descartes thought that he could show the evil demon story is false using his theism. Being perfectly good, God would seek to protect us from any evil demon that sought to psychologically manipulate us in this heinous way. Being omnipotent, God would be capable of protecting us from demons. And so the story must be false: a perfect God would not allow an evil demon to deceive us like that.

One can give similar responses to other skeptical arguments. For example, in response to the suggestion that the entire "physical" world is an extended hallucination, one may argue that God, who is a supremely perfect being, would protect us from hallucinations of this horrible kind. In this way, Descartes was able to defend his conviction that the physical world is real. Sense perception does sometimes mislead, but Descartes thought that he could show we are not victims of massive, systematic illusions.

5.6 The Cartesian Circle

Descartes's response to the evil demon problem was ingenious, but it is subject to an important objection. A crucial part of Descartes's theory was his account of clear and distinct perception:

> Whenever I clearly and distinctly perceive that something is true, it *is* true and I am entitled to believe it with complete certainty.

We've seen some powerful examples of clear and distinct perception—"I exist" and "I am a thinking thing"—but such examples do not show, in general, that whatever is clearly and distinctly perceived is true. What argument could there be for this general claim?

To see that there is a problem here, note that Descartes's own evil demon story seems to threaten his theory of clear and distinct perception. It would seem that a powerful, malicious demon might be able to psychologically manipulate someone, to give them a powerful compulsion to believe, say, that the sum of 2 and 3 is 8, or that frogs can speak ancient Greek. In a case like this, it seems, the person would clearly and distinctly perceive that something is true when in fact it is false. It's not clear that Descartes could rule out with certainty the hypothesis that his clear and distinct perceptions have been implanted in him by an evil demon and are misleading.

Descartes responded to this sort of concern by appealing to his theism. Descartes argued that God, being perfectly good, would not allow people to be led into error by clear and distinct perception:

> I see that it is impossible that God should ever deceive me. Only someone who has something wrong with him will engage in trickery or deception. That someone is able to deceive others may be a sign of his skill or power, but his wanting to deceive them is a sign of his malice or weakness; and those are not to be found in God. Next, I know from experience that I have a faculty of judgment; and this, like everything else I have, was given to me by God. Since God doesn't

want to deceive me, I am sure that he didn't give me a faculty of judgment that would lead me into error while I was using it correctly.⁵

For example, God would not permit an evil demon to implant in you the clear and distinct perception that the sum of 2 and 3 is 8, or that frogs can speak ancient Greek.

Ever since Descartes's *Meditations on First Philosophy* was first published, many of his readers have felt that there is something fishy about this reply. The first premise of Descartes's ontological argument was that whatever Descartes clearly and distinctly perceives to be true, is true. From this premise, he inferred that God exists. But at the same time, when defending the reliability of clear and distinct perception, Descartes appealed to his theism. And so Descartes seemed to be arguing in a circle. Philosophers call this the **Cartesian circle**,⁶ as shown in figure 5.1.

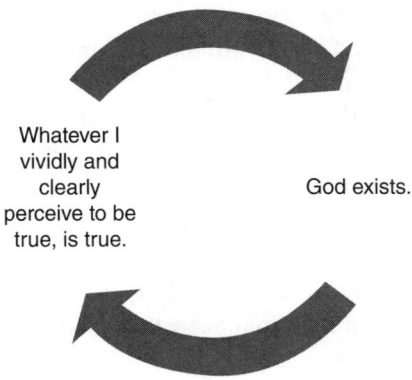

FIGURE 5.1 The Cartesian Circle

To establish the reliability of clear and distinct perception, Descartes attempted to prove that God exists. But his "proof" *used* clear and distinct perception—the reliability of which was still in doubt!

Despite its age, *Meditations on First Philosophy* is not such a difficult read. We encourage you to look at it and to think about whether Descartes can break out of the Cartesian circle.

5.7 Descartes's Legacy

Some of the arguments in Descartes's book look a lot like the arguments of the medieval philosophers who preceded him. We remarked on the similarity between Descartes's proof of the existence of God and Anselm's, for example. Even so, *Meditations on First Philosophy* is often said to be the founding work of modern, as opposed to medieval, philosophy. Why is this? We think it is because, in his *Meditations*, Descartes introduced a style of thinking that has been ubiquitous in philosophy ever since.

Anyone who's heard a past event described by several independent eyewitnesses will know that memory and perception are fallible. Anyone who's practiced long division knows that it can be easy to make mistakes in reasoning. But Descartes brought to the forefront of philosophical discussion the fear that these faculties may mislead us *radically* and *systematically*: perhaps all of our sense perceptions are hallucinations; perhaps all of our memories are inserted by a malicious demon; perhaps all of our reasoning is muddled by chronic cognitive disorder; and so on. Descartes thought that he could show our faculties do not, in fact, radically mislead us in this way. But many philosophers believed Descartes's argument was circular and, consequently, flawed. Since Descartes, it has often been thought that a central task of philosophy is to rebut such "skeptical" worries and to establish that we are justified in taking our perceptions and memories at face value and in trusting our own reasoning.

While philosophers have worried a great deal about memory, sense perception, and reasoning, those influenced by Descartes have often felt that our knowledge of our current conscious experience is secure: when you are in pain, are cold, or having the experience of yellow, you know it. So after Descartes, it has often been an aspiration of philosophers to show we can achieve knowledge of "external" things (i.e., things outside one's own current conscious experience) on the basis of one's knowledge of "internal" things (i.e., one's current conscious experiences). This is a philosophical project that will reappear in chapter 6.

This Cartesian way of thinking about the goals of philosophy has its critics, of course. The philosopher Richard Rorty thought that when confronted by radically skeptical questions such as "How do you know that you're not the victim of an evil demon?" the correct response is simply to tell the radical skeptic to get lost.[7] What's more, since the late nineteenth century, the trend in philosophy and psychology has been to emphasize that many of our mental processes are unconscious. So even if it's true that you can sometimes know for certain that you are in pain or that you are hungry, these are exceptional cases: much of what happens in the mind cannot be discovered by looking inward.

Conclusion

We began this chapter by asking whether it is ever rational to be *100 percent, not a shadow of a doubt, bet your life on it* certain. What have we learned?

Descartes came up with some plausible examples of truths of which we can be completely certain. Perhaps you can be completely certain you exist. Perhaps you can be completely certain you are a thinking thing. Perhaps you can be completely certain of some facts about your current conscious mental states.

But perhaps the most famous part of Descartes's *Meditations on First Philosophy* is his introduction of the evil demon thought experiment and his suggestion that it shows we can be certain of nothing or almost nothing. He wrote:

> I feel like someone who is suddenly dropped into a deep whirlpool that tumbles him around so that he can neither stand on the bottom nor swim to the top.[8]

It is ironic that, while Descartes set out to achieve certainty, he is remembered most for an argument that seems to show there is very little of which we can be certain.

Glossary

a priori/a posteriori: To understand these terms, contrast the design argument for theism with the ontological argument. The design argument relies on observations—more specifically, it relies on observations of plants and animals. To make these observations, we rely on sense perception—on sight, hearing, smell, touch, and taste. The ontological argument doesn't rely on sense perception in this way. The design argument is therefore an a posteriori argument, while the ontological argument is an a priori argument. More generally, an a priori argument is one that doesn't rely on observation. An a posteriori argument does involve observation.

Cartesian: "Cartesian" is an adjective derived from the Latin form of Descartes's name: Cartesius. It is used to describe things that are in some way associated with Descartes. For example, Descartes invented coordinate geometry, and so coordinate geometry is sometimes called "Cartesian geometry." Cartesian is always spelled with a capital C.

Cartesian circle: Some philosophers believe that Descartes's "proof" of the existence of God is circular. The circle in Descartes's argument is called the "Cartesian circle." See section 5.6 for more discussion.

clear and distinct perception: Descartes claimed that when he considered the claim *I exist,* he felt compelled to believe. He couldn't help believing that he existed. He referred to this inner compulsion as clear and distinct perception. It is important not to confuse clear and distinct perception with sense perception. See section 5.4.

evil demon: In the first chapter of his *Meditations on First Philosophy,* Descartes imagined that he is psychologically manipulated by an evil demon. Descartes's evil demon has become a stock character in modern Western philosophy.

ontological argument: Anselm's argument for the existence of God (see chapter 3) and other arguments similar to it are called "ontological arguments." In the fifth chapter of Descartes's *Meditations on First Philosophy,* Descartes gives an ontological argument.

skepticism: In ordinary English, a skeptic is someone who doubts. When philosophers talk about skepticism, they usually have in mind extreme forms of doubt. The philosophical skeptic might doubt that their body exists, that other people are conscious, or that the universe has existed for more than five minutes.

thinking: In this chapter, we use "thinking" to refer to all kinds of conscious mental activity—including such things as wanting to eat a muffin, wondering whether it is snowing, and feeling cold.

Comprehension Questions

1. Give an example of an a priori argument, and explain what it means to say that the argument is a priori.
2. Give an example of something that you *think* is true, without being completely certain. Why are you not completely certain?
3. Why did Descartes think we should not place complete confidence in our senses?
4. Descartes claimed to be completely certain that he existed. Why?
5. Descartes claimed to be completely certain that he was a thinking thing. Why?
6. What is clear and distinct perception?

7. Describe some differences between Descartes's version of the ontological argument and Anselm's version.
8. Consider the question "How do we know that the 'physical' world around us isn't just a vast computer simulation?" How would Descartes answer this question?
9. How did Descartes respond to the suggestion that his clear and distinct perceptions might be a result of an evil demon?
10. Some scholars believe Descartes's "proof" of theism is circular. Explain this objection.

Discussion Questions

1. The following statements are all generally believed to be true. In your opinion, which of them are *certainly* true? Why?
   (a) $2 + 2 = 4$.
   (b) France is in Europe.
   (c) There are no married bachelors.
   (d) $E = mc^2$.
   (e) At least one thing exists.
   (f) Not every statement is true.
   (g) You exist.

2. Suppose that someone offers you a bet:

   If the Notre Dame Cathedral is in Paris, I owe you ten cents. If the Notre Dame Cathedral is not in Paris, you owe me 100 million dollars.

   Would you accept this bet? If you did accept this bet, would you experience any fear of losing? Are you completely certain the Notre Dame Cathedral is in Paris?

3. In section 5.3, we claimed that nonexistent things can't dream and can't have hallucinations. But is this right? Here's an objection:

   In Shakespeare's play, Macbeth has a hallucination.
   Macbeth doesn't exist.
   Therefore:
   Nonexistent things can have hallucinations.

   What do you think of this argument?

4. (a) Is it always possible to figure out whether you are in pain?
   (b) Is it always possible to figure out whether you are in love?

5. (a) Can you think of any circumstances in which you might mislead a child for their own benefit?
   (b) Assuming that God exists, could there be circumstances in which God would want people to have false beliefs?
   (c) If so, what implications does this have for Descartes's argument?

6. Can you think of a time when you felt a compulsion to believe something and then later found out the belief was false? If you can, does this show that Descartes was wrong to think that clear and distinct perception is infallible?

7. Antoine Arnauld, one of Descartes's early critics, wrote:

    I have one further worry, namely how Descartes avoids reasoning in a circle when he says that it's only because [we know that] God exists that we are sure that whatever we [clearly and distinctly] perceive is true. But we can be sure that God exists only because we [clearly and distinctly] perceive this; so before we can be sure that God exists we need to be able to be sure that whatever we perceive [clearly and distinctly] is true.[9]

    This is a version of the Cartesian circle objection, which we discussed in section 5.6. Look at Descartes's reply to Arnauld.[10] Is it adequate?

8. In his discussion of the evil demon problem, Descartes suggested that God wants to protect us from false belief. But clearly, we sometimes have false beliefs. Why does God allow this? Why does God not always prevent us from forming false beliefs? Descartes discussed this issue in chapter 4 of the *Meditations on First Philosophy*. Evaluate his response.

9. People with Anton-Babinski syndrome are cortically blind, but they believe that they are able to see. Do some research on this syndrome. Does this show that Descartes was wrong to say that one can be certain about one's current conscious states?

What to Look at Next

- John Gribbin's *Science: A History* will help you understand the scientific background to Descartes's epistemological work. It also contains some information about Descartes's scientific work.

- Descartes's *Meditations on First Philosophy* is short and, despite its age, easy to read. You can find a translation of it at www.earlymoderntexts.com.
- Gary Hatfield's *Routledge Philosophy Guidebook to Descartes and the Meditations* is both authoritative and approachable.
- Bernard Williams's *Descartes: The Project of Pure Enquiry* is a classic discussion of Descartes's epistemology, written by one of the giants of twentieth-century philosophy. In chapter 7 of the book, Williams defends Descartes from the Cartesian circle objection, which we considered in section 5.6.
- For more on Descartes's arguments for theism, see chapters 2 and 3 of J. L. Mackie's *The Miracle of Theism*.
- Peter Unger's influential article "A Defense of Skepticism" in *The Philosophical Review*, Vol. 80, No. 2 (April, 1971), pp. 198–219, contains many echoes of Descartes's *Meditations on First Philosophy*.
- If you want to know about recent work on the evil demon problem and its variants, you should look at Duncan Pritchard's article "Contemporary Skepticism" in the *Internet Encyclopedia of Philosophy*.
- Lana and Lilly Wachowski's movie *The Matrix* can be thought of as an updated version of Descartes's evil demon thought experiment. After watching the movie, you might want to look at *Philosophers Explore The Matrix*, edited by Christopher Grau.
- The mind-bending book *Ubik*, by Philip K. Dick, is another science fiction work that echoes Descartes.

Notes

1. Oliver Sacks, *Hallucinations* (New York: Alfred A. Knopf, 2012), ch. 6.
2. In his translation of the *Meditations on First Philosophy*, which is available at www.earlymoderntexts.com, Jonathan Bennett writes "vivid and clear" instead of "clear and distinct." We think that Bennett's translation has much to recommend it, but "clear and distinct" is the standard translation, and so it's the translation we will use.
3. The first proof is given in the third meditation; the second proof is in the fifth meditation. We're considering the proof from the fifth meditation. We quote from Jonathan Bennett's translation, which is available at

www.earlymoderntexts.com. We have replaced Bennett's "vivid and clear" with our preferred "clear and distinct."

4. To repeat a point from chapter 3: if someone promised to set you up on a supremely perfect date, would you be satisfied if they provided you with a nonexistent date?
5. This quotation comes from the fourth chapter. See Bennett's translation at www.earlymoderntexts.com.
6. The word "**Cartesian**" comes from the Latin form of Descartes's name: Cartesius. Cartesian is always spelled with a capital C.
7. Admittedly, this blunt wording is Donald Davidson's characterization of Rorty's position. "Get lost" is not a direct quote. See Davidson, "Afterthoughts," in *Subjective, Intersubjective, Objective* (Oxford: Oxford University Press, 2001).
8. Descartes, Meditations on *First Philosophy*, second chapter.
9. Antoine Arnauld, *Fourth Objections*, CSM II 150/AT VII 214.
10. Many versions of the *Meditations on First Philosophy* come with selections from the objections and replies. Alternatively, you can find a translation of Descartes's response to Arnauld at www.earlymoderntexts.com.

CHAPTER 6

Can We Trust Our Senses?

6.1 Rationalism and Empiricism

Philosophers use the term **empirical evidence** for evidence acquired by sense perception—that is, by sight, touch, smell, hearing, or taste.[1] A biologist looking at bacteria through a microscope, a zoologist listening to bird calls, a food scientist smelling a sample: these people are gathering empirical evidence.

Philosophers distinguish **a priori** reasoning from **a posteriori** reasoning. A posteriori reasoning involves empirical evidence. A priori reasoning does not. To see the difference, compare a botany textbook with a pure mathematics textbook. The botany textbook will be filled with empirical evidence—botanists learn by making careful observations of plants. The mathematics textbook will contain little, if any, empirical evidence. So we might say that botanists mostly use a posteriori methods, while mathematicians mostly use a priori methods.

Now you might protest that mathematicians *do* rely on sense perception. Most mathematicians *look* at diagrams, and they *listen* to lectures, for example. That's true, but it is often thought that all of this is inessential to research in pure mathematics. In principle, one can learn mathematics without using sense perception. For example, you can establish that $25^2 = 625$ without using empirical evidence: you can carry out the calculation "in your head," eyes closed.[2]

In chapter 5, we said that when Descartes was developing his new scientific theory, he didn't want to rely on empirical evidence. Descartes thought that a posteriori methods couldn't give him certainty, and so he wanted to use a priori methods instead. Descartes was a **rationalist**: a philosopher who emphasized the importance of a priori reasoning. Rationalists are contrasted with **empiricists**: philosophers who emphasize a posteriori methods. In this chapter, we consider a trio of empiricists from seventeenth- and eighteenth-century Britain: John Locke (1632–1704), George Berkeley (1685–1753), and David Hume (1711–1776).

Hume expressed his empiricism with characteristic flair:

> If we take in our hand any volume . . . let us ask, *Does it contain any abstract reasoning about quantity or number?* No. *Does it contain any experiential reasoning about matters of fact and existence?* No. Then throw it in the fire, for it can contain nothing but sophistry and illusion.[3]

By "abstract reasoning about quantity or number," Hume meant *mathematics*. So what Hume was saying in this passage is that we should reject all a priori reasoning, except in mathematics. The British empiricists were influenced by the amazing success of Newton's work in physics. Newton himself was clear that (mathematics aside) his methods were a posteriori.

Despite this huge difference in philosophical outlook, the empiricists were troubled by some of the same skeptical puzzles that had bothered Descartes, as we will see in this chapter.

6.2 Indirect Realism

Find a rigid cube; a cubical box will do, or a Rubik's cube. Hold it so that one face is pointing directly at you. Concentrate very carefully on what you see. What shape is it? We predict you will see a square, as depicted in figure 6.1.

Now hold the cube so that one of the *corners* is pointing directly at you. Again, concentrate very carefully on the shape of what you see. We predict it will be a hexagon, as shown in figure 6.2.

So it seems that as you turn the cube in your hands, what you see changes shape. But of course, the cube itself doesn't change shape.

Can We Trust Our Senses? 103

FIGURE 6.1 A cube, viewed from one direction

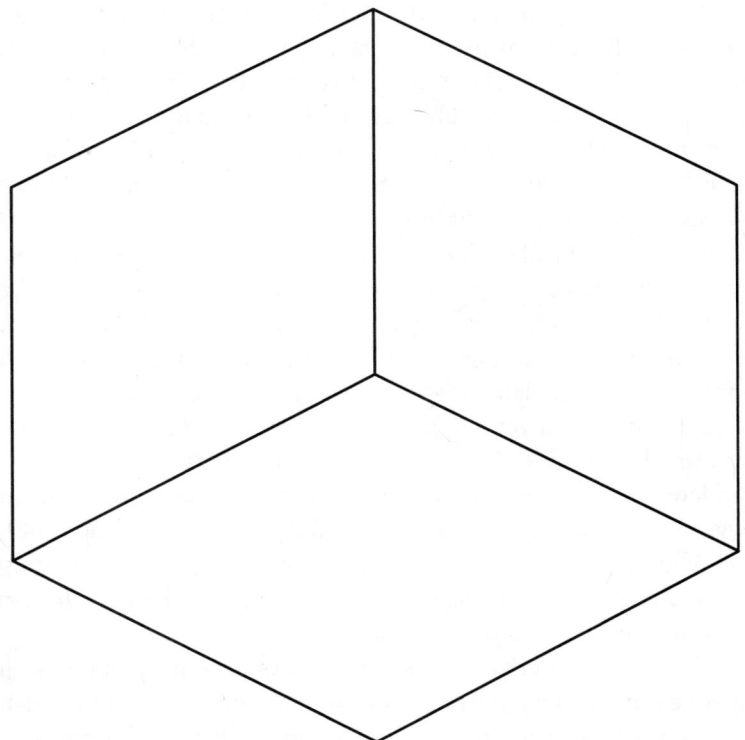

FIGURE 6.2 The same cube, viewed from another direction

(We told you to get a *rigid* cube, right?) So it might be argued that what you see is not the cube:

> What you see changes shape as you move the cube about in your hands.
>
> The cube doesn't change shape.
>
> *Therefore:*
>
> What you see is not the cube.

This is a version of the argument from perspectival variation.

The conclusion of the argument may seem ridiculous: of course you are seeing the cube! But bear with us for a moment. We're going to describe a theory of perception according to which this conclusion—strange though it may sound—is quite correct. The theory is most famously associated with the John Locke.[4] Philosophers today call it **indirect realism**, though Locke did not use this label.

This is what's going on in the cube experiment, according to indirect realists. Light from the cube enters your eye and is focused onto your retina by the lens at the front of your eyeball. The impact of light on your retina causes a certain image of the cube to form in your mind. The character of this mental image depends not only on the properties of the cube but also on the angle from which it is seen.[5] If you hold the cube so that one of its faces is pointed directly toward you, your mental image of the cube will be square. If you hold the cube so that one of its corners is pointed directly toward you, your mental image will be hexagonal. Strictly speaking, what you see is not the cube itself, but rather the mental image that is produced when light from the cube reaches your retina. This explains why what you see changes when you move the cube about; what you see, strictly speaking, is a mental image of the cube, which does indeed change shape as the cube is moved.

Here is an analogy. Your eyes are like cameras, and the mental images you see when you look at the cube are like photographs of the cube. Photographs of the same object taken from different angles usually look different. In the same way, two people looking at the same object may see different mental images.

We can make similar points about the other senses. Suppose that someone starts playing the bagpipes two feet from you, and you hastily walk away. As you get farther from the piper, what you hear gets quieter, even if the piper plays at a constant volume. Arguably, then, what you hear is not the bagpipes, but a certain mental representation of the bagpipe sound.

In Locke's terminology, a **material object** is an object that exists outside any mind (and is not itself a mind). According to Locke, trees, stones, and moons are all material objects. Locke used the term **idea** for mental objects, such as mental images, or the sensation of pain. When you look at the cube, the cube is a material object (outside the mind) while your mental image of the cube is an idea (inside the mind).

6.3 Primary and Secondary Qualities

To repeat, Locke's claim was that we can't perceive material objects—we can only perceive mental pictures of them. This leaves us with an important question: What are material objects like?

Grab a pencil and a glass of water. Submerge half of the pencil in water, and look at it from one side. You'll notice that the pencil appears bent—although, of course, the pencil is really straight. This is an "illusion": a case in which the evidence of the senses misleads. An indirect realist may say that, in this case, your mental image of the pencil is bent, although the pencil itself is straight—so the mental image fails to resemble the external object it represents. However, if you look at the pencil in normal conditions, when you are not subject to any illusion, both the mental image and the pencil itself are straight. In these normal cases, the mental image closely resembles the pencil. Examples like this suggest the following, more general hypothesis that we call **naïve representationalism**, although this is not a standard term:

> Setting aside occasional cases of illusion, the ideas generated in perception closely resemble the material objects they represent.

This is an appealing idea, but there are powerful objections to naïve representationalism. Here's one of them. It turns out that bee vision is very different from human vision. For one thing, bee eyes are insensitive to red light—so a bee may be unable to distinguish a red object from a gray one. As a consequence, a tile that looks stripy to a human might look plain to a bee (figure 6.3).

The same thing can happen in reverse. Bee eyes are sensitive to ultraviolet light, but human eyes are not. In consequence, a tile that looks plain to a human may look stripy to a bee.

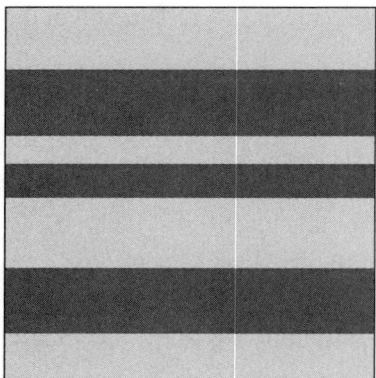 

FIGURE 6.3 On the left, a picture of a tile as seen by a person. On the right, a picture of the same tile as seen by a bee.

The visual systems of birds also differ from human visual systems, though in a more dramatic way. Humans have three different sorts of color receptors on their retinas. Consequently the colors that humans perceive seem to vary along three dimensions: red/green, blue/yellow, and light/dark. Most birds have *four* different sorts of color receptors on their retinas. So for a bird, colors vary along four dimensions. In consequence, two tiles that look identical to human observers may seem to differ in color to bird observers, with their extra color receptors.

For an indirect realist, what this suggests is that, even setting aside cases of illusion, the mental images of different animals differ enormously, even when those animals observe the same objects in the same conditions. This doesn't happen only in rare cases: the phenomenon is ubiquitous. Now since the perceptions of the different animals differ so greatly from one another, they can't all closely resemble the observed external objects. So it seems that, again, even setting aside cases of illusion, it can't be true in general that an organism's perception of an object closely resembles the object. So naïve representationalism seems to be false.

Perhaps, then, we should reject naïve representationalism. This brings us back to the question with which we started this section: What are material objects like? Locke looked to the sciences of his day for an answer to this question.

Locke noticed that scientists routinely supposed that external objects have shapes. For example, Newton had argued that the Earth is not quite spherical—it is, more or less, an oblate spheroid. Moreover, scientists assumed that different material objects are spatially related to one another. For example, astronomers of the time knew that the Moon is closer to the Earth than to the Sun. Scientists also supposed that material objects move around. For example, Johannes Kepler (1571–1630) had convinced astronomers that the planets have elliptical orbits. What's more, it was thought that many objects are solid, in the sense that they can't pass through each other. For example, the reason that a cup resting on a table does not fall downward toward the floor is that it cannot pass through the tabletop.

These observations may seem mundane, but Locke knew that scientists sometimes reach quite unexpected conclusions about the natures of material objects. Consider, for example, what Locke had to say about heat:

> Observing that merely rubbing two bodies violently together produces heat, and very often fire, we have reason to think that what we call heat and fire consists in a violent agitation of the tiny imperceptible parts of the burning matter.[6]

This idea—that heat is the "violent agitation of the tiny imperceptible parts" of an object—was not original to Locke. This was a common view in England in the seventeenth century.[7] The claim is striking because, while we can perceive heat using the sense of touch, our perception of heat does not make it apparent to us that heat is "violent agitation." Locke put it like this: our idea of heat does not resemble heat itself. He gave a helpful analogy to explain the point. The word "porcupine" represents porcupines, but it doesn't resemble a porcupine. You would never confuse a porcupine with the word "porcupine": the word and the animal are clearly very unlike each other. In the same way, Locke said, our idea of heat represents heat, but the idea of heat doesn't resemble heat itself.

Locke made rather similar claims about color:

> Observing that the different refractions of transparent bodies produce in our eyes the different appearances of various colors, and that the same effect can be produced by looking from different angles at velvet, watered silk, etc., we think it probable that the color and shining of bodies is nothing but the different arrangement and refraction of their minute and imperceptible parts.[8]

Locke's claim in this passage is that the color of an object is the arrangement of its "minute and imperceptible parts." In some passages, Locke expressed this theory by saying that a color of an object is a kind of "surface texture." We're used to the idea that we can detect the texture of a surface by touch: a smooth surface feels different from a ridged surface, which in turn feels different from a pockmarked surface. Locke's claim is that colors, too, are texture properties—albeit texture properties detected by sight rather than touch.

Locke's account of color is surprising. Our perception of color does not suggest to us that the color of an object is an arrangement of its imperceptible parts. As in the case of heat, Locke claimed that our ideas of color do not resemble the colors themselves. You can see, then, how a Lockean would account for the fact that a tile can look different to a bee observer and to a human observer. The Lockean will say that the tile has a certain surface texture. This surface texture is represented in different ways by the human visual system and the bee visual system: a human observer and a bee observer will have quite different ideas when looking at the tile. Neither the human's idea nor the bee's idea closely resembles the material tile itself.

Admittedly, Locke's account of color is now rather out of date. It is true that, in some rather special cases, the color of an object is a result of its surface texture. Certain beetles have ridges on their shells that act as diffraction gratings, and so in consequence, the beetles have an iridescent blue appearance when they are illuminated by a light source. However, in other cases, the color of an object has nothing to do with its surface texture. For example, the sky on a sunny day is blue because particles in the atmosphere preferentially scatter short-wavelength light. The blue of a rainbow is due to the refraction of sunlight through raindrops.[9] Water is slightly blue because, as light passes through it, more long-wavelength light is absorbed than short-wavelength light.[10] The details are too complicated for extended discussion here. However, it seems to us that this more recent science can be used to support Locke's thesis that our ideas of color do not resemble the colors themselves. When you look into a tank of water, it is not at all apparent to you that the liquid's blue is due to its absorbing more long-wavelength light than short-wavelength light. Plausibly, one's idea of blue in this case does not resemble the blue of the water itself.

Locke introduced some technical terms to summarize his conclusions. A **quality** is an observable characteristic of an object. For example, redness, squareness, sourness, and moistness are qualities. Locke distinguished two different kinds of quality: **primary qualities**, and **secondary qualities**:[11]

Primary Qualities	Secondary Qualities
Shapes	Colors
Solidity	Tastes
Motion and rest	Heat

In the case of primary qualities, one's idea of the quality resembles the quality itself. In the case of secondary qualities, one's idea of the quality does not resemble the quality itself (just as the word "porcupine" does not resemble a porcupine). Locke put it like this:

> The ideas of the primary qualities of bodies resemble them, and their patterns really do exist in the bodies themselves; but the ideas produced in us by secondary qualities don't resemble them at all. There is nothing like our ideas of secondary qualities existing in the bodies themselves.[12]

As we have said, some aspects of Locke's discussion are rather dated. However, these details should not blind us to the power of Locke's central point. It is surely true that the word "porcupine" does not resemble a porcupine. This shows that one thing can represent another without resembling it. And so perhaps our ideas of objects represent them without resembling them. Perhaps external objects are very unlike our ideas of them.

But we should not give you the impression that Locke's distinction between primary and secondary qualities has gone unchallenged. One of its most vigorous challengers was George Berkeley, whose work we discuss in section 6.5.

6.4 Do Material Objects Really Exist?

Indirect realists think that not all of our ideas represent material objects. Try closing and then gently rubbing your eyes with your fingers. After a few seconds, you should see swirling colored patterns, called "phosphenes." These phosphenes are mental images (or ideas), but they don't represent external objects.

Here is another illustration of the same point. Put this book down for a minute, close your eyes, and in as much detail as you can, bring to mind an image of a unicorn.

Finished?

You've just demonstrated that it's possible for a person to have a mental image (an idea) that does not represent any material object that actually exists. The idea is a product of your mind.

The same point can be established by thinking about dreams and hallucinations. You could dream, or hallucinate, that you are riding a unicorn. While having this dream or hallucination, you would experience mental images of a unicorn, and these mental images would not represent any material object that actually exists. Such mental images are generated in your mind.

Once you realize that it's possible to have a mental image that does not accurately represent any material object, you might start to worry: How do you know that *any* of your ideas accurately represent material objects? Indeed, how do you know that there even *are* any material objects?

Hume put it like this:

> By what argument can it be proved that the perceptions of the mind must be caused by external objects that are perfectly distinct from them and yet similar to them ... rather than arising from the energy of the mind itself[?] ... It is admitted that many of these perceptions— e.g. in dreams, madness, and other diseases—don't in fact arise from anything external, so how could we prove that others do arise from something external?[13]

If you have read chapter 3, you might recognize this puzzle: Descartes, too, was troubled by the question, "How do I know that I am not dreaming?"

It is tempting to reply to Hume's challenge by saying that it's *just obvious* that material objects exist. We don't think that this is obvious. In the next section, we discuss the work of a philosopher who denied that material objects exist.

6.5 Berkeley's Idealism

At the start of this chapter, we asked you to look at a rigid cube from different angles. We suggested that what you see changes shape as you move the cube around, while the cube itself does not change shape. The Lockean indirect realist infers that what you see is not the cube but only a mental image of the cube. The cube is a material object, on this view— that is, an object that exists outside of any mind. The thing you see is not the material object, according to the Lockean; rather, the thing you see is a mental image, an "idea," which *represents* the material object.

The terminology is this. An "idea" is a mental object, while a "material" object is a thing that exists outside of any mind and is not itself a mind. According to Locke, trees, stones, and Moons are all material objects.

Can We Trust Our Senses? 111

George Berkeley (1685–1753) believed that material objects do not exist.

George Berkeley (1685–1753) responded to Locke by arguing vigorously that *there are no material objects*. According to Berkeley, there are minds and there are ideas—but there are no material objects. This position is often called **idealism**. **Materialism** was Berkeley's name for the claim that material objects do exist.

At first glance, idealism may seem to be a rather far-fetched position, but don't be misled. Berkeley did not deny that trees, stones, moons, and so forth exist. He just denied that such things are material objects. According to Berkeley, trees, stones, and moons are ideas—or rather, collections of ideas.

Berkeley was greatly influenced by Locke; he agreed with Locke on some points but disagreed sharply on others. We start our discussion of Berkeley's arguments by looking at his work on color. On this topic, Berkeley and Locke were almost in agreement. Indeed, the argument against naïve representationalism that we rehearsed in section 6.3 is essentially due to Berkeley. After that, we look at what Berkeley had to say about Locke's "primary qualities"—here, Berkeley disagreed sharply with Locke. Finally, we explain Berkeley's case for idealism.

Berkeley presented his opponents,[14] the materialists, with a question: What colors do material objects have? This looks at first to be an easy question. It's tempting to reply that we can easily find out the colors of material objects just by looking at them. Bananas are yellow, oranges are orange, cucumbers are green, and so on. So what's the problem?

Well, one problem arises because sometimes objects appear to have different colors in different lighting conditions. It sometimes happens, for example, that a shopper buys a pair of pants and a jacket that seem to have the same color under fluorescent lights in the store. When the shopper gets the clothes outside, he finds that they appear to have different colors. You might be tempted to say that the "true" colors of the clothes are revealed in daylight—that the shopper was misled by poor lighting in the store. But why should we think it is daylight, rather than the light emitted by fluorescent lamps, that reveals the "true" colors of objects? And there are further problems. There is a certain amount of natural variation among the visual systems of different people. For example, an object that looks purely green to one human observer might look bluish-green to another.[15] In such a case, it's tempting to think that one of the observers must have defective eyesight—but how are we to know whose eyesight is accurate in a case like this? It gets worse. The differences between the visual systems of different humans are fairly small, but (as we said in section 6.3) the differences between the visual systems of different animals are dramatic. A tile that looks stripy to a person may look completely plain to a bee, or vice versa. How are we to know whether the tile in a case like this is *really* stripy or *really* plain?

These are tough questions for the materialist—but Berkeley had a solution. The resolution of the problem, Berkeley thought, is that colors exist only in the mind, not in material objects. For example, a tile might produce a stripy idea in the mind of a bee observer and a plain idea in the mind of a human observer. The tile itself is neither stripy nor plain. You may have heard the expression "beauty is in the eye of the beholder." Berkeley's proposal, in brief, is that color is in the eye of the beholder (though he would have preferred to say that color is in the *mind* of the beholder).

Berkeley thought that arguments of this kind can be used to force the materialist to concede that *all* qualities exist only in the mind. In each case, his strategy is the same: point out that an object presents conflicting appearances to different observers, and infer that the quality in question exists only in the mind. Berkeley devoted many pages to the development of variations on the theme; we'll give you some highlights:

- **Heat and Cold.** Here's another experiment for you. Prepare a bucket of ice water, a bucket of water that is so hot it's slightly unpleasant to touch, and a bucket of water at room temperature. Put your left hand in the bucket of ice water and your right hand in the bucket of very hot water, and hold your hands in place for thirty seconds. Then, plunge both hands in the bucket of room temperature water. You'll notice that your left hand feels hot and your right hand feels cold—even though they're in the same bucket of water. Berkeley thought that the materialist should conclude that heat is a property of ideas, not a property of material things.
- **Smell and Taste.** Berkeley thought that foods smell and taste different to different people, and to different animals. "Can you imagine," he asks, "that filth and excrement affect animals that choose to feed on them with the same smells that we perceive in them?"[16] Berkeley concluded that the materialist should infer that smells and tastes are properties of ideas, not of material things.
- **Solidity.** Water does not seem solid to people, but presumably, water does seem solid to water striders—bugs that can walk around on the surface of a pond. Berkeley concluded that the materialist should conclude that solidity is a property of ideas, not a property of material objects.
- **Size.** Something that seems very small to a person "will appear like a huge mountain to an extremely tiny animal."[17] Berkeley concluded that the materialist should infer that size is a property of ideas, not a property of material objects.

- **Shape.** An object that looks smooth to the naked eye may seem to have a rough surface when viewed through a microscope. Berkeley thought that the materialist should infer that shape is a property of ideas, not of material objects.

We could go on, but by now you've probably got the idea. In short, Berkeley argued that once materialists realize that objects look very different to different observers, they must concede that all qualities exist only in the mind, not in material objects.

We are now ready to look at Berkeley's critique of Locke. Remember that Locke had a rather subtle answer to the question, "Do material objects resemble our ideas of them?" Locke's view, you'll recall, is that material objects resemble our ideas with respect to their primary qualities, but not with respect to their secondary qualities:

> The ideas of the primary qualities of bodies resemble them, and their patterns really do exist in the bodies themselves; but the ideas produced in us by secondary qualities don't resemble them at all. There is nothing like our ideas of secondary qualities existing in the bodies themselves.

According to Locke, the primary qualities include geometrical properties. Locke also thought that solidity is a primary quality.

Berkeley thought that Locke could not sustain his claim that our ideas resemble material objects with respect to their primary qualities. He thought that a materialist must concede that even the so-called primary qualities like solidity and shape turn out to exist only in the mind. So an idea can't be similar in shape to a material object.

If you accept this Berkeleyan conclusion, the very idea that material objects exist comes to seem very mysterious. Material objects, if they exist, have no geometrical characteristics; they are not solid; they are not colored; they are neither hot nor cold; they have no smell and no taste ... it begins to seem that material objects are totally beyond imagination. We find ourselves completely unable to say anything helpful about the characteristics of the hypothesized material objects. As Berkeley put it, we're stuck with the conclusion that material objects are "unknown and inconceivable somethings."[18] If this line of thought is correct, materialism seems to be a rather unattractive position! Berkeley has turned things upside-down. At first glance, materialism seems to be the commonsense position, and idealism seems far-fetched. But if Berkeley is right, it is materialism that is contrary to common sense.

And so Berkeley rejected the idea that there are material objects. To repeat, he did not deny that trains, watches, mountains, or pebbles exist—it's just that he didn't think that these things are material objects. He said instead that each such object is a collection of ideas. Berkeley's idealism was the claim that there are minds and there are ideas, but there are no material objects. He summarized his position with a famous slogan, "For unthinking things, to exist is to be perceived."[19] This is often rendered in Latin as *esse est percipi*. There are no unperceived material objects, according to Berkeley; there are only ideas, which are perceived, and minds, which perceive them.

Now there's an obvious objection to the claim that "to exist is to be perceived." Put a ball in a completely opaque box for a few seconds. Now open the box and remove the ball. Now while the box was closed, it seems, the ball was not perceived. So if "to exist is to be perceived," it follows that while the box was closed, the ball didn't exist. Berkeley seems to be committed to the absurd conclusion that the ball ceases to exist when the box is closed, and then pops back into existence again when the box is opened!

Berkeley's responses to this challenge were slightly different in his various books, but we think that his most persuasive reply was this. The ball continues to exist, even when it is hidden in the opaque box, because God perceives it throughout. God perceives everything.

You may have thought about this old puzzle: When a tree falls in a forest and there's nobody around to hear it, does it make a sound? Berkeley would have responded: God is *always* around to hear a tree fall.

Here's another challenge to Berkeley's idealism. Suppose you are looking at a pineapple, so that you have a certain visual idea. You then touch the pineapple, so that you have a certain tactile idea. You then smell the pineapple, so that you have a certain olfactory idea. What causes these various ideas? The materialist has a ready answer to this question: the pineapple itself, a material object, causes the various ideas that represent it. But what can Berkeley say about the causes of the various pineapple ideas? He *could* say that these ideas are produced by your own mind, but this would be tantamount to saying that the pineapple ideas are hallucinatory or imaginary, and surely we want to preserve the distinction between hallucination and imagination on the one hand and perception on the other. Once again, Berkeley appealed to his theism to deal with the problem. Berkeley claimed that in perception it is God who causes your ideas.

At first, Berkeley's work was not well received.[20] However, views of a Berkeleyan character were influential at the end of the nineteenth century and the first half of the twentieth century. The British philosopher John Stuart Mill (1806–1873), the Austrian physicist and philosopher Ernst Mach (1838–1916), the British logician and philosopher Bertrand Russell (1872–1970), and the American psychologist and philosopher William James (1842–1910) were particularly significant. Some of these later writers (often called **phenomenalists** rather than idealists) in effect weakened Berkeley's doctrine from "to be is to be perceived" to "to be is to be perceivable." As Mill famously put it, objects are "permanent possibilities of sensation."[21]

It is not clear to us, however, that even the weaker claim that "to be is to be perceivable" is defensible. Consider, for example, black holes. The gravity of a black hole is so strong that no light can escape it. And so, arguably, it is impossible to see a black hole. As far as we know, it is also impossible to smell, taste, touch, or hear a black hole. And so black holes exist, but cannot be perceived. This seems to be a counterexample to the claim that to be is to be perceivable.

6.6 Direct Realism

As philosophers became aware of the challenges facing indirect realism and Berkeleyan idealism, some sought to revive the idea that we can see material objects *directly*. This position is known as **direct realism** (or **naïve realism**). Perhaps its most famous proponent was the Scottish philosopher Thomas Reid (1710–1796). According to direct realists, when you look at a giraffe, what you see is the giraffe itself, a material object, and not merely a giraffe-shaped mental image.

To defend this position, the direct realist must find some response to the argument from perspectival variation, which we discussed in section 6.2. Remember, the argument is that if you look at a rigid cube from different angles, what you see changes shape but the cube itself does not, and so what you see is not the cube:

What you see changes shape as you move the cube about in your hands.

The cube doesn't change shape.

Therefore:

What you see is not the cube.

The direct realist wishes to reject the conclusion of this argument. It seems clear, however, that the conclusion of this argument follows from the premises, and the second premise of the argument is clearly true. So the direct realist will have to reject the first premise of the argument. Typically, the direct realist insists that what you see *only seems* to change shape, but doesn't *in fact* change shape.

Even if this is an adequate reply to the argument from perspectival variation, there are further challenges for the direct realist. One of those challenges is this: Can a direct realist give a satisfactory account of color perception? A Berkeleyan might argue as follows:[22]

Only ideas can be colored.

The things we perceive are colored.

Therefore:

The things we perceive are ideas.

The conclusion of this argument manifestly follows from the premises, so the direct realist must reject one or the other of the premises (or both). We'll leave you to think about which of the two premises the direct realist should reject.

Conclusion

To wrap things up, we summarize the positions discussed in this chapter. Figure 6.4 summarizes these positions graphically.

Material objects, if they exist, are nonmental. Idealists deny that there are material objects. Typically, they endorse Berkeley's slogan "to be is to be perceived" or some variant such as "to be is to be perceivable."

Berkeley used the term "materialist" for those who think that material objects do exist, but today, the more common term is "realist." Those who believe in **realism** come in two varieties: direct realists and indirect realists. The indirect realists (e.g., Locke) believe we can't perceive material objects, we can only perceive mental representations of material objects. The direct realists believe that we can perceive material objects themselves.

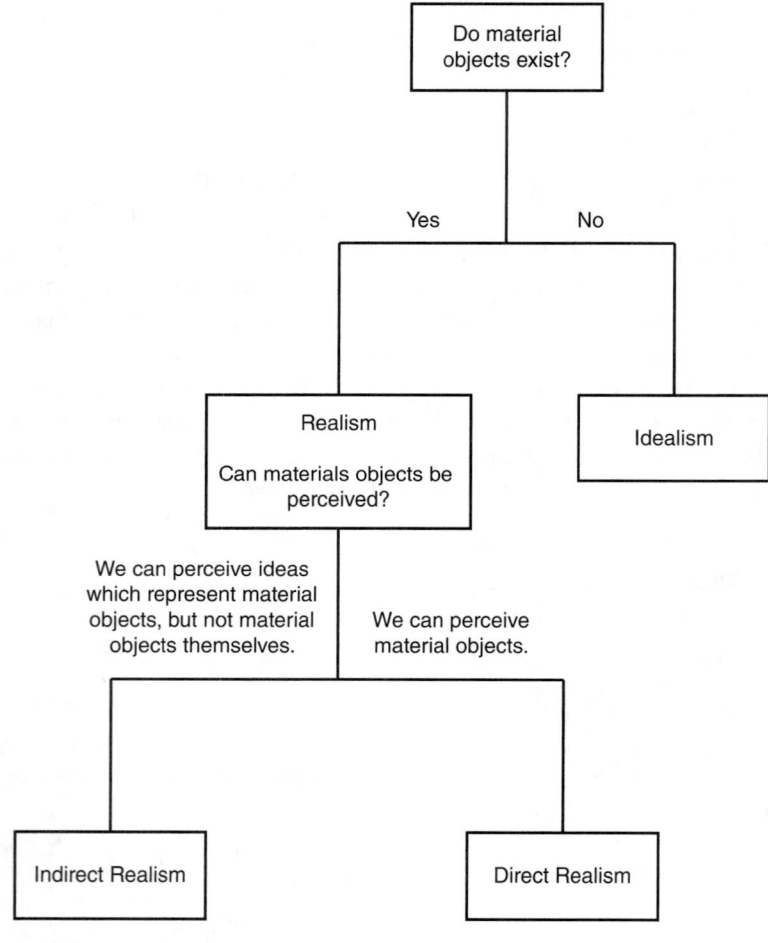

FIGURE 6.4

Glossary

a priori/a posteriori: To understand these terms, contrast the design argument for theism with the ontological argument. The design argument relies on observations—more specifically, it relies on observations of plants and animals. To make these observations, we rely on sense perception—on sight, hearing, smell, touch, and taste. The ontological argument doesn't rely on sense perception in this way.

The design argument is therefore an a posteriori argument, while the ontological argument is an a priori argument. More generally, an a priori argument is one that doesn't rely on observation. An a posteriori argument does involve observation.

direct realism: See realism.

empirical evidence: Empirical evidence is evidence acquired by sense perception—that is, by sight, touch, smell, hearing, or taste.

empiricist: Empiricist philosophers emphasize the importance of empirical evidence (i.e., the evidence of sense experience) and stress the limitations of a priori reasoning. Some empiricists believe that there can be no a priori knowledge at all. More moderate empiricists make an exception for logic and mathematics. Empiricism is usually contrasted with rationalism.

idea: An idea (as the term was used by Locke, and by us in this chapter) is an object that exists in a mind. For example, mental images are ideas. Sensations (e.g., sensations of pain) are also ideas.

idealism: Idealists deny that material objects exist. Typically, they endorse some variant of Berkeley's slogan "to be is to be perceived." Berkeley was an idealist.

indirect realism: See realism.

material object: A material object is an object that is not a mind and exists outside of any mind. It is plausible that trees, apples, mountains, moons, and ice cubes are material objects—though Berkeley denied this.

materialism: Materialism was Berkeley's name for the claim that material objects do exist.

naïve realism: This is another name for "direct realism." See realism.

naïve representationalism: This is our name for the claim that (setting aside the odd case of illusion) material objects closely resemble our ideas of them. This is not a standard term in philosophy.

phenomenalists: The phenomenalists were a group of philosophers in the mid to late nineteenth century and first half of the twentieth century. Their views were Berkeleyan. Some of them, however, weakened Berkeley's doctrine from "to be is to be perceived" to "to be is to be perceivable."

primary qualities and secondary qualities: Locke distinguished two sorts of quality: primary qualities and secondary qualities. Here are some examples:

Primary Qualities	Secondary Qualities
Shapes (round, square, etc.)	Colors
Solidity	Tastes
Motion and rest	Heat

According to Locke, in the case of primary qualities, one's idea of the quality resembles the quality itself, but in the case of secondary qualities, one's idea of the quality does not resemble the quality itself.

quality: A quality is an observable characteristic of an object. For example, redness, squareness, sourness, and moistness are qualities. This is a slight simplification of Locke's own definition: Locke said that a quality is "the power to produce an idea in our mind."

rationalist: Rationalist philosophers emphasize the value of a priori methods of reasoning, and they stress the limitations of empirical methods. Rationalism is usually contrasted with empiricism.

realism: The term "realism" is highly ambiguous in philosophy. In the sense that is important in this chapter, a realist believes that material objects exist. Realists come in two varieties: direct realists and indirect realists. The indirect realists (e.g., Locke) believe that we can't perceive material objects; we can only perceive mental representations of material objects. The direct realists believe that we can perceive material objects themselves.

secondary qualities: See primary and secondary qualities.

Comprehension Questions

1. Arrange these philosophers in chronological order: Berkeley, Descartes, Hume, Locke, Reid.
2. What is the argument from perspectival variation?
3. What is the difference between direct realism and indirect realism?
4. What is naïve representationalism? What grounds are there for rejecting naïve representationalism?
5. Explain Locke's distinction between primary and secondary qualities.
6. Why did Locke think that heat is a secondary quality?
7. Why did Locke think that motion is a primary quality?
8. Give an example of an idea that does not represent any material object.
9. What was Berkeley's complaint against Locke's ideas about the distinction between primary and secondary qualities?
10. What is the view that Berkeley called "materialism," and why did Berkeley reject it?

Discussion Questions

1. Here are some primary qualities and secondary qualities, according to Locke:

Primary Qualities	Secondary Qualities
Shapes (round, square, etc.)	Colors
Solidity	Tastes
Motion and rest	Heat

   Can you think of any properties that Locke could add to the list of primary qualities? Can you think of any properties that Locke could add to the list of secondary qualities?

2. As we said, Locke's claim that colors are "surface textures" is rather dated. Read up on modern color science and think about whether Locke's views about color can be updated.

3. Compare Locke's theory of color with Berkeley's. How are they different?

4. In *The Assayer,* Galileo wrote:

   If the living creature were removed, [tastes, odors, and colors] would be wiped away and annihilated.[23]

   Would Locke agree? What about Berkeley? Do you agree?

5. There is surely something to Berkeley's claim that a thing that seems very small to a person "will appear like a huge mountain to an extremely tiny animal." But was Berkeley right to draw the conclusion that size is a property of ideas, not a property of material objects? Read the first dialogue from Berkeley's *Three Dialogues Between Hylas and Philonous* before you make up your mind.

6. Here is a story from James Boswell's *The Life of Samuel Johnson*:

   After we came out of the church, we stood talking for some time together of Bishop Berkeley's ingenious sophistry to prove the nonexistence of matter, and that every thing in the universe is merely ideal. I observed, that though we are satisfied his doctrine is not true, it is impossible to refute it. I never shall forget the alacrity with which Johnson answered, striking his foot with mighty force against a large stone, till he rebounded from it—"I refute it thus."[24]

   Did Johnson succeed in refuting Berkeley's claim that physical objects are collections of ideas? How might a Berkeleyan respond?

7. Grab a straight pencil and a glass of water. Partially submerge the pencil in the water, and observe it from the side. Now consider the following argument:

   What you see is bent.
   The pencil is not bent.
   Therefore:
   What you see is not the pencil.

   Do you find this argument persuasive? How would a direct realist respond?

8. Consider the following dialogue between a theist and an atheist:

   Atheist: What grounds do you have for thinking that God exists?
   Theist: I know that *you* exist because I can see you—I know by perception that you exist. My grounds for thinking that God exists are similar. I perceive God when I pray. And so I know that he exists.
   Atheist: These experiences that you have when you pray: How do you know that they are caused by God and that they are not hallucinations?
   Theist: That's a tough question, I admit. I have to confess that I'm not completely certain that the experiences are not hallucinations. But then I'm not completely certain that *you're* not a hallucination either. Perhaps you are a phantasm created by an evil demon. I still maintain, however, that my grounds for believing that God exists are just as strong as my grounds for believing that you exist.

   What do you make of the theist's responses to the atheist's queries?

What to Look at Next

- The first few chapters of Betrand Russell's *The Problems of Philosophy* are concerned with the philosophy of perception. Although Russell was writing long after Locke, Berkeley, and Hume, their influence is clearly evident. The book is easy to follow.
- Locke's views about perception, which we discussed in this chapter, are presented in his *Essay Concerning Human Understanding*.

You can find a version of this, "translated" into modern English, at www.earlymoderntexts.com. You will find that Locke's writing is not so difficult to read. However, the *Essay* is extremely long, so you might prefer to start with one of the secondary texts listed below.
- E. J. Lowe's *Routledge Philosophy Guidebook to Locke on Human Understanding* is an excellent introduction. Unlike most commentators, Lowe thinks that Locke was *not* an indirect realist.
- Nicholas Jolley's *Locke: His Philosophical Thought* is another excellent introduction.
- J. L. Mackie's *Arguments from Locke* mixes together Locke exegesis with original philosophical argumentation. It is not an easy book, but it is well worth the effort!
- You can find versions of Berkeley's works "translated" into modern English at www.earlymoderntexts.com. We recommend that you start with his *Three Dialogues Between Hylas and Philonous*. Unlike Locke, Berkeley's writing is lively and concise.
- Berkeley's *A Treatise Concerning the Principles of Human Knowledge: An Introduction*, by Peter Kail, is an excellent source.
- If you would like to know about more recent work in the philosophy of perception, we recommend William Fish's book *Philosophy of Perception: A Contemporary Introduction*.

Notes

1. There are other senses too (e.g., proprioception), but for present purposes, these can be ignored.
2. Not all philosophers accept the idea that mathematics is an a priori science. If you want to explore this topic, check out Stewart Shapiro's book, *Thinking About Mathematics: The Philosophy of Mathematics* (Oxford: Oxford University Press, 2000).
3. David Hume, *Enquiry Concerning Human Understanding*, ch. 12. We have used Jonathan Bennett's "translation" of Hume's work into modern English, available at www.earlymoderntexts.com.
4. It should be noted that while *most* modern commenters agree that Locke was an indirect realist, there is not a complete consensus on this point. For an alternative interpretation, see E. J. Lowe, *Routledge Philosophy Guidebook to Locke on Human Understanding* (Abingdon: Routledge, 1995).
5. The character of your mental image also depends on the lighting, the distance between you and the cube, and a few other things.

6. John Locke, *Essay Concerning Understanding,* bk. 4, ch. 16, sec. 12.
7. For example, in the *Optics,* Newton claimed that heat consists in a "vibrating motion." For further references, see Robert Pasnau, *Metaphysical Themes, 1274–1671* (Oxford: Oxford University Press, 2011), 478.
8. Locke, *Essay Concerning Human Understanding,* bk. 4, ch. 16, sec. 12.
9. We owe these examples to C. L. Hardin, *Color for Philosophers: Unweaving the Rainbow* (Indianapolis/Cambridge: Hackett, 1988), 4–5.
10. It should be added that lakes are blue in part because they reflect blue light from the sky. Impure bodies of water can have other colors.
11. We have somewhat simplified Locke's definition. Locke said that a quality is "the power to produce an idea in our mind," *Essay Concerning Human Understanding,* bk 2, ch. 8, sec. 8.
12. Locke, *Essay Concerning Human Understanding,* bk. 2, ch. 8, sec 15.
13. Hume, *An Enquiry Concerning Human Understanding,* ch. 12.
14. The Berkeleyan case against materialism that we present here is based on the first dialogue in Berkeley's *Three Dialogues Between Hylas and Philonous.*
15. On this point, see Hardin, *Color for Philosophers,* 79–80. When we say "purely green," we have in mind what color scientists call "unique green."
16. George Berkeley, *Three Dialogues between Hylas and Philonous in opposition to Sceptics and Atheists,* The First Dialogue, available at https://www.earlymoderntexts.com/assets/pdfs/berkeley1713.pdf.
17. Ibid.
18. George Berkeley, Three Dialogues between Hylas and Philonous in opposition to Sceptics and Atheists, The Second Dialogue, available at https://www.earlymoderntexts.com/assets/pdfs/berkeley1713.pdf.
19. George Berkeley, *Principles of Human Knowledge,* sec. 3.
20. See Harry M. Bracken, *The Early Reception of Berkeley's Immaterialism 1710–1733* (The Hague: Martinus Nijhoff, 1965).
21. John Stuart Mill, *An Examination of Sir William Hamilton's Philosophy,* ch. 11.
22. See Bertrand Russell, *The Problems of Philosophy* (London: Williams and Norgate; New York: Henry Holt, 1912), ch. 3.
23. Stillman Drake, *Discoveries and Opinions of Galileo* (New York: Doubleday, 1957), 274.
24. Boswell's Life of Johnson is a classic work, easily found online. If you want a published copy, we recommend Boswell's Life of Johnson, by James Boswell, edited by G. Birkbeck Hill, revised and enlarged by L. F. Powell. (Oxford University Press, 1971).

CHAPTER 7
....

Will the Sun Rise Tomorrow?

Introduction

We often assume—to put it crudely for now—that what's happened in the past will keep on happening. Because the Sun has risen every day for as long as anyone can remember, we suppose it will rise tomorrow as well.[1] A friend who has always been trustworthy will be trusted again. When we see lightning we expect thunder because thunder has always followed lightning in the past.

Reasoning of this kind is apparently common in the sciences too. All species of spider discovered so far produce silk, and so we expect newly discovered spider species to produce silk as well. If a drug is given to a number of patients and no side effects are observed, it may be inferred that the drug is probably safe for other people also.

Though it may seem straightforward, this style of reasoning was questioned by the Scottish philosopher David Hume (1711–1776). Hume challenged us to justify our assumption that what's happened in the past will keep on happening—and later philosophers have found it very difficult to meet this challenge. To this day, the issue is central to philosophical discussions of scientific methodology.[2]

In this chapter, we present Hume's challenge in a little more detail; then, we look at some responses. But first, we need to introduce some terminology: "induction" and "necessary truth."

7.1 Making Predictions

The science fiction genre has now existed for so long that we are able to see how inaccurate its visions of the future have been. The world of 2001 did not resemble the world of *2001: A Space Odyssey*. *Back to the Future: Part II*'s depiction of 2015 turned out to be way off. Making predictions is difficult. And yet, somehow, we *do* make judgments about the relative likelihoods of future events. How do we do it?

According to Hume, we typically begin by noticing some pattern in observations we made in the past; we then predict that this pattern will continue in the future. We notice that it has always been true in the past that New York julys are hotter than New York februaries, and so we predict that the same will be true next year.

Another example. The vast majority of adult raccoons that we have observed in the past have weighed between four and thirty pounds. So we expect the next raccoon we find to weigh between four and thirty pounds. If a friend claims to have seen a raccoon the size of an elephant, we will suspect him of hallucination or deception.

For a more scientific example, consider Robert Boyle's (1627–1691) investigations of "the spring of the air." Boyle experimented with bodies of air in sealed containers; he noticed that, for a given body of the air at a fixed temperature, the pressure of the air was inversely proportional to the volume of the container. Having noticed this pattern in many cases, he expected further cases to conform to the same pattern.

In all these cases, we observe some pattern in observations that we've made in the past, and we predict that the pattern will continue in the future. These are cases of **enumerative induction**, or just induction for short. See chapter 2 for further discussion of enumerative induction.

Induction is persuasive only when it is based on a sufficiently large and diverse collection of observations. Here is a medical example. Suppose that the drug DP-80 has been given to a sample of patients and that no serious side effects have been detected. Would that justify us in concluding that the next patient to receive the drug will not experience serious side effects? That depends on the sample. If only two people so far have been tested, or if all the people in the sample are men aged fifty to fifty-five, it would be premature to conclude that the drug won't cause serious side effects in other patients. However, if the sample is both large and varied, a doctor might well predict that DP-80 is safe to prescribe to new patients.

It has to be admitted that—even when the sample is large and diverse—induction sometimes leads us astray. The philosopher John Stuart Mill (1806–1873) gave the following example, which has become so well-known it is now a cliché. For a long time, Europeans thought that all swans are white because they had only ever seen white swans. Then, they made it to Australia and discovered that some swans are black. Here's another example. The French chemist Antoine Lavoisier (1743–1794) was convinced by several examples that all acids contain oxygen; it turns out, however, that some acids (for example, hydrochloric acid) do not contain oxygen.

We shouldn't jump to the conclusion that induction should be abandoned, but these examples do show that induction should be used with some caution. If you make some prediction on the basis of induction, you should be less than certain that the prediction is correct, and you should be willing to revise your views as new evidence emerges.

We have seen that induction can be used to make predictions in a very wide variety of cases. This might lead us to conjecture that *all* predictions are based on induction. But this would be premature: as Hume pointed out, there are certain exceptional cases in which predictions can be made without induction. Here is one such case. Suppose that a commentator is asked to predict the outcome of a running race and says, "I predict that someone will win, unless of course nobody wins."

We can be very confident that this (rather unhelpful) prediction will be vindicated because we can see that the prediction *must* be true, whatever happens. If last year's champion has a repeat victory, the prediction will be correct. If there is a surprise victory by an outsider, the prediction will be correct. Indeed, the prediction will be correct even if something really bizarre or even magical happens. If all the competitors are kidnapped by aliens so that the race has to be cancelled, the prediction will still be correct. If one of the competitors uses a magic spell to finish in record-breaking time, the prediction will nevertheless be correct. No matter what happens—even if something weird and improbable happens—the prediction will be correct. To use the philosophical jargon, the prediction is a **necessary truth**. In this case, induction is not needed to justify the prediction. Just by thinking logically about the prediction, we can see that it is a necessary truth—induction is not needed.

Here is another, similar example: "In the future, any kitten we observe will be a cat." The word "kitten" just means *juvenile cat,* and so *of course* any kitten that we observe in the future will be cat. There's no way for this prediction to fail. The prediction is a necessary truth, and we can see this just using our understanding of English words and a little logic. Induction is not needed.

7.2 Hume's Problem

Now we're ready to take a look at Hume's problem of induction. First, a warning. We won't stick to the details of Hume's presentation. We're presenting the problem of induction as it is usually understood by philosophers today. We certainly won't use Hume's eighteenth-century language.

Recall that when we make predictions using induction, we proceed in the following way. We begin by noticing some pattern in observations that we have made in the past. For example:

- In past years in New York City, the average July temperature has been greater than the average February temperature.
- In the past, when a healthy adult raccoon has been weighed, it has typically been found that its weight is between four and thirty pounds.
- In the past, patients who have received the drug DP-80 have not experienced serious side effects.

We then infer, cautiously, that things observed in the future will conform to the same pattern:

- Next year in New York City, the average July temperature will be greater than the average February temperature.
- When a raccoon is weighed in the future, it will typically be found that its weight is between four and thirty pounds.
- The next patient to receive the drug DP-80 will not experience serious side effects.

Hume pointed out that when you reason in this way, you seem to presuppose that objects observed in the future will typically conform to patterns observed in the past. Let's give this presupposition a fancy name:

The Principle of Uniformity of Nature
Objects observed in the future will typically conform to patterns observed in the past.

Whenever you use an inductive argument, it seems, you rely on the **principle of uniformity of nature**, even if you don't make your commitment to the principle explicit. Now Hume asked, *What justifies us in accepting the principle of uniformity of nature?*

As Hume pointed out, the principle of uniformity of nature doesn't seem to be a necessary truth. We see no reason to think that it is *impossible* that the patterns we have noticed in the past will now break down. Perhaps next year in New York City there will be a freakishly cold July, colder even than the preceding February. And perhaps raccoons will increase in size so that most raccoons weigh more than thirty pounds. And perhaps patients will start experiencing severe side effects when they take DP-80. All of this seems very improbable, but there's no obvious reason for thinking that these freakish events are *impossible*.

Now the principle of uniformity of nature is a prediction, not a necessary truth, so it is natural to suggest that we can justify our accepting the principle using induction. At first, it might appear that an inductive justification of the principle of uniformity of nature is available. We need only point out that, in the past, objects observed later usually have conformed to patterns in earlier observations. And it seems reasonable to expect this trend to continue.

But this argument is highly problematic. As noted, it seems that all inductive arguments *presuppose* the principle of uniformity of nature. In consequence, to use induction in support of the principle of uniformity of nature is circular. Or so it seems.

An analogy may help. Suppose that you meet a man who makes a series of bold, confident predictions: he makes predictions about what the weather will be in six months, about who will win the next Super Bowl, and about who will be the president of the United States in 2040. Astonished, you ask him where his information is coming from. The man replies that he has a psychic parrot. He asks his parrot questions about the future, and the parrot replies either "yes" or "no." The man accepts the parrot's answers as faultlessly correct. You point out that the man presupposes:

The Parrot Principle
Whatever answer the parrot gives to a yes/no question is correct.

When you challenge the man to justify this presupposition, he responds by asking the parrot, "Do you invariably give correct answers to yes/no questions?" To which the parrot unhesitatingly replies, "Yes!" The man tells you that this is sufficient to establish the parrot principle. Of course, the man's argument is hopeless—it's circular. We wanted him to justify the parrot principle, but his method of justifying the principle is legitimate only if the parrot principle has already been established.

And so we reach the nub of the problem. Hume conjectured that (necessary truths aside) predictions can only be justified using induction. Since the principle of uniformity of nature is itself a prediction, it follows that the principle could only be justified by induction. But on pain of circularity, the principle can't be justified using induction. It then follows that the principle can't be justified at all. But this seems to establish that all induction rests on an unjustified presupposition. Hume concluded that one cannot show that a prediction is correct, or even that it is *probably* correct, using induction.

The conclusion of Hume's argument was very radical. Hume was *not* just making the uncontroversial point that sometimes inductive reasoning leads one to a false conclusion. Nor was he merely making the equally uncontroversial observation that beliefs based on inductive arguments should be held with some caution. Hume's claim was that inductive arguments do not justify us *at all* in accepting their conclusions.

To see how strange this conclusion is, think about this example again:

DP-80 has been given to a large and diverse sample of patients, and none of them has experienced serious side effects.

Therefore:

The next patient to take DP-80 will not experience serious side effects.

This argument seems to be persuasive. Assuming that we have indeed given DP-80 to a large and diverse sample of patients, and that none of them has experienced serious side effects, we really do seem to be justified in inferring—cautiously—that the next patient to take DP-80 will not experience serious side effects. But if Hume is right, we have *no reason at all* to believe it probable that the next patient to take the drug will not experience serious side effects. This is a counterintuitive conclusion, to say the least.

What's more, Hume's skepticism about induction put him at odds with the scientific establishment of his time. In his book *Novum Organum,* Francis Bacon (1561–1626) had argued that induction is central to the scientific method. The book was enormously influential, and

Bacon's claim was widely accepted in England in the seventeenth and eighteenth centuries. Newton himself described his method as inductive.[3] So when Hume argued that we are not justified in using inductive reasoning, he displayed skepticism about the scientific method as it was then understood.

To be clear, Hume did not advise us to give up on inductive reasoning. Hume thought that human beings will always use inductive arguments—inductive reasoning comes naturally to us, just as eating and sleeping come naturally. Even so, Hume thought that there is no rational justification for this practice. On this view, it is our nature as human beings to form beliefs using a method that cannot be rationally justified.

Most people find this conclusion unsettling. Hume certainly did:

> I am frightened and confused by the forlorn solitude in which my philosophy places me, and see myself as some strange uncouth monster who, not being able to mingle and unite in society, has been expelled from all human society and left utterly abandoned and disconsolate.[4]

Hume found a remedy, however, for his fear and confusion:

> I dine, I play a game of backgammon, I converse and I am merry with my friends; and when after three or four hours' amusement, I would return to these speculations, they appear so cold and strained, and ridiculous, that I cannot find in my heart to enter into them any further.[5]

But this is hardly a solution to the problem that Hume had uncovered. On the contrary, it seems that Hume needed to distract himself with backgammon precisely because he had no solution to his problem.

7.3 Karl Popper

Hume's conclusion is, to say the least, surprising. At the same time, his argument is powerful—so we should be willing to explore the suggestion that Hume was correct. One philosopher who *did* accept Hume's conclusion was Karl Popper (1902–1994). However, Popper was not willing to draw the conclusion that there is something wrong with the scientific method. So Popper offered a new account of scientific reasoning, arguing that induction is not, in fact, used in good scientific research.

Popper noted that the history of science is littered with refuted conjectures. Consider the contemporary scientific account of the structure

On the left is David Hume (1711–1776), who challenged us to justify inductive reasoning. On the right is Karl Popper (1902–1994), who thought that inductive reasoning is not needed in the sciences.

of the solar system. Astronomers reached this account only after many previous theories have been refuted. For example:

1. There are five planets.
2. All the celestial bodies (the Sun, the stars, and the planets) are perfectly uniform spheres.
3. The planetary orbits are perfectly elliptical.
4. The Earth sits at the center of the universe. Around it, "celestial spheres" rotate. Attached to them are the planets, the stars, the Moon, and the Sun.
5. The Earth travels around the Sun because they are both magnetic, and the force of magnetic attraction between them keeps the Earth in its orbit.

Theories (1) and (2) were refuted when sufficiently powerful telescopes were designed. These telescopes allowed astronomers to observe more than five planets. Galileo (1564–1642) made detailed observations of mountains on the Moon, thereby refuting (2). Theory (3), which was due to Kepler (1571–1630), was refuted by detailed observations of the trajectories of the planets in the seventeenth century, which showed that their orbits are not perfectly elliptical. And so on.

So Popper suggested that science advances by trial and error. A conjecture is proposed. Scientists then set out to refute this conjecture, and typically, they eventually succeed. They then set out a new conjecture, one which has not yet been refuted, and the cycle continues.[6]

Because he held that science advances in this way, Popper thought it was crucial that scientists maintain what he called a "critical attitude." By this, he meant that scientists should actively search for refutations of the prevailing theories. He railed against those who presented themselves as scientists but then failed to adopt this critical attitude—his criticisms of Marxists and Freudians were particularly severe.

Popper's account of the advancement of science was revolutionary because he avoided entirely the idea that scientific theories are justified by induction. Indeed, Popper denied that observations give us good reason to believe that scientific theories are true. According to Popper, Newton's theory of planetary motion was accepted not because eighteenth-century astronomers had empirical evidence for its truth—but simply because it was the only available theory which had not yet been refuted. Popper wrote:

> I think that we shall have to get accustomed to the idea that we must not look upon science as a "body of knowledge," but rather as a system of hypotheses; that is to say, a system of guesses or anticipations which in principle cannot be justified, but with which we work as long as they stand up to tests, and of which we are never justified in saying that we know that they are "true" or "more or less certain" or even "probable."[7]

Popper's work has been very influential. In particular, many philosophers (and, indeed, scientists) have been impressed by Popper's idea that scientists must maintain a "critical attitude." However, Popper's critics have argued that Popper did not have an adequate account of *applied* science.

Here's an example, to illustrate the problem. So far, every unbroken length of copper wire that's been investigated has conducted electricity. So the following theory has not (yet!) been refuted:

Theory One
It is always true that every unbroken length of copper wire conducts electricity.

However, there are very many other nearby hypotheses that have also not yet been refuted. For example:

Theory Two
It always has been true, and it will remain true until midnight tonight, that every unbroken length of copper wire conducts electricity. However, after midnight tonight, no copper wire will conduct electricity.[8]

Theory Three
It always has been true, and it will remain true until a year from now, that every unbroken length of copper wire conducts electricity. However, after one year from now, no copper wire will conduct electricity.

Theory Four
It always has been true, and it will remain true until midnight tonight, that every unbroken length of copper wire conducts electricity. After midnight tonight, unbroken copper wires in Europe will continue to conduct electricity, but copper wires elsewhere will no longer conduct electricity.

None of these four theories has been experimentally refuted. Nevertheless, we think that while theory one is probably true, theories two, three, and four are probably false.

These probability judgments are of enormous importance when science is applied. Suppose, for example, that an engineer is making a boat and uses copper wire to connect the battery to the boat's lights and to the starter motor for the engine. In doing this, the engineer manifests the expectation that unbroken copper wire will continue to conduct electricity long into the future. Someone's life may depend on it. The engineer will not take seriously the claim that the copper wiring will suddenly stop conducting electricity at midnight tonight or in a year's time. And the engineer's job would become impossible if such wild claims were to be taken seriously.

Popper claimed that "we are never justified in saying that we know that [a scientific theory is] 'true' or 'more or less certain' or even 'probable.'"[9] But such probability judgments appear to be vital in applied science.

7.4 Peter Strawson

The English philosopher Peter Strawson (1919–2006) proposed an intriguing and disarmingly simple response to Hume's challenge to justify inductive reasoning.[10] He began with a hypothesis about the meaning of the English word "reasonable."[11] He claimed that we have a shared conception of what constitutes a "reasonable" inference, and that to say an inference is "reasonable" is just to say it meets those shared standards. Now consider:

> In the past, when a healthy adult raccoon has been weighed, it has typically been found to weigh between four and thirty pounds.
> *Therefore:*
> When a raccoon is weighed in the future, it will typically be found that its weight is between four and thirty pounds.

Is this a reasonable inference? Strawson would say (assuming that we have weighed a sufficiently large and varied sample of raccoons) that this inference clearly *is* reasonable because it meets our shared standards for reasonable inference.

Here is an analogy. Anyone who understands the English word "bachelor" can figure out that all bachelors are unmarried. After all, part of what it *means* to say that someone is a bachelor is that he is unmarried. In much the same way, Strawson thought, anyone who understands the English word "reasonable" can see that the above inference about racoons is a reasonable one.

But it may be replied that this misses the point. Hume challenged us to *justify* our ordinary standards of reasoning—however, all we've done so far is dogmatically apply those very standards. To put it slightly differently, the objection is that Strawson is ignoring Hume's question, which is:

> (1) Are our ordinary standards of reasonableness themselves reasonable? In particular, are our ordinary standards for induction reasonable?

Strawson had an ingenious response to this objection. He used a legal analogy. Given a particular law in a country with a constitution, we can meaningfully ask whether the law is constitutional. But suppose we ask:

> (2) Is the constitution constitutional?

This is, it seems, a meaningless question—there is no "super-constitution" by which a constitution itself can be assessed. Now Strawson said that question (1) is meaningless, just like question (2). There is no higher standard by which our ordinary standards of reasoning can be assessed—just as there is no "super-constitution"—and so (1) doesn't make sense.

We're not totally convinced that (1) is a meaningless question, but we're prepared to grant the point, for Hume can instead ask:

> (3) Are inductive arguments *reliable?* That is, do inductive arguments with true premises usually have true conclusions?

It seems clear that (3) is a meaningful question, even if (1) isn't. Now a Strawsonian *could* respond to question (3) by arguing, inductively, that induction is reliable—but then his argument would be circular, and circular reasoning is impermissible even according to the ordinary standards that the Strawsonian professed to defend.

So the situation seems to be this. Strawson *may* have established that induction is *reasonable*, but he did not establish that induction is *reliable*. We'll leave you to think about whether this constitutes an adequate response to Hume's problem.

One philosopher who did *not* think that Strawson's response was adequate was Wesley Salmon (1925–2001). Salmon thought that, in the absence of some reason for thinking that inductive arguments "make correct predictions," to say that such arguments are "reasonable" is empty praise:

> It sounds very much as if the whole argument (that reasonable beliefs are, by definition, beliefs which are inductively supported) has the function of transferring to the word "inductive" all of the honorific connotations of the word "reasonable," quite apart from whether induction is good for anything. The resulting justification of induction amounts to this: If you use inductive procedures you can call yourself "reasonable"—*and isn't that nice!*[12]

7.5 Epistemically Basic Beliefs

Let's return to Hume's argument and have another go at identifying an error. Remember that Hume's argument went like this. Hume challenged us to present a justification for accepting the principle of uniformity of nature. Because the principle is not a necessary truth, Hume thought that it would have to be justified using induction. However, he argued that any attempt to justify the principle of uniformity of nature using induction would be circular because induction itself presupposes the principle of uniformity of nature. He concluded that the principle cannot be justified. He inferred that inductive reasoning relies on an unjustified presupposition and inferred that one cannot show that a conclusion is true, or even that it is probably true, using inductive arguments.

But why did Hume suppose that the principle of uniformity of nature *needs* to be justified? Perhaps there are certain beliefs that are warranted *without argument,* and perhaps the principle of uniformity of nature is one of these.

We use the term **epistemically basic belief** for a belief that is warranted without argument. The suggestion on the table, then, is that the principle of uniformity of nature is an epistemically basic belief. On this view, Hume was wrong to think that someone who uses inductive reasoning needs to provide some justification for accepting the principle of uniformity of nature: When a Humean challenges you to justify your acceptance of the principle, it suffices to reply, "I don't need to provide any justification—it's just *basic.*"

We have more to say in chapter 8 about the idea that there are epistemically basic beliefs. For now, we note an important challenge for proponents of this response to Hume's argument. There are surely cases in which it would be ridiculous to present one's opinions as epistemically basic. Suppose, for example, that someone you know spends all of their pension money on a certain stock, insisting that the stock will double in price within five years. You ask why the person believes this, and the answer is that it is epistemically basic. This would be a kind of madness. So someone who claims that the principle of uniformity of nature is a basic belief is stuck with difficult questions: *Which* beliefs are basic? *When* is it okay to claim that one's belief is basic?

Another way to see the force of these questions is to consider supposed examples of epistemically basic beliefs that have been presented by philosophers. Alvin Plantinga (1932–) has claimed that theism (i.e., belief in the existence of God) is basic.[13] Atheists, of course, reject Plantinga's claim.

Here is a second example:

> Anything that begins to exist must have a cause that produced it.

This is an important premise in some versions of the cosmological argument for the existence of God.[14] When challenged to justify this premise, a proponent of the cosmological argument may say that the premise is basic[15]—but, of course, opponents of the cosmological argument will allege that this is mere dogmatism.

Our third example is a little harder to grasp. G. E. Moore (1873–1958) once claimed that consequentialism is a basic belief, in the following form:

> It must always be right to do what has the best possible total effects.[16]

As we will discuss in chapter 15, many philosophers believe not only that this is not basic, but that it is also false. They say that there are certain sorts of acts which are *just wrong*, regardless of their effects. Such philosophers will say that, when Moore said consequentialism is basic, he was simply trying to cover up his failure to produce a justification for his views.

It seems to us that philosophers who believe there are basic beliefs need to find some method for dealing with disputes of this kind. Before such a method is specified, philosophers who insist that some of their own views are "basic" are open to the charge of dogmatism.

7.6 Beyond Enumerative Induction

As mentioned, Hume apparently believed that (necessary truths aside) all predictions must be justified using induction. This assumption, however, can be questioned. Perhaps there are other ways of justifying predictions.

Many philosophers of science today believe that a style of argument called **abduction** (or "inference to the best explanation") is crucial to scientific reasoning. When one gives an abductive argument, one begins with a number of observations, and one suggests an explanation for those various observations. If one judges that the proffered explanation is a *good* explanation, and is better than any available alternatives, one infers (cautiously) that the explanation is correct.

Here's an example. Suppose you return to your apartment after work. You find the front door ajar, some of yours drawers open and their contents strewn about, some of your most valuable possessions missing, and one of your windows broken from the outside. A good explanation of these observations is you have been burgled. What's more, this explanation is better than any alternative. And so you infer you probably have been burgled. In summary, your argument is this:

Premise 1: The front door is ajar.
Premise 2: Some of your valuables are missing.
Premise 3: Your drawers have been opened, and their contents strewn about.
Premise 4: One of your windows has been broken.
Conclusion: You have been burgled.

This is not an example of enumerative induction, but it is nevertheless a persuasive argument.

Many philosophers believe that abduction is often used in the sciences. Consider, for example, Newton's theory of gravity. Newton had before him a wide range of observations—concerning the trajectories of objects in free fall, the tides, the movements of the planets, and so on. Newton found he could explain all of these observations using his theory of gravity. Since this explanation was judged to be superior to rival theories offered by other scientists, Newton's theory was accepted.

Once Newton's theory of gravity was accepted, it could be used to make predictions, and these predictions were not based on induction. This seems to show that Hume was wrong to think that (necessary truths aside) all predictions are justified using inductions.

We seem now to have identified an important error in Hume's argument. One of the assumptions in Hume's argument was incorrect. It is not true that (necessary truths aside) all predictions are justified by induction.

However, this observation on its own does not constitute a solution to Hume's problem. We still do not have a convincing, noncircular justification for the principle of uniformity of nature or a cogent explanation of why no such justification is required.

The systematic investigation of different forms of reasoning is a thriving area of philosophical research today. Some philosophers in this area use mathematical tools—in particular, they draw on mathematical logic and the theory of probability. However, there is no still no consensus about how to deal with Hume's problem of induction.

We'll leave you to think about whether the principle of uniformity of nature can be justified using abduction, and whether the use of abduction itself requires justification. We're off to have a meal, conversation, and backgammon.

Glossary

abduction: When one gives an abductive argument, one begins with a number of observations, and one suggests an explanation for those various observations. If one judges that the proffered explanation is a *good* explanation, and better than any available alternatives, one infers (cautiously) that the explanation is correct. See section 7.6 for an example and chapter 2 for further discussion. Also called "inference to the best explanation."

enumerative induction: In an inductive argument, one starts by identifying some pattern in cases that have been studied; then, one suggests on this basis that the pattern will extend to other cases as well. In this chapter we focused on inductive arguments in which one identifies a pattern in past events and suggests that this pattern will continue in the future.

epistemically basic belief: A basic belief is a belief that is justified but is not derived from some other belief. Sometimes, basic beliefs are called "foundational beliefs," or "self-evident truths," or "axioms." See section 6 for more discussion. For even more, see the discussion of foundationalism in chapter 8.

necessary truth: Compare these two statements:
- The Philadelphia Eagles won the 2017 Super Bowl.
- Either some team won the 2017 Super Bowl, or no team did.

Both of these statements are true, but only the second is a *necessary* truth. The Philadelphia Eagles *did in fact* win the 2017 Super Bowl, but they could have lost—the New England Patriots could have beaten them. By contrast, it is *impossible* for the second statement to be false.

principle of the uniformity of nature: The claim that objects observed in the future will typically conform to patterns observed in the past. See section 7.2.

Comprehension Questions

1. (a) Suggest some examples of enumerative induction. (Don't repeat examples from the chapter.)
   (b) Suggest some examples of abduction. (Don't repeat examples from the chapter.)

2. Use examples to illustrate the point that, when constructing an argument by enumerative induction, one requires a sample that is both *large* and *varied*.
3. What is the principle of uniformity of nature?
4. (a) Hume thought that the principle of uniformity of nature is not a necessary truth. Why?
   (b) Hume thought that it is not possible to justify the principle of uniformity of nature using induction. Why?
   (c) Summarize Hume's problem of induction.
5. Karl Popper denied that scientists use enumerative induction. Explain his alternative account of scientific methodology.
6. According to Karl Popper, what is "critical attitude," and why is it important? What are some examples of the critical attitude in action?
7. In the chapter, we suggested that Popper did not have an adequate account of *applied* science. Explain this point.
8. Explain Peter Strawson's analogy between these two questions:
   (a) Are our ordinary standards of reasonableness themselves reasonable? In particular, are our ordinary standards for induction reasonable?
   (b) Is the constitution constitutional?
9. In our discussion of Strawson, we distinguished reasonableness and reliability. Explain this distinction.
10. What is an epistemically basic belief?

Discussion Questions

1. In section 7.1, we suggested that it was induction that convinced Boyle that the pressure of a fixed body of air at a fixed temperature is inversely proportional to its volume. Is it correct to think of this as an example of enumerative induction? Could it instead be classified as a case of abduction? Or as something else altogether?

2. Are there any scientific statements that have now been established beyond reasonable doubt so that it is no longer necessary to adopt a "critical attitude" toward them?

3. Popper has proposed, when applying scientific theory in medicine, engineering, and so on, that one should prefer to use whichever theory has been "best tested." That is, one should prefer to use, from

among unrefuted theories, whichever has been most thoroughly subjected to empirical trials.[17] What do you make of this proposal?
4. Strawson claims, in effect, that it is just part of what the word "reasonable" *means* that induction is reasonable—just as it is part of what the word "bachelor" means that all bachelors are unmarried. A haruspex in ancient Greece might similarly argue that it is just part of what "reasonable" means that making predictions by reading entrails is reasonable. Does this analogy discredit Strawson's position?[18]
5. This question is for people who have also read chapter 8: What might a coherence theorist say about the problem of induction?
6. Can you think of any plausible examples of epistemically basic beliefs?

What to Look at Next

- Hume presented his problem of induction in book 1, part 3, section 6 of the *Treatise of Human Nature*, and again in section 4 of his *Enquiry Concerning Human Understanding*. You can find versions of these works at www.earlymoderntexts.com. (We suggest you read the *Enquiry* first—it's easier.)
- For a more detailed presentation of Hume's work on induction, see Louis Loeb, "Inductive Inference in Hume's Philosophy," in Elizabeth Radcliffe's *A Companion to Hume*.
- Bryan Magee's *Philosophy and the Real World: An Introduction to Karl Popper* is a useful short introduction to Popper's philosophy.
- Popper presented his views on induction in many places. A good place to start is his "Conjectural Knowledge: My Solution of the Problem of Induction" in his *Objective Knowledge: An Evolutionary Approach*. This is a late paper and can be taken as a presentation of his mature position. For a broader understanding of Popper's epistemological views, check out his book *Conjectures and Refutations*.
- Strawson presented his views on the problem of induction in his book *Introduction to Logical Theory*. Salmon's objection is presented in his "Should We Attempt to Justify Induction?" *Philosophical Studies*, 8 (1957): 33–48.
- Many philosophers today think that probability theory can help us understand nondeductive reasoning. Two excellent introductions to this area of philosophy are *Choice and Chance* by Brian Skyrms and *A Critical Introduction to Formal Epistemology* by Darren Bradley.

Notes

1. We assume, for this example, you are neither in the Arctic nor the Antarctic!
2. You can find Hume's challenge in book 1, part 3, section 6 of his *Treatise of Human Nature* and in section 4 of his *Enquiry Concerning Understanding*. Translations of both works can be found at www.earlymoderntexts.com.
3. The claim is made in the "General Scholium." You may be able to find this work online. Alternatively, you can find it in Newton's *The Principia: The Authoritative Translation and Guide: Mathematical Principles of Natural Philosophy* (Berkeley: University of California Press, 2016). It should be stressed that Bacon and other early modern writers offered more sophisticated accounts of inductive reasoning than ours.
4. Hume, *Treatise of Human Nature*, bk. 1, pt. 4, sec. 7.
5. Hume, *Treatise of Human Nature*, bk. 1, pt. 4, sec. 7.
6. Karl Popper, *Conjectures and Refutations: The Growth of Scientific Knowledge* (Abingdon: Routledge, 2002).
7. Karl Popper, *The Logic of Scientific Discovery* (New York: Basic Books, 1959), 317.
8. Theories of this peculiar kind were first considered by Nelson Goodman. See his *Fact, Fiction and Forecast* (Cambridge, MA: Harvard University Press, 1983).
9. Popper, *The Logic of Scientific Discovery*, 317.
10. Strawson's discussion of induction can be found in chapter 9 of his book *Introduction to Logical Theory* (London: Methuen; New York: John Wiley and Sons, 1952).
11. His account was supposed to extend to other words too: "rational," "justified," and so on. For simplicity, we focus on "reasonable."
12. Wesley Salmon, "Should We Attempt to Justify Induction?" *Philosophical Studies*, 8 (1957): 33–48.
13. Alvin Plantinga, "Is Belief in God Properly Basic?" *Noûs* 15, no. 1 (1981).
14. In particular, it is a premise of the "Kalām cosmological argument," which is mentioned in the Discussion Questions at the end of chapter 3.
15. This was, essentially, Thomas Reid's position. See Dale Tuggy, "Reid's Philosophy of Religion" in *The Cambridge Companion to Thomas Reid*, ed. Terence Cuneo and René van Woudenberg (Cambridge, UK: Cambridge University Press, 2006). The claim "Anything that begins to exist must have a cause that produced it" is a first principle made in Reid's *Essays on the Intellectual Powers of Man*, essay 6, ch. 6.
16. G. E. Moore, *Ethics* (London: Williams and Norgate, 1912), ch. 4.
17. This suggestion is made in section 14 of Popper's "Replies to My Critics."
18. Of course, the ancient Greek haruspex would not use the English word "reasonable."

CHAPTER 8

What Is Knowledge?

Introduction

If you are reading this book, there is a good chance that you are a student in a college or university. Doubtless, you have many reasons for being there. One of them, surely, is that you want to acquire knowledge. But what, exactly, is knowledge? If you don't have a ready answer, you are not alone. It's a question that philosophers have been debating for 2,500 years. The branch of philosophy that tries to answer this question is called "**epistemology**."[1] Our project, in this chapter, is to look at some of the leading ideas and controversies about the nature of knowledge. The central question will be: When we say someone *knows* something, what do we mean?

8.1 Three Kinds of Knowledge

One point on which most philosophers agree is that there are several different kinds of knowledge, and thus the word "know" has several different meanings. Sometimes the word is used to indicate the possession of a skill or ability, like knowing how to drive a car or ride a skateboard, or read music. Philosophers often refer to this sort of knowledge as "knowledge how."

Another use of the word "know" indicates acquaintance. When we say things like "The Prime Minister of the United Kingdom knows the

Queen, but the Prime Minister of Australia has never met her," the word "knows" is being used in this sense—that is, "knowledge as acquaintance."

A third kind of knowledge is knowledge of facts. This sort of knowledge is typically expressed by the verb "know" followed by a that-clause, as in sentences like these:

(1) Lachlan knows that Ottawa is the capital of Canada.
(2) Shanice knows that there is no greatest prime number.
(3) Hyeon knows that John Quincy Adams was the sixth president of the United States.

Philosophers call this sort of knowledge "propositional knowledge." A **proposition** can be thought of as something that is expressed by a **declarative sentence** and that purports to state a fact.[2] Though propositions purport to state facts, not all of them do. False declarative sentences like

(4) Toronto is the capital of Canada.

and

(5) Andrew Jackson was the sixth President of the United States.

express propositions that aren't true and don't state facts. Though philosophers have been interested in all three kinds of knowledge, their main interest has always been on propositional knowledge, and that is the kind of knowledge we focus on in this chapter.

8.2 Analyzing Propositional Knowledge: The Easy Part—Belief and Truth

What do we mean when we attribute propositional knowledge to someone? How are sentences like (1) through (3) analyzed? Philosophers often describe these sentences as having the form

(6) S knows that p.

where S is a stand-in for a person's name and p is a stand-in for a declarative sentence. One point on which almost all philosophers agree is that if a sentence of this form is true, then the sentence replacing p must be true. No one can know that Andrew Jackson was the sixth president of the United States because Andrew Jackson *wasn't* the sixth president; he was the seventh president. Similarly, no one can know that 6 is the square root of 25, or that the Earth is flat. Of course, people can *believe* that the Earth is flat, and they can be quite confident of that belief. During the Middle Ages, many uneducated people believed that the Earth was flat, and most of these people thought they knew the Earth was flat. But they were wrong. Since the Earth is not flat, they couldn't know that it is.

Another point on which almost all philosophers agree is that if S knows that p, then S *believes* that p. To see why this seems so obvious, imagine that, on the day after the 2014 soccer World Cup, Alexis asks her friend Zach, "Hey, who won the World Cup yesterday, Germany or Argentina?" Zach, who is not a soccer fan, answers, "Gee, I don't have a clue." The answer, in case you don't know, is that Germany won. But since Zach doesn't believe that Germany won, he doesn't know that Germany won. We suspect that many readers are like Zach. If you had no beliefs at all about the winner of the 2014 World Cup until you started reading this paragraph, then until a minute or two ago, you didn't know that Germany won.

8.3 Analyzing Propositional Knowledge: The Hard Part—Justification

We now have two very plausible necessary conditions for knowledge. If S knows that p, then (i) S believes that p and (ii) p is true. Are we done? Is knowledge just true belief?

Well, since you're not even close to the end of this chapter, you probably guessed that the answer is no. Having propositional knowledge requires more than having a true belief. Philosophers often make the case that belief and truth are not enough for knowledge with rather implausible stories that go something like this:

> Joe is very superstitious. He thinks that a coin he keeps in his drawer has special powers. He believes that if he asks the coin an important question and then flips the coin, the answer is yes if the coin comes up heads and the answer is no if the coin comes up tails. Actually, there is nothing at all special about Joe's coin. It's just an ordinary quarter. Nonetheless, Joe has great faith in his special quarter. One day, Joe is looking for a good way to invest his life savings, $20,000, which is now in a bank account earning very low interest. He goes down the stock listings in the newspaper, and for each stock, he asks the coin, "Will this stock go up 100 percent or more over the next year?" For

the first three stocks, the coin says no—it comes up tails. But for the fourth stock, Aardark Advanced Technology (AAAT), the coin comes up heads. So Joe invests all of his savings in AAAT. A year later, the price of AAAT has gone up 104%. Joe sells his AAAT stock and gives his special coin a kiss to say thank you.

When Joe bought his AAAT stock, he believed it would go up at least 100 percent over the next year. And it did! So when he bought the stock, Joe had a true belief. But did he *know* that the AAAT stock would go up at least 100 percent? Most philosophers think that the answer is clearly no. Joe's belief wasn't an instance of knowledge. He was just lucky.

Now there is obviously something very far-fetched about this example. It's hard to believe that anyone would really base their beliefs about important matters on the flip of a coin. But there are lots of examples of similar phenomena in the real world. In some cultures, people make important decisions by casting lots or reading entrails. And in our culture, some people base important beliefs on horoscopes, palm readings, or Ouija boards. Sometimes, of course, beliefs formed this way turn out to be true. But those true beliefs, like Joe's belief, aren't instances of knowledge. Folks who end up with true beliefs in this way are just lucky. What these lucky-guess beliefs are missing, philosophers insist, is that they are not properly *justified*. So we need to add *justification* to our list of features required for propositional knowledge:

> An analysis of propositional knowledge: If S knows that p, then (i) S believes that p, (ii) p is true, and (iii) S's belief is justified. Conversely, if S believes that p, and S's belief is both justified and true, then S knows that p.

The idea that knowledge can be analyzed as justified true belief is a very old one. It was first proposed by Plato almost 2,400 years ago,[3] and it has been the dominant account of knowledge until very recently. However, when we say that a true belief must be justified in order to count as knowledge, we are doing little more than putting a label on the additional feature true beliefs must have to be instances of knowledge. The hard work comes when we try to say what it is for a belief to be justified. We do that in the next three sections. Since the term "justified" can mean different things in different contexts, philosophers often use the term "epistemic justification" for the sort of justification required if a true belief is to count as an instance of knowledge.

8.4 Foundationalism

Let's start our exploration of epistemic justification with another fictional example:

> Jill Kop is a police detective. She is investigating the murder of a man named Vince Victim and has come to believe that the crime was committed by Sam Suspect. (Hey, it's a made-up story, so we might as well have some fun with the names.) Had Jill formed her belief the way Joe did, by flipping a coin, we would surely protest that her belief is completely unjustified. But Jill is a very conscientious detective and wouldn't dream of forming a belief that way. She realizes that accusing the wrong person would be a very bad thing to do. So before filing charges against Sam Suspect, Jill reviews her reasons for thinking that Sam is the murderer. First of all, Jill believes that when Sam was arrested, he was in possession of the murder weapon. She was the arresting officer, and she remembers finding a gun in Sam's jacket pocket. The gun was sent to the ballistics laboratory and, Jill believes, the ballistics report said that the gun was the murder weapon. Jill also believes that a surveillance video, recorded a few minutes after Vince Victim was shot, showed Sam leaving the room where Vince's body was found. She remembers reviewing the video herself. Finally, Jill believes that Sam had a motive. She believes that Gina, Vince's girlfriend, used to be Sam's girlfriend, that she broke up with Sam when she met Vince, and that Sam was very jealous. Why does she believe this? Because she believes that's what Gina told her.

Clearly, Jill's belief that Sam Suspect murdered Vince Victim is a well-justified belief, in stark contrast to the beliefs that Joe forms with his special coin. What lessons we can learn about epistemic justification by thinking about Jill's belief?

A first observation is that Jill's belief that Sam Suspect killed Vince Victim is justified by *other* beliefs, including her belief that Sam had the murder weapon in his possession when he was arrested, her belief that Sam left the crime scene a few minutes after Vince was killed, and her belief that Sam was very jealous of Vince's relationship with Gina. Jill *inferred* her belief that Sam is the killer from these other beliefs. Many beliefs are justified in this way—they are inferred from other beliefs.

But it takes more than this for the inferred belief to be justified. When Joe invested $20,000 in AAAT, he believed that in a year he would have $40,000. He inferred that from his belief that the stock would go up

100 percent. But since his belief that the stock would go up 100 percent was itself not justified, neither is the belief he inferred from it. So for a belief (call it B1) to be justified by being inferred from another belief (call it B2), that second belief, B2, must *also* be justified.

Now let's return to Jill. One of the beliefs from which she inferred that Sam Suspect was the killer was her belief that Sam had the murder weapon in his possession when he was arrested. Is *that* belief justified? Well, Jill inferred that belief from a pair of further beliefs: she believed (a) that Sam had a gun in his pocket when he was arrested, and (b) that the ballistics lab report said that the gun was the murder weapon. For Jill's belief that Sam had the murder weapon in his possession when he was arrested to be justified, these additional beliefs, (a) and (b), must be justified.

Obviously, there is a pattern emerging here. Let's call Jill's belief that Sam killed Vince a Level-1 belief. Her Level-1 belief is justified by being inferred from other beliefs, let's call them Level-2 beliefs, provided that these Level-2 beliefs are themselves justified. The Level-2 beliefs are justified by being inferred from still other beliefs, Level-3 beliefs, provided that the Level-3 beliefs are justified. But where does all of this *stop*?

That question was first posed by Plato's student Aristotle.[4] As Aristotle noted, there seem to be three possibilities. The first is that it *doesn't* stop: the chain of beliefs that justify other beliefs is infinite. The second is that the chain of justifying beliefs has a circular structure and eventually returns to where it started. The third is that there must be some justified beliefs that are *not* justified by other beliefs. These beliefs would then serve as the foundation for all the rest of our justified beliefs. Directly or indirectly, all of our justified beliefs are inferred from these foundational beliefs.

Aristotle thought that the first two options were hopeless, and many contemporary philosophers agree. If the chain of justifications is infinite, then we have an infinite number of beliefs, which seems rather unlikely given the finite size of our brains. Even if we ignore that problem, the first option seems to require that, to have a justified belief, we have to have made an infinite number of inferences, each of which presumably takes a bit of time. But life, alas, is finite, so it is hard to see how we could succeed in making an infinite number of inferences. On the second option, the chain of justifications is circular—circular reasoning is notoriously bad reasoning because it can be used to justify *any* conclusion. From the proposition that you are a dill pickle, we can, with impeccable logic, infer that you are a dill pickle. But if we believe that you are a dill pickle, surely we can't justify our belief that way! Aristotle and many other philosophers concluded that the third option is the only viable one; there must be a class of justified beliefs that are not inferred from other justified beliefs. These beliefs—they are sometimes called **epistemically basic beliefs**—are the starting points from which all the rest of our justified beliefs are inferred. Because this picture of how beliefs are justified portrays our justified beliefs as structured like a building, with a foundation of epistemically basic beliefs supporting all the rest of our justified beliefs, it is called **foundationalism**.

In short, foundationalists claim that a belief is justified just in case it is basic or has been inferred (using good reasoning!) from basic beliefs. Foundationalism has been enormously influential throughout the history of philosophy. Descartes was a foundationalist, as was Locke, and the view has been endorsed and elaborated by a number of leading philosophers in the twentieth and twenty-first centuries.

Despite its popularity, foundationalism confronts some serious challenges. The most important of these is specifying *which* beliefs are epistemically basic, and explaining *why* those beliefs are justified. Where does their justification come from? Many foundationalists think that beliefs about our current perceptions—what we are seeing, hearing, touching, and so on—are epistemically basic, and some foundationalists insist that these beliefs are "self-justified." But the critics of foundationalism argue that this talk of "self-justification" is just a way of saying that we should accept those beliefs for no reason at all. If it is epistemically OK to accept perceptual beliefs for no reason at all, the critics continue, why isn't it epistemically OK to accept all sorts of other beliefs for no reason at all? Why, for example, isn't it epistemically OK to accept the belief that God exists for no reason at all? A few contemporary foundationalists have responded that it *is* epistemically OK. But their critics reply that this move erases the distinction between justified and unjustified beliefs. If it is epistemically OK for a theist to believe that God exists for no reason at all, why isn't it OK for Joe to believe that his coin will answer important questions for no reason at all, or for the soothsayer to believe, for no reason at all, that important questions can be answered by examining the entrails of sheep and chickens? Without some better account of which beliefs are basic and why, the critics insist, epistemic foundationalism can't do the job it is supposed to do. It can't tell us which true beliefs count as knowledge and which do not. Contemporary foundationalists have offered a variety of responses to this challenge, and a lively debate is ongoing. But the problems that foundationalism faces have led some philosophers to explore other accounts of epistemic justification.

8.5 Coherentism

One widely discussed alternative to foundationalism is **coherentism**. Philosophy of science was one major source for the coherentist account of epistemic justification. In science, observations of nature obviously play an important role. A scientist's beliefs about what she has observed don't play the role of foundationalist basic beliefs, however, because beliefs about what has been observed can be supported or undermined by more theoretical beliefs. For example, a scientist's belief that they saw a hitherto unknown star while peering through a telescope is supported by the belief that the telescope is working properly, the belief that atmospheric conditions were normal, and by a host of other beliefs. If any of these other beliefs prove to be mistaken, the scientist might well conclude that a hitherto unknown star hadn't actually been seen. The scientist's beliefs about the atmospheric conditions are justified by further observations using a variety of instruments, and those observations are in turn justified in part by more theoretical beliefs about how these instruments work. And this, of course, is not the end of the complex story about how a scientific belief is justified.

Coherentist epistemologists maintain that this complicated pattern of justification is not unique to science. Rather, they suggest, all epistemic justification works this way. So while foundationalists think that our justified beliefs are structured like a building, coherentists maintain that our justified beliefs are structured like a web, where the strength of any part of the web depends on the strength of the surrounding parts. For coherentists, an account of justification starts not with individual beliefs but with *systems* of interrelated beliefs. A system of beliefs is justified to the extent that the beliefs in that system are *coherent*. Individual beliefs are justified by virtue of their membership in a coherent system of beliefs.

To flesh out this picture, coherentists need to tell us what is required for a system of beliefs to be coherent. Logical consistency is an obvious place to start. A system of beliefs that includes both the belief that p and the belief that not-p is not a coherent system. But logical consistency can't be the whole story, since a collection of completely unrelated beliefs will easily pass this test. Consider, for example, the collection consisting of the belief that Paris is in France, the belief that Plato was Aristotle's teacher, and the belief that there is no greatest prime number. There are no logical inconsistencies in this set of beliefs, but surely, that's not enough to justify the set as a whole or any of its members. Coherentists have offered a number of accounts of what is required in addition to logical consistency. Though the details vary, they all require that beliefs in a coherent set be linked by a variety of logical, inductive, and explanatory relationships.

Regardless of how the idea of coherence is unpacked, however, coherentist theories face a number of objections. One objection turns on the fact that, no matter how coherence is spelled out, there will be *lots* of quite different coherent belief systems. To see this, let's suppose that, with a bit of patching here and there, *your* belief system gets reasonably high marks for coherence. Now consider the beliefs of a clever but deeply deluded person who believes that aliens from outer space regularly abduct our political leaders and replace them with realistic robots, that the Holocaust never happened and all those photos of concentration camp survivors are faked, and that global warming is a hoax. If our deluded character is inventive enough, this belief system will also get good marks for coherence. So if coherentism is right, this person's beliefs are as justified as yours. And of course, we could construct endlessly many other examples of people with very different but equally coherent delusions. The conclusion that many philosophers draw from examples like this is that the coherentist account of epistemic justification is far too permissive.

Another problem for coherentism emerges when we reflect on the implications of a thought experiment that has played an important role in many areas of philosophy. Imagine that scientists have developed a technology that enables them to remove a human brain from the skull of a living person and keep it alive and healthy in a vat of nutrients. Imagine further that they can connect the brain to a very sophisticated computer that provides the brain with completely realistic experiences. You have almost certainly heard a story like this before. It's the central idea of the film *The Matrix*, except that in the film the brain isn't actually removed from the body. But philosophers had the idea first. Now suppose that one night, ten years ago, a group of scientists anesthetized you while you were asleep, removed your brain, put it in one of their high-tech vats, and connected you to their supercomputer. All the experiences you have had since then have not been caused by the world around you; they have been generated by the supercomputer. So all of your beliefs about what has happened to you over the last ten years are false. You didn't graduate from high school. You didn't attend college. You are not actually taking a philosophy course. The experiences that led you to form those beliefs came from the supercomputer. It is plausible to suppose, as we did in the previous paragraph, that your current set of beliefs, with a bit of patching, gets reasonably high marks for coherence. So if coherentism is correct, your belief that you are attending college and your belief that you are taking a philosophy course are justified, even though you've been a brain in a vat for the last decade.

The argument we just sketched is sometimes called the "isolation objection" to coherentism. Since coherentism characterizes epistemic justification exclusively in terms of the structure of a person's system of beliefs, the account is isolated from what is going on in the external world. Because of that isolation, a person can have a complex set of beliefs about the external world that are epistemically justified but not true. So on the coherentist account, the fact that a set of beliefs is justified does not make it likely that the beliefs are true.

8.6 Internalism and Externalism

Coherentists believe that epistemic justification depends entirely on how a person's beliefs are related. Theories like this are called **internalist** because they only invoke states and processes internal to a person's mind. It is hard to see how an internalist theory of epistemic justification can avoid the isolation objection and provide a link between the epistemic justification of a belief and the truth of that belief, particularly when the belief is about something in the external world. Because of this, philosophers have explored accounts of epistemic justification that include factors external to the believer's mind, some of which the believer may not be aware of. Accounts of this sort are called **externalist**.

Contemporary philosophers have proposed a number of different externalist theories of epistemic justification. One of the most important is **reliabilism**. On one version of reliabilism, the epistemic justification of beliefs depends on the processes that produce the beliefs. Justified beliefs are those that are produced by *reliable processes,* where a reliable process is understood as a process that yields a relatively high proportion of true beliefs and a relatively low proportion of false beliefs. So a process that produces 80 percent true beliefs and 20 percent false beliefs is reliable, while a process that produces only 20 percent true beliefs and 80 percent false beliefs is unreliable.

What kinds of belief-forming processes do reliabilists have in mind? There is a wide variety. For most people, using visual perception to form a belief about the color of a well-lit object that is relatively nearby is a very reliable process. So reliabilists consider beliefs formed in this way to be epistemically justified. But for a color-blind person, identifying color using vision is much less reliable, and beliefs formed via this process are not epistemically justified. Of course, the reliability of a perceptual process—that is, its tendency to produce true beliefs—depends in part on facts about the perceiver's environment. For example, common sodium-vapor streetlights make white objects appear yellow. Reliabilism is externalist because its assessment of whether a belief is justified is sensitive to facts like these.

Many other beliefs are formed using valid deductive or inductive inference. Since deductive inference preserves truth and inductive inference usually preserves truth, beliefs formed in this way are justified provided that the premises are true. Other beliefs are formed using invalid reasoning. Over the last four decades, psychologists have invested a great deal of effort exploring the inferential strategies that people use in forming their beliefs. They have discovered that people often are unaware of the inference strategies they are using, and that many of those strategies are invalid.[5] However, some psychologists argue that in many situations these invalid strategies do quite a good job of producing true beliefs. Reliabilists urge that psychological research like this must play an important role in epistemology.

Reliabilism can also be used to assess the justification of beliefs produced by processes that involve our social and technological environment. Many of our beliefs are formed on the basis of what philosophers call "testimony." This includes what you hear on TV news programs, see on the Internet, or read in textbooks. Are beliefs formed in this way reliable? The answer is, of course, that it depends. If the article you are reading is on the National Institutes of Health's (NIH) website, the probability that the beliefs you form are true is quite high. But if the site you are reading is trying to sell you a "guaranteed secret formula miracle diet pill that will enable you to eat what you want and lose 20 pounds in ten days" (yes, we really did find this on the Internet!), and if you believe what you read, the probability that those beliefs are true is very low.

But there is a problem lurking here. For while the probability is high that beliefs formed when you read the NIH website are true, not *everything* on that website is true. In the thousands of pages on that site, there are bound to be errors. Suppose you are reading one of the quite rare error-plagued pages. In that case, the probability that the beliefs you form are true will be low. But not every paragraph on that page is error plagued. So how shall we describe the process that led to your beliefs while reading the website? Was it a process that began with reading a page on the NIH website? Or was it a process that began with reading an error-plagued page on the NIH website? Or was it a process that began with reading an error-free paragraph on an error-plagued page on the NIH website? It was all three, of course, and reliabilism offers different assessments about the justification of the beliefs formed depending on which description is chosen. What this example illustrates is that the same belief-forming process can be described in many ways, with some ways more general than others. So reliabilists must provide some principled way of deciding which one to choose. Epistemologists call this the "generality problem," and reliabilists are hard at work trying to respond to the challenge the generality problem poses.

8.7 Fallibilism and Skepticism

We've seen that philosophers can adopt different views about the link between the justification for a belief and the truth of that belief. Some internalists insist that no link is needed. On their view, a belief is justified if a person has fulfilled the epistemic obligations and met all reasonable standards in forming the belief. So an epistemically conscientious person can have justified beliefs even if that person is a brain in a vat. Other philosophers, including most externalists, insist that justification must be linked to truth; having a justified belief must make it likely that a belief is true. But *how* likely?

One possible answer is that the justification a person has for a belief must *guarantee* that the belief is true. This is a very demanding standard. Moreover, it is a standard that may be impossible to attain in many areas. Our best scientific theories are supported by a great deal of convergent evidence, but that evidence does not guarantee that the scientific theory is true. Scientists might discover new evidence that leads them to conclude that the theory is mistaken. Your everyday beliefs about the external world are in much the same boat. Those beliefs are supported by a variety of perceptual experiences, but you might suddenly wake up and realize that the perceptual experiences you were having a few minutes ago were part of a dream. Worse yet, you might be a brain in a vat and never discover that your perceptual experiences tell you nothing about external reality. How about mathematical beliefs? Well, many mathematical beliefs are justified by long and complex proofs, and it is not uncommon for mathematicians to discover errors in proofs they had previously accepted. So the fact that mathematicians have a proof that they believe to be error free does not guarantee that the conclusion of the proof is true. Most of us are not mathematicians, however, and many of our mathematical beliefs are based on what we remember from classes we took long ago. Could your memory be mistaken? Of course it could. Thus, it does not guarantee that the mathematical propositions you remember are true.

Do we have *any* beliefs that are justified in a way that guarantees the truth of the belief? Philosophers disagree about this. Some think that beliefs about your own current mental states—or at least some of them—are guaranteed to be true. If you believe you are in pain because you seem to feel the pain, then, these philosophers insist, your belief is guaranteed to be true. Other philosophers are convinced that Descartes's *cogito* argument is ironclad.[6] If you go through the steps of the argument and conclude that you exist, the conclusion is guaranteed to be true. While there is considerable disagreement about these cases, and about others that have been proposed, there is widespread agreement that, for the vast majority of our beliefs, the justification we have does not guarantee that the beliefs are true.

What conclusion can we draw from this? If knowledge requires the kind of justification that guarantees the truth of the belief that it justifies, then it follows that we have very little knowledge—and perhaps none at all. This view is known as **skepticism**. While there have been some important skeptics, most philosophers reject skepticism. To derail the argument for skepticism we have been discussing, they reject the very demanding requirement that adequate justification must guarantee the truth of the belief that it justifies. Rather, these antiskeptical philosophers insist, knowledge is compatible with a level of justification that does not guarantee the truth of the belief that it justifies. A *fallible* justification—one that does not guarantee truth—is all that is required for knowledge. Philosophers who endorse this view, called **fallibilism**, maintain that we have a great deal of knowledge, since we have many true beliefs and many of those true beliefs are adequately justified. Their justification does not guarantee their truth. But that, these fallibilists insist, is not required for knowledge.

8.8 Gettier Cases—A Challenge to the Justified True Belief Account of Knowledge

Thus far in this chapter, we have assumed that knowledge can be analyzed as justified true belief, and we have tried to better understand what the justification condition amounts to. But fallibilism, which allows that justification does not guarantee truth, opens the door for a powerful challenge to the venerable justified true belief analysis of knowledge.

The challenge was famously articulated in 1963 by the American philosopher Edmund Gettier (1927–2021), and the sorts of hypothetical cases he used became known as "Gettier cases." Here is an example:

> One morning Eleanor is walking through the train station, having just arrived on her usual commuter train. She glances up at the big clock in the center of the station and sees that it says 8:45. Eleanor has noted the time on that clock on many occasions over the last several years, and it has always been accurate. So without looking at her watch or checking the time on her cell phone, Eleanor forms the belief that it is 8:45. And her belief is true; it is 8:45. However, at 8:45 the previous evening, the clock broke, and it has not yet been repaired. So it has said it is 8:45 for the last twelve hours. It is just a lucky accident that Eleanor happened to glance at the clock at exactly 8:45. Thus, it is just a lucky accident that the belief she formed is true.

Does Eleanor *know* that it is 8:45? Many philosophers think that the answer is no, she does not know that it is 8:45. If that's right, then the justified true belief account of knowledge is in trouble. Eleanor believes it is 8:45, her belief is true, and her belief is justified. It is not justified in a way that guarantees the truth of the belief. Had she glanced at the clock a minute later, she would have formed a false belief. But if fallibilism is correct, then justification can be adequate for knowledge even if it does not guarantee truth. So Eleanor has a justified true belief that is not an instance of knowledge, and the justified true belief analysis is mistaken.

After Gettier brought this problem to philosophers' attention, many philosophers concluded that there must be some fourth condition that has to be added to justification, truth, and belief in order to have an adequate analysis of knowledge. Lots of fourth conditions have been proposed, but to date, none has found wide acceptance. Epistemologists are still hard at work on the problem. Now that we have brought you to the cutting edge of research in epistemology, we encourage you to try your hand at constructing a fourth condition. What, besides justification and truth, is required for a belief to be an instance of knowledge?

Glossary

coherentism: Coherentists believe that a system of beliefs is justified to the extent that it is *coherent*—that is, to the extent that the beliefs fit together in the right kind of way. (Explaining in detail what "coherence" consists of is an important task for coherentists.) See section 8.5 for more details.

declarative sentence: Contrast these sentences:

Declarative	Not declarative
Alba is tall.	Is Alba tall?
It is summer.	If only it were summer!
The door is closed.	Close the door!

The sentences on the left are declarative; the sentences on the right are not. "Is Alba tall?" is interrogative, "If only it were summer!" is optative, and "Close the door!" is imperative. Note that only declarative sentences are capable of being true or false. For example, the sentence "Is Alba tall?" is not true, and it is not false. Note also that a sentence of the form "S knows that p" is grammatical only when "p" is replaced by a declarative sentence:

Grammatical	Not grammatical
Ella knows that Alba is tall.	Ella knows that is Alba tall?
Shanice knows that it is summer.	Shanice knows that if only it were summer.
Raul knows that the door is closed.	Raul knows that close the door.

epistemically basic belief: An epistemically basic belief is a belief that is justified, but not because it is has been inferred from some other justified belief. Sometimes, basic beliefs are called "foundational beliefs," or "self-evident truths," or "axioms." See section 8.4.

epistemology: A branch of philosophy, traditionally defined as the "theory of knowledge". This chapter is an introduction to epistemology.

externalist and internalist: An internalist believes that whether a person's belief is justified depends only on how that belief is related to the person's other mental states. And externalists denies this. Reliabilism is an example of an externalist position. See section 8.6.

fallibilism: Fallibilists think that a belief can be justified even when the belief is justified in a way that does not *guarantee* the truth of the belief. For example, our memories are not 100 percent reliable. Nevertheless, the fallibilist may insist, a belief may be justified on the basis of memory. See section 8.7 for more details.

foundationalism: Foundationalists think that, to be justified, a belief must either be epistemically basic or be inferred (using good inferences) from epistemically basic beliefs.

internalist: See externalist and internalist.

proposition: A proposition is the *meaning* of a declarative sentence. Arguably, these three different sentences express the same proposition:

"Cats are mammals."

"Chats sont des mammifères."

"Los gatos son mamíferos."

Some propositions are true; some are false. Many philosophers think that in cases of propositional knowledge, the thing that is known is always a true proposition.

reliabilism: According to reliabilists, a belief is epistemically justified just in case it was produced by a reliable process—that is, a process that produces true beliefs most of the time.

skepticism: In ordinary English, a "skeptic" is someone who doubts. When philosophers talk about skepticism, they usually have in mind rather extreme forms of doubt. The philosophical skeptic might claim that we know nothing at all, or that we know nothing about the external world.

Comprehension Questions

1. In section 8.2, we distinguished (i) knowledge as acquaintance, (ii) knowledge how, and (iii) propositional knowledge. Classify these examples:

    > Jorge knows that Mexico is south of the United States.
    > Jorge knows Maria.
    > Jorge knows how to make a donut.

2. Give three examples of people who *believe* something but don't *know* it. In each case, try to explain why the belief is not knowledge.
3. Consider the following claim:

    > Suppose that S believes p, that p is true, and that S's belief is justified. Then S knows that p.

    We presented a counterexample to this analysis in section 8.8. Can you think of another counterexample?
4. What is foundationalism?
5. Give an example in which one belief (B1, say) is justified by being inferred from another belief (B2), which is in turn justified by being inferred from another belief (B3).
6. Give some examples of beliefs that might count as epistemically basic.
7. What is coherentism?
8. Are there epistemically basic beliefs? Answer from the point of view of a foundationalist and from the point of view of a coherentist.
9. Briefly outline some objections to foundationalism and some objections to coherentism.
10. Reliabilism is an externalist theory. Explain what this means.
11. Illustrate reliabilism by (a) giving an example of a belief that is justified and which was produced by a reliable process and (b) giving an example of a belief that is not justified and was not produced by a reliable process.
12. What is the generality problem?
13. Suggest an example of a belief that is justified, but which is justified in a way that does not guarantee the truth of the belief.

Discussion Questions

1. Are knowledge how, acquaintance knowledge, and propositional knowledge the only kinds of knowledge? Consider sentences like these:

   - Tyrone knows the Pythagorean theorem.
   - Kenny knows when to hold 'em and knows when to fold 'em.

   Do they fit into one of the three categories? Can you think of some other examples that don't seem to be knowledge how, acquaintance knowledge, or propositional knowledge?

2. Consider these three sentences:

   - Jorge knows that Mexico is south of the United States.
   - Jorge knows Maria.
   - Jorge knows how to make a donut.

   If you speak another language, think about how to translate these sentences. Is the word "know" translated in the same way in all three cases?

3. The critics of foundationalism insist that foundationalists must provide some account of *why* epistemically basic beliefs are justified. Can you help the foundationalists? How do you think that epistemically basic beliefs can be justified?

4. In section 8.5, we suggested that a deluded person who believes

   I. that aliens from outer space regularly abduct our political leaders and replace them with realistic robots,
   II. that the Holocaust never happened and all those photos of concentration camp survivors are faked, and
   III. that global warming is a hoax

   might have a consistent system of beliefs. Is this really true? If you think it is, what other strange beliefs would our deluded person require to make this beliefs system cohere with what the person sees in newspapers and reads on the Internet? If you think our deluded friend could not possibly have a coherent set of beliefs, explain why.

5. We argued that the brain-in-the-vat thought experiment poses a major problem for internalist theories of epistemic justification. What about externalist theories? Does the brain-in-the-vat case pose a problem for reliabilism? Explain why it does or why it doesn't.

6. The justification for most of our beliefs is fallible; it does not guarantee the truth of the belief. In section 8.7, we mentioned two possible exceptions. Can you come up with other plausible candidates of beliefs whose justification is *not* fallible?

7. This question is for people who also read chapter 7. A reliabilist says:

   > Enumerative induction is a *reliable* form of reasoning, in the sense that beliefs formed by enumerative induction are usually true. (They're not *always* true, of course, but they're true in most cases.) This is sufficient to ensure that beliefs formed using enumerative induction are justified. And that's the end of the matter. Hume's problem of induction therefore has a very simple solution.

   What do you make of this?[7]

8. Epistemic cultural relativists claim that a belief is justified just in case it is justified *according to the norms prevalent in that person's culture*. For example, suppose that a person makes predictions about next year's harvest by inspecting the entrails of a dead animal. If that person lived in our culture, his belief would *not* be justified because we don't recognize reading entrails as a legitimate way of making predictions. However, if that person were in ancient Greece, this beliefs might be justified. What do you make of this position?

What to Look at Next

- Robert M. Martin's *Epistemology: A Beginner's Guide* is an excellent introduction to epistemology. It is short and very clearly written.
- To learn about the history of epistemology, check out Stephen Hetherington's *Key Thinkers: Epistemology*.
- Once you're ready for a more advanced work on the topic, you might consider *Contemporary Theories of Knowledge* by John Pollock and Joseph Cruz.
- Daniel Kahneman's best-seller *Thinking, Fast and Slow* contains fascinating information about psychological research on the processes that underlie our reasoning.
- Edmund Gettier's 1963 paper "Is Justified True Belief Knowledge?" is unusually short! We suggest you check it out in *Analysis*, 23(6): 121–123.
- Many philosophers today believe that mathematics (especially probability theory) can be tremendously helpful in epistemology.

If you're interested in this sort of work, we suggest you start with Darren Bradley's *An Introduction to Formal Epistemology* and/or Brian Skyrms' *Choice and Chance*.
- If you're interested in the idea that some beliefs are epistemically basic, you might like to look at Alvin Plantinga's paper "Is Belief in God Properly Basic?" *Noûs* 15, no. 1 (1981).
- Peter Unger's "A Defence of Skepticism" is an important discussion of skepticism and fallibilism.

Notes

1. *Episteme* is the Greek word for knowledge.
2. Grammarians distinguish "declarative" sentences from "interrogative" sentences (i.e., questions) and "imperative" sentences (i.e., commands).
3. Plato addresses this topic in his *Theaetetus* (Oxford: Oxford University Press, 2014). Note that Plato eventually *rejects* the analysis. For details, see Nicholas Smith, "Plato's Epistemology," in *Key Thinkers: Epistemology*, ed. Stephen Hetherington (London: Continuum, 2012) pp. 29–49.
4. *Posterior Analytics* 1.2. A translation of this work can be found in *The Complete Works of Aristotle, The Revised Oxford Translation*, ed. Jonathan Barnes (Princeton, NJ: Princeton University Press, 1984).
5. *Thinking, Fast and Slow* (New York: Farrar, Straus and Giroux, 2011) by Nobel laureate Daniel Kahneman provides a very readable account of this research.
6. See chapter 5 for a discussion of Descartes's *cogito* argument.
7. If you want to explore this issue in detail, start by looking at Hugh Mellor's essay "The Warrant of Induction." This essay is easy to find online. Alternatively, you can find it in his book *Matters of Metaphysics*.

CHAPTER 9

Do We Have Free Will?

9.1 What Is Determinism?

Historians sometimes like to imagine what would happen if time could be "rewound" and then run again from a slightly different starting point: How would history have been different if gunpowder had been discovered earlier? How would American history have gone if there had been no George Washington? What would have happened if Columbus's ships hadn't made it across the Atlantic? These questions are interesting, but we want to talk about a slightly different one: What if we could rewind history back a few hundred years and run it again, *from exactly the same starting point*? What would happen?

If **determinism** is true, then the answer is simple: if the starting point is the same, down to the smallest detail, then history will proceed in exactly the same way.

Here's an analogy. Suppose you type a sum (123 + 456, say) into a calculator and press the = button. The calculator blinks, and then the answer (579) appears on the screen. If you type the same sum into the calculator again, of course, you'll get the same result. This is because the calculator runs according to a set of instructions called a "program." This program is "deterministic," which means that given the same input, the calculator will perform the same calculations, in the same order, and then produce the same output. The program leaves nothing to chance; it completely determines what the calculator does.

According to determinists, the laws of physics are deterministic and govern everything. They completely determine what happens in the universe, in much the same way that the calculator's program completely determines what the calculator does. Given the state of the universe at any one time, the laws of physics fix the whole of the rest of history. So if you could rewind history and run it again from exactly the same starting point, history would be exactly repeated.

Here's another way of thinking about it. Pierre-Simon Laplace (1749–1827), a French mathematician and astronomer, imagined a supernatural "demon" with unlimited memory, an unlimited ability to calculate, and a complete knowledge of the laws of physics. Laplace claimed that given a complete description of the world at some particular time, the demon could figure out the whole subsequent course of history—including all human actions.

You might be thinking "Determinism is crazy! Surely there are *chance events*, which can't be predicted in advance—dice rolls and coin flips for example?" A determinist will agree that we can't predict the outcomes of these so-called chance events ahead of time, but then will say that this is just because our abilities to calculate and measure are limited. Suppose, for example, that you throw two dice. We can't measure the *exact speeds* at which you throw them or the *exact rates* at which they spin as they leave your hand. And we don't know the *exact shape* of the surface on which the dice land. Even if we could measure these things (and the wind speed, and the precise shape of the dice, and . . .), we *still* couldn't predict the outcome in advance because the math would be too difficult. The motions of the dice are too complicated to calculate ahead of time. However, the determinist will say that *if* we could make all the right measurements in advance, and *if* we could make all the difficult calculations fast enough, then we could predict the outcome of the dice roll.

Human thought processes are much more complicated than dice rolls: our brains each contain about 100 *billion* interacting neurons. Even so, if the determinists are right, Laplace's demon could predict not only dice rolls and coin flips but also all human behavior. If you were to play rock-paper-scissors against Laplace's demon, it would beat you every time—because it would always be able to predict your move in advance (even if you tried to choose your move at random). According to determinists, every one of your actions could, in principle, have been predicted before you were even born. This is a spooky thought: it seems to conflict with our feeling that we are "in charge" or "in control" of the way we behave. We normally think that we have a choice about whether to go to college, or who to marry, or what to have for dinner; but if determinism is true, the whole course of our lives was settled before we even existed. So there seems to be a conflict between determinism and our belief that we have "free will." Perhaps free will is an illusion.

But is determinism true?

In the eighteenth and nineteenth centuries, it was generally thought that the laws of physics are deterministic. For example, it was thought that Newton's law of gravity completely determines the motions of the planets in the solar system, which was sometimes compared to a giant clock. So philosophers and scientists at the time thought that if determinism is false, this must be because there are some things—human minds, perhaps—which are not governed by physical laws.

In the first part of the twentieth century, there was a dramatic development in physical theory—what's sometimes called the "quantum revolution." Now it is considered an open question whether the laws of physics are deterministic. According to some physicists, there are events (e.g., radioactive decay) that cannot be predicted in advance, even by Laplace's demon. According to these physicists, radioactive decay is a *genuinely random* process. (We'll say more about this later in the chapter.)

In this chapter, we discuss whether free will is an illusion. Since it is not known whether determinism is true, we'll have to work in stages. We'll begin by thinking about whether we have free will, on the assumption that determinism is true. Then, we'll think about the issue again, without this assumption.

9.2 Incompatibilism

Suppose you have a job as a waiter in a restaurant. One night, you discover that one of the other waiters, a friend of yours, has stolen a crate of expensive wine from the cellar. A few days later, your boss accuses your colleague of the theft. He defends himself by saying that he didn't *steal* the crate: he dropped it, and all the bottles smashed. Being too embarrassed to admit the mistake, he cleaned up the mess and told nobody about it. Your boss asks you what you know . . .

We'll talk about ethics later in the book, so for now we won't think about what you *should* say to your boss. The point here is that this story is an example of a situation in which you are *free to choose,* or so it seems. But what does this mean? There are three apparent features of the situation that are relevant:

(a) First, you seem to have several different courses of action available to you:
- You could tell your boss that your friend stole the wine.
- You could back up your friend's story.
- You could deny all knowledge of what happened.

Perhaps there are other things you could do too, but there's no need for a complete list: the point is that there are, or seem to be, several different things you could choose to do.

(b) Second, it seems to be *up to you* which of these various courses of action you take. You seem to be *in charge* or *in control* of what you do.

(c) Third, it seems that because you have control over which option you choose, you are morally responsible for your action. What this means is that if you do the wrong thing, it's your fault, and you can reasonably be blamed for your bad decision; if you do the right thing, you deserve credit for it. It's on you.

Of course, this is just one example. There are lots of situations that have, or seem to have, these three important features. In these situations, it seems (a) you have a number of different options, (b) you are in control of which option you go for, and (c) you are responsible for the decision. This seems to be all or part of what we have in mind when we say that we have "free will."

Two points of clarification. First, nobody's saying that we can do *anything* we'd like to do. Obviously, we can't go back in time or fly unaided. When we make a free choice, there is only ever a limited range of open alternatives. It's important, too, that other people can restrict your freedom by doing things that limit the number of alternative courses of action open to you; for example, jailers make sure their prisoners have rather few choices available to them. Second, it's obvious that we are not *always* in control of ourselves. People having an epileptic seizure, for example, may not be in control or in charge of what they do. The claim, more modestly, is that *some of the time* we are in control of what we do.

Incompatibilists think that IF determinism is true, IT FOLLOWS THAT we don't have free will. To understand this, we can look at (a), (b), and (c) in turn.

> (a) Assuming determinism, the laws of physics completely determine what happens in the universe, including all of your actions. So in principle, everything you do could have been predicted before you were even born. It seems that if this is true, you are wrong to suppose that you are sometimes able to choose between different options. There's only ever been one path through life open to you.
>
> (b) Incompatibilists say that you can't be "in control" of what you do if you only ever have one option. One of Henry Ford's customers, who could have a car of "any color he wants so long as it's black," wasn't in charge of the color of his car. In the same way, according to the incompatibilists, you're not in charge of your actions if you never have more than one option.
>
> Here's another way of seeing the point. Assuming determinism, all of your actions are determined by the laws of physics and the state of the universe before you were born. Now, of course, you are not in control of the laws of physics or the state of the universe before you were born. So it seems that if determinism is true, you are not in control of your actions either.
>
> (c) Determinism also seems to threaten the idea that we are responsible for what we do—that is, that we are *at fault* for the things we do wrong or *deserve credit* for the good things we do. This is because we don't hold people responsible for things they do when they are not in control of themselves. For example, if someone knocks over a precious vase while having an epileptic seizure, we wouldn't blame him for the damage. As we've just seen, determinism seems to imply that we are not in control of our actions. So if determinism is true, it seems that we are not responsible for what we do. Any criminal can defend himself from blame by saying "the laws of physics made me do it."

The French philosopher Baron d'Holbach (1723–1789) was a determinist and an incompatibilist. He said:

> Man is a purely physical being . . .[He is] subject to . . . immutable laws. . . . Man's life is a line that Nature commands him to describe upon the surface of the Earth: without his ever being able to swerve from it even for an instant. He is born without his own consent [and] he is unceasingly modified by causes, whether visible or concealed, over which he has no control. . . . Nevertheless, despite of the shackles by which he is bound, it is pretended he is a free agent, or that independent of the causes by which he is moved, he determines his own will; regulates his own condition.[1]

When they first confront these ideas, some people are incredulous. They insist that they know from personal experience that their own decisions aren't determined in advance. And it's true that, for example, when you're at a restaurant choosing your meal, it doesn't appear that the outcome of your decision-making is already determined. You don't feel you are bound by shackles, as d'Holbach claimed.[2]

In reply, d'Holbach and those who share his views will insist that this is only because in everyday life we have very little awareness of the workings of our own minds. The human brain is a spectacularly complicated organ, and even the world's greatest neuroscientists are a long way from achieving a complete understanding of how it works. Because we are unable to see the processes that determine the outcomes of our decision-making, it appears to us, wrongly, that the outcome is not predetermined.

9.3 Compatibilism

So d'Holbach can't be refuted with the simple observation that we *feel* free. Nevertheless, it has to be admitted that his conclusions are highly counterintuitive—indeed, they are shocking. It is alarming to think that we don't deserve credit for the good things we've done, that we are not the authors of our own life stories. And if we took seriously the claim that people who act wrongly aren't responsible for their misdeeds, this would have dramatic implications—e.g. for the criminal justice system. For this reason, we should take a serious look at the works of those philosophers who suggested that determinism does not imply that we lack free will. This position is known as **compatibilism**.

Many compatibilists have offered theories of the nature of free will, which are supposed to show that one can have free will even if determinism is true. The great Scottish philosopher David Hume (1711–1776) gave a characterization of free will that has become particularly famous. Note that he uses the term "liberty" rather than "free will."

> By "liberty," then, we can only mean a power of acting or not acting according to the determinations of the will; i.e. if we choose to stay still we may do so, and if we choose to move we may do that.[3]

"The will" is Hume's term for the part of the mind in which desires are formed and decisions made. So when Hume says that a free person acts "according to the determinations of the will," he means that a free person's actions are a result of their decisions, in pursuit of their desires. What's more, Hume insists that we are free only to the extent there are no obstacles in our way that prevent us from acting as we choose: "if we choose to stay still we may do so, and if we choose to move we may do that."

As we interpret him, then, Hume's suggestion is that a person is free to the extent that person meets two conditions:

(1) The person is acting in pursuit of what they desire, and their actions are a result of their own decisions.
(2) There are no obstacles in the person's way, which prevent the person from acting as desired.

Consider again the epileptic person who has a seizure and knocks a precious vase to the floor. The epileptic person in this case doesn't *decide* to knock over the vase. Indeed, the person's movements aren't the result of any decision. They are random movements triggered by the seizure. So applying condition (1), Hume would say that the epileptic person is not free in this case. Condition (2) is more straightforward. A prisoner locked in a cell is not free, according to Hume, because the jailer has put obstacles in the way that prevent the prisoner from going where he wants.

Now think again about the story about the restaurant from the beginning of section 9.2. In this case, it is *your* decision that will determine what you will do. What's more, no obstacle will prevent you from telling your boss the truth, if that's what you choose to do, and no obstacle will prevent you from protecting your friend, if that's your decision.

So according to Hume, you are free in this case. The crucial point is that, for Hume, you are free in this case *even if determinism is true*. Hume saw no incompatibility between determinism and the claim that we have free will.

Many philosophers today admire Hume's writing on this topic; however, few think that Hume's theory is adequate as it stands. Here's an example to explain why. Suppose that a criminal mastermind slips a psychoactive pill in your drink that gives you a very strong desire to rob a jewelry store. You try hard to resist this desire, but it is overwhelming—so you get yourself a gun, make your way to the store, and steal a bag of diamonds.

In the story, your decisions and your desire to steal diamonds cause your actions. What's more, no obstacle prevents you from acting on your criminal impulses. So if we apply Hume's theory in this case, we reach the conclusion that your action is free. But this doesn't seem right. It seems that you are not free, or not fully free, in the story because you are not fully "in charge" of your own actions. The pill has caused you to "lose control of yourself"; you are a slave to a desire implanted in you by the criminal mastermind.

An incompatibilist may say that this story shows our actions are not free if they are caused by desires we are unable to control. They may add that if determinism is true, our desires are *always* caused by factors beyond our control, since our entire mental life was determined before we were even born.

Perhaps the story about the pill strikes you as too silly to be taken seriously—too much like the plot of a 1950s B-movie. Well, perhaps you are right—but philosophers like to talk about far-fetched examples like this because it helps them clarify the issues, without being distracted by the subtleties and complexities of real-life cases. And in fact, there are real-life cases like the pill story. For example, people with obsessive-compulsive disorder, or OCD, sometimes feel that they are not free as they act on their compulsions, precisely because those compulsions are beyond their control.

Here's another real-life example: a medical case.[4] The patient was a man who at the age of forty started experiencing sexual desires for young children—desires of a kind he never had before. He began to download child pornography and made sexual advances on his prepubescent stepdaughter. He knew what he was doing was wrong, but (in the words of doctors who studied the case) he "could not restrain" himself. A tumor was discovered in the man's brain; when the tumor was removed, his pedophilic desires disappeared. It seems that the tumor caused his pathological desires—desires so strong that he lost control of his behavior. Now it seems clear the man was not responsible (or not fully responsible) for his actions because he was not free. But Hume's theory implies that he was free, because his actions were a result of his own desires and decisions, and there were no obstacles in his way preventing him from acting on his criminal desires.

Can we improve upon Hume's version of compatibilism? The philosopher Harry Frankfurt (1929–2023) has suggested that, in cases like that of the man with the tumor, the agent is not free (or not fully free) because the agent acts on a desire that the agent doesn't want to have.[5] The fully free person, Frankfurt suggests, acts only on desires that the person wants to have.

Inspired by Frankfurt, we want to suggest a modified version of Hume's compatibilism. We suggest that a person's action is free only to the extent that it meets the following *three* conditions:

(1) The person is acting in pursuit of what they desire, and their actions are a result of their own decisions.
(2) No obstacles prevent the person from acting as desired.
(3) The desires on which the person acts are desires that the person wants to have.

The first two conditions are Hume's. The third is inspired by Frankfurt.

This new theory seems to us to be an improvement on Hume's theory, but we're not sure that it's completely correct. To explain why, we'd like to look at a variant of the pill story.

A criminal genius hypnotizes you and causes you to have a strong desire to rob a bank. What's more, the genius causes you to *want* this first desire. Once the hypnosis is finished, you grab a gun and a mask and make your way to the bank to rob it. In this story, you meet conditions (1), (2), and (3), and yet it is at least arguable that your actions are not free.

The compatibilist may attempt to get around this problem by modifying condition (3), or adding a condition, or replacing condition (3) with some alternative condition. Whether it is possible to come up with an adequate compatibilist theory of freedom is still an important topic of conversation in philosophy, but we won't pursue the question any further. We want to turn to a very different way of thinking about free will.

9.4 Libertarianism

Recall that incompatibilists argue that IF determinism is true, THEN we lack free will. As we've said, the conclusion that we lack free will is shocking—so perhaps incompatibilists have reason to *hope* that determinism is false.

The American philosopher William James (1842–1910) found determinism disturbing for another reason. He argued that if determinism is true, then all the horrors of the past were *inevitable*—no other course of history was possible. James thought that this is a "pessimistic conclusion," saying:

> Determinism, in denying that anything else can be in its stead, virtually defines the universe as a place in which what ought to be is impossible,—in other words, as an organism whose constitution is afflicted with an incurable taint, an irremediable flaw.[6]

People like James who find determinism depressing will be attracted to the position that philosophers call **libertarianism**. Libertarians think that determinism is false and that (in part for this reason) we are capable of free action.

Libertarianism in this sense should not be confused with *political* libertarianism. Political libertarians emphasize individual rights, especially property rights. They think that the state may restrict the individual freedom of a citizen only to prevent the violation of another person's rights. None of this has much to do with the denial of determinism.

Two versions of libertarianism should be distinguished. We'll call them **scientific libertarianism** and **radical libertarianism**, though these are not standard terms. We will look at them one by one.

Scientific libertarians know that, according to many contemporary physicists, the universe is *not* deterministic. These physicists say there are some physical processes that are random. Take, for example, the decay of the radioactive substance carbon-14. Suppose we have just created a nucleus of carbon-14 and arranged for it to be left undisturbed indefinitely. Carbon-14 is an "unstable" substance, so our particle will eventually decay, even in the absence of any outside interference. When the nucleus decays, it will emit an electron and an electron antineutrino, and in so doing, it will turn from a carbon-14 nucleus into a nitrogen-14 nucleus. Now according to many contemporary physicists, there is no way for us to know how long it will be before the carbon-14 nucleus decays. We *can* calculate *odds*; for example, we know that there's a fifty-fifty chance the particle will decay within the first 5,700 years (this is the "half-life" of carbon-14). But we cannot know exactly how long it will take. These physicists say that our ignorance about this is not due to ignorance about what the laws of nature are, or lack of knowledge about the current physical state of the universe, or inability to perform the relevant calculations. They think that it is impossible even in principle to know how long the particle will take to decay. Even Laplace's demon couldn't figure this out. The reason is that the current state of the universe, together with the laws of physics, is compatible with lots of different possible futures. There's a possible future in which the particle takes one year to decay; another possible future in which the particle takes two years to decay, and so on. The laws of physics don't determine the outcome; they only determine the probabilities of the various different outcomes. So determinism is false, according to many physicists today.

Scientific libertarians think that there is randomness of something like this kind in our neural processes, and so our decision-making is not deterministic. If this is right, perhaps you could win a game of rock-paper-scissors against Laplace's demon after all. Randomness in your choices would make it impossible for the demon to figure out your moves in advance, giving you the opportunity to win. The scientific libertarian thinks that, in part because our decisions are indeterministic in this way, we are free.

Back in section 9.2, we described three apparent features of human decision-making that people often have in mind when they talk about "free will":

(a) It seems that we often have several different alternative courses of action available to us.
(b) In these situations, we often seem to be in control or in charge of which option we choose. How we act is up to us on these occasions.
(c) When we make choices of this kind, we are morally responsible for the choices that we make.

Scientific libertarians are able to accommodate feature (a): because there is randomness in our decision-making, they say, the laws of physics don't fix in advance what we are going to do, so there is more than one course of action that is possible. However, we're not sure whether scientific libertarians can accommodate feature (b). If the scientific libertarians are right, our actions are caused in part by random events in our brains. Now surely these random events are beyond our control (because they are random!), so if the scientific libertarians are correct, it would seem that our actions are caused by things outside our control. And again, this seems to imply that we are not in control or in charge of how we act. What is more, if we're not in charge of what we do, it would seem we are not responsible for our actions—so scientific libertarians will also have a hard time accommodating feature (c). We think, then, that scientific libertarianism is problematic.

In section 9.2, we looked at some powerful arguments for the conclusion that if our decision-making processes are governed by deterministic laws, we don't have free will. If the argument in the previous paragraph is correct, we also don't have free will if our decision-making processes are governed by probabilistic laws (like the probabilistic laws that are sometimes said to govern radioactive decay). This could lead you to think that, in order to be free, it's got to be that our decision-making processes aren't governed by any causal laws at all. This is the basic thought behind radical libertarianism.

Immanuel Kant (1724–1804) developed a particularly extreme form of radical libertarianism. When we think about morality, Kant thought, we need to think of ourselves as morally responsible, and so we need to suppose that we have free will. However, he was convinced, by arguments similar to those in section 9.2, that *if* our decision-making processes are governed by deterministic laws, we lack free will. Because the generally accepted laws of physics at the time *were* deterministic, he concluded that we could have free will only if we are not just physical objects. His response was to say that we each have a nonphysical, "transcendental" self, which is outside space and time and is ungoverned by the laws of physics. It is the transcendental self that makes free decisions for which we are morally responsible.[7]

Immanuel Kant (1724–1804) was a radical libertarian.

Not all forms of radical libertarianism are quite *this* radical. Most recent radical libertarians would reject Kant's claim that we have transcendental selves, outside space and time. However, they would agree with Kant that human decision-making is not governed by physical law. To assess this position, we need to turn to another branch of philosophy. In the chapter 11, we will look at the philosophy of mind, which is about mental states and processes. Among other things, we will criticize the view that the mind is a nonphysical thing.

Glossary

compatibilism: Compatibilists believe that determinism is compatible with the claim that we have free will.

determinism: According to determinists, given the state of the universe at any one time, the laws of physics fix the whole of the rest of history. So if you could "rewind" history and run it again from exactly the same starting point, history would be exactly repeated.

hard determinism: Hard determinists think that determinism is true and infer that we lack free will.

incompatibilists: Incompatibilists think that if determinism is true, it follows that we do not have free will.

libertarianism: Libertarians think that *if* determinism is true, we lack free will. But they also think that we have free will. So they conclude that determinism is false.

radical libertarianism: Radical libertarians think that our actions are not governed by physical law. (This is not a standard term.)

scientific libertarianism: Scientific libertarians think that we can have free will because our neural processes are not deterministic. There is some kind of randomness in our brain processes, and in consequence, we have free will. (This is not a standard term.)

Comprehension Questions

1. What does determinism claim?
2. What is Laplace's demon? What did Laplace claim that the demon could do?
3. We have proposed three conditions that must be met for a person to have free will. What are those three conditions?
4. Incompatibilists argue that if determinism is true, then we do not have free will because none of the three conditions for having free will are met. What is their argument that each of these conditions is unmet in a deterministic universe?
5. What is compatibilism?
6. According to Hume, what two conditions must be met for an action to count as free? Use examples to illustrate these two conditions.
7. Most philosophers reject Hume's account of free will. Sketch an imaginary case in which a person meets Hume's conditions but does not seem to have free will. (Don't repeat a story from the chapter—come up with a new example.)

8. Use examples to illustrate Frankfurt's idea that a person is free only if the person acts on desires that the person wants to have.
9. Why did William James find determinism disturbing?
10. What do scientific libertarians claim? Why do scientific libertarians think that we are free?
11. Can scientific libertarianism accommodate the three features of human decision-making that are required for free will? Consider each of the three features, and explain why scientific libertarianism can (or can't) accommodate that feature.
12. What does radical libertarianism claim about human decision-making?

Discussion Questions

1. Many people find the idea that the universe may be deterministic to be disquieting or spooky. Do you? How do you think it would affect your life if you became convinced that determinism is true and that everything you did throughout your life, down to the smallest detail, was determined—and could have been predicted—long before you were born?
2. Some philosophers have argued that if determinism is true, then it makes no sense to punish criminals for their crimes, since their behavior was determined by the state of the universe long before they were born. Do you agree that punishing criminals makes no sense in a deterministic universe? If not, why not? If you do agree, how do you think the laws should be revised if the universe is deterministic?
3. At the end of section 9.3, we proposed a revision to Hume's version of compatibilism, developing an idea from Harry Frankfurt. We finished the section by suggesting that even this new version of compatibilism is problematic. Can you suggest some further improvement to our compatibilist theory to deal with these problems?
4. Radical libertarians think that, in order to have the sort of free will that is required for morality, it must be the case that human decision-making is not governed by the laws of physics. Do you think they are right? Do you think it makes sense to claim that human decisions are not governed by the laws of physics? Do you think it is *true* that human decision-making is not governed by the laws of physics? If

human decisions are brain processes that are governed by the laws of physics, what implications does this have for morality?

5. Theists in the Abrahamic tradition believe that God is omniscient; he knows everything. If that's right, then God knows everything we are going to do, and he has known it since . . . well, forever. Yet most theists in the Abrahamic tradition also believe that God gave humans free will, and it appears that these two beliefs are incompatible. Do you think it is possible to have free will if God is omniscient? If so, how is it possible? If you think God's omniscience is incompatible with human free will, then which belief should a theist give up? If you find yourself intrigued by this problem, check out the last item in the What to Look at Next section.

What to Look at Next

- Hume's version of compatibilism is set out in "Of Liberty and Necessity," section 8 of his *Enquiry Concerning Human Understanding*. We recommend the translation into modern English by Jonathan Bennett available online at http://www.earlymoderntexts.com/authors/hume.
- William James's essay "The Dilemma of Determinism" is included in his book *The Will to Believe and Other Essays in Popular Philosophy*, which has been reprinted a number of times. There is a free e-copy available at https://archive.org/details/thewilltobelieve00jameuoft.
- Harry Frankfurt's essay "Freedom of the Will and the Concept of a Person" appeared in the *Journal of Philosophy* 68, no. 1 (1971). It is reprinted in Frankfurt's book *The Importance of What We Care About*, along with several additional essays Frankfurt has written on free will. The volume also includes Frankfurt's famous essay "On Bullshit."
- Robert Kane's book *A Contemporary Introduction to Free Will* provides a readable and reliable introduction to recent philosophical work on free will.
- Peter Strawson's article "Freedom and Resentment" introduced a new way of defending compatibilism that has been enormously influential. The paper originally appeared in the *Proceedings of the British Academy* in 1962. It has been reprinted many times and is available at http://www.ucl.ac.uk/~uctytho/dfwstrawson1.htm.

- Daniel Dennett, a well-known philosopher and cognitive scientist, develops another new approach to compatibilism in his lively and readable book *Elbow Room: The Varieties of Free Will Worth Wanting*.
- If free will does not exist, what are the implications for morality, law, and personal relationships? These issues are insightfully explored by Derk Pereboom in his book *Living Without Free Will*.
- Some famous experiments by the neuroscientist Benjamin Libet have been interpreted as showing that we do not have free will and that our sense of having free will is an illusion. Libet's work is reported in "Unconscious Cerebral Initiative and the Role of Conscious Will in Voluntary Action," which appeared in *Behavioral and Brain Sciences* in 1985. Psychologist Daniel Wegner examines the implications of Libet's work in his widely discussed book *The Illusion of Conscious Will*.
- J. T. Ismael's recent book *How Physics Makes Us Free* is both creative and readable.
- Linda Zagzebski's book *The Dilemma of Freedom and Foreknowledge* provides a detailed discussion of the apparent conflict between God's omniscience and human free will.

Notes

1. d'Holbach, *The System of Nature* (New York: Garland Press, 1984), pt. 1, ch. 11. We have modified the translation to make it slightly easier to read.
2. d'Holbach was both a determinist and an incompatibilist. He thought that determinism is true, and he inferred that we lack free will. This view is sometimes called "hard" determinism. "Soft" determinists think that determinism is true, but they insist that we have free will even so.
3. David Hume, *Enquiry Concerning Human Understanding*, sec. 8.
4. See Jeffrey M. Burns and Russell H. Swerdlow, "Right Orbitofrontal Tumor with Pedophilia Symptom and Constructional Apraxia Sign," *Archives of Neurology* 60, no. 3 (2003): 437–440.
5. See his paper "Freedom of the Will and the Concept of a Person," *Journal of Philosophy* 68, no. 1 (1971): 5–20.
6. This quotation comes from "The Dilemma of Determinism." This paper is easy to find online. Alternatively, you can find it in *The Will to Believe and Other Essays in Popular Philosophy* (Cambridge, UK: Cambridge University Press, 2014).
7. For an accessible description of Kant's views about free will, see Ralph Walker, *Kant* (London: Routledge and Kegan Paul, 1978).

CHAPTER 10
....

Race

Introduction

In recent years, heated moral and political debates involving race have been headline news in the United States and many other countries. The issues raised in these debates are enormously important. But they are not the issues we will be focusing on in this chapter. Instead, our focus will be on a cluster of conceptual and metaphysical issues that underlie the moral and political debates. The questions we will be asking are:

1. Do races really exist?
2. If races do exist, what are they?

The answer to our first question might seem obvious. And indeed, some philosophers who have written about race maintain that it *is* obvious. According to philosophy professor Lucius Outlaw:

> For most of us that there are different races of people is one of the most obvious features of our social worlds.[1]

If you walk down a crowded street in any city in North America or Western Europe you will have no trouble identifying some people as Black, others as White, and still others as Asian. But a number of philosophers think that this is an illusion. Kwame Anthony Appiah is perhaps the best known advocate of this view. "The truth" Appiah has written, "is that there are no races: there is nothing in the world that can do all we ask 'race' to do for us."[2]

10.1 Racialism

Why does Appiah think that there are no races? The answer he offers begins with the history of the concept of race. When that concept was first introduced and elaborated, in the late eighteenth and early nineteenth centuries, it incorporated a cluster of claims—a theory—that Appiah and other contemporary scholars call **racialism**. According to the racialist theory,

> we could divide human beings into a small number of groups, called "races," in such a way that the members of these groups shared certain fundamental, heritable, physical, moral, intellectual, and cultural characteristics with one another that they did not share with members of any other race.[3]

Racialism should not be confused with **racism**. There's some controversy about what racism is, but roughly, we might say racists are those who think that some races are inferior to others, or that racism is a system of oppression in which some racial groups are subordinated to others.

Borrowing an idea from the biology of their time, early racialists believed that all members of a race share a **racial essence**, which was taken to be an underlying natural property of people that is inherited from their parents and that is causally responsible for the unique physical, moral, intellectual, and cultural characteristics of members of that race. Early racialists did not have a clear idea of what these underlying racial essences were, or of how, exactly, they were conveyed from parents to their children. But with the emergence of the science of genetics in the early decades of the twentieth century, it became clear that what parents convey to their children are genes, and that genes play an important role in determining the physical and psychological characteristics of the organisms that have them. So if racialism is true, it must be the case that each member of a race has a substantial race-specific cluster of genes that it does not share with members of other races. The genes in these race-specific clusters must play a central causal role in producing both the easily identifiable physical characteristics that enable us to recognize a person's race and the sort of fundamental, physical, moral, intellectual, and cultural characteristics that racialists believe are distinctive of each race.

A critique of racialism plays a central role in the case made by Appiah and others for the conclusion that there are no races. That critique can be divided into two parts. The first focuses on familiar racial terms, terms like "Black," "White," "Asian," and "Native American." The use of these terms varies from time to time and from place to place. At one point in American history, there were places where the **one drop of blood rule** meant that having one Black ancestor was enough for a person to be labeled "Negro" or "Black."[4] At other times and places, the number of Black ancestors required for a person to be classified as Black varied enormously. In the United States for much of the nineteenth century, people of Irish descent were not considered to be "White."[5] Examples like this abound.[6] Since who would count as members of racialist races would not vary from time to time and from place to place, it follows that familiar racial terms do not pick out racialist races.

The second part of the critique of racialism maintains that racialist races do not exist at all. One argument for that conclusion focuses on facts about how physical characteristics that allegedly characterize races are distributed. Imagine that we undertook a long hike from the Democratic Republic of the Congo (DRC) through Sudan and Egypt and then along the Mediterranean coast to Greece, where we would head northwest toward Germany, and then on to Scandinavia, ending in Norway. If racialism were true and humans could be divided into a small number of distinct racial groups, we would expect to find sharp discontinuities in skin color, hair texture, and the other physical characteristics that racialism claims to be unique to each race. But that is not what we would see. Rather, skin color, hair texture and other features would change gradually, from the very dark skin and kinky black hair that is common in the DRC to the very light skin and straight blond hair that is common in Norway.

Another widely discussed and influential argument against racialism relies on the findings of modern genetics. In a seminal paper published in 1972, the eminent geneticist Richard Lewontin (1929–2021) found that the portion of human genetic diversity that falls within commonly recognized races is much larger than the portion that falls between races. This finding invokes some rather sophisticated statistical ideas. To make them more readily understandable, philosophy professor Edouard Machery has suggested a useful analogy with some readily understandable facts about height. Contemporary German men are quite tall; the average German man is about 6 feet tall. But the Dutch are currently the tallest people in the world; the average Dutch man is almost 6.1 feet tall. Of course, in both groups, there are men who are taller than average and men who are shorter than average. Figure 10.1 is a (slightly idealized) representation of these facts. There is a great deal of diversity in the height of the German and Dutch men shown in figure 10.1. However, most of the diversity in height is *within* the two groups represented, and only a small part of the diversity is between the two groups. The Aka people, who live in the Central African Republic and nearby, are currently among the shortest people in the world. The average Aka man is about 4.9 feet tall, and as one would expect, some are taller and some are shorter. Figure 10.2 compares the height of Dutch and Aka men. Though there is a great deal of diversity in the heights of the men represented in figure 10.2, most of that diversity is *between* groups rather than *within* groups. What Lewontin found is that that the genetic diversity in groups picked out by familiar racial labels is like the height diversity in figure 10.1, not like the height diversity in figure 10.2. And that looks like bad news for racialism, which maintains that each race has a substantial race-specific cluster of genes that it does not share with members of other races. If that were true, we would expect much more genetic diversity between commonly recognized racial groups.

In the years following Lewontin's pioneering work, there have been may other studies using newer technologies and more sophisticated methods. Most of them have reached the same conclusion. This

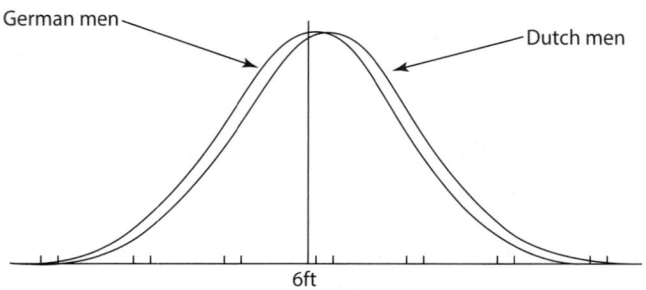

FIGURE **10.1** A comparison of the heights of Dutch and German men

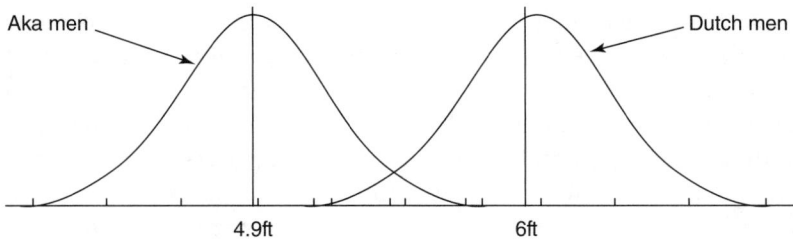

FIGURE 10.2 A comparison of the heights of Dutch and Aka men

research has convinced most scientists and scholars that racialist races simply do not exist. There isn't enough genetic variation between races to support systematic differences in physical, moral, intellectual, and cultural characteristics.

10.2 Nonracialist Meanings of "Race"

We began this chapter by sketching the disagreement between two leading philosophers who have written about race. Lucius Outlaw claims that the existence of different races of people is obvious. Kwame Anthony Appiah claims that there are no races. We then noted that the theory of racialism was embedded in the concept of race when that concept was first introduced, and went on to argue that racialism is false. Should we conclude that Appiah was right and Outlaw was wrong? No, that would be much too hasty. For while Appiah may be right that racialism was embedded in the concept of race when that concept was first introduced, it is far from clear that racialism is embedded in the concept (or concepts) of race used by many contemporary speakers of English. It is, for example, very implausible that, when Outlaw insists that races exist, he is using the term "race" in a way that commits him to the truth of racialism. And if, like many contemporary students, you had never heard of the theory of racialism and found it to be very implausible, then it is hardly likely that racialism is embedded in the meaning of "race" as you use the term.

So what do contemporary students mean when they use the term "race"? That turns out to be a very hard question. Part of the problem is that both linguists and philosophers disagree about what determines the meaning of the terms we use. Do all of our beliefs about race count as part of our meaning of the term? If not, which beliefs are relevant? Another part of the problem is that there may well be quite different meanings of the term in common use, and speakers like us may uses different meanings at different times. After conducting in-depth interviews with undergraduate students at four American universities, sociologist Ann Morning concluded that "we cannot assume that individuals hold a single definition of race. Instead they may carry around a 'tool kit' of race concepts from which to draw."[7]

In recent years, a number of philosophers have proposed definitions of "race" that, they urge, capture commonly used meanings of the term. Here is one proposed by philosophy professor Joshua Glasgow:

> Races, by definition, are relatively large groups of people who are distinguished from other groups of people by having certain visible biological traits (e.g., skin colors) to a disproportionate extent.[8]

And here is another proposal, by philosophy professor Michael Hardimon:

> A race is a group of human beings
>
> (1) that, as a group, is distinguished from other groups of human beings by *patterns of visible features*
> (2) whose members are linked by a *common ancestry* peculiar to members of the group, and
> (3) that originates from a *distinctive geographic location*.[9]

One important feature that these definitions share is that both are most definitely nonracialist definitions. They say nothing about members of a race sharing moral, or intellectual, or cultural characteristics.

Glasgow's definition readily avoids the problem posed by our imaginary hike from the center of Africa to Norway, since it doesn't require that races have sharp boundaries or that they can't overlap. If, as imagined in figure 10.3, we were to arrange photos of all the people in the countries we walked through on a line, with their place on the line determined by their skin color—very dark on one end and very light on the other—there are lots of different ways to divide them into groups having dark skin or light skin to a "disproportionate extent." And since Glasgow's definition does not specify *which* visible biological traits distinguish one racial group from another, it can readily accommodate the fact that different cultures characterize races in quite different ways.

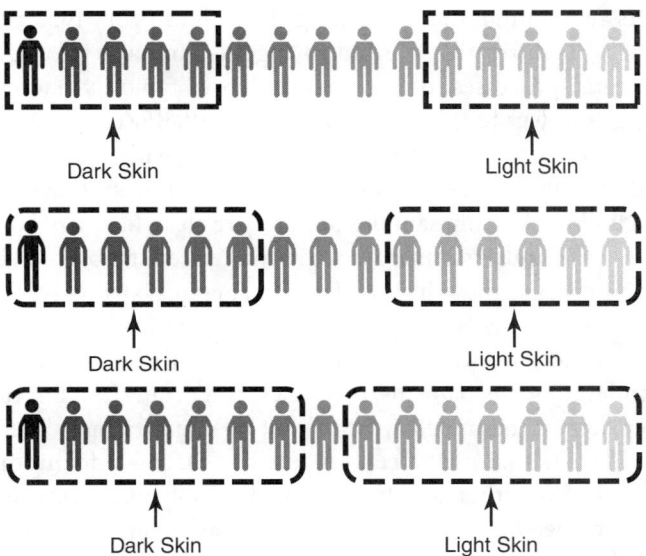

FIGURE 10.3

To better understand how these definitions differ, use your favorite web browser to find images of "people from Nigeria today" and "people from Papua New Guinea today." The people portrayed in these images will be very similar in skin color, hair texture, and facial features. But they have no recent common ancestry in a distinctive geographic location. So Glasgow's definition would classify them as members of the same race, but Hardimon's definition would not classify them as members of the same race. We, the authors, are inclined to think that both of these definitions, or something close to them, are included in our tool kit of racial concepts. In some circumstances, we'd be inclined to say that the people from Nigeria and from Papua New Guinea are the same race; in other circumstances, we'd say they aren't; and in still other circumstances, we wouldn't be comfortable making either claim. What do you think? Are both Glasgow's definition and Hardimon's included in your conceptual tool kit?

There is another important feature of Glasgow's definition that requires a bit of explaining. When scientists characterize categories of things in nature—animal and plant species, for example, or chemical elements and compounds—the things in each category typically have a cluster of features that are linked together because of underlying mechanisms, processes, or properties. Zebras typically have stripes, four long thin legs, a long head, and a tufted tail. Zebras share these properties because they share many genes along with complex mechanisms that enable the genes to regulate the building and maintenance of zebra bodies. All pure samples of water are clear, have a pH of 7, and freeze at 32°F under standard conditions. Water samples have these properties because they share a common chemical structure. Philosophers of science use the term **natural kind** for categories of things like zebras and pure water samples that share attributes because they share underlying mechanisms, processes, and properties. But races, as Glasgow defines them, will typically not be natural kinds. The visible biological traits that play a central role in Glasgow's definition need not be linked together due to the operation of underlying systems. Indeed, they need not be linked together at all. Someone could introduce a Glasgow-style label, "Blukies," for people who have blue eyes, curly hair, and "outie" belly buttons. If others started to use the term "Blukies" for these people, Glasgow would classify "Blukies" as a racial term and the people it applied to as a race. The traits that characterize this newly labeled race have no shared causal explanation. They are grouped together only because some people found that collection of traits to be of interest and created a label for people with those traits. So on one interpretation of a rather overused term, Blukies would be a **socially constructed group**, and races, as Glasgow characterizes them, are social constructions.

So far, the story we've told about the creation of the category of Blukies is innocuous enough. But all too often, when a group of people are labeled, it is because other people wish to treat them differently from people to whom the label is not applied. And that group-specific treatment can have profound effects. If Blukies are only allowed to do certain kinds of arduous and unhealthy work, if they must live in specified undesirable neighborhoods, if they are not allowed to educate their children, Blukies will gradually (or perhaps not so gradually) become increasingly different from non-Blukies. And if their social interactions are mostly with other Blukies, they may well develop traditions, art forms, clothing styles, hair styles, a cuisine, a dialect, and a belief system that differ from those of non-Blukies. What began as a socially constructed way of labeling people may develop into a multi-faceted socially constructed culture.

Many race theorists, including the path-breaking African American scholar and civil rights leader, W.E.B. Du Bois[10] (1868–1963), insist that a group should not be counted as a race unless it is culturally, economically, or politically distinct from other groups. This view, which we'll call **strong social constructionism**, has the apparent implication that if the political, economic, and cultural differences between groups that we now call races were to disappear, races would disappear! But Glasgow has proposed an intriguing thought experiment he thinks shows that this is not the case, and thus that all forms of strong social constructionism are mistaken. Here is Glasgow's thought experiment:

> Imagine a world of only babies. Everyone else has died off. A new technology keeps the newborns alive and cares for them until they can care for themselves. Before the adults perished, they acted to prevent the terror wrought by centuries of unjust racist behavior. Wanting their children to avoid the same racial struggles with which humanity had plagued itself, the parents decided to wipe any trace of racialization. They destroyed any records that refer to our racially fraught history. In fact, just to be safe, they erased all history and culture other than what was needed to provide the babies with enough science to maximize their well-being. All babies are given equal resources. A variety of therapies become available to allow them the equal chance for equal health outcomes. And so on. . . .
>
> Because *every* racial practice, along with *every* result of our racialized past dies off with the adults, [strong social constructionism] is forced to say that a (racially) Asian baby stops being (racially) Asian when the last adult dies [and a Black baby stops being Black when the last adult dies]. . . . But this is not how race purports to work. Surely the babies would still have their races after the last adult perishes. . . . [Thus strong social constructionism] fails to capture race in the ordinary sense of the term.[11]

Do you share Glasgow's intuition about this case? Do you think that the babies would still be Black, or Asian, or White even when *all* cultural, economic, and political distinctions were eliminated? If so, it may be the case that none of the concepts of race in your conceptual tool kit is a strong social constructionist concept. If, on the other hand, you think it's plausible that the babies in Glasgow's thought experiment would have no race, then at least one of the concepts of race in your conceptual tool kit may be a strong social constructionist concept.

Hardimon's definition of "race" is more demanding than Glasgow's, since it requires that members of a race are linked by a common ancestry and that the group originates from a distinctive geographic location. Those added requirements make it more likely that members of a race will share some distinctive genetic material. And in the early years of this century, research by the biologist Noah Rosenberg and his colleagues found that this was indeed the case for five commonly recognized races: Black, White, East Asian, Native American, and Pacific Islanders.[12] The genetic material that Rosenberg and colleagues found were short segments of DNA that do not code for proteins, so they are not involved in producing skin color, hair texture, or other features commonly associated with race. But they enabled scientists to identify the race, and geographic origin, of people with impressive accuracy. These results, and other similar studies, led Hardimon to conclude that "it is possible to assign individuals to . . . races on the basis of genetic information alone," and thus that "there are differences between . . . races 'at the level of the gene.'"[13] Because of this, Hardimon offers a very different account of the implications of our imaginary walk from Africa to Norway:

> [T]he fact that it is possible . . . to demarcate . . . races solely on the basis of genetic information means that the fact of continuity, that is, the fact that "people occupy very many different locations on a spectrum of shades, from very light to very dark" and the fact that "similar points are true of our facial features and hair types" do not entail that there is no nonarbitrary way of demarcating the boundaries of races.[14]

The conclusion that Hardimon offers is that, on his definition of race, race is biologically real. However, he also stresses that

> real does not mean deep. Compared to the biological differences associated with *sex* . . ., the biological differences associated with . . . race are superficial. . . . The fact that for hundreds of years . . . *race* was *taken to be* a big deal biologically makes the fact that *it is **not** a big deal* a big deal.[15]

Quayshawn Spencer, another leading philosopher of race who has been impressed by Rosenberg's research and other, more recent studies that report similar findings, offers a more guarded account of the implications of these findings. The biologically based theory of race he proposes "does not imply that . . . races differ in any socially important traits (e.g., intelligence, beauty, moral character, etc.) . . . and it does not imply that . . . races don't differ in any socially important traits. Determining whether . . . races differ in any phenotypically important ways requires a separate empirical investigation."[16]

Summary

Let's finish with a short summary of the views we've looked at in this chapter.

Racialists once argued that there are genetic differences between the races, and that these genetic differences result in important moral, intellectual, and cultural differences between the races. Even today, some defend racialism, but it is overwhelmingly rejected by scientists in the field (and, indeed, by philosophers). All of the philosophers we've discussed in this chapter reject racialism.

Kwame Anthony Appiah argued that our categorization of people into different races is based on racialism, in such a way that when one rejects racialism, one should also reject this categorization. Appiah denies that there are different races of people; for Appiah, "there are no races."

Others argue that we can reject racialism while retaining the idea that there are different races of people:

- Joshua Glasgow argues that a race is just a large group of people who look alike in certain ways: perhaps in skin color, or the shapes of the facial features, or the texture of the hair.
- Michael Hardimon agrees with Glasgow that the people in a certain race look alike in certain ways, but he adds that they must have a common ancestry that originates from a distinctive geographic region.
- Some philosophers (most notably W. E. B. Du Bois) argue our racial categories depend not only on appearance and ancestry, but on today's politics, economy, and culture. They argue that a group of people should not be considered a race unless they differ from others politically, economically, or culturally.

Perhaps you are eager to move on to political and economic questions about race—questions about policing, disparities in wealth and income, or university admissions. We hope you do. But when you do, we hope, too, that you remember the racial categorizations they so often presuppose are far less straightforward, and far more controversial, than they might first seem.

Glossary

natural kind: A category of things that share attributes because they share underlying mechanisms, processes, and properties. Biological species and chemical elements and compounds are widely viewed as being natural kinds.

one drop of blood rule: A rule for classifying people as Negro that specified if a person had one Negro ancestor, that person would be classified as Negro. Also known as the "hypodescent rule."

racial essence: Prior to the emergence of modern genetics, racialism maintained that racial essences were underlying natural properties of people that are inherited from their parents and that are causally responsible for the unique physical, moral, intellectual, and cultural characteristics that members a race were thought to have.

racialism: The theory that human beings can be divided into a small number of groups, called "races," in such a way that the members of these groups share a number of fundamental, heritable, physical, moral, intellectual, and cultural characteristics with one another that they do not share with members of any other race.

racism: There's some controversy about what racism is, but roughly, we might say it is the belief that some races are inferior to others, or we might say that racism is a system of oppression, in which some racial groups are subordinated to others.

socially constructed group: A group whose members do not constitute a natural kind. The members of a socially constructed group are included in the group only because they have a cluster of properties that some people found of interest.

strong social constructionism: The view that a group should not be counted as a race unless it is culturally, economically or politically distinct from other groups. Strong social constructionism entails that if the political, economic, and cultural differences between groups that we now call races were to disappear, races would disappear.

Comprehension Questions

1. What is racialism? How does racialism differ from racism?
2. What are the arguments for the claim that familiar racial terms, like "Black," "White," "Asian," and "Native American," do not pick out racialist races?
3. If we traveled from the center of Africa through the Middle East and southern Europe and then on to Scandinavia, we would find that skin tone, hair texture, and other physical features commonly associated with race would change gradually. We would not find any sharp discontinuities. Explain why these facts pose a problem for racialism.
4. Explain what Richard Lewontin and others have found about the genetic diversity within and between groups picked out by familiar racial labels.
5. Explain why Lewontin's finding about the genetic diversity within and between groups has been taken to be a powerful argument against racialism.
6. Explain why the falsity of racialism would not be sufficient to establish Appiah's claim that there are no races.
7. The fact that skin color, hair texture, and other physical features commonly associated with race vary continuously poses a problem for racialism, but it doesn't pose a problem for races as Glasgow defines them. Why not?
8. What are natural kinds?
9. What are Blukies? Why aren't Blukies a natural kind? Why are Blukies a socially constructed group?
10. Explain how labeling a group and treating that group differently can lead to the labeled group becoming increasingly different from those to whom the label does not apply.
11. In what ways is Hardimon's definition of "race" more demanding than Glasgow's? Why do the requirements Hardimon adds make it more likely that members of a race will share some distinctive genetic material?
12. What did Noah Rosenberg and his colleagues discover about five commonly recognized racial groups?
13. Why does Hardimon think that the fact that biological differences associated with race are superficial is a "big deal"?
14. How does Spencer's view about the biological importance of race differ from Hardimon's?

Discussion Questions

1. Thomas Jefferson (1743–1826) was both a racialist and a racist. It was his "suspicion" that "the blacks, whether originally a distinct race, or made distinct by time or circumstances, are inferior to the whites in the endowments of both body and mind."[17] What reasons might Jefferson have had for this "suspicion"? What evidence for the falsity of racism do we now have that was unavailable to Jefferson? What evidence for the falsity of racism would have been available to Jefferson?
2. Many people believe that racial discrimination and racial injustice have been, and continue to be, major problems in the United States and in other countries. However, Kwame Anthony Appiah and others have argued that human races don't really exist. Are these two views compatible? Can racial discrimination and racial injustice really exist if there are no races? What implications does Appiah's view have for programs aimed at addressing the problems that many people take to be caused by racial discrimination?
3. In the most recent census, over 30 million people in the United States reported that they viewed themselves as being of more than one race. What would racialists say about these people? Does racialism allow for the possibility that someone could be of more than one race? Some racialists were surely aware of the existence of multiracial people. Indeed, there is excellent evidence that the ongoing sexual violation of Sally Hemings, a woman enslaved by Thomas Jefferson, resulted in six children. Was Jefferson's racialism consistent with what he knew about Sally Hemings and their children?
4. Racialism is not the only theory of race that has difficulty dealing with the existence of biracial and multiracial people. What would Glasgow's definition of race say about these people? What would Hardimon's definition say about them?
5. Some race theorists maintain that, in order to count as a race, a group must be socially constructed and culturally and economically distinct from other groups. But Joshua Glasgow has argued that this can't be right, since it entails that if cultural and economic differences were to disappear, races would no longer exist. Do you agree with Glasgow that races would continue to exist even in a world with no cultural and economic differences?

6. Are Hispanics a race? Are Jews a race? Are Indian castes races? In each case, explain why or why not. Do you think there are correct and incorrect answers to these questions, or can they only be settled by providing a more or less arbitrary definition of race?

What to Look at Next

- As we noted in section 10.2, there is some controversy about what racism is. For a useful discussion of the issue, see chapter 1 of Lawrence Blum's book *I'm not a Racist, But . . . The Moral Quandary of Race*.
- The view that race is an illusion is presented in an engaging and accessible way in the three-part video documentary *Race: The Power of an Illusion*. The first episode, "The Difference Between Us," considers some of the scientific evidence that has been used to support the claim that races do not exist. . You may be able to access the documentary through a library. For more information see https://www.racepowerofanillusion.org/.
- Kwame Anthony Appiah's argument that races don't really exist is developed in detail in his elegant and sophisticated essay "Race, Culture, Identity: Misunderstood Connections," in K. Anthony Appiah and Amy Gutmann, *Color Conscious: The Political Morality of Race*. There is an online version available at https://philpapers.org/archive/apprci.pdf.
- The view of four leading contemporary philosophers of race are presented and debated in Joshua Glasgow, Sally Haslanger, Chike Jeffers, and Quayshawn Spencer, *What Is Race? Four Philosophical Views*.
- In "'Race': Normative, Not Metaphysical or Semantic," *Ethics*, 116, (2006): 525–551, Ron Mallon, another leading philosopher of race, argues that much of the philosophical disagreement about the existence and the nature of human races is actually an illusion.
- Michael Hardimon's "deflationary realism" about race is developed in detail in his book *Rethinking Race: The Case for Deflationary Realism*.
- Philosophers have developed many more accounts of race than we have discussed in this brief introduction to the topic. Some of the books that have contributed to this lively debate include:

- Linda Martín Alcoff, *Visible Identities: Race, Gender and the Self*
- Sally Haslanger, *Resisting Reality: Social Construction and Social Critique*
- Charles Mills, *Blackness Visible: Essays on Philosophy and Race*
- Paul Taylor, *Race: A Philosophical Introduction*
- Naomi Zach, *Philosophy of Science and Race*
- Cognitive psychologists and evolutionary psychologists have written a great deal about why we perceive people to fall into different racial groups, why we treat members of different groups differently, and what, if anything, can be done about it. For an overview of this literature, see Daniel Kelly, Edouard Machery, and Ron Mallon, "Race and Racial Cognition," in *The Moral Psychology Handbook*, edited by John Doris and the Moral Psychology Research Group. There is an online version available at https://web.ics.purdue.edu/~drkelly/KellyMacheryMallonRaceRacialCognition.pdf.
- Quayshawn Spencer argues that his biologically based theory of race "does not imply that . . . races differ in any socially important traits (e.g., intelligence, beauty, moral character, etc.) . . . and it does not imply that . . . races don't differ in any socially important traits. Determining whether . . . races differ in any phenotypically important ways requires a separate empirical investigation." One important attempt to determine whether races differ in intelligence can be found in *Intelligence and How To Get It* by the eminent psychologist Richard Nisbett.

Notes

1. Lucius Outlaw, "Toward a Critical Theory of 'Race," in *Anatomy of Racism*, ed. David Theo Goldberg (Minneapolis: University of Minnesota Press, 1990): 58–82.
2. K. Anthony Appiah, "The Uncompleted Argument: DuBois and the Illusion of Race," in *Overcoming Racism and Sexism*, ed. Linda A. Bell and David Blumenfeld (Lanham, MD: Rowman & Littlefield, 1995): 59–78.
3. K. Anthony Appiah, "Race, Culture, Identity: Misunderstood Connections," in *Color Conscious: The Political Morality of Race*, ed. K. Anthony Appiah and Amy Guttmann (Princeton, NJ: Princeton University Press, 1996), 30–105.

4. The one drop of blood rule was also know was the hypodescent rule, and those who endorsed the rule were unaware of the more recent anthropological findings indicating that *all* humans are descended from a relatively small group of humans living in Africa. So according to the one drop of blood rule, all humans are Black!
5. For an engaging account see Noel Ignatiev, *How the Irish Became White* (New York: Routledge, 1995).
6. See, for example, Karen Brodkin, *How Jews Became White Folks & What That Says About Race in America* (New Brunswick, NJ: Rutgers University Press, 1998).
7. Ann Morning, "Toward a Sociology of Racial Conceptualization for the 21st Century," *Social Forces* 87, no. 3 (2009): 1167–1192.
8. Joshua Glasgow, "Is Race an Illusion or a (Very) Basic Reality?" in Joshua Glasgow, Sally Haslanger, Chike Jeffers, and Quayshawn Spencer, *What Is Race? Four Philosophical Views* (New York: Oxford University Press, 2019): 111–149.
9. Michael O. Hardimon, *Rethinking Race: The Case for Deflationary Realism* (Cambridge, MA: Harvard University Press, 2017).
10. Du Bois, who was one of the founders of the NAACP and the first African American to earn a doctorate at Harvard, was a towering figure in American history. For an excellent biography, we recommend David Levering Lewis' *W. E. B. DuBois: A Biography*.
11. Glasgow, "Is Race an Illusion," 133.
12. Noah A. Rosenberg et al., "Genetic Structure of Human Populations," *Science* 298, no. 5602, (2002): 2381–2385.
13. Hardimon, *Rethinking Race*, 91.
14. Hardimon, *Rethinking Race*, 90.
15. Hardimon, *Rethinking Race*, 84.
16. Quayshawn Spencer, "How To Be a Biological Racial Realist," in Joshua Glasgow, Sally Haslanger, Chike Jeffers, and Quayshawn Spencer, *What Is Race? Four Philosophical Views* (New York: Oxford University Press, 2019): 104.
17. Thomas Jefferson, *Notes on the State of Virginia*, 1785.

CHAPTER 11
....

How Is Your Mind Related to Your Body?

Introduction

If you've seen the *Star Wars* films, you're sure to remember R2-D2, the three-foot-tall robot who moved around on its own, communicated in beeps and chirps with its robot friend C-3PO, and regularly helped Luke Skywalker when help was needed. Before we begin our discussion of the philosophy of mind, we'd like to introduce you to another robot who looks a lot like R2-D2. We'll call this robot R1-D1 (or R1, for short). Like R2-D2, R1 moves on its own and occasionally emits beeps and chirps. But you should not assume R1 is as clever, or as useful, or as loveable as R2-D2. We'll tell you more about R1 as the chapter unfolds.

The philosophy of mind is the area of philosophy that deals with a cluster of fundamental questions about the mind and mental states. But before we explain them, we'd like you to help us by undertaking a few very simple exercises. One of them is a bit unpleasant, so let's get that out of the way first. What we'd like you to do is to kick yourself—not too hard, we don't want you to end up with a bruise, but hard enough so that it is a little bit painful. OK, now that you've done that, we'd like you to find something that is blue and roughly rectangular and stare at it for about ten seconds. It doesn't much matter what it is; a blue piece of paper or a blue computer screen will do, or pair of blue jeans folded into something that approximates a rectangle. If nothing blue is available, you can substitute a white rectangle—a blank piece of printer paper, for example, or an empty page of this book. Your third exercise is to taste something sweet—put a little bit of sugar in your mouth, or enjoy a bite of chocolate. For your next exercise, we'd like you to spend a minute or two imagining doing something that you've never done before, but that you would really like to do. Don't worry, we won't ask you to reveal what it is. Done yet? We hope it was fun. For your final exercise, we'd like you to do some simple mathematical reasoning. But we'd like you to do it in your head—don't use pencil and paper, or a calculator, or a computer. Here's the question: If $A = 17 + 13$ and $B = 50 - 23$, is A greater than B?

OK, that's the end of our set of exercises. What we've asked you to do in these five exercises is to have some very common mental states—a mild pain (when you kicked yourself), a visual experience, a taste experience—and to engage in some familiar mental processes—imagining and reasoning. If you've been indulging us and playing along with our exercises, then you know that you had the experience of mild pain, of seeing a blue rectangle, and of tasting sweetness, and that you reasoned about numbers and imagined . . . well, whatever it was (we promised we would not ask). You know this via **introspection**, a process that enables you to know a great deal about what's going on in your mind.

Now let's think about R1-D1. Suppose someone kicked it. Would R1 experience mild pain? Or suppose we held a blue piece of paper in front of R1. Would the robot have the experience of seeing blue? Obviously, the answer is that you don't know because we haven't told you enough about R1. But how about your mom, or the person who sits next to you in philosophy class, or the authors of this book? If someone gave these people a kick or showed them a blue piece of paper, would they have the same experience that you had? If your answer is yes, as we expect it would be, how do you know? Obviously, you can't use introspection to obtain knowledge about other people's mental states. So why are you confident that they have mental states like yours? Indeed, why are you confident that they have any mental states at all? The questions we've been asking:

(i) Do other people (and things like robots or fish) have mental states?
(ii) Are their mental states similar to yours?
(iii) How can we know?

are the central questions in the part of the philosophy of mind that's often called the "problem of other minds."

The other part of the philosophy of mind that we'll discuss—the part that's called the "mind-body problem"—is closely linked to the problem of other minds. To see how they are linked, it will be helpful to return to robot R1. At this point, you haven't a clue whether R1 has mental states or what they are like, since we've told you very little about it. But suppose we offered to tell you more about R1. We'll tell you what R1 is made of, how it works, and how it behaves under any set of circumstances you care to describe. What information should you use to determine whether R1 has mental states—whether it experiences pain, has blue visual experiences, experiences sweetness, thinks about events that have not actually occurred, and reasons about math? The answer, of course, depends on what experiences (of pain, or blue, or sweetness) and thoughts and reasoning *are* and on how they are related to the physical and biological and behavioral facts about human beings and animals and robots like R1. In other words:

(iv) How are mental states and processes related to physical and biological and behavioral phenomena?

That's the central questions of the mind-body problem.

The mind-body problem falls squarely in the part of philosophy known as "metaphysics," which tries to give an account of the most general features of reality and how they are related. The problem of other minds, by contrast, is something of a hybrid. Though the first two of its central questions concern what is the case, the third asks how we can *know*. Thus, the problem of other minds has an important epistemological component. In this part of philosophy, as we'll see, epistemological issues and metaphysical issues are closely connected. Since the middle of the twentieth century, many philosophers have urged that we can make progress on traditional philosophical problems, in metaphysics, epistemology and elsewhere, by attending carefully to the language we use in discussing those problems. So to better understand how mental states and processes are related to physical, biological, and behavioral facts, and how we can know whether other people (and animals and robots) have mental states, we'll also be asking some questions about language; we'll be asking what terms for various mental states *mean*.

11.1 Cartesian Dualism

The French philosopher René Descartes (1596–1650), who is widely considered to be the first "modern" philosopher, proposed a solution to the mind-body problem that dominated philosophical thinking until the twentieth century and continues to influence how many people think about minds and mental states. In his sixth *Meditation*, Descartes offers a very simple argument. Descartes claims that he can imagine[1] his mind existing without his body (perhaps *you* can imagine your mind continuing to exist after you have died and your body has been destroyed). Descartes also claims that he can imagine his body existing without his mind. He then infers that his body and his mind are, in fact, distinct. They are different things.

Philosophers continue to debate whether Descartes's argument for the distinctness of the mind and the body is a good one. Some maintain that it is just a logical fallacy. To make the case, they draw our attention to arguments that seem to have the same logical form. It seems that we can imagine water existing in the absence of H_2O, and that we can imagine H_2O existing without water. Nevertheless, water and H_2O are the very same chemical. Other philosophers, most notably David Chalmers, have urged that, with some careful updating, Descartes's argument can be made valid and persuasive.[2]

We won't take a stand on whether Descartes's conceivability argument can be successfully updated. But this argument was not the only consideration that led Descartes, and many philosophers who followed him, to believe that the mind and the body are distinct things. Equally important, and more compelling to many, is the fact that mental states and processes seem to have some extraordinary properties that nothing in the physical world possesses. Think back to our five exercises. The first three, and perhaps the fourth as well, required you to have **conscious** experiences, like having pain and experiencing sweetness. The fourth exercise required you to *think about* something that has never happened—something that does not exist. (Philosophers apply the term **intentional** to mental states that are *about* something, perhaps a nonexistent thing.) The final exercise required you to engage in a bit of *rational* thought. These three phenomena—consciousness, "aboutness" or intentionality, and rationality—seem to be unique to minds. We don't think that rocks, or slabs of metal, or planets are conscious; they are not able to think *about* anything; and they don't engage in rational thought. Moreover, for Descartes, and for many other people, both philosophers and nonphilosophers, it seemed inconceivable that physical stuff could have these properties. How could a physical object—a collection of atoms and molecules, no matter how complex, possibly have consciousness or intentionality, or exhibit rationality?

Descartes's answer was that it couldn't. Being conscious, being about something, and being rational are not the kinds of properties that physical things—things made of matter—can have. Thus, Descartes concluded, there must be another, fundamentally different category of things in the universe—minds. Minds are the kinds of things whose nature enables them to have conscious experiences, have thoughts that are about things, and be rational. Matter obeys the laws of physics, but minds are not made of matter. Minds belong to a quite distinct metaphysical category. They are, in the terminology of Descartes's day, a fundamentally different **substance**. The metaphysical theory that claims minds and matter are fundamentally different kinds of things is often called **substance dualism**.[3] For Descartes, the division between the mental and the physical goes back to the origin of the universe. When God created the universe, he created two types of things. He created minds, which are things capable of consciousness, intentionality, and rationality, and he created matter, which obeys the laws of physics. But appeal to God is not essential for substance dualism—one can be a dualist and an atheist. What is essential is that minds and matter are two basic and different categories of reality.

For Descartes, and for most other dualists, the fact that minds and matter are basic and distinct metaphysical categories does not mean that they do not interact. Indeed, Descartes thought it was obvious that they did. Think back to our first exercise. Your foot, a hunk of matter, kicked your leg, another hunk of matter, and this resulted in something happening in your mind—you felt pain. Descartes, and most other dualists, think it is obvious that this is a causal process—the kick causes the pain. So events in the domain of matter ("material events," as philosophers sometimes say) can cause mental events. And it seems equally plausible that the causal links can go in the other direction as well. To see this, here's another exercise. Touch your nose with either your right hand or your left hand; you decide which one to use. Ready? Go. If you went along with our exercise, you made a decision (a mental event), and then one of your hands moved toward your nose. Here, it seems obvious that a mental event is causing a physical event. Simple observations like this led Descartes and most other dualists to believe that there is two-way causal interaction between the mental and the physical.

As we noted earlier, the sort of mind-matter dualism that Descartes was the first to articulate had a profound influence on Western philosophical thought. Most of the philosophers we've discussed in this book who wrote prior to the twentieth century were dualists. (Can you name one who *wasn't*?)[4] But though it was, and remains, a quite popular metaphysical view, philosophers have raised a number of serious challenges to dualism. Here, we will mention only two.

The first was raised forcefully by Princess Elisabeth of Bohemia (1618–1680), who conducted a long and penetrating philosophical correspondence with Descartes. If minds and matter are totally different kinds of thing, if they are metaphysically distinct substances, then how, Elisabeth asked, is it possible for them to causally interact with one another? For Descartes, this was a particularly vexing question, since on his view, minds exist in time but do not exist in space; mental states, for Descartes, do not have *any* spatial location.[5] It is, Elisabeth noted, deeply puzzling how something that is not located in space at all can interact causally with some hunk of matter, since hunks of matter always have a spatial location. But even if, along with many dualists, one does not accept Descartes's view that minds are not located in space at all, Elisabeth's question remains very difficult to answer. Descartes speculated that the interaction takes place deep inside the brain, in the pineal gland. But he acknowledged that he could offer no good response to Elisabeth's request for an account of how this is possible.

The second objection to Cartesian dualism that we'll mention is that it makes the problem of other minds exceedingly difficult to solve. Let's start with the question of whether other people have minds at all. If they do, obviously you have no introspective access to them. You can't literally feel your friend's pain or think your friend's thoughts. All you can do is observe what your friend says and does, and in doing this, you are observing the body, not the mind. If the Cartesian dualist is right, your friend's mind is not a physical substance, so you can't see it or feel it. Why, then, should you believe it exists? Why don't you believe that your friend is a mindless biological robot with no conscious life at all? Of course, Descartes might reply that your friend is obviously rational—able to do math problems and make sensible decisions just as well as you can—and that only minds can be rational. But Descartes and

Princess Elisabeth of Bohemia (1618–1680) formulated an influential challenge to Cartesian dualism.

his fellow dualists have offered no *argument* for the claim that only a nonmaterial mind can be rational. And though Descartes would surely be amazed by them, we now have machines that are remarkably good at solving math problems; we call them "computers." So perhaps your friend is just a sophisticated bio-computer who can solve math problems and engage in other sort of rational behavior, but who has no consciousness or intentionality at all.

The problem is more obvious for things like our imaginary robot, R1-D1. Suppose you take R1 apart and see that there is nothing squishy and biological inside. It is a mechanical device—a robot controlled by a sophisticated object that seems to be a computer. Does R1 have a mind? Is it capable of consciousness and intentionality? If the dualists are correct, the answer depends on whether R1 is linked up with a nonmaterial mind in the way they think our human brains are. Do events in R1's control mechanism cause conscious experiences and intentional thoughts in a nonmaterial mind? Since minds, for the dualist, are not physical things, it seems we have no way of determining whether R1 has one. So if dualism is true, then the mind-body problem for R1 seems very difficult indeed. And note that much the same problem looms for nonhuman animals. Do chickens or fish have mental states? Are they conscious? How about insects? If having mental states requires being linked up with a nonmaterial mind, it is hard to see how we could ever discover the answers to these questions.[6]

Thus far, we have been focusing on the first of the three questions that comprise the problem of other minds: Do other people (and nonhuman things) have minds at all? But dualism poses equally difficult obstacles to the second question: Are other people's mental states similar to yours? There is a venerable philosophical thought experiment, first proposed by John Locke (1632–1704), that makes the problem particularly vivid. Suppose there is group of people whose visual color-processing system works in a way that is systematically different from yours. When they look at an object that causes a conscious experience of red in you—a ripe Red Delicious apple, for example—they have a conscious experience just like the one you have when you look at something at the opposite end of the color spectrum—like a ripe blueberry. And similarly for all the other colors. These people have what philosophers have dubbed an "inverted spectrum." People with an inverted spectrum are not aware that their perceptual experience is different from other people's. They have no introspective access to what other people experience when looking at a Red Delicious apple. And when they acquired color words as young children, they learned to use the word "red" for the experience they get when looking at a ripe Red Delicious, even though that *experience* is the one that you, and other people without an inverted spectrum, have when looking at blueberries. So their linguistic behavior doesn't differ from yours.

This appears to be an entirely possible state of affairs. There *might* be people with inverted spectrums. But if dualism is true, then it seems we could never know whether another person had an inverted color spectrum. For according to the dualist, the visual experience that a person has when looking at a ripe Red Delicious apple is an event taking place in the non-physical mind, and there is no physical test that will reveal the nature of these nonphysical events. A person with a brain exactly like yours might nonetheless be spectrum inverted, and a person with a visual system that looked suspiciously different from yours might *not* be spectrum inverted. The second of the three questions that comprise the problem of other minds asks whether other people's mental states are similar to yours. If dualism is true, then it seems there is no way to answer this question. We have no way of knowing what other people's mental states are like.

11.2 Philosophical Behaviorism

In the decades just before and just after the Second World War, philosophers who had become profoundly dissatisfied with the dualist account of the nature of mental states developed a radically different account, known as **philosophical behaviorism**.[7] The English philosopher Gilbert Ryle (1900–1976), who was one of the most influential advocates of philosophical behaviorism, proposed a memorably disparaging epithet for the dualist view; according to the dualists, Ryle said, the mind is "the ghost in the machine."

One major reason for the behaviorists' dissatisfaction with dualism was the impasse it led to in trying to deal with the problem of other minds. But for many of them, the path to their alternative account of the nature of mental states began with a philosophical view about language and what is required for a sentence to be meaningful. According to this philosophical view, which is called **verificationism**, a declarative sentence is literally meaningful if and only if it is either true or false, and there are two (and only two) ways in which a sentence can be literally meaningful. Some sentences are true or false solely by virtue of the meanings of the words they employ. "All bachelors are unmarried" is an example of a sentence that is *true* in virtue of meaning. "Some uncles are female" is an example of a sentence that is *false* in virtue of meaning. The other category of meaningful sentences are those that are verifiable (or falsifiable) by observation. "It will rain in Chicago on July 4, 2035" is an example of a verifiable sentence. More interesting examples, according to advocates of the verificationist theory of meaning, include the sentences to be found in legitimate scientific theories. However, the verificationists also maintained that some putatively scientific theories, and a great deal of philosophy, include sentences that are neither true or false by virtue of meaning nor verifiable or falsifiable by observation. Favorite examples were some of the wilder claims of psychoanalysts, like the claim that all little boys want to have sex with their mother, and philosophical pronouncements like Martin Heidegger's account of what "nothingness" is up to: "The Nothing itself nothings." This stuff, the verificationists insisted, is literally meaningless.[8]

That's all sort of interesting, you may be thinking, but what does it have to do with the philosophy of mind? The answer is that behaviorists, along with just about everyone else, think that most ordinary claims about mental states are clearly meaningful. Sentences like "Fred is experiencing a pain in his shin" and "Cynthia is having a visual experience of a blue rectangle" are either true or false. Moreover, neither these sentences nor other common sentences about people's mental states are true or false by virtue of meaning. So they must fall into the other category of meaningful sentences—they must be verifiable (or falsifiable) by observation. And if that's right, then dualism must be wrong, since as we saw in the previous section, if dualism is correct, there is no way of determining whether claims about other people's mental states are true or false. If mental states like a pain in the shin and the experiences of seeing a blue rectangle are events occurring in a nonphysical mind, then there is no way of observationally verifying claims about other people's mental states. And that, the behaviorists insisted, is surely mistaken. We verify claims about other people's mental states all the time.

How do we do it? Well, the behaviorists urged, it's obvious: we observe their behavior. If, after Fred is kicked in the shin, he says "Ouch!", rubs his shin soothingly, and walks with a limp for the next few minutes, that's evidence confirming the claim that Fred has a pain in his shin. Additional confirming evidence might be obtained by evoking some additional verbal behavior from Fred. Suppose, after he's been kicked, you ask him, "Hey, Fred, why are you rubbing your shin?" He will say, "Because it hurts!" (or perhaps something more forceful, and unprintable in a book like this). Why does all of this behavior count as evidence confirming the claim that Fred has a pain in his shin? The answer, according to the behaviorists, is that these behavioral descriptions are part of the *meaning* of the sentence "Fred has a pain in his shin."

This is just a single example of what, according to the behaviorists, is a quite general phenomenon. The meaning of sentences attributing any mental state to a person is given by the verification conditions for that sentence, and those verification conditions will be a set of claims about the person's behavior. So at the core of philosophical behaviorism is a *semantic* claim:

> (1) The meaning of sentences attributing mental states to an individual can be analyzed into a set of sentences about how the individual would behave under a variety of circumstances.

This is a clear illustration of the trend, noted in the chapter Introduction, for ideas about language and meaning to play an important role in philosophical discussions. But the central question posed by the mind-body problem is a metaphysical question, not a semantic question. It asks how mental states and processes are related to physical, biological, and behavioral phenomena. The behaviorists' semantic thesis suggests an answer to that metaphysical question:

> (2) Mental states and processes are **behavioral dispositions**.

To return to our example, Fred's pain is his disposition to say "Ouch!", to rub his shin soothingly, and so on. If Seo-Yun is happy, a behaviorist might say that her happiness is her disposition to smile, to whistle chirpy tunes, to walk with a bouncy gait, and so on. If Jeandré is tired, a behaviorist might say that his tiredness is his disposition to yawn, to close his eyes, to speak slowly, and so on.

A conspicuous advantage of this this account, in contrast to the account proposed by dualists, is that it offers a straightforward solution to the problem of other minds. Do other people have mental states? Yes, of course they do, since they have pretty much the same behavioral dispositions that you do. Are their mental states similar to yours? Yes again, and for the same reason: they share much the same behavioral dispositions. How do we know? It's easy, just observe their behavior. And if any doubt arises, you can do a few simple (though sometimes dangerous) tests. Does your philosophy professor feel pain? Kick your professor in the shin and watch what happens.

All this makes a simple and tidy package. But many philosophers came to think it was a bit *too* simple, and that it leads to very counterintuitive consequences. To see the point, let's go back to the *Star Wars* robots. R2-D2 isn't the best example, since the sounds it emits are unfamiliar to us, and it is not clear whether they are really a language at all. But C-3PO, the one who looks more like a human, also behaves like a human, albeit a rather annoying and subservient one. And according to the philosophical behaviorists, if something behaves like a normal human under a wide variety of conditions, then it has mental states. So C-3PO and robots like him really are conscious and they really think about things, including things that don't actually exist. You might have thought that, in order for an individual to feel pain, or have a blue visual experience, or taste sweetness, something rather special has to be going inside that person. But the behaviorist denies this. If C-3PO behaves like he is in pain, then he *is* in pain. End of story!

There are a number of other ways in which the behaviorist's account seems to lead to very counterintuitive consequences. Consider the inverted spectrum problem. For centuries, many philosophers took it to be a serious puzzle, and we expect that, when you first heard about it, you thought it was puzzling as well. But behaviorists have a simple way to dispatch the problem; they maintain that people with an inverted spectrum are impossible. After all, if someone's behavioral dispositions (including dispositions to verbal behavior) are the same as yours when viewing that ripe Red Delicious apple, then that person is having the same red visual experience you are having. How do we know? That's simple. It follows from the meaning of "having a red visual experience."

One reason why many people find these consequences of behaviorism to be so counterintuitive is that we think that mental states—particularly the ones that involve a conspicuous consciousness component, like feeling a pain—are states and processes that go on inside a person, and that merely exhibiting the behavior characteristic of someone in pain is not enough to make it the case that someone is really in pain. The philosopher Hilary Putnam (1926–2016) underscored this concern by asking us to imagine an excellent actor who is highly motivated to act as though he is in pain, even though he is not.[9] If the actor does a perfect job of exhibiting the behavior characteristic of someone in pain, then the behaviorist is committed to saying that the actor really is in pain. But surely, Putnam argued, putting on a great act is not the same as being in pain.

There are many other examples of the counterintuitive consequences of behaviorism. Our favorite is due to the philosopher and cognitive scientist Daniel Dennett. Dennett asks you to imagine that you need to have an operation—an appendectomy, perhaps. The anesthesiologist who will be assisting the surgeon offers you a choice of drugs. The first choice is a traditional one, a drug that is believed to induce a coma-like state where the patient is completely unconscious. The second is a new product, a mixture of two chemical compounds. The first is a compound similar to curare. When administered by itself, it leads to temporary paralysis of all the voluntary muscles, though it does not affect breathing or heartbeat. That temporary paralysis is important, the anesthesiologist explains, because it would obviously be a very bad thing for you to squirm or scream as the surgeon is cutting open your abdomen. The other compound is a newly developed amnestic drug that, when administered by itself, has no effect at all for about two hours. But two hours after the drug has been administered, it completely removes all memories of anything that has occurred during the last two hours. That's also important, the anesthesiologist explains, because it will take about two hours for the paralytic effects of the curare to disappear. By the time you are able to talk and move your arms and legs, you will have no memory at all of the surgery. "Which option would you prefer?" the anesthesiologist asks.

What makes this a philosophically important thought experiment, Dennett notes, is that if behaviorism is correct, then you should be completely indifferent. If you select the first option, you will lie motionless while the surgeon cuts you open and removes your infected appendix, and afterward, you will have no memories at all of what happened after the anesthetic was administered. And if you select the second option, exactly the same thing will be true. But, you might protest, the second option does nothing to prevent the horrible pain you would feel while the surgeon is cutting you open. Don't be silly, the behaviorist responds, if you accept the second option, you will exhibit no pain behavior during the surgery, and if you are asked about it afterward, you will say that you have no memory at all of anything that happened during the two hours after the drugs were administered. There will be no pain behavior and no pain reports, so there will be no pain. If you are like us, you will find this ghoulishly counterintuitive. If we discovered that our anesthesiologist was a behaviorist, we would get another anesthesiologist, *fast*.

For the last few paragraphs, we have been detailing counterintuitive consequences of philosophical behaviorism; there are many more. But while most behaviorists will acknowledge that their view leads to counterintuitive consequences, they have a brief, and potentially persuasive, rejoinder to arguments based on these intuitions. Yes, the behaviorists may reply, our view sometimes does not comport with commonsense intuition, but why should we care about *that*? In lots and lots of other areas, ranging from physics and biology to economics and history, we think it is wise to be very skeptical of ordinary people's intuitions. When we rely on intuitions at all in these areas, the intuitions we take seriously are those of experts. And when the topic at hand is the meaning of mental state terms, the behaviorists may argue, *we* are the experts. We are the people who have studied the meaning of mental state terms most carefully and systematically. So if the intuitions of ordinary people, who are not experts, differ from ours, we should simply ignore their intuitions and the antibehaviorist arguments based on them.

Debates about the use of intuitions as evidence in philosophy have become more common, and more heated, in recent years. Fortunately, for those who are skeptical about behaviorism, another argument poses a major challenge to behaviorism without relying on anyone's intuitions. Behaviorists claim that sentences about mental states can be analyzed into a cluster of sentences about behavior and behavioral dispositions. And in our exposition of behaviorism earlier in this section, we offered a few very sketchy examples of what these analyses might look like. But those sketchy analyses are clearly not accurate. If Fred gets a painful kick in the shin, he may say "ouch," but he may *not*. Perhaps Fred wants to conceal the fact that he is in pain. If that's the case, then he *won't* say "ouch." Or perhaps Fred believes that if he says "ouch," the person standing next to him will take out a gun and shoot him. Here, again, Fred won't say "ouch" even if he is in pain. So it looks like we can't analyze a statement about Fred's pain into statements about Fred's behavior and his behavioral dispositions. The analysis also has to include *statements about Fred's other mental states*—what he wants, what he believes, and perhaps many others was well. Moreover, there is nothing unique about this example. When philosophers began to take the behaviorists' claim about the meaning of mental state statements seriously, they found that it was almost always impossible to give a purely behavioral analysis. We can't say how a person's beliefs will affect their behavior without saying something about what that person wants. And we can't say how what a person wants will affect their behavior without saying something about what that person believes. Moreover, the same is true for just about every mental state. But if that's right, if the analysis of mental state-statements will always include other mental state statements, then proposition (1), the semantic claim that is central to philosophical behaviorism, is false. And if the behaviorists' semantic claim is mistaken, so, too, is proposition (2), the behaviorists' metaphysical account of the nature of mental states. As philosophers became convinced that these problems could not be solved, philosophical behaviorism lost just about all of its adherents. But as we'll see in section 11.4, the problems that scuttled philosophical behaviorism suggested a new, and much more plausible, account of the nature of mental states.

11.3 The Mind-Brain Identity Theory

As philosophers became increasingly aware of the problems that confronted philosophical behaviorism, a new theory, called the **mind-brain identity theory**, emerged and quickly attracted a growing number of adherents. Descartes used the conceivability argument—which maintains that our minds and our bodies are distinct because we can conceive of each one existing without the other—as one argument in support of dualism. But as we noted earlier, many contemporary philosophers think that the conceivability argument is fallacious, since there are lots of examples of things that science has discovered to be identical even though we can conceive of each one existing without the other. The example we gave earlier was water and H_2O. It is easy to imagine that water exists and H_2O doesn't. Nonetheless, chemists have discovered that water is the same stuff as H_2O; water and H_2O are identical.

The core idea of the mind-brain identity theory is that science is on the way toward making a similar discovery about mental states. What contemporary neuroscience suggests is that mental states are identical with brain states. Of course, the philosophers who defend the mind-brain identity theory do not claim to know which brain state is identical with a particular type of mental state. That's an empirical question that must be answered by neuroscientists. What the philosophers are offering is a metaphysical theory, an answer to question (iv), which is the central question of the mind-body problem. According to these philosophers, every type of mental state (every type of pain, every type of visual experience, every thought) is identical with some specific type of brain state or a specific type of brain process. And different types of mental states (like a visual experience of blue and a visual experience of green, or the thought that it's raining and the thought that the Sun is shining) are identical with different brain states or different brain processes.

Though the mind-brain identity theory is intended primarily as an answer to the core question of the mind-body problem, it also suggests an answer to the questions posed by the problem of other minds. Do other people have mental states? If they have brains like yours, then yes, they do. So if your friend Tom has a brain like yours, then you can rest assured that he is not a mindless biological robot. Are his mental states similar to yours? When he looks at a ripe Red Delicious apple, does he have a visual experience like the one you have when you look at the same apple. Here, again, the answer is yes, provided that you and your friend Tom have the same sort of brain state or brain process when you look at things with that shade of red. If you *don't* have the same sort of brain state when looking at that shade of red, then you and your friend *don't* have the same visual experience. But how can we know whether other people have the same sorts of mental states that we do? How, for example, can you know whether you and your friend have inverted spectrum experiences? The behaviorist's answer seemed too easy. If your friend behaves the way you do when confronted with colored objects, then he is experiencing what you are. The mind-brain identity theorist's answer makes it harder to know. With the help of neuroscientists, you have to find out what's going on in your brain when you see colored objects and what's going on in your friend's brain. So it is not easy to determine whether or not you and your friend have inverted spectrums. But in contrast with the dualist account, it is empirically possible to find out.

Many contemporary students find the mind-brain identity theory to be very attractive. But the theory confronts a number of problems, some of which are more easily handled than others. Perhaps the most obvious problem is that brain states and mental states *seem* to be very different. A pattern of firing of neurons seems to be a very different thing from an experience of a blue rectangle. So how could they be identical? The identity theorist's response is to draw our attention to other scientifically discovered identities. Two molecules of hydrogen bonded with one molecule of oxygen *seems* very different from the stuff that fills our lakes and comes out of the tap in the kitchen. Nonetheless, chemists have made an overwhelming case that they really are identical. So, the identity theorist insists, we should not be troubled by the fact that mental states and brain states seem very different.

But what about the content of mental states, things like the blue rectangle that you saw in our second exercise. As we noted in endnote 5, there is no blue rectangle in your brain—or if there is, then you are very, very ill. So how could the experience of a blue rectangle be a brain state? Here, the identity theorist replies that, according to this theory, some brain state is identical with the *experience* of a blue rectangle; it is the experience that is occurring somewhere in your brain. And although that experience presents itself as being blue and rectangular, the experience is not actually composed of anything blue and rectangular; a blue rectangle is not a *part* of the experience in the way that a blue rectangle might be part of a painting. But where is the blue rectangle that you experience? Well, the identity theorist replies, there is a blue rectangular piece of paper in front of your eyes that causes the visual experience, and there is no puzzle about where *that* is, and that's the only blue rectangle involved in having a visual experience of a blue rectangle. Are you convinced? Some philosophers are persuaded by a response along these lines. Others are not. They note that people sometimes have experiences of blue rectangles (in dreams or hallucinations, for example) when there are no blue rectangles in front of their eyes. That experienced blue rectangle surely exists, they insist, and the identity theorist has no plausible account of where it is. We'll let you decide whether you think this is a serious problem for the identity theory.[10]

A problem of a rather different sort is that even if the identity theorist, with the help of some high powered neuroscience, can tell us which brain state is identical with a specific sort of mental state, the identity theorist provides no explanation of *why* a brain state of this type is identical with that mental state. Why, for example, does a particular brain state lead to the experience of blue rather than the experience of green or yellow, or the experience of a sweet taste? If identity theorists and their neuroscientist colleagues can't explain why a particular brain state is identical with a particular mental state, then, the critics maintain, the theory suffers from an important *explanatory gap*.

In response, the identity theorist might point to analogous situations in the history of other areas of science. Chemists discovered that water is H_2O long before physical chemists discovered *why* a collection of H_2O molecules would turn from liquid to solid at 0°C and from liquid to gas at 100°C. So, the identity theorist continues, there is, indeed, an explanatory gap, but it is one that we can reasonably expect to be filled as science advances. Some philosophers are doubtful that an explanation will be forthcoming, however, since we currently have no idea what such an explanation would look like. And a few philosophers (they have been dubbed "mysterians") have suggested that the correct explanation might be the sort of thing that minds like ours simply cannot understand. Our view is that it is far too early in the development of neuroscience to draw any skeptical conclusions about the explanatory gap remaining a permanent mystery. Predicting the future of scientific theorizing and scientific discoveries, we believe, is an all-but-impossible task. So we don't think that the (current) existence of an explanatory gap poses a major problem for the mind-brain identity theory. But other philosophers disagree. What do you think?[11]

We are much more impressed by a very different problem that some philosophers have posed for the identity theory. Earlier in this section, we sketched the identity theory's answers to the questions posed by the problem of other minds. If your friend Tom has a brain like yours, then he is not a mindless biological robot and he has mental states like yours. That's the unproblematic part of the story. The problematic part emerges when we think about creatures that *don't* have brains like ours. If the identity theory is correct, then they *don't* have mental states like ours. To make this problem vivid, some philosophers have asked that we imagine there are creatures in another galaxy whose basic chemistry is very different from ours. Perhaps they evolved with a silicon-based chemistry rather than a carbon-based chemistry. If that's the case, then their brains are made of very different stuff, and they do not share any of our brain states. But if our pains of various sorts are specific sorts of brain states, then these imagined extraterrestrials can't experience pain. That seems like an odd thing for a philosophical theory to entail. It seems plausible to think that whether these extraterrestrials feel pain is an open empirical question. But if their brains are silicon based, then it follows from the identity theory that they *don't* feel pain. No further investigation is needed. Perhaps you're OK with that. But there is worse to come. For if the identity theory is right, then thinking about the math problem we asked you to solve back in the chapter's Introduction is a specific set of states and processes in your brain, and believing that 17 plus 13 is greater than 50 minus 23 is also a specific state in your brain. However, since you share no brain states with the extraterrestrial (or with robots like R2-D2 and C-3PO), it follows that neither the extraterrestrial nor the robots can think about math problems or believe that 17 plus 13 is greater than 50 minus 23. And for many philosophers, this is an unacceptable result. What it shows, they maintain, is that the mind-brain identity theory is unacceptably *chauvinistic*. It entails that only creatures very like us have mental states such as beliefs, desires, thoughts, and experiences. And that, the critics argue, is a major shortcoming.

11.4 Functionalism

The last theory about the relation between mind and body that we'll consider in this chapter is also the most recent, and for much of the last few decades has been the theory most widely held by philosophers. This theory, called **functionalism**, comes in a variety of forms. We'll focus on two with daunting labels: **analytic functionalism** and **psychofunctionalism**. Though the philosophers who developed analytic functionalism had a variety of motivations, we think the view is best understood as an attempt to avoid the problem that scuttled philosophical behaviorism, while at the same time avoiding the sort of chauvinism that, in the opinion of many, makes the mind-body identity theory unattractive.

Let's start with the problem that led to the demise of behaviorism. Though their view has lots of very counterintuitive consequences, behaviorists, you'll recall, can argue that we should ignore those intuitions. The problem that behaviorists cannot ignore is that, when we try to actually give definitions of mental state terms like "pain" in terms of behavior, we find that this just can't be done without including other mental state terms like "believes," "wants," and so on. To give a plausible account of how we think pain is connected to behavior, we have to give a commonsense theory in which pain, various sorts of behavior, and other mental states all play a role. It is this widely shared, commonsense theory, the analytic functionalist maintains, that captures what we mean when we talk about pain. Moreover, this theory not only provides an implicit definition of the term "pain," it also provides an implicit definition of all the other mental state terms that are invoked in the commonsense theory. This may sound a bit abstract, so let's look at a simplified account of what this commonsense theory would look like.

What sorts of environmental stimuli can cause pain? There are, alas, lots of them, but let's focus on just one: touching a hot stove. We all know that that touching a hot stove will cause the mental state of pain. What does the pain cause? Well, it causes many things. It typically causes us to wince and to shout "ouch" (or something more colorful). It also causes us to have a desire that the pain stop. If we also believe, as most people do, that running one's hand under cold water stops a burning pain, then this belief, along with the desire for the pain to stop, leads to the desire to run one's hand under cold water. And if there is a source of cold water available, that desire leads us to engage in some more behavior—we run our hand under cold water. Figure 11.1 depicts the commonsense causal network that we've just recounted; the arrows in the diagram indicate causation. Of course, this isn't a complete account of our commonsense view about the ways that pain can lead to behavior. We also think there are a number of circumstances under which the desire to run one's hand under cold water won't actually lead to that behavior. If the person whose mental states are depicted in figure 11.1 believes that if he runs his hand under cold water, then the man next to him will shoot him, and if he desires not to be shot, then the causal link between the desire to run one's hand under cold water and the behavior will be blocked. With a bit of effort, you can probably add a number of other commonsense elaborations to the picture of the causes and effects of pain in figure 11.1. Give it a try, and see how many elaborations you can come up with.

Now the fundamental claim of the analytic functionalist is that a causal flowchart diagram like figure 11.1—though with lots more detail added to reflect *all* of our widely shared commonsense beliefs about the connections between environmental stimuli, mental states, and behavior—can be viewed as an implicit definition of "pain" and of all the other mental state terms included in the diagram.[12] Behaviorism faltered because it tried to define mental state terms exclusively in terms of behavior. On the functionalist account, the definition of "pain" invokes not only behavior, but all the other commonsense mental state terms as well.

Thus far, we've been portraying analytic functionalism as a semantic theory that, like behaviorism, offers an account of the meaning of mental state terms. But this semantic theory also suggests an answer to the metaphysical question posed by the mind-body problem. If the word "pain" is defined by a causal flowchart like the one in figure 11.1,

How Is Your Mind Related to Your Body? 221

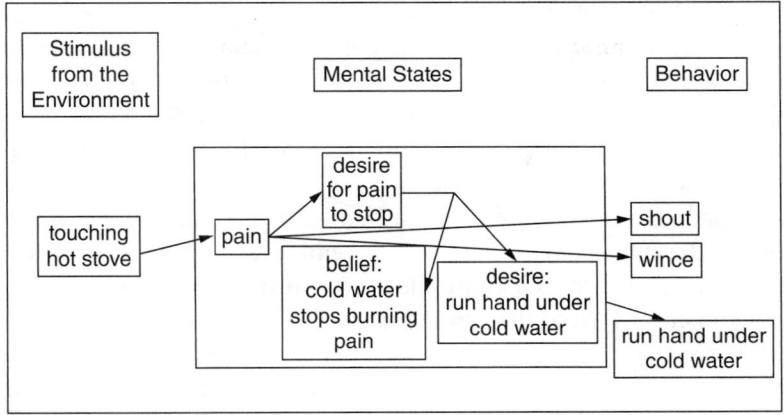

FIGURE 11.1 A depiction of the commonsense causal network that begins when we touch a hot stove

then pain (the mental state, not the word denoting it) is any state that exhibits the pattern of causal connections depicted in a more complete and detailed version that diagram. Pain, the functionalist maintains, is anything that plays the pain-role in a complex causal system that captures our widely shared commonsense beliefs about pain, other mental states, environmental stimuli, and behavior.

We said earlier that functionalism was motivated in part by the desire to avoid the sort of chauvinism that makes the mind-brain identity theory problematic. Let's see how this works. For the functionalist, pain is any state that plays the pain-role in a complex causal system like the one in figure 11.1 (though much more detailed). And of course, functionalists give an entirely parallel account for all the other mental states. So, for example, the mental state of believing that 17 plus 13 is greater than 50 minus 23 is any state that plays the believing-that-17-plus-13-is-greater-than-50-minus-23-role in a complex causal system that captures our shared commonsense beliefs about mental states, thinking about Abraham Lincoln is any state that plays the thinking-about-Abraham-Lincoln-role in such a causal system, and so on. OK, now let's think about *your* mental states. When you are in pain, the functionalist maintains, you are in a state that plays the pain-role in a complex causal system that captures our commonsense beliefs about pain and other mental states. What kind of state plays that role? In you (and in all other humans), that role is played by a brain state of some kind—a complex firing pattern of interconnected neurons whose exact details are still being worked out by neuroscientists. That sounds a lot like what the identity theorist would say. The crucial difference comes when we think about the imagined extraterrestrial invoked in the argument aimed at showing the identity theory is chauvinistic. Neurons are cells made of proteins and other carbon-based organic chemicals. But the extraterrestrial has a silicon-based chemistry, so it has no proteins in its body, and its behavior controlling mechanism contains nothing like human neurons. According to the identity theorist, it follows that the extraterrestrial can't feel pain or believe that 17 plus 13 is greater than 50 minus 23. But the functionalist confronts no such difficulty. For while the extraterrestrial's body includes no proteins and no neurons, there may well be states in its silicon-based behavior controlling mechanism that play the pain-role, and other states in that silicon-based system that play the believing-that-17-plus-13-is-greater-than-50-minus-23-role. So for the functionalist, having a physical and chemical composition very different from ours is no obstacle at all to having mental states like pains and beliefs and thoughts. If an extraterrestrial has a behavior controlling system that exhibits the pattern of causal interactions represented in a suitably elaborated version of figure 11.1, then the extraterrestrial can have all the mental states that we can have. In contrast with the identity theory, functionalism does not entail that extraterrestrials with silicon-based chemistry can't believe that 17 plus 13 is greater than 50 minus 23 or think about Abraham Lincoln. Note that everything we've said about extraterrestrials applies equally to robots like R1-D1, R2-D2, and C-3PO. If the mechanism that controls their behavior—we assume it is some sort of advanced computer—has states that exhibit the pattern of causal interaction depicted in a suitably elaborated version of figure 11.1, then our robot friends can believe that 17 plus 13 is greater than 50 minus 23 and think about Abraham Lincoln. And they can also feel pain, have the visual experience of blue, and experience the taste of sugar!

Since functionalism avoids some of the problems of behaviorism and the identity theory, it is no surprise that many philosophers found it very attractive. But philosophers soon noted that functionalism faces problems of its own. We will discuss two of them. The first of these derives from the fact that the definition of mental state terms, according to the analytic functionalist, is constructed from our widely shared commonsense beliefs about mental states. This cluster of interconnected commonsense beliefs constitute a commonsense theory about mental states, a theory that is often called **folk psychology**. But it is no secret that folk theories are often rather seriously mistaken. Folk theories about the causes and cures for common diseases are no match for modern scientific medicine. And psychologists have shown that our widely shared commonsense theory of physics is rather similar to a medieval theory that was common prior to Newton! Some philosophers maintain that we have good reason to believe our commonsense folk psychology is also a badly mistaken theory. Paul Churchland, who has long been a leading critic of folk psychology, suggests that folk psychology is so badly mistaken that we should simply discard it. According to Churchland,

> [folk psychology] suffers explanatory failures on an epic scale . . . it has been stagnant for at least twenty-five centuries, and . . . its categories appear (so far) to be incommensurable with or orthogonal to the categories of background physical sciences whose long term claim to explain human behavior seems undeniable. Any theory that meets this description must be allowed a serious candidate for outright elimination.[13]

Other philosophers are less pessimistic about folk psychology. However, if folk psychology does turn out to be a seriously mistaken theory about the processes intervening between stimuli and behavior, the consequences for analytic functionalism would be catastrophic. For according to analytic functionalism, pains, beliefs, desires, and thoughts are the states that play the pain-role, the belief-role, the desire-role, and the thought-role, respectively. And if folk psychology is mistaken, it follows that *nothing* plays these roles, so pains, beliefs, desires, and thoughts *do not exist*! Churchland and a few like-minded philosophers are happy to embrace this conclusion. These **eliminativists** think commonsense mental states, including beliefs, desires, and pains, are like witches: they are the posits of a mistaken folk theory, and we should come to grips with the fact that they do not exist. But many other philosophers take this to be an absurd conclusion. If analytic functionalism, along with the findings of psychology and neuroscience, entail that beliefs, desires, pains, and thoughts do not exist, these philosophers urge that we must abandon analytic functionalism.

One response to the challenge posed by the eliminativists is to retain the basic functionalist idea that mental state terms are implicitly defined by a theory, but switch the focus from folk psychology to scientific psychology. Psychologists and neuroscientists offer a much richer account of the causal processes intervening between stimuli and behavior. And in contrast with commonsense folk psychology, their account of the ways that the states posited by their theory interact is constantly tested in the laboratory and revised when necessary. So some philosophers who think that functionalism is on the right track urge that we should use scientific psychology and neuroscience rather that commonsense psychology to define our mental state terms and specify the causal roles that mental states play. This version of functionalism is called psychofunctionalism. In contrast with the analytic functionalists, the psychofunctionalists obviously need not worry that the theory they use to characterize the role of mental states will be in conflict with the findings of science.

There is, however, a problem that has led many philosophers to doubt that either version of functionalism gives the correct account of the nature of many mental states. As we saw earlier, a virtue of analytic functionalism is that it is not chauvinistic. Much the same is true of psychofunctionalism. The mental state roles characterized by either version of functionalism can be filled by lots of different things. In us, they are filled by the firing of neurons made of organic molecules; in extraterrestrials and robots, they might be filled by the activity of components that contain no organic molecules at all. But many philosophers think that functionalism's permissiveness about the sorts of things that can fill mental state roles is a two-edged sword. Though it addresses the concern about chauvinism, it allows in too much and thus attributes mental states to systems that, these philosophers maintain, surely don't really have mental states.

One particularly vivid example of this problem was proposed by the philosopher Ned Block.[14] Block notes that the current adult population of China is now roughly the same as the number of neurons in a human brain. So, Block suggests, it would be possible to build a functional analog of a human brain using one Chinese person to play the role of each neuron. If we organized this bizarre system in the right way, then the billion people of China would pass messages to each other in exactly the way messages were passed in your brain when, in our first exercise, you kicked yourself and felt pain, though no doubt the messages would be passed more slowly. What makes this problematic is that, according to the functionalist, this elaborate system made up of a billion Chinese people would feel pain. Similarly, if we got the people of China to simulate the activity in your brain when, in the second exercise, you experienced a blue rectangle, then the system composed of a billion Chinese would experience a blue rectangle. And if we got them to simulate what went on in your brain when, in the third exercise, you tasted something sweet, then the system of interacting Chinese people would experience something sweet. But this, Block argues, is absurd. Surely it is not the case that this system of a billion people passing messages to one another would experience the same thing that you did when you kicked yourself, or looked at a blue rectangle, or tasted something sweet. If that's right, then neither functionalism nor psychofunctionalism succeeds in giving an adequate account of mental states like these in which conscious awareness is particularly salient.

11.5 Physicalism, Zombies, and a Revival of Dualism

In the nineteenth century, as the science of physics became increasingly sophisticated and explanatorily powerful, many scientists came to believe that physics could ultimately explain everything that occurs in the universe, and that if two objects are physically identical, then they are identical in every respect. This view is often called **physicalism**, and if physicalism is true, then **philosophical zombies** are impossible. In the movies, zombies are hulking creatures that move awkwardly and speak in monosyllables or grunts. But philosophical zombies are exactly like ordinary people in every physical, biological, and behavioral respect. They move and talk and interact just like ordinary people, and they are physically and biologically indistinguishable from ordinary people. What makes them philosophical zombies is that, unlike ordinary people, they have no conscious experiences. They don't feel pain or pleasure; they have no visual or auditory experiences, or any other sort of experience; they never feel giddy, or fearful, or nauseous; they never feel anything at all. A zombie (we'll drop the "philosophical" from here on) could be an exact physical replica of you now, but it would have no conscious experiences.

Physicalism entails that zombies are impossible, since physicalism insists that if two things are physically identical, then they are identical in every respect. Identity theorists and functionalists will also insist that zombies are impossible. The argument is simplest for identity theorists. Anything that is physically identical with you will have the same mental states you have, since for identity theorists, mental states *are* physical states. And since anything that is physically identical with you will also be functionally identical, your physical replica will have all the same functional states that you do. But as we've seen, both the identity theory and functionalism confront daunting challenges. And that has led some philosophers to challenge physicalism and revisit dualism.

One widely discussed argument against physicalism is inspired by Descartes and has been elaborated and defended with great sophistication by philosopher David Chalmers. The first premise of the argument is this:

(1) Whatever is conceivable is possible.

We should explain what this means. As far as we know, nobody has ever made a five-meter-high statue of Bugs Bunny entirely of gold—and we're confident that nobody ever will. However, we think that this statue is possible: an eccentric billionaire *could* make a statue like this, if they really wanted. What makes us think that this statue is possible? Part of the answer is that we can *conceive* of a statue like this. It's not easy to explain precisely what the word "conceive" means, but roughly, the idea is that to conceive something is to form a clear idea of it in one's mind, without coming across any contradiction. Examples like this motivate the claim that whatever is conceivable is possible. To put it the other way around, the claim is that whatever is *im*possible is *in*conceivable. For example, we are unable to conceive of a round square, or of a woman who is taller than herself.

The next premise in the argument is this:

(2) Zombies are conceivable.

There may or may not be good reason for thinking that there are no *actual* zombies, but it does seem that we can clearly imagine them, without coming across any contradiction.

From (1) and (2), we infer:

(3) Zombies are possible

Since physicalism entails that zombies are impossible, if zombies are possible, then physicalism is false. The three-step argument that zombies are possible is clearly valid. But it is far from clear that the premises, (1) and (2), are true, since both "conceivable" and "possible" can be interpreted in many ways. On some interpretations, (1) is very plausible, but (2) is not. On other interpretations, (2) is plausible, but (1) is not. Can you come up with an interpretation on which both (1) and (2) are likely to be true?[15]

Though debate over the zombie argument has led some philosophers to revisit dualism, these modern dualists typically don't adopt Descartes's view that the universe is divided into two kinds of substances. Rather, they suggest that ordinary matter may have two quite different kinds of properties. Some of the properties of matter are the familiar (and sometimes not so familiar) physical properties studied by physics. But in addition to these physical properties, these philosophers suggest that a primitive form of consciousness is also a basic property of all of the matter in the universe. Since it claims that consciousness is present in all matter, this view is often called **panpsychism**. Of course, no one thinks that atoms or rocks have the sort of conscious experiences that you do. No one thinks that atoms taste sweetness or that rocks feel pain. Rather, modern panpsychists suggest that pain and the taste of sweetness are somehow constructed from the more primitive consciousness that all matter possesses. Whether this idea makes sense and how the process of constructing complex conscious states from primitive consciousness might work are topics of lively debate in contemporary philosophy. These are exciting times in the philosophy of mind!

Glossary

analytic functionalism: See functionalism.

behavioral dispositions: We'll start by explaining what a disposition is, in general. Then, we'll look at *behavioral* dispositions in particular. Consider *fragility, solubility in water,* and *elasticity*. These are dispositions. When an object has a disposition, it has a propensity to respond in a particular way to events of particular kinds:
- Barring special circumstances, a fragile object will break if it is struck.
- Barring special circumstances, an object that is soluble in water will dissolve when put in water.
- Barring special circumstances, an elastic object will return to its original shape after it has been deformed.

Now a *behavioral* disposition is a special kind of disposition—a disposition where the response is a particular sort of behavior. Here are some examples:
- Mortimer will close his eyes when he is sitting.
- Li breaks into song when she is in the shower.
- Shanee sighs when someone mentions money.

conscious: "Conscious" is a difficult and contested term in philosophy. In this chapter, we have been using the term in the following way: a person's mental state is conscious when the person can detect the state by introspection. For example, *being hungry* is a conscious state because you can find out whether you are hungry by introspection (at least in typical cases).

dualism: Substance dualists believe that each human being is composed of two fundamentally different parts: a mind and a body. These two parts may interact, but they are nevertheless fundamentally different. Cartesian dualism is the version of substance dualism that was espoused by the French philosopher René Descartes. See section 11.1 for more details.

eliminativists: Eliminativists think that folk psychology is a *false* theory, and that the mental states posited by folk psychology (e.g., beliefs) don't really exist. See section 11.4.

emotive meaningfulness: See literal meaningfulness and emotive meaningfulness.

folk psychology Here are some banal, everyday claims about our psychology:
- A toothache is a kind of pain.
- Disgust often causes retching.
- Prolonged exposure of the skin to very cold or very hot objects causes pain.
- Sufficient eating causes the cessation of hunger.

All banal psychological claims of this kind, together, constitute "folk psychology." Folk psychology is often contrasted with scientific psychology.

functionalism: Functionalists believe that a mental state can be entirely characterized by describing (a) its characteristic causes, (b) what effects it has on other mental states, and (c) what behaviors it can produce, on its own or when combined with other mental states. For example, perhaps we can characterize pain by collecting together such observations as these:

- Pain is caused by bodily damage (e.g., burns on the skin).
- When someone is pain, they typically desire that the pain stop.
- Pain often causes people to scream or yell.

> Functionalists come in at least two varieties: there are "analytic functionalists" and "psycho-functionalists." For more on this distinction, see section 11.4.

intentional: An intentional state is a mental state that is "about" something—something which may or may not be real. Here are some examples:
- Thinking about New York City
- Admiring the President
- Wanting a pet unicorn

introspection: The process of "looking inwards" to investigate one's own mental states. For example, if you are asked "How are you feeling today?" you might introspect to find out that you are feeling happy but slightly stressed.

literal meaningfulness and emotive meaningfulness: A declarative sentence is literally meaningful[16] if it succeeds in expressing a proposition that is either true or false. A declarative sentence that is not literally meaningful might nevertheless evoke some emotional or imaginative response in a reader. Think, for example, of sentences in nonsense poetry. Such sentences have emotive meaning, but not literal meaning.

mind-brain identity theory: Mind-brain identity theorists claim that mental states are brain states. For example, a mind-brain identity theorist might say that *pain* is a certain pattern of neural activity in the brain. The mind-brain identity theory is often just called "identity theory" for short. For more details, see section 11.3.

panpsychism: Panpsychists claim that some form of consciousness is present in all matter—even in trees, even in pebbles.

philosophical behaviorism: Philosophical behaviorists make the following two claims:
  (1) The meaning of sentences attributing mental states to an individual can be analyzed into a set of sentences about how the individual would behave under a variety of circumstances.
  (2) Mental states and processes are behavioral dispositions.
  See section 11.2 for examples and for further discussion.

philosophical zombies: Philosophical zombies are exactly like ordinary people in every physical, biological, and behavioral respect. They move and talk and interact just like ordinary people. What makes them philosophical zombies is that, unlike ordinary people, they have no conscious experiences. We usually drop the "philosophical" and just call them "zombies."

physicalism: Physicalism is the view that physics can ultimately explain everything that occurs in the universe, and that if two objects are physically identical, then they are identical in every respect.

psychofunctionalism See functionalism.

substance: The term "substance" has a complicated history, and is used differently by different philosophers. For the purposes of this chapter, all you need to know is that if a dualist claims that the mind and the body are distinct "substances," this means that a human being is not an entirely physical system. On the contrary, the dualist thinks that a human being has two parts: a physical part (the body) and a mental part (the mind).

substance dualism: Substance dualists believe that each human being is composed of two fundamentally different parts: a mind and a body. These two parts may interact, but they are fundamentally different. Cartesian dualism is the version of substance dualism espoused by the French philosopher René Descartes.

verificationism: Verificationists think that all literally meaningful declarative sentences fall into one of three categories:

- Sentences that are true in virtue of the meanings of the words they contain (e.g., "All kittens are juvenile cats").
- Sentences that are false in virtue of the meanings of the words they contain (e.g., "Oscar is a kitten but not a cat").
- Sentences that can be verified or falsified empirically (e.g., "It will rain sometime today in Times Square").

Verificationists sometimes claim that an obscure philosophical claim is not literally meaningful because it doesn't fall into one of these three categories. For example, the philosopher A. J. Ayer argued in this way that Heidegger's claim that "The Nothing nothings" is not literally meaningful.

Comprehension Questions

1. What is the problem of other minds? What is the mind-body problem?
2. Give three examples of *conscious* states. (Don't repeat examples from the chapter).
3. Give three examples of *intentional* states. (Don't repeat examples from the chapter).
4. What is Cartesian dualism?
5. What was Princess Elisabeth's objection to Cartesian dualism? What other objections to Cartesian dualism are there?
6. What is pain? Answer from the point of view of a behaviorist.
7. Opponents of behaviorism have argued that the theory has some highly counterintuitive consequences. Explain one of these.
8. Consider the following behavioristic analysis of the sentence "John is in pain":

    "John is in pain" means *John is disposed to scream.*

    Is this an adequate analysis? Why or why not?
9. What is the mind-brain identity theory?
10. Briefly describe the causal role of *disgust*. Now consider this question:

    What is disgust?

    Answer from the point of view of a mind-brain identity theorist, an analytic functionalist, and a psychofunctionalist.
11. Some analytic functionalists allege that the mind-brain identity theory is "chauvinistic," and that their own theory is not. Explain these claims.
12. What is the difference between analytic functionalism and psychofunctionalism?
13. An eliminativist and a psychofunctionalist are likely to agree that folk psychology is false, at least in part. What is the difference between eliminativism and psychofunctionalism?
14. Explain Ned Block's objection to functionalism.
15. What is a philosophical zombie? How do philosophical zombies differ from ordinary people?

Discussion Questions

1. We began the chapter by listing four questions which are central to the philosophy of mind:
   (i) Do other people (and things like robots or fish) have mental states?
   (ii) Are their mental states similar to yours?
   (iii) How can we know?
   (iv) How are mental states and processes related to physical and biological and behavioral phenomena?
   Answer these questions from the point of view of a dualist, a behaviorist, a mind-brain identity theorist, and a functionalist. And what do *you* think about these four questions?

2. Close your eyes, and visualize a red cube. Now that you've done that, consider this question:

   Where is that red cube located?

   Before you commit yourself to an answers, read endnote 5 and section 11.4.

3. Have a go at producing a behaviorist analysis of "Fred is in pain." What obstacles do you find?

4. Suppose that a person is permanently paralyzed, in such a way that they can no longer operate their skeletal muscles. Is it possible for this person to have mental states? Answer from the point of view of (a) a dualist, (b) a behaviorist, (c) an identity theorist, and (d) a functionalist.

5. Suppose that we make contact with an alien civilization. After a great deal of effort, we find that we can translate back-and-forth between their language and our own. We are then able to trade with them, learn about their achievements in science and engineering, study their social and political systems, and so on. As we do all of this, we find it natural to attribute mental states to the aliens. We say things like:
   - The aliens believe that our understanding of physics and mathematics is rudimentary.
   - That alien is jealous.
   - That alien is cheerful.

One day, however, we get to look inside one of these aliens—and we find nothing inside the alien that looks anything like a human brain. Does this establish that the aliens don't really have mental states? Answer from the point of view of (a) a dualist, (b) a behaviorist, (c) an identity theorist, and (d) a functionalist.

6. In science fiction stories, it is sometimes suggested that, in the distant future, it will be possible to transfer a person's mind into a computer. (The procedure might be performed, for example, if the person's body was irreparably damaged.) Is this really possible?

7. Suppose that an eliminativist (in the course of everyday life) says things like "I'm tired" and "That baby is crying because it is hungry." A critic might accuse the eliminativist of inconsistency. Is this an important objection to eliminativism?

8. Some people believe that their minds will continue to exist after they have died—and, indeed, after their bodies have rotted away. Discuss whether this is really possible.

9. You have been in charge of a zoological research team. Your job is to figure out whether lobsters experience pain. How would go about your task? What experiments would you need to perform? (For a discussion of the moral significance of animal pain, see chapter 16.)

10. You have been in charge of a research team. Your job is to figure out when fetuses first become conscious. How would go about your task? (For a discussion of the moral significance of the consciousness of fetuses, see chapter 16.)

11. You have been in charge of a research team. Your job is to figure out whether anyone in your city is a zombie. How would you go about your task?

What to Look at Next

- Many textbooks on the philosophy of mind have been written. Here are three of our favorites:
  - *Mindware: An Introduction to the Philosophy of Cognitive Science* by Andy Clark.

- *Matter and Consciousness* by Paul Churchland.
- *Philosophy of Mind: A Contemporary Introduction* by John Heil.
- You can find a translation of Descartes's *Meditations on First Philosophy* at www.earlymoderntexts.com. Descartes discusses the philosophy of mind in meditations V and VI.
- Selections from the correspondence between Descartes and Princess Elisabeth can be found in Margaret Atherton, ed., *Women Philosophers of the Early Modern Period*.
- For a much more recent defense of dualism, see Karl Popper and John C. Eccles, *The Self and Its Brain*.
- The most important presentation of philosophical behaviorism is *The Concept of Mind* by Gilbert Ryle. Bear in mind as you read this book that Ryle's version of behaviorism was sophisticated and complex—so it diverges in some ways from the simple version of behaviorism that we described in section 11.2.
- Two classic presentations of the mind-brain identity theory are:
  - U. T. Place, "Is Consciousness a Brain Process?", *British Journal of Psychology*, 46, no. 1 (1956): 44–50.
  - Herbert Feigl, *The "Mental" and the "Physical": The Essay and a Postscript* (Minneapolis: University of Minnesota Press, 1967).
  Though historically important, both of these papers are quite difficult. For much more accessible discussions of the mind-brain identity theory, see Steven Schneider's article "Identity Theory" in the *Internet Encyclopedia of Philosophy* and "The Case for Physicalism," which is chapter 5 in Peter Carruthers's book *The Nature of the Mind: An Introduction*.
- Hilary Putnam was an early proponent of functionalism. His most important papers on the topic are collected in his *Mind, Language and Reality: Philosophical Papers Volume Two*. See also Jerry Fodor's *Psychological Explanation*.
- Ned Block presents some important objections to functionalism in his "Troubles with Functionalism"; it includes the "China brain" thought experiment, which we discussed in section 11.4.[17]
- Thomas Nagel's "What Is It Like to Be a Bat?"[18] is one of the most famous papers ever written in the philosophy of mind—and not only because it has such an arresting title.
- Some philosophers believe that we can make progress in the philosophy of mind only by paying detailed attention

to neuroscience. One of the leaders of this group is Patricia Churchland. Two of her books have been particularly influential: *Neurophilosophy: Toward a Unified Science of the Mind-Brain* and *Brain-Wise: Studies in Neurophilosophy*.
- Many science fiction films explore the question of what it would take to manufacture a conscious thing. One of the best is *Blade Runner*, directed by Ridley Scott. The central character in the movie is tasked with finding and "retiring" a number of "replicants"— synthetic humans. See the director's cut if you can, and try to spot a quote from Descartes. The movie was based on the novel *Do Androids Dream of Electric Sheep?* by Philip K. Dick.

Notes

1. For simplicity, we have used the word "imagine" in our description of Descartes's argument, but it is arguably a slightly inaccurate term to use. In Jonathan Bennett's translation, the crucial premise of Descartes's argument is "[T]he fact that I can vividly and clearly think of one thing apart from another assures me that the two things are distinct from one another." For a more detailed discussion of this argument, see Gary Hatfield's *Routledge Philosophy Guidebook to Descartes and the Meditations* (London: Routledge, 2003).
2. We'll discuss Chalmers's argument in section 11.5.
3. There are other sorts of mind-body dualism, but we won't discuss them until the final paragraphs of this chapter. Until then, when we use the term "dualism," we'll always mean substance dualism.
4. George Berkeley was not a dualist. He didn't believe in the existence of matter! See chapter Six for discussion.
5. This is not as strange as it might seem. Think about the second exercise, the one in which you had the visual experience of a blue rectangle. Where, in space, does this experience exist? Many contemporary readers are inclined to respond that it exists in their brain. But this response faces an obvious objection: there is nothing in your brain that is blue and rectangular! (If there is, then we strongly urge that you stop reading immediately and go to the emergency room at the nearest hospital.) Perhaps there is a good response to this objection; philosophers have made a number of proposals. However, we think that the problem the objection raises is enough to show that Descartes's view is far from unmotivated. If one thinks that perceptual experiences and other mental states are located in space, it is not easy to give a plausible account of where they are.

6. These questions are important in ethics. We normally suppose that horses can feel pain, and we try to avoid causing pain to horses gratuitously. But what about fish? What about lobsters? What about crickets? See chapter 16 for a discussion of animal pain and vegetarianism.
7. At about the same time that philosophical behaviorism was being developed, psychologists, led by J. B. Watson and B. F. Skinner, were advocating another view that is also called "behaviorism." To distinguish the two, we'll call the psychologists' view "psychological behaviorism." Psychological behaviorism is a methodological doctrine that urges psychologists not to posit unobservable mental states of the people and other organisms they study, but to focus on observable phenomena that impinge on organisms (sounds, patterns of light, electric shocks, etc.) and observable patterns of behavior. For the remainder of this chapter, when we use the term "behaviorism," we'll be talking about philosophical behaviorism.
8. This particular example is taken from Ayer's *Language, Truth and Logic* (London: Gollancz, 1946). The verificationists acknowledged that what they called **literal meaningfulness** (being either true or false) was not the only kind of meaning. Some declarative sentences that are not literally meaningful can evoke an emotional response in listeners and thus have **emotive meaning**. Favorite examples were sentences from the great English writer of nonsense, Lewis Carroll (1832–1898). This is the first stanza of Carroll's "Jabberwocky":

'Twas brillig, and the slithy toves
Did gyre and gimble in the wabe:
All mimsy were the borogoves,
And the mome raths outgrabe.

Obviously, this is neither true nor false. But many readers find it amusing, and it evokes a happy smile.
9. See his discussion of "super-spartans" in "Brains and Behavior," in his *Mind, Language and Reality: Philosophical Papers, Volume 2* (Cambridge, UK: Cambridge University Press, 1975).
10. A variation on this argument goes like this. As you look at a blue cube from different angles, the blue thing you see changes shape. However, the physical blue cube doesn't change shape. Therefore, the blue thing you see is not the physical cube. The thing that you see, then, must be a mental object—but the identity theorist has no plausible account of where this mental object is located. You might recognize this argument from chapter 6.
11. In his book *The Mysterious Flame* (New York: Basic Books, 1999), Colin McGinn makes the case for mysterianism.
12. With some sophisticated logical machinery, the implicit definition provided by the causal flowchart can be transformed into an explicit definition. If you'd

like to see how this works, see David Lewis, "How to Define Theoretical Terms," *Journal of Philosophy* 67, no. 13 (1970): 426–446.
13. Paul Churchland, "Eliminative Materialism and the Propositional Attitudes," *Journal of Philosophy* 78 (1981): 67–90.
14. See his "Troubles with Functionalism," in C. W. Savage, ed., *Perception and Cognition: Issues in the Foundations of Psychology* (Minneapolis: University of Minnesota Press, 1978).
15. For Chalmers's initial version of the argument, see his book *The Conscious Mind: In Search of a Fundamental Theory* (Oxford: Oxford University Press, 1996), Section II. Robert Kirk's "Zombies" in the *Stanford Encyclopedia of Philosophy* (https://plato.stanford.edu/archives/spr2021/entries/zombies/) provides a readily accessible guide to the ongoing debate that the argument has provoked.
16. Sometimes the term "cognitively meaningful" is used instead.
17. Ned Block, "Troubles with Functionalism," *Minnesota Studies in the Philosophy of Science* no. 9 (1978): 261–325.
18. Thomas Nagel, "What Is It Like to Be a Bat" in *Mortal Questions* (Cambridge: Cambridge University Press, 1991): 165–180.

CHAPTER 12

Will You Be the Same Person in Ten Years? Could You Survive Death?

12.1 The Philosophical Issue and Its Practical Importance

"Ivan the Terrible" was the grim nickname of one of the most brutal and sadistic guards at Treblinka, a Nazi death camp where almost a million innocent people, mostly Jews, were murdered. Ivan was notorious for torturing prisoners with pipes and whips as they headed to the gas chamber, and for cutting off people's ears, then forcing them to continue working as blood flowed from their wounds. In 1975, John Demjanjuk, a Ukranian-born auto worker in Michigan who had emigrated to the United States in 1952, was accused of being Ivan the Terrible. After a long legal battle, Demjanjuk was stripped of his American citizenship and deported to Israel, where he was convicted in 1988 and sentenced to death. Demjanjuk, who insisted he was not Ivan the Terrible, appealed to the Israeli Supreme Court, and on the basis of documents that had only become available after the collapse of the Soviet Union in 1991, the court overturned Demjanjuk's conviction. They ruled there was reasonable doubt that Demjanjuk and Ivan the Terrible were the same man.[1]

The story of Ivan the Terrible illustrates both the philosophical issue that will be center stage in this chapter and its importance. The question that the courts had to decide was whether Ivan the Terrible and John Demjanjuk were the same person—or, as philosophers sometimes say, whether they were *identical*. But this terminology is all too easy to misunderstand. The question is *not* whether the man on trial in Israel and the barbaric guard at Treblinka are the same in every respect. Of course they are not. Ivan the Terrible was in his mid-twenties when he committed his crimes; Demjanjuk was in his seventies when the Israeli Supreme Court threw out his conviction. Ivan had a full head of hair; Demjanjuk was bald. Demjanjuk spoke English; Ivan did not. The term "identical" sometimes means something like *completely similar in every respect*. That's what we mean when we say that two TV sets, on sale at two different stores, are identical. When this sense of the term is intended, philosophers often say that the objects in question are qualitatively identical—that is, they have **qualitative identity**. But that is not what the courts were trying to determine. What the courts needed to know is whether the brutal prison guard and the retired auto worker were identical—whether they were the same person—in a sense of these terms that does not require similarity in every respect. To make the distinction clear, philosophers sometimes use the expression **numerical identity** for the kind of identity that the courts were interested in. What the courts had to decide was whether Ivan the Terrible and John Demjanjuk were numerically identical.

We use this idea of numerical identity frequently in our daily lives. Is that young woman at the frat party the girl who sat in front of you in third grade? Is the woman being interviewed on TV, who has just won a Nobel Prize, the star student in Stich's Introduction to Philosophy course back in 1980? Although these questions, and endlessly many like them, rarely use the terms "same" or "identical," what they are asking is whether the people in question are numerically identical. Though the idea of numerical identity is familiar and widely used, in this chapter we'll see it is an idea that is very hard to analyze. What, exactly, has to be the case for it to be true that the young woman at the frat party is numerically identical with the kid who sat in front of you in third grade? That's the question we will be trying to answer. The issue is sometimes called the "problem of personal identity."

One part of the answer that is accepted by many, though not all, of the philosophers who have thought about this topic is that numerical identity is what logicians call **equivalence relation**—it is **reflexive**, **symmetric**, and **transitive**.[2]

There are many reasons why the notion of personal identity is of great practical importance. One of them is clearly illustrated by the story of John Demjanjuk. Ivan the Terrible was a monster who committed hideous crimes. There is a good case to be made that Ivan should be punished for his crimes. But of course, it would be a horrible miscarriage of justice to punish Demjanjuk for Ivan's crimes if Ivan and Demjanjuk are not the same person. The numerical identity of the perpetrator and the accused seems to be a **necessary condition** that our moral and legal principles place on holding an accused person responsible and punishing them.[3]

Personal identity can also be enormously important for reasons having nothing to do with responsibility and punishment. The film *Philomena* tells the true story of Philomena Lee, an unwed mother whose child, Anthony, was born in a Catholic convent in Ireland. When the child was a toddler, the nuns gave (or perhaps sold) the boy to an American couple, who adopted him and renamed him Michael. Philomena was given no choice or warning of the adoption and was not even allowed to say goodbye to her son. Fifty years later, Philomena joined forces with a British journalist in an attempt to track down her son. Tragically, they discover that he had died of AIDS some years earlier, and that he had spent the final months of his life in an unsuccessful effort to find his mother. At Michael's request, his lover arranged for him to be buried in the graveyard of the Irish convent where he was born. The movie ends with Philomena visiting her son's grave. At the end of his life, Michael was, of course, very different from the little boy that Philomena cherished. But for Philomena, those differences were unimportant. What she desperately wanted, but never achieved, was to be reunited with her son, the man who was numerically identical with the toddler who had been taken from her decades earlier.

Thus far, we have been focusing on the practical importance of the personal identity of other people. But for most of us, our own personal identity is also of great practical importance. To see the point, let's consider a rather fanciful example. Suppose an eccentric billionaire announces that he plans to give one of the students at your university 20 million dollars five years from now. The recipient has been selected by lottery, and the person's identity will be revealed in five years. That's intriguing news, of course, though it probably would not make much of an impact on your current life. But now suppose you learn from a reliable source that the person who will get the money in five years is *you*. That would, no doubt, make you very happy, and it might well have a major impact on your current plans and decisions. What this story illustrates is that, like everyone else, you have a special concern about your own future self—the person in the future who is numerically identical to you.

We all know that, at some time in the future, we will die. Your future self—a person numerically identical to you, though hopefully a lot older—will pass away, and your body will be buried or cremated. However, most of the world's major religions maintain that when your body dies, *you* do not go out of existence permanently. Rather, these religions insist, after a person dies there is an afterlife that may be extraordinarily pleasant or unimaginably horrible. What these religions are claiming is that after your body dies, you can continue to exist—there will be a being somewhere in the universe who is numerically identical to you. Though many people are skeptical of the claim that they will exist after the death of their body, most people strongly *desire* that it be true. But it is no easy job to say what would satisfy this desire. To see why this is so, consider the prediction, made in a number of places in the Bible, that on judgment day, the dead will be resurrected.

What, exactly, would God have to do to resurrect you a few hundred (or a few thousand) years after your body decays? One obvious thought is that God would have to create a living human body that was exactly similar to you a moment before your death (or perhaps at some earlier time). But even if God did this, it is far from clear that this living human body would be *you*. To see why, imagine that, as you are on your death bed, God appears and reassures you that you will not cease to exist when your body dies. And to prove the point, God creates, there in front of you, a living human being who is an exact replica of you. "There you are," God says, "resurrected even before you die. In a few hours, after you die, I will miraculously cure all the illnesses that afflict your resurrected body."

People have quite different reactions to this philosophical thought experiment. One widespread reaction is that if *that* is what God proposes to do, then the promise of an afterlife is a sham. Those who have this reaction insist that, while the replica is an exact copy of you, it isn't really *you*. You and the replica are not numerically identical. Thus, the fact that the replica will continue to exist after your body dies is no solace at all. If that's all that God is offering, then when your body dies, you will no longer exist. Now, of course, no one in the Christian tradition suggests that, in order to fulfill the promise of resurrection, God will create a replica of you while you are still alive. Rather, they claim, the resurrection will occur at some time in the future, on judgment day. But if an exact replica of you isn't you a few hours before you die, then it is hard to see why an exact replica of you *is* you on judgment day. The upshot of all this is that it is far from clear that God could fulfill the promise of life after death merely by creating a perfect replica of you on judgment day, since you and the replica would not be the same person; you would not be numerically identical. If this is right, then exact similarity (or qualitative identity) is neither necessary nor sufficient for numerical identity, or for continued existence. So what *is* required? That is the question that philosophical theories of personal identity try to answer.

12.2 The Soul Theory

The oldest theory of personal identity, and the one that is probably most widely accepted by nonphilosophers around the world, explains personal identity by invoking the **soul**. According to this theory, the soul is a nonphysical, nonmaterial part of a person. For our purposes, the claim that the soul is **nonmaterial** means that it is not made of matter, and the claim that it is **nonphysical** means that it cannot be detected or studied by physics or any of the other natural sciences. The soul is claimed to be the **seat of consciousness**—it is the part of us that is conscious, the part that has conscious experiences. But the soul is not itself ever perceived in our conscious experience; though we are consciously aware of lots of things, we are never consciously aware of our own soul. The soul is also, according to many soul theorists, the part of us that engages in thought—so it is the part of us that is conscious and thinks. If you have read chapter 11, you will have noticed that when characterized in this way, the soul seems to be a lot like the mind, as conceived by Descartes and those in the Cartesian dualist tradition. And while those who think the soul holds the key to personal identity need not endorse everything Descartes says about the mind, in this chapter we can take the soul to be very similar to the **Cartesian mind**.

According to soul theorists, under ordinary circumstances each normal living human body is linked to a soul, and it is the soul that determines personal identity. If a body at one point in time and a body later in time are linked to the same soul, then the complex consisting of the body and the soul at the earlier time is numerically identical with the complex consisting of the body and the soul at the later time; they are the same person, no matter how physically similar or dissimilar the bodies may be. But if a body at an earlier time and a body at a later time are linked to different souls, then there are two persons, not one.

To get a clearer idea of what, exactly, the soul theory of personal identity is claiming, we'll apply it to two of the examples discussed earlier. Let's start with Ivan the Terrible. According to soul theory, the perpetrator of the sadistic crimes at the Treblinka death camp was a person who, like all people, consisted of a body and a soul. Many decades later, a person called "John Demjanjuk" appeared before a court in Israel. That person, too, consisted of a body and a soul. The body was in many ways different from the body of the concentration camp guard. It was older, heavier, bald, and so forth. But was the person on trial Ivan the Terrible? The answer, according to the soul theory, is that it was Ivan if and only if the soul linked to the twenty-five-year-old body of the concentration camp guard was the same as the soul linked to the much older body of the person on trial. If Ivan the Terrible and John Demjanjuk did not have the same soul, then the Israelis had the wrong man.

Next, let's consider the biblical promise of resurrection. In one of our hypothetical scenarios, we imagined that God creates an exact replica of your body a few hours before you die. Many people would insist that's not *you*, and soul theorists would surely agree. For if that replica body is conscious and capable of thinking, soul theorists maintain, it must be linked to a soul. And while it may be linked to a soul that is very similar to your soul, it is not linked to *your* soul. You don't have the replica's perceptions or feel the replica's pains. So the person God has created is someone else.

But what could God do to fulfill the promise of resurrection on judgment day? The soul theorist has a clear answer: God could create a living human body, preferably one that was reasonably similar to your body at some point in your life, and *attach your soul to that body*. For the soul theorist, it is the last step, which was not mentioned in our earlier discussion of resurrection, that is crucial. If God is going to bring *you* back to life many years after you die, he has to link *your soul* to a new body.

So far, we've been assuming that what your soul gets linked to at resurrection is a human body. But that's not essential. Some theologians in the Christian tradition think your soul will get linked to a spiritual body of some sort. And many Hindus believe that the soul, after a person's body dies, is sometimes linked to the body of a nonhuman animal. So while a person may be reincarnated with a human body, he may also be reincarnated as a cow, or even an insect.

12.3 Problems for Soul Theory

One of the virtues of the soul theory of personal identity is that it gives a clear and simple account of when a person existing at one time is numerically identical with a person existing at another time: they are the same person if and only if they are linked to the same soul. However, philosophers and scientists have raised some serious objections to the soul theory. The first of these is that there is arguably a substantial body of evidence suggesting that souls *do not exist*. According to the soul theory, the soul is an immaterial thing that is the seat of consciousness and the part of a person that thinks. It is, near enough, a Cartesian mind. But most contemporary neuroscientists, and most philosophers as well, think that the *brain* is the part of us that thinks and is the seat of consciousness. If these neuroscientists and philosophers are correct, then the part of us that thinks and is conscious is not immaterial. Quite the opposite. It is about three pounds of enormously complicated neural circuitry, made up of something in the vicinity of 100 billion neurons. Clearly, if souls like those that the soul theory invokes to explain personal identity do not exist, then the soul theory of personal identity is mistaken.

Even if immaterial souls do exist, however, it is far from clear that soul theory provides the right account of personal identity. One influential argument against soul theory focuses on our beliefs about personal identity and the extent to which those beliefs are justified. In unusual cases, like that of Ivan the Terrible, we may be very unsure about a question of personal identity. But in most cases, we have no doubt at all about our personal identity judgments. Suppose, for example, that you live on campus and go home to visit your family every few weeks. The next time you go home, there will be a man weeding in the garden. He'll look very similar to the man you saw the last time you went home. He answers to the name "Dad," and he remembers lots of things about what you did and talked about on your previous visits. (He also remembers some pretty embarrassing things you did when you were younger, but fortunately, he rarely mentions them.) Though there may be a bit of variation in his mood from one visit to the next, his personality and temperament are much the same as they were on previous visits. Under these circumstances, after a few minutes of conversation, you would be quite certain that this man is your dad. He's the same person who cooked dinner for you on your last visit home, and the same person who took care of you when you were little. There's nothing surprising about any of this. Indeed, under ordinary circumstances, if you have any doubt at all that this man is your dad, we might well begin to worry about you!

But if the soul theory of personal identity is correct, then it would be entirely reasonable to doubt that this man is your dad. According to the soul theory, when you judge that this man is the same person as the man who raised you, what you are judging is that this man and the man who raised you are connected to the same soul. Since that soul is immaterial, neither you nor anyone else can see it or touch it, or detect it in any other way. So it seems that you don't have any evidence at all that this nice man weeding the garden is the same person as the man who raised you. Perhaps it is the same body (though older and with a bit more gray hair and a few more wrinkles) linked up to a soul that is different from the one that was linked to the man you called "Dad" when you were ten! It looks like you don't have, and perhaps can't have, any evidence that this is not the case.

Confronted with this problem, a soul theorist might argue that the soul, in addition to being the locus of thought and consciousness, is also the locus of memory and personality. And because of this, the soul theorist might claim, the facts about Dad's personality now and his memory of you as a ten-year-old count as evidence that Dad now and Dad back then are really the same person. But this argument does not really handle the objection. To be sure, if Dad now had a very different personality from Dad back then and could not remember what Dad back then did, that might be evidence that Dad now and Dad back then are linked to different souls and are different people. But if Dad now has the same personality as Dad back then and remembers what Dad back then did, that's not evidence that they share a soul. For these facts are compatible with the hypothesis that the soul of Dad now is very similar to the soul of Dad back then, though it is a numerically different soul. And that's the hypothesis that needs to be ruled out. Unless soul theorists can show that the existence of similar but numerically distinct souls is impossible or unlikely, they have not shown that you are justified in believing that Dad now and Dad back then are the same person.

The problem we have just posed for the soul theory is not, of course, restricted to your beliefs about your dad. It applies equally to your beliefs about anyone, including *yourself*! You may have a memory of taking a tough final exam last term and of being very pleased with yourself when you learned that you got a good grade. But do you really deserve that grade? Not if someone else took the exam and wrote your name on it. Right, you say, but that did not happen. Well, what evidence do you have that you really took the exam? Perhaps on the day of the exam your body was linked to a soul that was disconnected from your body on the night after the exam, and your body was then linked up to another soul that was very similar (or qualitatively identical) to the old one, packed with similar memories but numerically distinct. If that happened, then, if the soul theory is correct, you should not get credit for the good grade because the person who took the exam was someone else. Moreover, since neither you nor anyone else can perceive your immaterial soul, it is hard to see how you or anyone else could justify your belief that *you* took the exam. Indeed, neither you nor anyone else can justify your belief that you (the body-plus-soul complex that is reading this sentence) existed on the day of the exam. If these consequences of the soul theory strike you as implausible or absurd, then you'll need a different account of personal identity.

12.4 Memory Theories

According to the contemporary philosopher Sydney Shoemaker (1931–2022), "the history of the topic of personal identity has been a series of footnotes to [John] Locke."[4] While this may be something of an exaggeration, it is clear that Locke had, and continues to have, an enormous influence on thinking about personal identity. The puzzles about resurrection that we considered earlier were hotly debated in Locke's time, and for reasons like those we just discussed, Locke rejected the soul theory of personal identity. Rather, he suggested, personal identity is determined by a cluster of psychological properties, the most important of which is memory. In this section, we'll explain both the attractions and the problems of theories in the Lockean tradition.[5]

To begin, we'll present our own version of one of Locke's most famous thought experiments. Imagine there is a town in which the prince lives in a grand castle and the cobbler lives in a humble cottage. One night, as usual, the prince goes to bed in the castle, and the cobbler goes to bed in his cottage. But somehow, the prince's memories are transferred overnight to the cobbler, and the cobbler's memories are transferred to the prince. So when the morning arrives, the cobbler's body wakes up with the memories of the prince, and the prince's body wakes up with the memories of the cobbler. Which of these people, Locke asks, is *really* the prince? Is it the one who knows his way around the palace and remembers what the prince has done in the past, or is it the one who has no memory of ever being in the palace and who only remembers events that occurred in the cobbler's life? Locke thinks the answer is obvious: the prince is the person who has the prince's memories and the cobbler's body. He's the one we would hold responsible for deeds the prince has done in the past; he's the one we would praise or blame for those deeds. It would, Locke suggests, be a great injustice if the man who woke up in the palace with the prince's body and the cobbler's memories were to be punished for some past deed done by the prince, since he has no memory of doing that deed. If the prince committed a crime a week before the memory switch, it's the person with the cobbler's body who remembers committing the crime and who may well feel guilty about what he did. Before reading further, pause for a minute and ask yourself whether you agree with Locke. Which of these men do you think is the prince? Which one should be held accountable for the things the prince did in the past?

Locke suggests that memory is a crucial determinant of personal identity. But there are many ways in which this idea might be unpacked. We'll start by setting out a very simple version of a Lockean memory theory, and noting some of the problems that theory confronts. We'll then propose a series of modifications, each aimed at dealing with the problems posed for earlier versions. In setting out these theories, the idea of a **person stage** will be very useful. A person stage is just a short, temporal segment of the life of a person. If we arbitrarily stipulate that the length of a person stage is ten seconds, then you will pass through six person stages in the next minute. A person's life, then, is a long sequence of person stages, such as those shown in figure 12.1. Using the idea of a person stage, we can pose the central question of personal

John Locke (1632–1704) pioneered the memory theory of personal identity.

identity in the following way: When are two person stages parts of the life of the same person?

We can now formulate the following very simple version of the memory theory:

Memory theory—Version 1
A person stage at an earlier time (for example, t_2) and a person stage at a later time (for example, t_{102}) are parts of the same person's life if and only if the later person stage can remember an experience that the earlier person stage had.

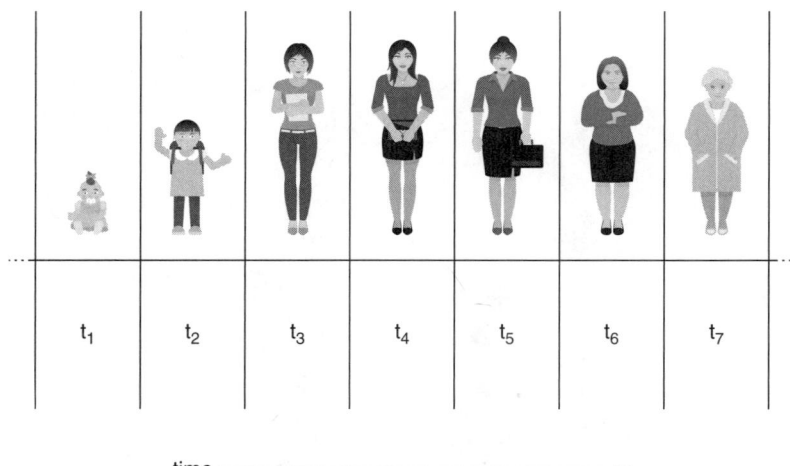

FIGURE 12.1 Life as a series of person stages

On this theory, if there was a person who took an exam with your name on it a month ago, you are that person if and only if you remember taking the exam. This application of the theory is depicted in figure 12.2.

Though it is a promising start, a number of philosophers during the century after Locke's death pointed out what look to be very serious problems with this version of the memory theory. Two of Locke's most acute critics were Bishop Joseph Butler (1692–1752) and Thomas Reid (1710–1796).[6] We'll look at two of their objections in turn.

To explain the first objection, we need to draw a distinction between **real memories** and **apparent memories**. From time to time, memory plays tricks on us. We have what seems to be a real memory, but the event we seem to be remembering never actually happened. Have you ever had an experience like this? If not, ask around; you'll probably find that some of your friends have. Here's an example that one of us can share with you. As a seven-year-old, Stich went to summer camp with one of his cousins, and one day, the cousin got into a rather messy food fight. At the end of the summer, one of the counselors told Stich's parents about the fight. But the counselor had gotten confused about who actually took part in the fight. She said that it was Stich, not his cousin, who was throwing bread and shooting spoonfuls of chocolate pudding

Will You Be the Same Person in Ten Years? Could You Survive Death? 251

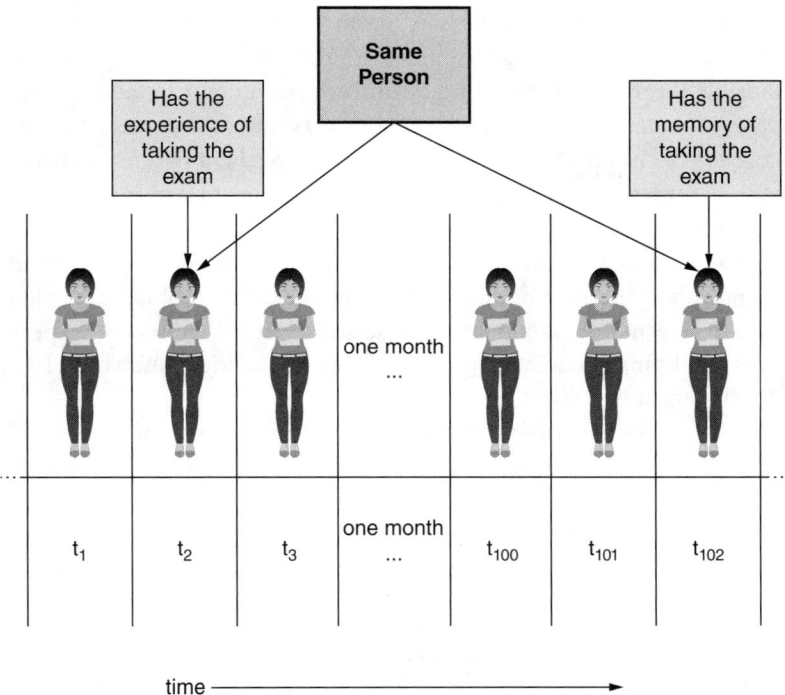

FIGURE 12.2 An illustration of the *Memory theory—Version 1*

across the dining room. A few years later, Stich's parents told this story, with some amusement, over the dinner table. Stich didn't remember the event. But the story was a great hit and so was repeated many times over the years. By the time Stich was an adult, he had what seemed to be a vivid memory of engaging in the summer camp food fight. But it was just an apparent memory, not a real one—a fact Stich only discovered when he was in his fifties and told the story about the food fight to his cousin, who assured Stich that he had not participated in the dining hall debacle. Stich never really had the experience of lobbing chocolate pudding in the summer camp dining room. It was his cousin who had that experience!

OK. Now that you know what an apparent memory is, the problem is easy to see. Version 1 of the memory theory implies that if a person stage at a later time remembers experiences of an earlier person stage, then the two person stages are parts of a single life. But this claim is only plausible if the "memories" in question are *real* memories and not just *apparent* memories. This means that our version of the memory theory is useless in the absence of some explanation of the difference between real and apparent memories. Locke's critics challenged him to provide just such an explanation.

Some Lockeans have suggested that real and apparent memories are distinguished by their *origin*. Stich's "memories" of lobbing chocolate pudding are merely apparent because they weren't caused by experiences of lobbing chocolate pudding—they were formed much later, long after the event had taken place.

We use the term **s-memory** as a label for things that *seem* to be memories, whether real or not. Real memories are s-memories; apparent memories are also s-memories. Using this new word, we can formulate a new version of the memory theory:

> *Memory theory—Version 2*
> A person stage at an earlier time (for example, t_2) and a person stage at a later time (for example, t_{102}) are parts of the same person's life if and only if the later person stage has an s-memory of an experience that the earlier person stage had and the s-memory is caused by the experience.

On this account, person stages of the prince's body before the memory swap and of the cobbler's body after the swap are stages of the same person's life because the s-memories that the person with the cobbler's body has after the swap are caused by experiences that the person with the prince's body had before the swap.

Version 2 of the memory theory is a clear improvement over Version 1, but it is still imperfect. You can see this by thinking about the fact that memories often disappear over time. Suppose, for example, that you took that exam we used as an example in figure 12.2, and that you still remember it clearly at a rather wild and joyous graduation party a month later. For reasons best not discussed, the graduation party was *very* memorable. You remember it clearly and reminisce about it at your twenty-fifth class reunion. However, by that time, you have completely forgotten about the exam. All of this seems quite plausible. But it creates a major problem for Version 2 of the memory theory. Let's say that

t_E is the time of the exam, t_P is the time of the graduation party, and t_R is the time of the reunion. Then, according to the theory we are considering, the person who took the exam at t_E is the same—that is, is numerically identical with—the person who went to the wild party at t_P. And the person who went to the party at t_P is numerically identical with the person who went to the reunion at t_R. But since by the time your twenty-fifth reunion rolls around you have completely forgotten about the exam, the person who took the exam is *not* numerically identical with the person who went to the reunion. And that's impossible! For as we noted earlier, numerical identity is an equivalence relation, and equivalence relations are *transitive*. If A (the exam-taker) is identical with B (the partygoer), and if B is identical with C (the person at the reunion), then A must be identical with C.

To deal with this example, we can exploit the fact that there is a segment of your life during which you remember the exam, and that there is a segment of your life during which you remember the party, *and that these segments overlap*, as shown in figure 12.3.

Specifically, the exam-taker (at t_E) is numerically identical to the partygoer (at t_P) because the partygoer has an appropriately caused s-memory of taking the exam; the person at the reunion (at t_R) is numerically identical to the partygoer because the person at the reunion has an appropriately caused s-memory of being at the party. What's more, because the exam-taker is numerically identical to the partygoer and the partygoer is numerically identical with the person at the reunion, the exam-taker is numerically identical to the person at the reunion.

Here is another example. Suppose that Sam was ten in 1960, and suppose that since 1960 his memory has always stretched back only ten years. A Lockean might say that the Sam of 1970 is numerically identical to the Sam of 1960, because 1970-Sam has an s-memory of an experience that 1960-Sam had and the s-memory is caused by the experience. In the same way, the Lockean may argue that 1980-Sam is numerically identical to 1970-Sam, and that 1990-Sam is numerically identical to 1980-Sam. Putting this together, the Lockean may infer that 1990-Sam and 1960-Sam are the same person—even though by 1990, Sam's memories of the 1960s were long gone, as depicted in figure 12.4.

To put it metaphorically, 1990-Sam is connected to 1960-Sam by a chain of overlapping person segments. Here's one way of setting out the idea in detail.

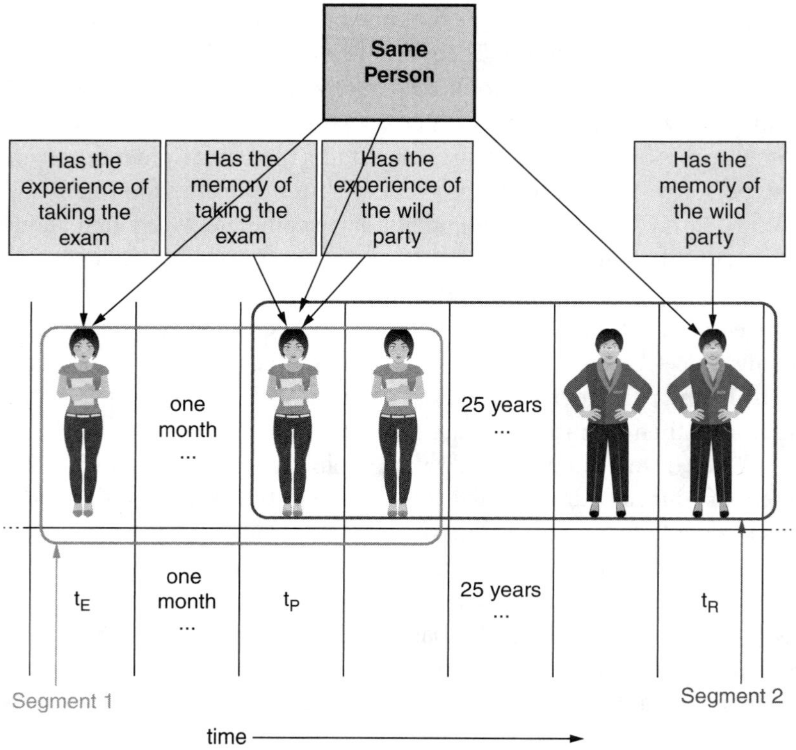

254   Philosophy: Asking Questions—Seeking Answers

FIGURE 12.3 An illustration of the *Memory theory—Version 3*

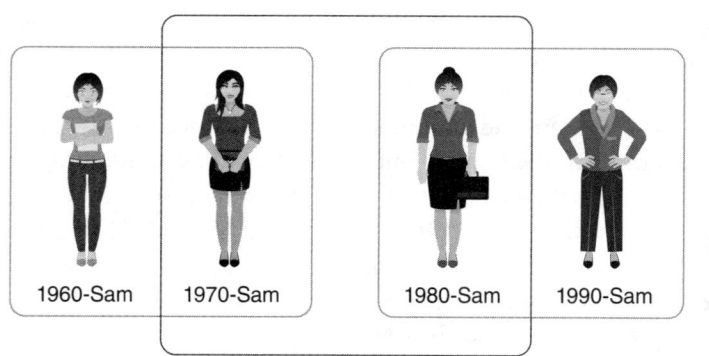

FIGURE 12.4 An illustration of the *Memory theory—Version 3*

Memory theory—Version 3
  (i) A person stage at an earlier time and a person stage at a later time are stages of the same *person segment* if and only if the later person stage has an s-memory of an experience that the earlier person stage had and the s-memory is caused by the experience.
  (ii) Two person segments *overlap* if there is some person stage that is part of each of them.
  (iii) A person stage at an earlier time and a person stage at a later time are parts of the same person's life if and only if *either* (a) the two person stages are parts of the same person segment *or* (b) the earlier person stage is part of a person segment S_1, which overlaps with a person segment S_2, which overlaps . . . which overlaps with a person segment S_n, which contains the later person stage.

Though Version 3 of the memory theory can sidestep some of the problems that were posed by Bishop Butler, Thomas Reid, and other historically important critics of Locke's memory theory, contemporary philosophers have posed additional problems based on thought experiments inspired by contemporary science fiction. In the long-running *Star Trek* television series, and the dozen or so movies it inspired, a piece of equipment known as a "transporter" often plays an important role. (Philosophers sometimes use the longer term "teletransporter" when discussing the device.) For our purposes, the teletransporter can be thought of as a device that makes a precise scan of every atom in a person's body. In the process, the body is destroyed. However, the information recorded in the scan is sent to a second device that builds an atom-for-atom copy of the body that was destroyed. Since the information can be sent from the first device to the second via radio waves, it enables a person to travel from one place to another at the speed of light. Or does it? Some philosophers, and some science fiction buffs as well, have insisted that the person who steps out of the receiving teletransporter is not the same person as the one who stepped into the sending teletransporter unit. But Version 3 of the memory theory seems to say otherwise. The s-memories of the person who steps out of the transporter are caused by the experiences of the person who steps in. So on Version 3 of the memory theory, the person who arrives at the new destination is the same person as the one who was scanned and destroyed. Do you agree? Would you be willing to take a trip using the teletransporter, or do you think that people who travel in this way are actually killed and replaced by another person who is exactly like them?

One way of casting doubt on our memory theory's claim that people survive teletransportation is to consider a thought experiment, depicted in figure 12.5, in which the teletransporter malfunctions. You step into the teletransporter, and as usual, it scans you and sends the information to the receiving unit many miles away. But on this occasion, the sending unit does not destroy the body that steps into the unit. Indeed, it does not harm that body in any way. As a result, there are now two people with exactly the same bodies and exactly the same memories. If, as our current version of the memory theory maintains, the person who steps out of the receiving unit really is you, then it seems that you have been duplicated. There are now two of you. Moreover, as time passes, these two people become increasingly different from one another, since they are in different locations and will have different experiences leading to different memories. After a few days, and certainly after a few years, the person who stepped out of the teletransporter receiving unit (person C) and the person who stepped out of the malfunctioning sending unit (person B) are clearly different people. However, according to our current version of the memory theory, they are *both* numerically identical to the person who stepped into the sending unit (person A). And since numerical identity is an equivalence relation, this entails that they are numerically identical to each other. Clearly, something has gone wrong.

One way in which some philosophers in the Lockean tradition have dealt with this problem is to impose an added constraint on Version 3 of the memory theory. The constraint specifies that, at any given time, there can only be one person who is numerically identical to a person at an earlier time. If, at a later time, there are two people who, according to Version 3, are numerically identical with a person at an earlier time, then *neither* of these is the same person as the person at the earlier time. This constraint, which is sometimes called the **no-branching constraint**, avoids the problem that we noted at the end of the previous paragraph. We no longer have to say that the person who leaves the teletransporter receiving unit (person C) and the person who leaves the sending unit (person B) are both numerically identical to the person who entered the sending unit (person A). But this way of avoiding the problem has what many people think is a very counterintuitive consequence. If we impose the no-branching constraint, then, if you happen to step into a malfunctioning teletransporter sending unit and then step out again, you have ceased to exist. And this is not because of any change in you, but simply because your body has been duplicated in the receiving unit!

Some philosophers who find memory theories of personal identity congenial have reacted to this counterintuitive result by trying to construct a version of the memory theory that avoids it. We encourage you to try your hand at this. Can you come up with a formulation of the memory theory that does not entail that duplication is death?

Other philosophers have proposed a very different way of dealing with the counterintuitive implications of the no-branching constraint. They accept the implication that if you are duplicated, you will not be numerically identical with either of the people who exist after the duplication event. But they try to take the sting out of this result by urging that numerical identity is actually much less practically important than we have been assuming. You might have thought that you cared deeply about whether there would be a person in the future who is numerically identical with you. But now that we have a clearer idea of what numerical identity amounts to, these philosophers argue, it turns out that you are not really troubled by the fact that there may be no person in the future who is numerically identical with you. If you are person A in figure 12.5, it is not at all troubling that B, a person with your body and memories a few minutes later, is not numerically identical with you. Of course, there are other ways in which it might happen that no one in the future is numerically identical with you that would be deeply troubling. But saying what those ways are is a project that is quite distinct from providing a theory of personal (i.e., numerical) identity. If you are tempted by this response, you should try to say *which* ways of failing to be numerically identical to any person in the future you would find troubling.

For another illustration of the suggestion that numerical identity, as analyzed by Version 3 of the memory theory plus the no-branching constraint, is not as practically important as it has often been assumed, let's return to the themes of moral responsibility and punishment. Earlier, we proposed that it would be a gross miscarriage of justice if we punished a person for a crime committed by someone not numerically identical to the person being punished. But if our best account of

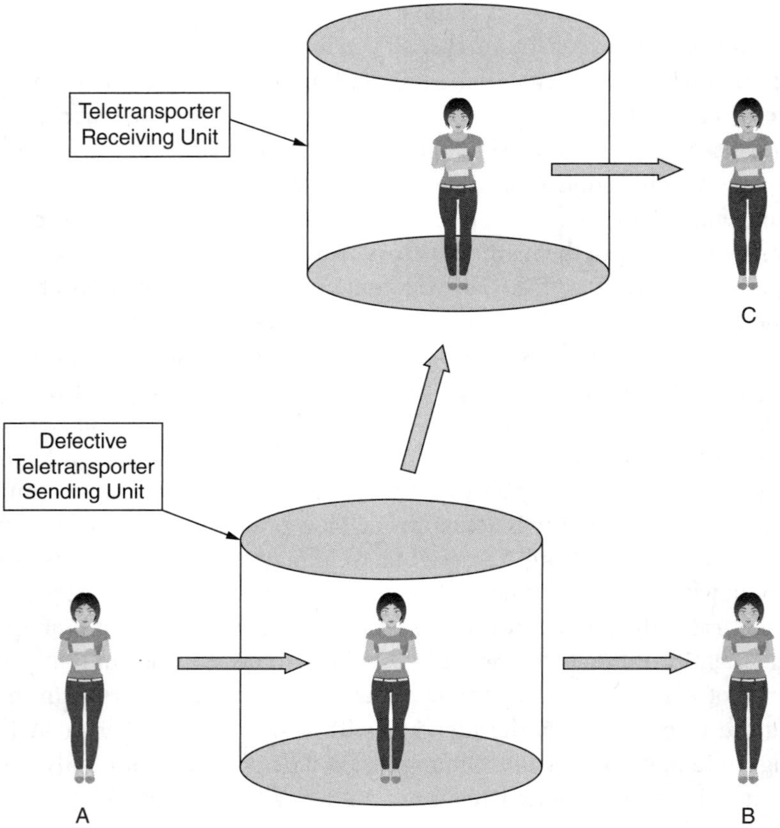

FIGURE 12.5 Which of B and C is numerically identical to A?

numerical identity includes the no-branching constraint, then perhaps it would not be a miscarriage of justice at all. To see why, consider the case of Adolf Eichmann, a Nazi leader who organized the mass deportation of Jews to the Nazi death camps. At the end of the Second World War, Eichmann disappeared. But in 1960, Mossad, the Israeli intelligence service, captured a man in Argentina who they believed to be Eichmann and smuggled him out of the country to stand trial in Israel. In this case, unlike in the case of John Demjanjuk, there was no dispute about the identity of the man on trial. He admitted that he was Adolf Eichmann, though he insisted that, in arranging for the mass murder of Jews, he was only following orders. Ultimately, Eichmann was convicted and hanged, and most people who followed the trial believed that the punishment was entirely appropriate. But now suppose that, on his way to trial, Eichmann had passed through a defective teletransporter sending unit, and that a duplicate had been created on a planet in a distant solar system. If our account of personal identity includes the no-branching constraint, then the man who stepped out of the defective sending unit is not numerically identical with the Nazi leader who organized the Holocaust. Would it then be unjust to hold that man responsible for Eichmann's crimes or to punish him? Surely, the answer is *no*—the fact that the prisoner now has a duplicate on a far off planet has no bearing at all on his responsibility, or guilt, or punishment. So here, too, it seems that personal identity is of much less practical importance than we earlier assumed.

12.5 Personal Identity and the Brain

We've considered quite a few philosophical thought experiments in this chapter. Here's our last one. Suppose you and a close friend, Pat, are riding in a car and are involved in a terrible accident. You are both taken by ambulance to a major university medical center, where the head of the trauma unit comes to your bedside and explains the situation. Pat has sustained a catastrophic head injury, and his brain (or hers—you should assume that you and Pat are the same sex) has been damaged beyond repair. But the rest of Pat's body has only a few cuts and bruises. Your body, however, has sustained massive damage. Your heart, liver, lungs, and other vital organs are all seriously injured. Within an hour or so, all of these organs will cease to function, and your body will die. But miraculously, your brain has not been damaged at all. After explaining the grim situation to you, the head of the trauma unit introduces you to the hospital's acclaimed neurosurgeon, who makes a startling proposal. She has been developing a new surgical procedure, hitherto tested only on dogs, that implants the brain of one dog in the skull of another dog and connects the transplanted brain to the nervous system of the recipient. The results have been excellent. After a brief recovery period, the dogs with the new brains are completely normal. Indeed, the neurosurgeon's family has adopted one of them as a pet. Moreover, just a few days ago, the neurosurgeon got permission to try this surgery on humans for the first time, and she offers you the opportunity to be the first person whose brain is transplanted into another person's skull. Pat's family has already been contacted, and they have given their permission to use his (or her, or their—remember that you and Pat were the same sex) body in the experimental procedure. The decision is now up to you. Would you give your approval for your brain to be transplanted into Pat's skull? Or would you decide to forego the procedure, and let your body and brain die in the next hour?

It's been our experience that most students who are confronted with this question say that they would opt for the surgery, so we'll assume that's what you would decide. We'll also assume that the surgery goes exactly as planned. A few hours after the surgery, the person consisting of Pat's body and your brain is able to see and hear and talk. A few days later, that person is encouraged to get out of bed and take a few steps. Within a week he (or she) is ready to leave the hospital. Since this person has your brain, he (or she) also has your memories and your personality; but he (or she) also has Pat's fingerprints, Pat's blood type, Pat's hair, and a scar on the left knee that Pat got in a skiing accident a few years ago. Before this person can leave the hospital, an important issue must be settled. Who is he (or she)? Is the person who is about to be checked out of the hospital you or Pat?

In recent years, a number of philosophers who work on personal identity have defended a view, often called **animalism**, that maintains the person who is checking out of the hospital is Pat. On their view, prior to the accident, both you and Pat were human animals, and one of those animals, you, has died. The other one, Pat, has received a transplanted organ, a new brain. According to the animalists, the situation is similar to one in which a person receives a kidney transplant or a heart transplant, though the brain transplant has some very unusual side effects. Pat now has your memories and personality, and mistakenly thinks that he (or she) is you! We won't discuss the arguments that animalists offer for this view.[7] But most philosophers who defend animalism admit that thought experiments like this one pose a serious challenge to their view, since most people have the very strong intuition that the person who leaves the hospital is *you*, not Pat. And of course, Lockean memory theorists share this view. The person leaving the hospital has the same memories that you had prior to the surgery, and those memories are caused by the experiences remembered, just as our final version of the memory theory requires. According to Lockean memory theories of personal identity, having the same brain that you had prior to the surgery, with its memories intact, is a **sufficient condition** for the person with that brain being you.

Some philosophers, however, are inclined to go a step further. They propose that, having the same brain, with its memories intact, is not only sufficient for personal identity, it is also *necessary*—that is, a **necessary and sufficient condition**. So if you are to exist at some time in the future, the person who is you will have to have your current brain (allowing for the normal small changes that naturally occur over time) with your memories intact (again allowing for normal gradual changes). Though requiring "brain continuity" may seem to be a small change to the Lockean memory theory, the implications are momentous. For if brain continuity is necessary for personal identity, then the hope for life after death is bound to be unfulfilled. Sooner or later, your brain will die and decompose. So if brain continuity is a necessary condition for personal identity, then not even God could grant you life after death, after your brain meets its inevitable fate. Another consequence of requiring brain continuity for personal identity is that, when they are working properly, teletransporters are deadly. If your entire body is destroyed by the sending unit, then no matter how precisely your body is copied by the receiving unit, the brain in that body is not *your* brain. So the person who steps out of the receiving unit is not you.

As we noted earlier, some philosophers have argued that personal identity is actually much less practically important than many people think. Some of these philosophers embrace the brain-continuity condition and then point to the teletransporter as a way of making their point. If you use a teletransporter, then the person who steps out of the receiving unit, they argue, is not you. But from a practical point of view, you should not care at all, since he (or she) will have your memories and personality and goals and values. Do you agree? Do you think that the person who steps out of the receiving unit isn't really you, and that this is of no practical importance? Or do you, perhaps, think that, from your perspective, nothing could be more practically important, since the teletransporter has ended your existence?

Glossary

animalism: Animalism is a theory of personal identity that holds people are biological organisms, and that the criteria for numerical identity of people are the same as the criteria for numerical identity of biological organisms. Animalists maintain that a person after a kidney transplant is numerically identical to the person who receives the kidney transplant. They hold the same is true for a person who has a brain transplant. The person after the transplant is numerically identical to the person who receives the transplant.

apparent memories: See real and apparent memories.

Cartesian mind: Descartes held that the mind is a nonmaterial thing that is capable of consciousness, intentionality, and rationality. See chapter 11 for more discussion.

equivalence relation: An equivalence relation is a relation that is reflexive, symmetric, and transitive (see their entries in this glossary). Most philosophers think that personal identity is an equivalence relation.

necessary and sufficient condition: A is a necessary and sufficient condition for B if and only if A is a necessary condition for B and A is a sufficient condition for B. Being a number that is divisible by two without a remainder is a necessary and sufficient condition for being an even number, for example.

necessary condition: A is a necessary condition for B if and only if everything that is B must also be A. For example, being male is a necessary condition for being an uncle.

no-branching constraint: The no-branching constraint is a component of some versions of the memory theory of personal identity. Proponents of the no-branching constraint say that, at any given time, there can only be one person who is numerically identical to a person at an earlier time. Thus, if you step into a machine that produces an exact duplicate of you, then you cease to exist.

nonmaterial: In this chapter, we use the term "nonmaterial" for things that are not made of matter.

nonphysical: In this chapter, we use the term "nonphysical" for things that cannot be detected or studied by physics or any of the other natural sciences.

numerical identity and qualitative identity: Objects A and B are qualitatively identical if and only if they are very similar to each other. Two cell phones with the same model number are usually qualitatively identical. When a retailer says that all the cell phones in a display are identical, this means that they are qualitatively identical. If you buy a cell phone and use it for several years, it will typically not be qualitatively identical to the cell phone you bought, since you will have added apps, scratched the surface, and made other sorts of changes.

Objects A and B are numerically identical if and only if they are the *very same thing*, even if they have significantly different properties. If you have broken the screen on your cell phone, it is not qualitatively identical to the phone you bought. But it is numerically identical.

The job for a philosophical theory of personal identity is to explain what is required for a person at one time and a person at another time to be numerically identical.

person stage: A person stage is a short temporal segment of the life of a person. In this chapter, we arbitrarily assumed that a person stage is a ten-second segment. Thus, you pass through 360 person stages every hour. Theories of personal identity try to specify the conditions under which two person stages are stages of the same person's life.
qualitative identity: See numerical identity and qualitative identity.
real memories and apparent memories: A real memory is a mental state representing an experience that the person having the memory actually experienced. An apparent memory is a mental state representing an experience that the person having the memory did not experience, though it seems to the person that it did. People cannot distinguish real memories from apparent memories by introspection.
reflexive relation: A relation is reflexive if and only if everything stands in that relation to itself. *Having the same birthday* is a reflexive relation, since everybody has the same birthday as themselves.
s-memory: In this chapter, we use the term "s-memory" as a label for an experience that is either a real memory or an apparent memory.
seat of consciousness: The seat of consciousness is the part of a person that has conscious experiences. Descartes and soul theorists think that the seat of consciousness is a nonmaterial, nonphysical thing— the soul or the Cartesian mind. Many contemporary philosophers and scientists think that the seat of consciousness is the brain.

soul: Soul theorists maintain that the soul is a nonphysical, nonmaterial part of a person that is the seat of consciousness and the part of a person that engages in thought. Soul theorists believe that a person at time t_1 and a person at time t_2 are numerically identical if and only if they have the same soul.

sufficient condition: A is a sufficient condition for B if and only if everything that is A must also be B. For example, being an uncle is a sufficient condition for being male.

symmetric relation: A relation is symmetric if and only if for any objects a and b, if a stands in the relation to b, then b stands in the relation to a. *Being married to* is a symmetric relation; if a is married to b, then b is married to a.

transitive relation: A relation is transitive if and only if for any objects a, b, and c, if a stands in the relation to b and b stands in the relation to c, then a stands in the relation to c. *Being taller than* is a transitive relation; if a is taller than b and b is taller than c, then a is taller than c.

Comprehension Questions

1. What is qualitative identity? Give an example. (Don't repeat examples from the chapter.)
2. What is numerical identity? Give an example. (Don't repeat examples from the chapter.)
3. Give an example illustrating the practical importance of personal identity. (Don't repeat examples from the chapter.)
4. Explain the soul theory of personal identity.
5. What is a person stage?
6. Explain Version 1 of the memory theory of personal identity, illustrated in figure 12.2. Explain why the fact that memories sometimes disappear over time poses a problem for this version of the memory theory. Explain why apparent memories pose a problem for this version of the memory theory.
7. Explain Version 2 of the memory theory of personal identity. Explain how this version of the theory avoids the problem of apparent memories.
8. Explain Version 3 of the memory theory of personal identity, illustrated in figure 12.3. Explain how this version of the theory deals with the problem that memories sometimes disappear over time.

9. Sketch Locke's thought experiment about the prince and the cobbler. What would a soul theorist say about this case? What would a memory theorist say?
10. Why does the malfunctioning teletransporter thought experiment, illustrated in figure 12.5, pose a problem for memory theories of personal identity?
11. Explain the no-branching constraint. How does the no-branching constraint deal with the malfunctioning teletransporter case? Do you think this is a good way of dealing with that case? Why or why not?
12. Some philosophers have argued that if the memory theory plus the no-branching constraint is the correct account of personal identity, then personal identity may be of little practical importance. Use an example to explain this view.
13. What does the animalist theory of personal identity entail about cases in which a brain is transferred from one living human body to another? Do you think this is plausible?
14. Some philosophers have proposed that brain continuity is both necessary and sufficient for personal identity. What implication does this proposal have about the possibility of life after death?

Discussion Questions

1. Most major world religions maintain that people can continue to exist after their bodies die. Do you want to continue existing after your body dies? If not, explain why. If you do want to continue existing after your body dies, what would be needed for you to get what you want? Suppose that 1,000 years after you die, God creates an atom-for-atom replica of your body (including your brain, of course) on your twenty-first birthday. Would that be sufficient for life after death? (If you would prefer some other birthday, that's OK. Just change the question.) Why or why not? Suppose that God creates an atom-for-atom replica of your body on your twenty-first birthday and that he uses *exactly the same atoms*—that is, numerically identical atoms. Would *that* be sufficient for life after death? Why or why not?

    Over the course of time, almost all the atoms in your body are replaced by different atoms as your body ages. Suppose that 1,000 years after you die, God collects all the atoms that composed your body when you were sixteen and builds an exact replica of you at sixteen. Suppose he also collects all the atoms that composed your body when you were sixty-six and builds an exact replica of you at sixty-six. Would either of these be you? Would *both* of them be you?

2. Suppose that Garrett, a thirty-five-year old man, robs a bank and kills one of the bank guards. While driving away from the scene of the crime, Garrett loses control of his car and crashes into a brick wall. He is not wearing a seat belt, and he sustains a serious head injury, which results in a total and permanent loss of memory of everything that has happened for the last three years. A year after the robbery, Garrett is brought to trial. His lawyer argues that since Garrett has no memory of the robbery or of the events leading up to it, he can't be held responsible for the crime. Is the man on trial numerically identical with the man who robbed the bank and killed the guard? What would a soul theorist say about this? What would a memory theorist say? What do you think? Do you think it is reasonable for Garrett to be punished for the bank robbery and murder?

3. Here's another question about a bank robber. This one is named Aarav. Like Garrett, Aarav robs a bank and kills a bank guard. He is not involved in an auto accident, but he is captured a few hours after the robbery. While he is in prison awaiting trial, Aarav undergoes a religious conversion that profoundly changes his preferences and his values. However, he has a clear memory of the bank robbery and the killing and is genuinely ashamed and remorseful about what happened. A year after the robbery, Aarav is brought to trial. His lawyer argues that, since he has undergone a profound change in his preferences and values, the man on trial is not the same person as the man who robbed the bank and killed the guard. What would a soul theorist say about this? What would a memory theorist say? What do you think? Do you think it is reasonable for Aarav to be punished for the bank robbery and murder?

4. Suppose that we have begun to colonize other planets in the solar system. You need to travel from the Earth to the colony on Neptune. The voyage by spaceship will take several years. However, you can also use a teletransporter. That trip only takes a few minutes. Assume that the teletransporter will work perfectly. It will destroy your body and create an atom-for-atom copy of you on Neptune. Would you use it? Explain your decision. Now find some classmates who make the opposite decision. Try to convince them that they should make the same decision you did.

5. Throughout this chapter, we have been assuming that numerical identity is an equivalence relation. But some philosophers have been tempted to abandon that assumption. Here's a thought experiment that might tempt you. Suppose you step into a teletransporter that scans (and then destroys) your body and sends the information to two receiving units on two different planets. Atom-for-atom copies of you with your full set of memories and personality traits appear in both receiving units. Would you be tempted to think that you had been divided and that *both* these copies are numerically identical with you (but not with each other)? If not, why not?

Now consider a slightly different case. In this one, you step into the teletransporter, it scans you, and it sends the information to a receiver on a distant planet that creates an atom-for-atom duplicate. But in this case, the sending unit fails to destroy the body that stepped into it (the situation depicted in figure 12.5). Have you divided in this case? Are both these people you? If not, why not? Suppose one of them will have to suffer great pain next week. Are you indifferent about which one suffers? If not, why not?

What to Look at Next

- John Perry's little (51-page!) book *A Dialogue on Personal Identity and Immortality* provides an accessible and engaging discussion of major theories of personal identity.
- Locke developed his theory of personal identity in *An Essay Concerning Human Understanding*, bk. 2, ch. 27, "Of Identity and Diversity." We recommend the translation into modern English by Jonathan Bennett, available at http://www.earlymoderntexts.com/authors/locke.
- For Thomas Reid's criticism of Locke's theory, see "Locke's Account of Our Personal Identity" in Reid's *Essays on the Intellectual Powers of Man*, Essay 3, Chapter 6. We recommend the translation into modern English by Jonathan Bennett, available at http://www.earlymoderntexts.com/authors/reid.
- For discussion of the contemporary response to Locke, see M. Ayers, *Locke: Epistemology and Ontology*.
- Two very useful collections of essays on personal identity are John Perry, ed., *Personal Identity* and Amelie Rorty, ed., *The Identities of Persons*.

- Another useful and more recent collection of essays is Raymond Martin and John Barresi, eds., *Personal Identity*.
- Derek Parfit's book *Reasons and Persons* has had a profound influence on contemporary philosophical discussions of personal identity.
- Bernard Williams is another very influential contributor to contemporary debates. A number of his important essays are collected in his book *Problems of the Self*.
- For an explanation and defense of animalism, see Eric Olsen's book *The Human Animal: Personal Identity Without Psychology*.
- The movie *Blade Runner*, directed by Ridley Scott, touches on Locke's memory theory. If you haven't seen the movie yet, look for the director's cut, and try to spot a quote from Descartes. Once you've seen the movie, check out Helen Beebee's article "Who Is Rachael? Blade Runner and Personal Identity" in IAI news. You can find the article at https://iainews.iai.tv/articles. The movie was based on the novel *Do Androids Dream of Electric Sheep?* by Philip K. Dick.

Notes

1. Some years later, Demjanjuk was convicted in Germany of being a guard at Sobibor, another Nazi death camp. He died, at age ninety-one, while his legal team was appealing that conviction.
2. For definitions of **reflexive relation**, **symmetric relation**, and **transitive relation**, see the glossary.
3. On some theories of personal identity, this claim turns out to be rather implausible. We'll return to the link between personal identity, responsibility, and punishment in section 12.3.
4. Sydney Shoemaker, "Persons, Animals, and Identity," *Synthese* 162, No. 3 (June, 2008): 313.
5. For Locke's discussion of this topic, see his *An Essay Concerning Human Understanding*, bk. 2 ch. 27, available at http://www.earlymoderntexts.com/authors/locke.
6. For discussion of the contemporary response to Locke, see M. Ayers, *Locke: Epistemology and Ontology*, vol. 2 (London: Routledge, 1991), pt. 3, sec. 24.
7. If you're curious, you can find an influential defense of the animalism in Eric Olsen's book *The Human Animal: Personal Identity Without Psychology* (Oxford: Oxford University Press, 1999).

CHAPTER 13

Are There Objective Truths About Right and Wrong?

Introduction

You may have noticed that debates about morality very often go nowhere. Take debates about vegetarianism. The vegetarian insists that it is wrong to eat meat and presents arguments for this view. The meat-eater responds by rejecting one or more of the premises of the vegetarian's argument. The meat-eater then presents arguments from the other side, and the vegetarian rejects the meat-eater's premises. And so it goes, until they give up. In the end, no headway has been made, and everyone is frustrated. Debates about abortion, euthanasia, or capital punishment often have a similar character. Debates among professional ethicists are often just as unconstructive (though with more footnotes).

It is perhaps instructive to compare ethics with the sciences. Entomology, for example, may not be completely free from controversy. Nevertheless, the entomologists share a large corpus of uncontested knowledge about insects, and they know far more about insects than they did a century ago. In ethics, however, there is very little uncontested knowledge, and many of the controversies of a century ago still rage today.

Because questions about the ethics of abortion, vegetarianism, and so on have not yet been settled, despite extensive and detailed discussion, it can be tempting to think that they will *never* be settled. Perhaps we simply have no way of reaching a consensus about whether it is wrong to eat meat, or about whether it is okay to abort a fetus. And one might begin to suspect that none of us really knows the answers to such questions. Perhaps we are unavoidably, permanently ignorant. This **moral skepticism** is alarming. We want to do the right thing—but how can we if we don't know what the right thing is?

Alternatively, it might be suggested that we are unable to figure out the correct answer to these ethical questions because the questions *don't have* a "correct" answer. Ethical questions, it may be said, have different answers from different perspectives. From a vegetarian perspective, it is wrong to eat meat. From the meat-eater's perspective, it is okay to eat meat. There are no "correct" or "incorrect" views here—only different perspectives. As it is sometimes put, ethics is not objective.

In this chapter, we will talk about whether there are objective truths in ethics, and whether we are capable of finding them if they exist. But first, we should clarify what we mean by "objective."

13.1 Objective Truth

The term **objective** is used in a confusing miscellany of different ways in philosophy. In this section, we want to explain how we will use the word in this chapter. Here are two claims which are objective and true:

> One hundred is an even number.
>
> Ducks are birds.

These claims are objective because they are true no matter who makes them, no matter when they are made, and no matter where they are made. Here are two claims that are objective and false:

> One hundred is an odd number.
>
> Ducks are reptiles.

These claims are objective because they are false no matter who makes them, no matter when they are made, and no matter where they are made. Here is another example:

> There is (or will be, or has been) life on a planet other than Earth.

This claim is objective because it is either true or false, and because its truth or falsity doesn't depend on who makes the claim, on where the claim is made, or on when the claim is made. In this case, we don't know whether the sentence is true or false. Even so, we're confident that the claim is objective.

In summary, a claim is objective if it is either true or false and its truth or falsity doesn't depend on who makes the claim or the time or place at which the claim is made. You should note that a claim can be objective in our sense even if it is hotly disputed. Consider, for example, this claim:

> The planets go around the Sun, and their orbits are approximately elliptical.

This claim was once highly controversial; even so, it is objective and true.

Now let's look at some sentences that are *not* objective in this sense. Questions and commands aren't objective, in our sense, because questions and commands are neither true nor false. The sentence "I am tall" is also not objective. This claim is true if it is made by a tall person, but it is false if made by a short person. Much the same goes for "It is raining here." This claim is true if it is made by a person standing drenched in a thunderstorm, but it is false if it is made by a person under clear blue skies. The sentence "It is legal for a nineteen-year-old to buy beer" is similar. This sentence is false if the country under discussion is the United States. If the country under discussion is, say, France, Germany, or the United Kingdom the sentence is true.

Here is a more controversial example. Consider the sentence "*Aliens* is a better movie than *Singin' in the Rain.*" It could be argued that this sentence is true for some people but false for others. Different people have different aesthetic standards: beauty is in the eye of the beholder, as they say. On this view, the sentence is not objective.

Back to ethics. It is uncontroversial that many ethical claims are not objective. Consider, for example, the sentence "You shouldn't drive faster than the speed limit." We suppose that this claim would be true in many contexts. But suppose that you're talking to a friend who is driving someone having a stroke to the hospital. In this case, it might well be that breaking the speed limit is the right thing to do. In this special case, if you were to say, "You shouldn't drive faster than the speed limit," your claim would be false. It's easy to come up with similar examples, so it seems clear that many ethical claims are not objective in our sense.

Nevertheless, many people think that there are objective truths in ethics. We explain why with a true story. The narrator, who lived in the American South before the Civil War, is known to us only as Miss G.:

> I had a young slave, who was, without exception, the prettiest creature I ever saw. She used to tend table for us, and almost always attracted the attention of visitors. A gentleman, who was often at our house, became dreadfully in love with her, and tried to make her accept handsome presents. One day she came to me, and asked me to speak to that gentleman, and forbid his saying anything more to her; for he troubled her very much, and she could not get rid of him. I promised to speak to the gentleman about it; and I did so, telling him that his attentions were very unpleasant to my slave, and begged him to refrain from offering them in the future. For a few weeks he desisted; but at the end of that time, he came to me and said, "Miss G., I must have that girl! I cannot live without her!" He offered me a very high price. I pitied the poor fellow, and so I sold her to him.[1]

It's hard to deny that "Miss G. was wrong to sell her slave to the gentleman" is objective and true. To be sure, Miss G. and some of her friends would have insisted that it was okay for her to sell the slave—but arguably, they would have simply been wrong about this. As we've said, a claim can be objective and true even if it is contested.

Some theists would claim that Miss G.'s action was wrong because it violated God's law. This is an application of the divine command theory, which we'll discuss in the next section.

13.2 The Divine Command Theory

It is natural to think that, when an action is morally wrong, it is wrong because it violates a moral law. For example, it was immoral for Miss G. to sell her slave because in doing so she violated such laws as *Don't sell slaves* and *Don't facilitate rape*. Perhaps our statements of these laws could be refined, but for now, what concerns us is not the exact content of the laws, but rather their origin. *Where do moral laws come from?*

Plausibly, every law must have a lawmaker. Laws don't spring into existence on their own: they have to be brought into existence by some person, or some group of people, with appropriate authority. Now it seems that human lawmakers always have limited jurisdictions: laws created by the US Congress only apply to people within the United States, laws created in the Russian Federal Assembly only apply to people in Russia, and so on. Moral laws are apparently rather different: they apply to all people everywhere and at all times. What the story about Miss G. illustrates is that laws like *Don't facilitate rape* and *Don't sell slaves* apply even in places where they are not recognized. And so it seems that moral laws do not have human lawmakers.

We've now claimed that moral laws have lawmakers, but that they don't have *human* lawmakers. From here, it's a short step to the conclusion that God is the creator of the moral law. And this is the **divine command theory**. On this picture, God is a legislator whose jurisdiction has no edges.

The divine command theory

When an action is morally wrong, it is morally wrong because it is forbidden by God.

When an action is morally okay, it is morally okay because it has not been forbidden by God.

The argument for the divine command theory that we have just rehearsed could certainly be contested. One might, for example, deny the claim that every law must have a lawmaker—insisting instead that the moral law is a fundamental feature of reality. Even so, the divine command theory has some extremely attractive features.

For one thing, the theory accommodates our sense that there are objective truths about right and wrong. When she sold her slave, Miss G. didn't violate the laws of her state (buying and selling slaves was legal in South Carolina at the time), nor did she violate the moral norms that she and her peers accepted. Nevertheless, we have a strong sense that what she did was wrong. The divine command theorist accommodates this by insisting that what Miss G. did was wrong because it violated God's commands.

Linda Zagzebski suggests a further argument for the divine command theory:

We must have more to go on in the moral life than our own human faculties. In particular, the possibility of success in the moral life requires something which enables us to get out of skepticism. The Christian God has such a function.[2]

As Zagzebski says, the divine command theory is attractive in part because it yields an attractive response to the challenge of moral skepticism.

The divine command theorist may insist that in principle it is possible to settle ethical questions by figuring out what God commands. This might involve praying, or reading scripture, or consulting someone with authority on religious matters. Now it should be conceded that in practice this can be very difficult. Different religious authority figures have different opinions; scripture is often hard to interpret; speaking to God in prayer is not like speaking on the phone. Even so, it is perhaps an attractive feature of the divine command theory that it suggests that difficult moral questions are all answerable *in principle*. The divine command theory seems to undermine moral skepticism.

We've seen that the divine command theory has some attractive features. Nevertheless, the theory is highly controversial, even among theists. To see why, consider the following fiction.[3] God issues a command to some people that an innocent person is to be chosen at random, and then tortured, and then killed. At first, it is assumed that God anticipates some long-term benefit to this horrible act. But God replies that he anticipates no such long-term benefit. He has simply decided, arbitrarily, that someone at random is to be tortured and killed. After some discussion, the people decide that they will not follow God's instruction.

Arguably, it was morally okay for the people in the story to ignore God's instruction. Indeed, it seems that, in this case, it would be *wrong* to do what God says: it is wrong to torture and murder innocent people, even when you are asked to do so by a person in authority. But the divine command theorist is apparently stuck with the conclusion that it would be right for the people in the story to follow God's command—because according to the divine command theory, it is God's commands that determine what is right and what is wrong.

We think that the divine command theorist's best response to this objection is to insist that what is described in the story is simply impossible. God has not, will not, and could not issue such a grotesque command. Now it is not easy to square this claim with the doctrine that God is omnipotent. If God is omnipotent, presumably, he can do anything—and in particular, he can issue grotesque commands. Perhaps the divine command theorist can avoid the objection by giving a suitably qualified definition of "omnipotent."[4] But even then, the reply is deeply puzzling. *Why* would God never issue this command? What would stop him?

The divine command theorist might be tempted to answer that God would never command us to torture and kill an innocent person at random because to murder and torture innocent people is morally wrong—and God would never command us to sin. But this reply is confused. To say that God would not command us to murder because murder is morally wrong is to say that God is *constrained* by the moral law. But this is not consistent with the divine command theory, which implies that God is the *creator* of the moral law. An analogy may help. Why did the writers of the US Constitution insist that there must be no religious test for public office in the United States? It would clearly be confused to reply that they did this because religious tests for public office are unconstitutional. The people who wrote the US Constitution were not, as they wrote, bound by the Constitution. In the same way, the divine command theory implies that, as God creates the moral law, he is not constrained by it.

Some proponents of the divine command theory have suggested that God's commands are simply arbitrary. For example, John Calvin (1509–1564) wrote:

> If His will has any cause, there must be something antecedent to it, and to which it is annexed; this it were impious to imagine. The will of God is the supreme rule of righteousness, so that everything which He wills must be held to be righteous by the mere fact of His willing it. Therefore, when it is asked why the Lord did so, we must answer, *because He pleased*. But if you proceed farther to ask *why* He pleased, you ask for something greater and more sublime than the will of God, and nothing such can be found.[5]

According to this way of thinking, God's commands seem to be the product of whim or caprice. But it's hard to see why, on this view, God's commands deserve our respect.

We'll leave it to you to think about whether the divine command theorist can find a solution to these challenges. We'd like to finish our discussion by suggesting that a theist need not accept the divine command theory: it is perfectly coherent to say that God exists, and that we should do what he says, but to reject the divine command theory. Here is an analogy. A novice carpenter making their first table might follow the instructions of a helpful expert. This is not because the expert carpenter somehow has the power to determine right and wrong. More simply, it is because the expert carpenter knows how to make a table properly and will instruct the novice accordingly. One can understand the relation between

God and human beings in the same way. Because he is omniscient, God knows how we should live. Being perfectly good, he will give us instructions in such a way that, if we follow them, we will lead good lives. And so we should follow his instructions. On this view, God doesn't *determine* what is right and wrong, but he is an *expert* on morality.

But we are left with a question: *If moral rules are not created by God, where do they come from?* One answer to this question is that moral rules are created by groups of people. We will explore this idea in the next section.

13.3 Cultural Relativism

Ruth Benedict (1887–1948) opened her book *Patterns of Culture* by saying, "Western civilization . . . has spread itself more widely than any other local group" and "standardized itself over most of the globe." In consequence, she wrote, most people who have grown up in Western cultures are hardly aware that alternative ways of life are possible. They are therefore prone to mistake "local normalities" for "the inevitable necessities of existence." Benedict set herself the task of showing her readers the enormous diversity of cultures around the world. She hoped that, once people became more aware of this diversity, they would become more tolerant of other cultures. She called for a "more realistic social faith, accepting as grounds of hope and as new bases for tolerance the coexisting and equally valid patterns of life which mankind has created for itself."[6]

Since this chapter is about ethics, we are particularly interested in the differences between the ethical codes of different cultures. For example, Benedict described the disparate views about the ethics of sex prevalent in different cultures. Both authors of this book live in cultures in which it is generally considered wrong for a person to have sex with a cousin. But in many other cultures—for example, in many parts of the Middle East—this is not considered wrong. In some cultures, sex between people from the same settlement is frowned upon; in other cultures, it is sex between people from *different* settlements which is taken to be wrong. Observations like these form the basis of **descriptive cultural relativism**:

Descriptive cultural relativism

Different cultures around the world have different ethical codes. What is considered wrong in one culture is not considered wrong in other cultures.

This claim is uncontroversial, once a couple of caveats have been made. First, there is diversity in moral opinion *within* cultures as well as *between* cultures. So we need to be careful when talking about "the" moral code of a culture. Second, there are commonalities as well as differences between cultures. Every culture enforces *some* putatively moral restrictions on who may have sex with whom. In almost every culture, sex between siblings is regarded as wrong.[7]

As we said, descriptive cultural relativism is not a controversial claim. However, in some of her work, Benedict presented a form of relativism that is highly controversial. To say that an action is wrong, she suggested, is just to say that it is prohibited by the relevant culture. For example, if an American says to another American that it is morally wrong to have sex with a cousin, all that is meant is that the moral code prevailing in America forbids a person from having sex with a cousin. At the same time, if a Saudi says to another Saudi that it is morally okay to have sex with a cousin, all that is meant is the moral code prevailing in Saudi Arabia does not forbid a person from having sex with a cousin. The American and the Saudi might seem to have endorsed conflicting opinions—but in fact they have not. Each has correctly characterized the moral code of their own culture.[8]

It is not hard to see why a person who seeks to promote tolerance between different cultures might find this position attractive: perhaps it is easier to tolerate people in other cultures if their views do not contradict one's own. And indeed, Benedict was not the only anthropologist in the first part of the twentieth century to endorse **metaethical cultural relativism** (as we will call it).[9] Nevertheless, the position has deeply problematic consequences. To see this, it helps to distinguish two different versions of metaethical cultural relativism.

The first is **agent relativism**:

Agent relativism

When it's said that a person's action is morally wrong, what's meant is that the action is condemned by the ethical code of that person's culture.

When it is said that a person's action is morally okay, what's meant is that the action is not condemned by the ethical code of that person's culture.

Ruth Benedict (1887–1948) was a pioneering anthropologist.

Agent relativism implies that many moral claims are objective, in the sense we discussed earlier. If Dave and Sarah are two first cousins in the United States today, then agent relativism implies that the claim "It is morally wrong for Dave and Sarah to have sex" is true, and the truth of this claim does not depend on who makes the claim, when they make the claim, or where they make the claim. Moreover, agent relativism offers a straightforward solution to the problem of moral skepticism. According to the agent relativist, we can always, in principle, figure out whether an action is morally okay or morally wrong by finding out about the moral code prevalent in the relevant culture. Though these might be thought to be attractive features of agent relativism, the view also has some extremely counterintuitive implications. Consider once more Miss G. The ethical code of Miss G.'s culture did not forbid Miss G.'s action, and so agent relativism implies that Miss G.'s action was morally okay. We think that this implication of agent relativism is implausible, to say the least.

The relativist may respond to the example by saying that, when we say Miss G. was wrong to sell her slave, we are retrospectively evaluating her action by the ethical code of our own culture. This suggests a rather different version of relativism, known as **speaker relativism**:

> *Speaker relativism*
>
> When it's said that a person's action is morally wrong, what is meant is that the action is condemned by the ethical code of the speaker's culture.
>
> When it is said that a person's action is morally okay, what's meant is that the action is not condemned by the ethical code of the speaker's culture.

This maneuver may postpone the problem, but it doesn't solve it. Suppose that Miss G. said, "It was not wrong of me to sell my slave to the gentleman." According to speaker relativism, what this would have meant was that the sale was not condemned by the ethical code of her culture—and this is surely true. So speaker relativism implies that Miss G.'s claim was true, which seems implausible at best. Like agent relativism, speaker relativism is counterintuitive in such cases, to say the least.

The relativist may reply that in making these complaints we are guilty of the mistake that Benedict warned us about: we are mistaking "local normalities" for "the inevitable necessities of existence." Even if this reply is successful, there is a further important problem with cultural relativism. We will illustrate the problem with an example. In Europe, eating meat is not considered morally wrong, except by a few vegetarians who advocate reform of the prevailing moral code. Now suppose that one of these vegetarians tells fellow Europeans that they should not eat meat. What are we to make of this claim from a relativist point of view? Well, according to the relativist, the vegetarian's claim is that the moral code of Europe condemns eating meat. But this is straightwardly false: the European moral code doesn't condemn eating meat. From a relativist point of view, then, we can conclude that the vegetarian's claim is false, *without having to consider the arguments put forward in favor of this position*. This relativist attitude strikes us an unacceptably glib. In this sort of case, relativism acts a barrier to moral discussion.

The relativist may be tempted to reply that, when saying that eating meat is wrong, the European is not reporting the ethical code of her culture. Instead, she is reporting her own personal attitudes. However, to say this is to move away from cultural relativism and toward subjectivism, a view we discuss in the next section.

13.4 Subjectivism and Expressivism

Simple subjectivism is our name for this position:

> *Simple subjectivism*
>
> When someone says that an action is morally wrong, this means that the person disapproves of it personally.
>
> When someone says that an action is morally okay, this means is that the person does not disapprove of it personally.

If, for example, you say, "It was wrong of Miss G. to sell her slave," what you mean is that you personally disapprove of her action.

Like relativism, simple subjectivism has deeply counterintuitive consequences. For the simple subjectivist, if Miss G. said, "It was not wrong of me to sell my slave," all she would have meant is she personally did not disapprove of the sale—and she would have been right.

A further problem with simple subjectivism is this: it is extremely difficult for the simple subjectivist to give a credible account of moral disagreement and discussion. Suppose that Ashni says, "It is morally wrong to eat meat," and that Baldev says, "It is morally okay to eat meat." It is natural to think that Ashni and Baldev *disagree* about the ethics of eating meat, and that it would make sense for them to give arguments for their different views. The simple subjectivist must disagree. For the simple subjectivist, when Ashni says, "It is morally wrong to eat meat," all she means is that *she* disapproves of eating meat, and when Baldev says, "It is morally okay to eat meat," all he means is that *he* doesn't disapprove of eating meat. On this view, Ashni and Baldev don't disagree at all—they may well both be correct. What's more, it's not at all clear on this view why Ashni and Baldev should bother giving arguments for their views: Ashni and Baldev can find out what their attitudes are just by introspection. If simple subjectivism is true, it is totally unclear what the point of moral argument is.

For these reasons, simple subjectivism is not a common view today. However, a closely related position, **expressivism**, remains popular. Here is an early statement of expressivism from the philosopher A. J. Ayer (1910–1989):

> If I say to someone "You acted wrongly in stealing that money," I am not stating anything more if I had simply said "You stole that money." In adding that this action is wrong . . . I am simply evincing my moral disapproval of it. It is as if I said "You stole that money," in a particular tone of horror, or written it with the addition of some special exclamation marks. This tone, or the exclamation marks, . . . [serves] merely to show that the expression of it is attended by certain feelings in the speaker.[10]

Ayer's claim in this passage is that moral claims are expressions of emotion. For example, according to Ayer, "stealing is wrong" means more or less the same as "boo to stealing!" And "honesty is virtuous" means much the same as "hoorah for honesty!" Ayer's expressivism is accordingly sometimes called the **Boo! Hurrah! theory**.

Ayer's claim is clearly a relative of simple subjectivism, but there's an important difference between the two views. Consider, for example, the sentence "stealing is wrong." According to the simple subjectivist, someone who uses this sentence asserts that they disapprove of stealing. According to Ayer, the sentence is used to *evince* or *exhibit* disapproval of stealing. The difference between *asserting* that one has some emotion and *evincing* this emotion should be clear, at least in simple cases like these:

Asserting that one is in pain	vs.	screaming
Asserting that one is amused	vs.	laughing
Asserting that one loves the Boston Red Sox	vs.	cheering in the stands of Fenway Park

Ayer further distinguished his position from simple subjectivism by adding the suggestion that some moral claims are really commands.

For example, "It is your duty to look after your aunt until she recovers" might mean the same as "Look after your aunt until she recovers!"

One of our objections to simple subjectivism was that the simple subjectivist is unable to give a plausible account of moral discussion and disagreement. Expressivists claim that their theory does not have the same flaw. Let's go back to Ashni and Baldev. Suppose that Ashni says, "It is wrong to eat meat." According to the expressivist, this means something like "Boo to eating meat! Don't eat meat!" And suppose that Baldev says, "It is good to eat meat." According to the expressivist, this means something like "Hurrah for eating meat! Eat meat!" Notice that there is, in some sense, a conflict between Ashni and Baldev: they are issuing commands that can't both be followed. So unlike the simple subjectivist, the expressivist can perhaps account for the fact that Ashni and Baldev disagree. What's more, the expressivist may be able to make sense of what Ashni and Baldev are doing when they give arguments for their views: they are attempting to modify each other's emotional responses to eating meat.

Ayer's view did have one rather peculiar feature. Commands aren't capable of truth or falsity. It makes no sense, for example, to say, "It is true that you look after your aunt." Similarly, expressions of emotion, such as sighs and groans, aren't capable of truth or falsity. If a friend expresses joy by laughing, it would not make sense to reply, "That's true!" So Ayer inferred that moral claims are also not capable of truth or falsity, and thus they are not objective, as we have been using that term. Moral judgments, he said, are "pure expressions of feeling and as such do not come under the category of truth and falsehood."[11] Some philosophers have found Ayer's claim that moral sentences are neither true nor false objectionable. Once again, suppose that Miss G. said, "It was not wrong of me to sell my slave." It is natural to say that this claim is false, but Ayer would have to deny this.

We think that expressivism is a significant improvement over simple subjectivism. However, there is a major problem with the view—a problem that has been at the center of much philosophical work over the past few decades. So far, we've given expressivist accounts of some very simple moral sentences, such as "stealing is wrong" and "it is your duty to look after your aunt until she recovers." It is difficult, however, to give an expressivist treatment of more complicated sentences. Consider this sentence, for example:

> If it is wrong to do something, it is also wrong to pay someone else to do it on your behalf.

This sentence is an important premise in our argument for vegetarianism in chapter 16. However, this premise on its own doesn't express disapproval of inflicting pain on animals, or of buying meat, or of eating meat. Indeed, it is hard to see the sentence as an expression of any kind of approval or disapproval. Nor is the sentence easily construed as a command. And even if the expressivist finds some way of dealing with this one sentence, there are others to deal with. Here are some examples:

- Mr. Chang left the company because of the management's immoral business practices.
- I suspect that eating meat is morally okay, but I might be mistaken.
- Luci is very brave.

Expressivists have devoted a great deal of effort over the past few decades attempting to explain systematically the meanings of sentences like these. Philosophers still disagree about whether this project can succeed.

13.5 The Qualified Attitude Theory

We don't know whether an adequate version of expressivism can be devised. So in this section, we're going to look at a different approach. Like expressivism, the qualified attitude theory may be thought of as a sophisticated descendant of simple subjectivism.

An important problem with simple subjectivism is that its proponents underestimate the prevalence of error in moral judgment. Here is a story to illustrate the point. Andy went out to a bar and drank several beers and shots. While still drunk, he decided to go out on his motorbike. His friends discouraged him, but he told them that there's nothing wrong in his going out for a joyride. After riding around the city at great speed, he got home and went to bed. When he woke up the following morning—sober, with a headache—he was horrified by his own stupidity the night before.

Now when drunk Andy said to his friends, "It's okay for me to go for a joyride," for the simple subjectivist all this meant was that he did not disapprove of his going for a joyride. And this was true, of course—Andy didn't disapprove of his own actions at the time. But it seems clear that the simple subjectivist is wrong about this. As Andy himself realized the following morning, he was mistaken when he said that it was okay for him to go for a joyride.

The story shows once more that simple subjectivism is false. It also illustrates the point that we are prone to make errors in moral judgment, especially when we are in suboptimal circumstances. For example, we make mistakes when we are drunk, tired, uninformed, or biased. The **qualified attitude theory** can be thought of as a modified version of simple subjectivism, designed to accommodate these simple points. The simple subjectivist says that moral claims are claims about *current* attitudes; the qualified attitude theorist says that moral claims are claims about what one's attitudes *would be in ideal conditions*. To be explicit:

The qualified attitude theory

When a person says that an action is morally wrong, this means that the person would disapprove of it, given ideal conditions.

When a person says that something is morally okay, this means that the person would not disapprove of it, given ideal conditions.[12]

By **ideal conditions**, we mean conditions in which the speaker is fully informed, sober, unbiased, alert, unhurried, and so on. When Andy said, "It's okay for me to go for a joyride," what this meant (according to the qualified attitude theory) is that, given ideal conditions, he would not have disapproved of his going for a joyride. And of course, this was false: Andy approved of his joyriding only because he was drunk.

The qualified attitude theory also scores over simple subjectivism in that it offers a far more satisfying account of moral deliberation and discussion. Ashni may be quite certain that she *currently* disapproves of eating meat. However, when she says, "It is wrong to eat meat," she may speak falsely because she may be missing some relevant information or may be biased in some way. So it makes sense for Ashni to listen carefully to Baldev's arguments: she may learn something from him. In the same way, Baldev may worry that his attitudes about eating meat may be in error because he may be lacking information, may be prejudiced, or may have missed some important considerations. And so it makes sense for Baldev to listen to Ashni's arguments: he may learn something from her. And so the proponent of the qualified attitude theory is able to explain the value of reasoned discussion about moral issues between people with differing views.

The qualified attitude theorist may also claim to have a solution to the problem of moral skepticism. Perhaps we are never in truly ideal conditions. Still, perhaps we are sometimes in conditions that approximate the ideal. The qualified attitude theory implies that the attitudes we have on such occasions are a good guide to the moral truth. Thus, the qualified attitude theory implies that some degree of moral knowledge is possible.

What does the qualified attitude theory imply about objectivity in ethics? As an example, let's think about slavery in the United States in the first part of the nineteenth century. It could be argued that those who defended the institution did so only because they were misinformed about race or were prejudiced by self-interest. On this view, perhaps, they would have recognized the wrongfulness of slavery if they were to think through the issue carefully under ideal conditions. On this basis, a qualified attitude theorist might argue that it is true and objective that the institution of slavery was immoral. On the other hand, it could be argued that there have been people whose racism was so deeply ingrained that they would have continued to support the institution of slavery even if they were to think through the question in the best possible conditions. If this is right, then it's a consequence of the qualified attitude theory that it is not an *objective* truth that the institution of slavery was wrong. Can you think of a claim that is, for the qualified attitude theorist, true and objective?

Conclusion

It is sometimes suggested that ethics can't be objective because there is so much controversy about it. This argument is mistaken—at least if the word "objective" is intended in our sense. Indeed, we think that, by giving examples, we can make a powerful case for the claim that there are objective truths in ethics. We find it hard to deny that "it was morally wrong of Miss G. to sell her slave to the gentleman" is both true and objective.

At the same time, it is hard to explain what moral statements *mean* in a way that accommodates the idea that there are moral claims which are objective and true. Perhaps to say something is morally wrong is to say that it is a violation of a moral law. But then where do these moral laws come from? Not from social convention, it seems—these are too variable. It could be suggested that the moral laws don't come from anywhere: they are fundamental features of the universe. But this flies in the face of the intuition that every law must have a lawmaker. A popular view, of course, is that the lawmaker is God. But as we've seen, the divine command theory has its own problems.

According to another way of thinking, moral claims are descriptions of expressions of the speaker's attitudes. This is an attractive idea, but it remains unclear whether proponents of such views can account for objectivity in ethics, or whether they can properly explain the role of rational argument in ethics.

The problem, we think, remains unsolved.

Glossary

agent relativism: Agent relativism consists of the following two claims:
- When it's said that a person's action is morally wrong, what's meant is that the action is condemned by the ethical code of that person's culture.
- When it's said that a person's action is morally okay, what's meant is that the action is not condemned by the ethical code of that person's culture.

Boo! Hurrah! theory: Expressivism is sometimes referred to as the "Boo! Hurrah! theory" because, according to expressivists, saying that X is morally bad is a bit like saying "Boo!" to X, and saying that X is morally good is a bit like saying "Hurrah!" to X.

descriptive cultural relativism: Descriptive cultural relativism maintains that different cultures around the world have different ethical codes, and that in many cases what is considered wrong in one culture is not considered wrong in another culture.

divine command theory: Divine command theorists make the following two claims:
- When an action is morally wrong, it is morally wrong because it is forbidden by God.
- When an action is morally okay, it is morally okay because it has not been forbidden by God.

Most theists believe that something is morally bad *if and only if* God disapproves of it, since they think that God is omniscient and perfectly morally good. But divine command theory makes a much stronger claim. It says that things are bad *because* God disapproves; it is God's disapproval that *makes* it wrong. Many theists disagree with this much stronger claim.

expressing or evincing a feeling or emotion vs. asserting that one has a feeling or emotion: This distinction is best explained by example. If you accidentally hit your thumb with a hammer, you might shout "Ouch!" (or perhaps something more colorful and unprintable). If you did that, you would be expressing or evincing your pain. You might also say, "My thumb really hurts!" If you did that, you would be asserting that you are in pain. Note that when a person asserts that they have a feeling or emotion, what the person says is typically either true or false. But when a person expresses or evinces a feeling or emotion, what the person does is neither true nor false.

expressivism: Expressivists maintain that moral claims are expressions of emotion, or commands. For example, the expressivist might say that "stealing is wrong" expresses disapproval of stealing or is equivalent to the command *Don't Steal!*

ideal conditions: The qualified attitude theory explains the meaning of "morally good" and "morally bad" in terms of the attitudes people would have under ideal conditions. Under ideal conditions, a person
- is fully informed about the relevant facts;
- has thought through the issue carefully;
- is psychologically normal, not drunk, not under the influence of psychoactive drugs, and not suffering from a psychological disorder that affects moral feelings or reasoning; and
- is not biased by self-interest.

metaethical cultural relativism: According to metaethical ethical relativism, claims about the ethical rightness or wrongness of an action are actually claims about whether that action is condoned or condemned by the ethical code of a culture. There are two versions of metaethical relativism: agent relativism and speaker relativism. They differ on which culture's ethical code is relevant, the code of the speaker's culture or the code of the "agent"—that is, the person whose action is being assessed.

moral skepticism: Moral skeptics claim that we have no way of knowing whether moral claims are true or false.

objective: Beware! The term "objective" is used in many ways in philosophy. In this chapter, we define "objective" as follows: a claim is objective if and only if (i) it is either true or false and (ii) the truth or falsity of the claim does not depend on who makes the claim, where the claim is made, or when the claim is made.

qualified attitude theory: According to the qualified attitude theory:
- When a person says that an action is morally wrong, this means that the person would disapprove of it, given ideal conditions.
- When a person says that something is morally okay, this means that the person would not disapprove of it, given ideal conditions.

simple subjectivism: According to simple subjectivism:
- When someone says that an action is morally wrong, what this means is that the person disapproves of it personally.
- When someone says that an action is morally okay, what this means is that the person does not disapprove of it personally.

speaker relativism: Speaker relativism is a version of metaethical cultural relativism. According to speaker relativism:
- When it is said that a person's action is morally wrong, what's meant is that the action is condemned by the ethical code of *the speaker's* culture.
- When it is said that a person's action is morally okay, what's meant is that the action is not condemned by the ethical code of *the speaker's* culture.

If speaker relativism is correct, then most moral claims are not objective, since they are claims about the moral code of the person making the claim. If two speakers, S_1 and S_2, both say that P's action is wrong, and if S_1 and S_2 come from different cultures with different ethical codes, then it is possible for S_1's statement to be true and S_2's statement to be false.

Comprehension Questions

1. Without repeating examples from the chapter, give (a) three examples of statements which are objective and true, (b) three examples of statements which are objective and false, and (c) three examples of statements which are *not* objective.
2. Are there claims that are objective and true but nevertheless controversial?
3. It is uncontroversial that some ethical claims are not objective. Why is this?
4. What is the divine command theory?
5. Is it true that all theists accept the divine command theory?
6. Briefly list the motivations for the divine command theory.
7. We finished section 13.2, by presenting an objection to the divine command theory. Briefly describe this challenge.
8. Describe the following views, being careful to explain the differences between them: (a) descriptive cultural relativism, (b) agent relativism, and (c) speaker relativism.
9. Is it true that different people around the world have different opinions about morality? Illustrate this point with examples (without repeating an example from the chapter). Does this, on its own, show that there are no objective truths in ethics?
10. Briefly describe our objections to agent relativism and speaker relativism.
11. Describe the following views, being careful to explain the similarities and differences between them: (a) simple subjectivism, (b) expressivism, and (c) the qualified attitude theory.
12. Describe some challenges to simple subjectivism and expressivism.
13. Consider the sentence "It was wrong of Miss. G. to sell her slave to the gentleman." Is this sentence true or false? Is it objective? Answer from the point of view of (a) a divine command theorist, (b) an agent relativist, (c) a speaker relativist, (d) a simple subjectivist, and (e) an expressivist.

Discussion Questions

1. In the introduction to this chapter, we implied there has been rather little progress in ethics. A critic might reply that this is ridiculous: just in the last few hundred years, slavery has been banned across the world, rates of violent crime have decreased hugely, the rights of women have been increasingly recognized, and democracy has spread across much of the world. Can you think of further examples? Do examples of this kind establish that there has been, overall, moral progress?[13]

2. The economist Lionel Robbins wrote:

    > If we disagree about ends, it is a case of thy blood or mine—or live and let live, according to the importance of the difference, or the relative strength of our opponents. But, if we disagree about means, then scientific analysis can often help us to resolve our differences. If we disagree about the morality of the taking of interest . . . then there is no room for argument. But if we disagree about the objective implications of fluctuations in the rate of interest, then economic analysis should enable us to settle our dispute.[14]

    If we take this passage at face value, Robbins's position is that when two people disagree about "ends" (i.e., moral values), they will not be able to settle their disagreement through argument. They therefore have two choices: they can "live and let live," or they can fight. Can you think of a case in which two people (or groups of people) who initially disagreed about some moral topic reached agreement through rational argument?

3. There is a famous passage in Dostoevsky's *The Brothers Karamazov* in which Ivan Karamazov insists, "if there is no God, then everything is permitted." If God does not exist, Ivan seems to suggest, nothing is morally wrong. Do you agree? If so, explain why. If you don't agree, can you explain why, in a universe in which there is no God, some things are morally wrong?

4. William Lane Craig wrote:

    > If God does not exist, then objective moral values do not exist. When I speak of objective moral values, I mean moral values that are valid and binding whether anybody believes in them or not. Thus, to say,

for example, that the Holocaust was objectively wrong is to say that it was wrong even though the Nazis who carried it out thought that it was right and that it would still have been wrong even if the Nazis had won World War II and succeeded in exterminating or brainwashing everyone who disagreed with them. Now if God does not exist, then moral values are not objective in this way. . . . But . . . objective values do exist, and deep down we all know it. There's no more reason to deny the objective reality of moral values than the objective reality of the physical world. . . . Actions like rape, cruelty, and child abuse aren't just socially unacceptable behavior—they're moral abominations. Some things are really wrong. Similarly love, equality, and self-sacrifice are really good. But if moral values cannot exist without God and moral values do exist, then it follows logically and inescapably that God exists.[15]

Do you find this argument persuasive?

5. Suppose that Becci and Sam want to have sex even though they are not married. They live in New York City, where premarital sex is not generally disapproved of. However, they are part of a very conservative community, where premarital sex is frowned upon. From an agent relativist point of view, is it okay for Becci and Sam to have sex?

6. How might a speaker relativist respond to the objection presented in the penultimate paragraph of section 13.3?

7. Consider the following story:

> Julie and Mark are brother and sister. They are traveling together in France on summer vacation from college. One night they are staying alone in a cabin near the beach. They decide that it would be interesting and fun if they tried making love. At the very least it would be a new experience for each of them. Julie was already taking birth control pills, but Mark uses a condom too, just to be safe. They both enjoy making love, but they decide not to do it again. They keep that night as a special secret, which makes them feel even closer to each other. What do you think about that? Was it OK for them to make love?

> When Jonathan Haidt and his colleagues gave this paragraph to participants in an experiment, they found that the participants condemned Julie and Mark's action but could not justify this condemnation. The participants were "dumbfounded."[16]

Using examples like this one, Haidt argues that our moral views are typically based on emotions, and that these emotions are not responsive to rational argument.[17] On this view, when people give arguments for their views, these arguments are typically only *post hoc* rationalizations. For example, people are disgusted by the thought of incest, and this causes them to say that incest is morally wrong.

Now answer the following questions:
- Do you think that what Julie and Mark did is morally wrong?
- If so, can you produce an argument for this conclusion, or is your judgment based on emotion, or both?
- Might a moral conclusion be justified by emotion?

8. Consider the sentence "If it is wrong to do something, it is also wrong to pay someone else to do it on your behalf." Suggest an expressivist account of the meaning of this sentence.

9. Consider the sentence "It was wrong of Miss G. to sell her slave to the gentleman." Do you think that this sentence is objective and true? Answer from the point of view of a qualified attitude theorist.

What to Look at Next

- Walter Sinnott-Armstrong's book *Moral Skepticisms* examines a variety of versions of moral skepticism and the arguments for and against them.
- The objection to the divine command theory that we present in section 13.2 has its origins Plato's dialogue *Euthyphro*. The dialogue is easy to find online. Alternatively, you can find a translation in *Five Dialogues,* edited by John Cooper.
- For two sophisticated contemporary defenses of the divine command theory, see William Alston's article "Some Suggestions for Divine Command Theorists," in *Christian Theism and the Problems of Philosophy,* ed. Michael Beaty, and Phillip Quinn's book *Divine Commands and Moral Requirements*. For a contemporary critique of the divine command theory, see Kai Nelson's book *Ethics Without God*.
- W. G. Sumner's 1906 book *Folkways* is a classic defense of moral relativism by an anthropologist.

- Neil Levi's book *Moral Relativism: A Short Introduction* is an engaging and accessible volume. Both descriptive and metaethical moral relativism are discussed insightfully by David Wong in his book *Natural Moralities: A Defense of Pluralistic Relativism.*
- Chapter 6 of A. J. Ayer's book *Language, Truth and Logic* is a bold and bracing statement of expressivism. C. L. Stevenson's book *Ethics and Language* is a classic. For a sophisticated contemporary discussion, see M. Schroeder's *Noncognitivism in Ethics.*
- The version of the qualified attitude theory that we present is borrowed from chapter 10 of Richard Brandt's book *Ethical Theory*. A related account was developed by Roderick Firth in "Ethical Absolutism and the Ideal Observer," *Philosophy and Phenomenological Research* 12, no. 3 (1952): 317–345.
- Woody Allen said that, in his movie *Crimes and Misdemeanors*, he wanted to "illustrate, in an entertaining way, that there is no God, that we're alone in the universe, and that there is nobody out there to punish you, that there's not going to be any kind of Hollywood ending to your life in any way, that your morality is strictly up to you."[18]

Notes

1. This quotation is taken from Lydia Maria Child's *Authentic Anecdotes of American Slavery* (Newburyport, MA: Whipple, 1838).
2. Linda Zagzebski, "Does Ethics Need God?" *Faith and Philosophy* 4, no. 3 (1987): 294–303.
3. Debates on this topic are often traced to Plato's *Euthyphro*. Many of Plato's dialogues are extremely difficult to understand, but the *Euthyphro* is more approachable. The text is easy to find online.
4. As we discussed in chapter 4, it is rather difficult to explicate "omnipotent" adequately.
5. John Calvin, *Institutes*, bk. 3, ch. 23, quoted in James Fieser, *Moral Philosophy through the Ages* (Mountain View, CA: Mayfield, 2001).
6. Ruth Benedict, *Patterns of Culture,* (New York: Houghton Mifflin, 1934), quotes at 5, 271, and 278.
7. Donald Brown, *Human Universals,* (New York: McGraw-Hill, 1991), ch. 5.
8. For Benedict's statement of this position, see her "Anthropology and the Abnormal," *Journal of General Psychology* 10, no. 1 (1934): 59–82.

9. See also M. Herskovits, *Man and His Works,* (New York: Knopf, 1948), ch. 5; E. Westermarck, *Ethical Relativity* (New York: Littlefield, Adams & Company, 1932); and W. G. Sumner, *Folkways* (Boston: Ginn & Company, 1907).
10. A. J. Ayer, *Language, Truth and Logic,* (Harmondsworth: Penguin Books, 1971), ch. 6.
11. Alfred Jules Ayer, *Language, Truth and Logic* (London, England: Dover Publications, 1936), 108.
12. Versions of the qualified attitude theory have been offered by many authors. The version we present and the label "qualified attitude theory" are borrowed from R. Richard Brandt, *Ethical Theory* (Englewood Cliffs, N.J.: Prentice-Hall, 1959).
13. See Steven Pinker, *The Better Angels of Our Nature* (New York: Viking, 2011), on the rates of violent crime.
14. Lionel Robbins, *An Essay on the Nature and Significance of Economic Science* (London: Macmillan, 1932), ch. 6.
15. William Lane Craig, *Does God Exist?* (Colorado Springs: David C. Cook, 2018), 17–18.
16. Jonathan Haidt, *The Righteous Mind,* (New York: Pantheon, 2012), ch. 2.
17. Haidt, *The Righteous Mind,* ch. 2.
18. The quote comes from R. Schickel's book, *Woody Allen: A Life in Film* (Chicago: Ivan R. Lee, 2003).

CHAPTER 14

What Really Matters?

Introduction

Dev and Otávio are going to the movie theater, and they are arguing. They're both fully informed about the price of the tickets, the parking, the popcorn, and so on; their disagreement is not about price. Rather, it's about value: about what's good, and about what's important. Otávio wants to see the latest gross and raunchy comedy: the one with the nudity, the dog, and the vanilla pudding. Dev wants the see the arty Scandinavian classic: the one with the Palme d'Or, the subtitles, and the melancholy Swedes staring into the middle distance. Otávio says:

> I took that film class too, so I totally understand the artistry that goes into those films. But—to be honest—I just don't enjoy them. And I don't think you really enjoy them either. The raunchy movie will be fun.

Dev replies:

> I agree with you that the raunchy comedy would be more fun, and I agree with you that it's good to have a laugh. But I want more than fun. The Scandinavian movie is profound. It will make us think, and it will elevate us. These things are more important.

In this chapter, we take a look at what philosophers have had to say about value. We consider hedonism, which is, roughly speaking, the view that pleasure is the only good and pain is the only bad. We'll then consider Jean-Paul Sartre's idea that it is *up to you* what is good and important in your life. Finally, we'll consider Susan Wolf's attempt to understand what's involved in living a *meaningful* life.

14.1 Hedonism

We begin with a distinction between **direct value** and **indirect value**.

Suppose that you have a ticket to see your favorite band. The ticket is a good thing for you to have—but not because the ticket per se is a valuable thing: the ticket is valuable to you because you can use it to gain admission to a concert. In other words, the ticket is not valuable for its own sake; it is valuable as a means to something else. We will say that the ticket is only "indirectly" good. Fertilizer is another example. Nobody values fertilizer in its own right; we value fertilizer because it increases crop yields. Fertilizer is also only indirectly good. We would say the same thing about toilet brushes, twenty-dollar bills, and printer ink.

Now consider the **pleasure** you get when you eat a piece of chocolate. (If you don't like chocolate, choose a different example.) This feeling of pleasure is good, we suggest, for its own sake. It's good not as a means to something else, but in its own right. It is "directly" good. Plausibly, other pleasures, too, are also directly valuable. For example:

- The thrill that a downhill skier feels when plummeting down a mountainside
- The satisfaction that someone takes in finishing a crossword
- The awe that a mountaineer feels when admiring the view from the summit

It's worth noting, in passing, that there are things which are good *both* directly *and* indirectly. Suppose, for example, that you derive pleasure from eating chocolate; this puts you in a good mood, which helps you to do well on an exam. The pleasure of eating chocolate, in this case, was good both in its own right and as a means to a further good (a high score on the exam).

To recapitulate, we can distinguish direct goodness from indirect goodness. Some things are good only indirectly (e.g., concert tickets, fertilizer). These things are good only as a means to some other good thing. Some things are good directly (e.g., the pleasure of eating chocolate or finishing a crossword). These things are valuable for their own sakes. Some things may be good both directly and indirectly.

We can draw a similar distinction between direct and indirect badness. Suppose, for example, that you put out a trap for pantry moths in your kitchen. You do so not because the presence of pantry moths is in itself a bad thing—you do it because you know that the pantry moths can lay eggs from which hatch larvae that spoil food. The presence of pantry moths is bad indirectly.

Just as pleasure seems to be directly good, **pain** may be directly bad. For example, the throbbing pain you feel when you stub your toe is in itself a bad thing. Here are some other pains, all of which seem to be directly bad:

- The heartache of the person whose love is unrequited
- The feeling of humiliation a bullied child experiences when being mocked in public
- The sensation of being too cold that you get when you are not properly dressed for the snow

So far, we've suggested that pleasure is directly good and that pain is directly bad. Are there any direct goods besides pleasure? And are there any direct bads besides pain? Hedonists say "no" in response to both of these questions. **Hedonists** think that pleasure is always directly good, and that pleasure is the *only* direct good; they think that pain is directly bad, and that pain is the *only* direct bad. Finally, hedonists think that other things are good or bad indirectly only insofar as they bring about pleasure and/or pain. For the hedonist, something that brings about a good deal of pleasure but little or no pain is very good, something that brings about a good deal of pain but little or no pleasure is very bad, and something that brings about pain and pleasure in equal amounts is neither good nor bad.

As an example, let's think about Dev and Otávio's decision from a hedonistic point of view. According to the hedonist, the most valuable experience for Dev and Otávio is whichever one will give them the most pleasure overall.[1] This might be the raunchy comedy—this movie, after all, would be very amusing, and amusement is a sort of pleasure. But it might also be that seeing the arty classic would produce the most pleasure overall. Perhaps the raunchy comedy would be quickly forgotten, while the arty classic would stay in the memory and bring pleasure to Dev and Otávio for years to come. Hedonism, then, does not provide us with a quick answer to the question of which movie would be more valuable to see. Hedonism does, however, give Dev and Otávio a way of thinking through the issue.

We should note that some people use the word "hedonist" rather differently—to describe people who devote themselves to thrill-seeking, sexual promiscuity, the consumption of drugs, and so on. But a "hedonist" in our sense need not choose to live this way. A hedonist, after all, may decide that other people's pleasures matter as much as their own, and so may choose to devote their time to helping other people. Or the hedonist may decide that, in the long run, the life of decadence does not produce the best balance of pleasure over pain. Epicurus (341–270 BCE)—probably the most famous of all hedonists—chose to lead a simple, almost ascetic life with his friends in a commune they set up together. He said that "the things which produce certain pleasures entail annoyances many times greater than the pleasures themselves."[2] Anyone who's suffered a serious hangover will know what he meant.

So far, we've focused on cases involving only a small number of people. However, policymakers can also apply hedonism. The economist and hedonist Richard Layard develops this idea in his book *Happiness: Lessons from a New Science*. (Layard prefers the word "happiness" to the word "pleasure," which we use.) Layard claims that researchers can measure levels of **happiness**, using surveys, and that policymakers should make it their goal to increase the average level of happiness. Layard recommends this as an alternative to the goal of increasing gross domestic product, or GDP, per capita. On this basis, Layard makes several policy recommendations; for example, he recommends increased spending on treatment for mental illness, which he considers "probably the largest single cause of misery in Western societies."[3]

Some critics of hedonism have urged that pleasure is not always good. Imagine, for example, a cruel man who takes great pleasure in the suffering of others. When he hears that his neighbor fell off a roof and broke her back, for example, he enjoys an invigorating surge of warm *schadenfreude*. The hedonist is committed to thinking that this cruel man's pleasure is directly good—but the critic may say that this is wrong. The critic may say that the cruel man's pleasure is clearly not good; it may even be bad.

A more common objection to hedonism is that, while pleasure is directly good, it is not the *only* direct good. For example, it seems plausible that honest, loving relationships are directly good. The hedonist will reply, of course, that such relationships *are* good—but only indirectly. Honest, loving relationships, the hedonist will say, are good because they produce pleasure and reduce pain, and *only* because they produce pleasure and reduce pain.

We don't know who's right about this, but we have a thought experiment that might help you think the issue through. Imagine two married couples: Sam and Alex, and Ed and Jessie. The two couples, we suppose, were equally happy—they experienced the same mixture of pleasure and pain. However, Sam and Alex were happy in part because they were dishonest with each other: they hid from each other various misdeeds and nasty feelings. Ed and Jessie, by contrast, were not deceitful with each other in this way. Now from a hedonist's point of view, these two couples were equally well off because they experienced the same mixture of pleasure and pain. Those who are not hedonists, however, are free to say that Ed and Jessie were better off than Sam and Alex. We'll leave you to think about this.

Another objection to hedonism—closely related to the last—is that hedonists neglect *meaningfulness*. The good life—or so this objection goes—is meaningful as well as pleasurable. One way to see the force of this is to think about what we might call "tough projects"—that is, projects we pursue because we consider them to be meaningful and important, even though we know that there are more pleasurable ways of spending time. Think, for example, of raising children, or writing a novel, or running a restaurant. Or think of training to swim the English Channel. This is a physically strenuous process: the swimmers' training sessions are typically very tiring and very cold. What's more, any time one spends training for a Channel swim is time *not* spent doing other, more pleasurable activities—such as eating chocolate cake while watching movies. So why do people do it? Arguably, people do it because they understand that pleasure is not the only thing that matters—meaningful endeavor also matters.

14.2 Sartre

In this section, we'll look at some of what the French philosopher Jean-Paul Sartre (1905–1980) had to say about value, meaning, and authenticity. But first, a warning. Sartre's views on these topics changed substantially throughout his career, and we don't have anything like the space to discuss the development of his views. Instead, we focus on his position as it was presented in a single essay, "Existentialism Is a Humanism."[4]

Sartre summarized his central thesis by saying that, for human beings like us, "existence precedes essence." The aphorism is obscure at first sight, but in fact, Sartre's claim is not difficult to understand. The term **essence** is used in a confusing variety of ways in philosophy, but in "Existentialism Is a Humanism," it means, more or less, *purpose*. So when Sartre said that, for human beings, "existence precedes essence," what he meant is that we *first* exist and only *later* do we acquire a purpose.

Think about a sieve. The maker of the sieve starts off with a purpose ("I want a tool for getting the lumps out of flour"). The maker then designs and constructs an object to achieve the predefined purpose. So the purpose of the sieve (its "essence") precedes the object itself. Sartre claimed that theists tend to think about human beings in much the same way. God had a purpose for us, and he created human beings to meet that purpose. On this view, people are like sieves—the purpose comes first, the object comes later. Sartre, however, was an atheist: he denied that human beings were created by a god. For Sartre, we are products of blind evolution: we come into existence without a purpose (without an "essence"). However, Sartre does not draw the nihilistic conclusion that our lives are purposeless. Instead, he concludes that it is up to each person to *create* their own essence. For example, you might decide that your goals in life include (a) raising children, (b) writing a book about zoology, (c) maintaining friendships, and (d) staying healthy. These goals are not imposed upon you by God, or by your family, or by society at large, or by any other external thing; instead, these goals are freely chosen by you. So a human being exists first, and only later creates a purpose for their life.

Hence, for human beings, "existence precedes essence." People are not like sieves:

> If I have excluded God the Father, there must be somebody to invent values. . . . [Life] is yours to make sense of, and the value of it is

nothing else but the sense that you choose. In short: each of us is *free* to choose his own values.⁵

How do you feel about this freedom? Sartre stressed that it can also be *frightening* to understand that one is responsible for creating value. He illustrated the point with an example from his own experience. The story is so cinematic, and philosophically rich, that it is worth quoting in full:

> [The student's] father was quarrelling with his mother and was also inclined to be a "collaborator"; his elder brother had been killed in the German offensive of 1940 and this young man, with a sentiment somewhat primitive but generous, burned to avenge him. His mother was living alone with him, deeply afflicted by the semi-treason of his father and by the death of her eldest son, and her one consolation was in this young man. But he, at this moment, had the choice between going to England to join the Free French Forces or of staying near his mother and helping her to live. He fully realized that this woman lived only for him and that his disappearance—or perhaps his death—would plunge her into despair. He also realized that, concretely and in fact, every action he performed on his mother's behalf would be sure of effect in the sense of aiding her to live, whereas anything he did in order to go and fight would be an ambiguous action which might vanish like water into sand and serve no purpose. For instance, to set out for England he would have to wait indefinitely in a Spanish camp on the way through Spain; or, on arriving in England or in Algiers he might be put into an office to fill up forms. Consequently, he found himself confronted by two very different modes of action; the one concrete, immediate, but directed towards only one individual; and the other an action addressed to an end infinitely greater, a national collectivity, but for that very reason ambiguous—and it might be frustrated on the way.⁶

Sartre's only advice to the student was that *he* had to decide what to prioritize. He could choose to put his mother's health first, or he could choose to prioritize his desire to avenge his brother's death. The student could be forgiven for thinking that this advice is not very helpful. When he left his conversation with Sartre, the student was stuck with the same horrible decision.

The student might have been tempted to avoid having to make the decision by "outsourcing" it to someone else. For example, if the student was a Christian, he could have asked a priest. However, according to Sartre, it was not really possible to avoid the decision in this way. After all, if the student asked a priest for advice, it would have been the student's decision to ask a priest for help, and if the student chose to follow the priest's advice, that, too, would have been his decision. So the student was stuck with the decision: he could not pass his burden on to someone else.

The student might possibly have been able to reduce the emotional toll of this horrible situation by engaging in self-deception. The student could lie to himself, pretending that he had no choice about what to do. For example, the student might say to himself, "I am a devoted son, and I always have been. It's in my nature to put family first. And so it is inevitable that I will stay with my mother rather than leaving home to fight with the Free French Forces." Since the prospect of having to make a decision was so frightening, this maneuver might well have been comforting.

This is, of course, a singular example, but it illustrates two Sartrian concepts with very broad application: "anguish" and "bad faith." **Anguish** is the pain we experience when forced to make difficult decisions about what to value. Sartre said that we are "condemned to be free." We are "free" because each of us is able to choose their own essence. But this freedom is often painful, and we are unable to escape it, and so, paradoxically, freedom is forced upon us. **Bad faith** is—according to Sartre, anyway—a common response to anguish. When people live in bad faith, they delude themselves into thinking that they are not free to make their own decisions.

In an earlier book, *Being and Nothingness*, Sartre had described in detail what he took to be a particularly frequent form of bad faith. It is common, according to Sartre, for people to hide their freedom from themselves by identifying with their social roles. A waiter, for example, might start to think of himself as *just a waiter*, neglecting to attend to the fact that he could choose some other way of life.[7] The waiter rises at five in the morning, thinking, "As a waiter, I *must* get up at five." He gets to the café and sweeps the floor, thinking, "As a waiter, I *must* sweep the floor." As he serves his customers, he does so with certain mannerisms, thinking, "These are the mannerisms characteristic of waiters like me." All the time, he fails to notice that he is free to behave differently. This process of self-deception, Sartre thought, is made easy because there is social pressure on people to conform to particular social roles. "A grocer who dreams is offensive to the buyer," Sartre wrote, "because such a grocer is not wholly a grocer. Society demands that he limit himself to his function as a grocer."[8]

It is clear in Sartre's writing that he disapproved of people who live in bad faith. What is less clear is the basis of this disapproval. We think that his argument went something like this. It is a consequence of Sartre's position that things are of value only when they are *given* value by free agents. For an object that lacks freedom, nothing is good, and nothing is bad. This is, we think, a plausible claim. Nothing is good or bad from the point of view of a rock, for example, because the rock is not capable of conferring value on things. Now consider the waiter who lives in bad faith. The waiter chooses to deceive himself, by pretending that he is not free. According to Sartre, the waiter, by choosing to deny his own freedom, commits himself to the conclusion that nothing is valuable for him. But, of course, the waiter will continue to value things—perhaps he will continue to value his job, his marriage, and so on. The waiter's position is thus *contradictory,* according to Sartre. The waiter values certain things, but at the same time, he denies his freedom, which is the very basis of that value.

Back to Dev and Otávio. Which movie would it be more valuable for them to see? Or rather, what would Sartre say about the question?

We think Sartre would say that it is up each of them, individually, to make a decision about what's most important. Let's focus on Otávio. Otávio may decide that what is most important is belly-laughs, in which case he should see the raunchy movie. Alternatively, he may decide that what is most important is intellectual depth, in which case he should choose the arty classic.

But Sartre would urge Otávio *not* to make the decision in bad faith; that is, he should not pretend that one of the options is closed off to him by virtue of his social position. He shouldn't say:

> I'm an educated person, and educated people like me always prefer arty films to gross and raunchy comedies. Therefore, I will certainly choose the Scandinavian classic.

Similarly, he shouldn't say:

> I'm a young person, and art films are only for old people. So I will certainly choose the raunchy comedy.

Sartre's claim that we "invent" values has struck some people as contrary to our everyday experience. Typically, we seem to *find* value, not *invent* it. For example, suppose that you're leaving your apartment to go to work. You step outside and see that one of your car's tires is flat. You don't then think to yourself, "I hereby declare that this is a bad thing"—you just *see* that it's a bad thing. The disvalue is *perceived*, not created.

Sartre saw this objection coming, and he had a response.[9] Sartre claimed that it is only because we have chosen, freely, to take on certain life projects that we are able to perceive value in this way. To return to the example, the fact that your car has a flat tire only strikes you as a bad thing because you have already freely chosen to pursue the project of being a punctual worker. In this way, Sartre could maintain his claim that value is invented rather than discovered.

It seems to many people, however, that pleasure and pain are counterexamples to Sartre's theory. If you hit your thumb hard with a hammer, the pain will immediately seem bad to you—and this doesn't seem to be a consequence of some project that you have chosen. Pain, it seems, *just is* bad—regardless of your personal commitments. The badness of pain is discovered, not created.

A further objection to Sartre's position goes like this. Imagine someone who devotes her life to a single project: amassing a gargantuan collection of completely ordinary rubber bands.[10] She devotes many hours of each day to this project, stopping only to take care of biologically necessary tasks like sleeping and eating. There is no bad faith involved: she fully understands that *she chose* to devote herself to collecting rubber bands, and that she could instead have chosen a more conventional kind of life. But she is entirely happy with her choice. The rubber-band collector's life is in some ways enviable. She is happy, and she has had the opportunity to pursue a goal that she cherishes. Even so, one might feel that there is something wrong with the way she lives. Her project—however much she enjoys it, however sincerely she values it—is *pointless*. She is wasting her time. Appealing to examples like this, one might say that something is missing from Sartre's account. We may be able to "invent value," but our power to do so is limited. Certain projects—for example, collecting rubber bands—are simply not worthwhile, even if they are pursued without any bad faith.

14.3 Susan Wolf on Meaningfulness

We have now considered two different theories of value: Sartre's theory, and hedonism. We have suggested that neither theory includes a satisfactory account of *meaning*. The hedonist, arguably, cannot account for the value of "tough projects"—projects that may not be pleasurable but may be deeply meaningful for the people involved. Sartre, critics have alleged, cannot account for the fact that a life entirely devoted to the collection of rubber bands is lacking in meaning—even if the person is not guilty of bad faith. We took this last point from Susan Wolf, whose views about meaning we discuss in this section.[11]

Wolf summarizes her position with the slogan "meaningful lives are lives of active engagement in projects of worth."[12] There are two expressions here that require discussion: "active engagement" and "projects of worth." Let's start with **active engagement**. Wolf claims that one cannot derive meaning from activities that are "boring or mechanical." For example, it's good to donate money to effective charities, and it's good to recycle. Even so, Wolf says, few people "get meaning from recycling or from writing checks to Oxfam"[13] because these activities do not involve active engagement:

> A person is actively engaged by something if she is gripped, excited, involved by it. Most obviously, we are actively engaged by the things and people about which and whom we are passionate. Opposites of active engagement are boredom and alienation. To be actively engaged in something is not always pleasant in the ordinary sense of the word. Activities in which people are actively engaged frequently involve stress, danger, exertion, or sorrow (consider, for example: writing a book, climbing a mountain, training for a marathon, caring for an ailing friend). However, there is something good about the feeling of engagement: one feels (typically without thinking about it) especially alive.[14]

So far, it may seem that Wolf is merely echoing the graduation-day cliché "Find Your Passion!" But in fact, Wolf thinks that, in order to lead a meaningful life, it is not enough to be "actively engaged" in one's projects. Some projects, Wolf thinks, are just not important enough to confer meaning on a person's life, even if they are pursued with active engagement. For example, one might be actively engaged while riding a

Susan Wolf thinks that one can lead a meaningful life by actively engaging in projects of worth.

rollercoaster or while meeting a movie star—but according to Wolf, one would not derive much meaning from these trivial pleasures.

This brings us to **projects of worth**. According to Wolf, a project can only confer meaning on a person's life if it is "worthwhile." We've already mentioned some of Wolf's examples of projects that are not worthwhile: collecting rubber bands, riding rollercoasters, and meeting movie stars. Other examples include making handwritten copies of

War and Peace, memorizing the dictionary, eating chocolate, attending aerobics classes, and watching sitcoms. Examples of projects that *are* worthwhile (according to Wolf) include scientific research, political activism, building relationships with friends and family members, and creating and appreciating works of art.

To sum up: for Wolf, in order to lead a meaningful life, it is not enough to pursue worthwhile projects, and it is not enough to be actively engaged. These two things *together* are needed: meaning occurs "where subjective attraction meets objective attractiveness."[15]

Back to Dev and Otávio. What would Wolf say about which movie they should choose?

Wolf doesn't directly address the question of whether watching movies is worthwhile, so we'll have to extrapolate from examples she does discuss. Wolf *does* indicate that watching sitcoms is not worthwhile, and presumably, watching gross and raunchy movies is relevantly similar to watching sitcoms. So we think Wolf's position would be that watching gross and raunchy movies is not worthwhile. By contrast, Wolf says that appreciating art is worthwhile, which suggests that she would say that appreciating the best art movies is worthwhile.

Does Wolf's view imply, then, that it would be more valuable for Dev and Otávio to see the Scandinavian movie? Not quite. For one thing, Wolf's position implies that Dev and Otávio will only find meaning in watching the Scandinavian movie if they are able to watch it with active engagement. If they find the movie boring, they won't derive meaning from watching it. And there's a second complication. We've been talking exclusively about Wolf's theory of **meaningfulness**. However, according to Wolf, meaningfulness is not the only thing that is important in life. She says that there are two "aspects" to the good life: meaning is one, happiness is the other. So perhaps when Dev and Otávio think about which movie to go to, they should think about happiness as well as meaning. They may find that they face a trade-off: if they choose the raunchy comedy, they get more happiness but less meaning; if they choose the Scandinavian art film, they get more meaning but less happiness.

As we've said, Wolf thinks that appreciating art is a project of worth, but watching sitcoms is not. But what is the basis for such judgments? How does she know that appreciating art is a project of worth but watching sitcoms isn't? Here is another example. Kayla and

Sydney, two Wolfian gymnasts, are relaxing with a drink after a training session. Kayla says:

> Practicing on the uneven bars is good for me in the short run because it makes me happy. And it's good for me in the long run because it helps me meet new friends, and it keeps me fit. When I'm practicing, I'm certainly actively engaged. Even so, I don't think that practicing or competing on the uneven bars per se brings meaning to my life. After all, it's just a game. It's fun, but it's not meaningful.

Sydney winces at the claim that competing on the uneven bars is "just" a game. She insists that competing on the uneven bars is worthwhile, in Wolf's sense, and that, in consequence, it can bring meaning to a person's life.

How could this dispute be settled? More generally, how can we figure out which activities are of worth?

Wolf suggests that, when we address this question, we should start with our "pretheoretical judgments" about what is of worth. We should then try to improve our judgments with an "open-minded, concentrated, and communal effort to examine and articulate the basis for them."[16] In particular, Wolf suggests, we should *compare* our judgments one with another in an attempt to identify and remove anomalies. For example, Sydney might say:

> Creating art is a paradigmatically worthwhile activity, and presumably, ballet is an art form. So I think we can agree that performing in the ballet is of worth. Now performing on the uneven bars is in all relevant respects just like performing in the ballet. Both activities require a great deal of strength and balance. Both are graceful. In both cases, it takes many years of practice to achieve competence. And so on. So we can infer that performing on the uneven bars is worthwhile.

Kayla might reply that performing on the uneven bars differs only in degree from such mundane exercises as push-ups, squats, and planks.

We'll leave you to think about how much progress can be made using this kind of reasoning. Wolf herself is somewhat pessimistic:

> Our culture-bound, contemporary judgments of which activities are worthwhile are bound to be partly erroneous. History is full of unappreciated geniuses, of artists, inventors, explorers whose activities at their time were scorned, as it is full of models of behavior and accomplishment that later seem to have been overrated.[17]

Wolf makes two points in this passage that are worth separating. The first point is that our judgments about which activities are worthwhile are "culture-bound"—that is, judgments about which activities vary greatly from one culture to another. For example, people in martial cultures and people in pacifist cultures have very different opinions about whether waging war is "worthwhile" in Wolf's sense. The next point is that if we look back through history, we are likely to conclude that people in the past made many errors in their judgments about which activities were worthwhile.

Wolf goes on to suggest it is likely that we, too, make such errors. It would be "overly optimistic," she writes, to hope for a "reliable method for generally distinguishing worthwhile from worthless activities."[18] This is, we think, a rather unsettling thought: perhaps some of us are in the unfortunate situation of the rubber-band collector but have no "reliable method" for seeing the problem.

Conclusion

We finished our discussion of hedonism by suggesting that the hedonist does not have an adequate account of what it is to lead a meaningful life. We made the point by considering people who take on "tough projects," such as raising children, writing a novel, or running a restaurant. A project of this kind might greatly enrich a person's life—such a project is *meaningful*—even if it produces a lot of pain and not much pleasure. The hedonist, it seems, has no way of explaining the value of such projects.

Sartre's position is not vulnerable to this same complaint. He claimed that "each of us is *free* to choose his own values." In particular, a person might choose as most valuable raising children, writing a novel, or running a restaurant (even if the chosen activity is far from pleasurable). However, Sartre's position is vulnerable to a different complaint. It seems that a life devoted entirely to the collection of perfectly ordinary rubber bands is not a meaningful life, no matter how sincerely the person values the project. And apparently, Sartre could not accommodate this point. So perhaps, like the hedonist, Sartre did not have an adequate account of meaningfulness.

Susan Wolf's position is appealing because it avoids these problems. Unlike the hedonist, she thinks that happiness is not the only thing that matters: meaningfulness is important too. And unlike Sartre, she thinks that certain endeavors are not meaningful, even if they are sincerely and whole-heartedly pursued. As she puts it, only some projects are "worthwhile." However, Wolf's position has one rather unnerving feature.

She says that it would be "overly optimistic" to hope for "a reliable method for generally distinguishing worthwhile from worthless activities." On this view, some of us may be wasting our lives on worthless activities, with no "reliable method" for uncovering the error.

We have to admit that we find all of this unsettling: we don't know how to figure out how to lead a meaningful life. But perhaps you can do better.

Glossary

active engagement: Susan Wolf says that, to lead a meaningful life, one must be "actively engaged" in "projects of worth." She writes, "[a] person is actively engaged by something if she is gripped, excited, involved by it." See section 14.3 for more details.

anguish and bad faith: Sartre claimed that "it is we who give [life] meaning, and value is nothing more than the meaning we give it." He also claimed that it can be frightening to recognize this truth, especially when we face big decisions. He called this particular fear "anguish"—that is, anguish is the pain we experience when forced to make difficult decisions about what to value. Sartre went on to claim that sometimes people respond to anguish with self-deception: they pretend they are not free to choose what to value. He called this particular sort of self-deception "bad faith." See section 14.2 for more details.

direct value vs. indirect value: Something is *indirectly* valuable if it is valuable as a means to something else. For example, a concert ticket is valuable because you can use it to gain access to a concert. Something is *directly* valuable if it is valuable, not as a means to something else, but in its own right. It is plausible that pleasure is directly valuable. Philosophers use a number of synonyms for "direct" and "indirect":

Synonyms for "directly valuable"	Synonyms for "indirectly valuable"
intrinsically valuable	extrinsically valuable
noninstrumentally valuable	instrumentally valuable
inherently valuable	
valuable for its own sake	
valuable in its own right	

See section 14.1 for more discussion of this distinction.

essence: The term "essence" is used in many different ways in philosophy. In section 14.2, "essence" means *purpose*. For example, we might describe the essence of a sieve by saying that it is for getting lumps out of flour.

happiness: "Happiness" is a contested term in philosophy. Some people use the term "happiness" as a synonym for "pleasure." Other people use the term as a near synonym of "well-being" or "welfare."

hedonists: Hedonists think that pleasure is always directly good, and that pleasure is the *only* direct good; they think that pain is directly bad, and that pain is the *only* direct bad. Finally, hedonists think that other things are good or bad indirectly only insofar as they bring about pleasure and/or pain. For the hedonist, something that brings about a good deal of pleasure but little or no pain is very good, something that brings about a good deal of pain but little or no pleasure is very bad, and something that brings about pain and pleasure in equal amounts is neither good nor bad. See section 14.1 for more details.

indirect value: See direct value vs. indirect value.

meaningfulness: We won't attempt a succinct characterization of meaningfulness in the glossary. See the end of section 14.1 for a preliminary characterization, and see section 14.3 for a description of Susan Wolf's theory of meaningfulness.

pain and pleasure: Roughly, pleasures are positive sensations. This includes:

- The taste of chocolate
- The thrill a skier feels going down a mountainside
- The satisfaction one takes in finishing a crossword
- The awe a mountaineer feels when admiring the view from the summit

Pains are negative sensations. This includes:

- The heartache of the person whose love is unrequited
- The feeling of humiliation a bullied child experiences when being mocked in public
- The sensation of being too cold that you get when you are not properly dressed for the snow

projects of worth: Susan Wolf says that, to lead a meaningful life, one must be "actively engaged" in "projects of worth." She gives the following as examples of projects of worth: scientific research, political activism, building relationships with friends and family members, and creating and appreciating works of art. She gives the following as examples of activities that are not projects of worth: collecting rubber bands, riding rollercoasters, and meeting movie stars. See section 14.3 for more details.

Comprehension Questions

1. Explain the distinction between "direct" and "indirect" value, using examples. (Don't repeat examples from the text.)
2. What is hedonism?
3. One dictionary defines "hedonism" as *sensual self-indulgence*. Explain the difference between hedonism in this sense and the philosophical theory known as hedonism.
4. Suppose that someone who has lied to a friend later experiences unpleasant feelings of guilt. Are these feelings good or bad? Answer from the point of view of a hedonist.
5. Briefly list some objections to hedonism.
6. In "Existentialism Is a Humanism," Sartre uses some obscure expressions. Write brief explanations of the following: "Existence precedes essence"; "anguish"; "bad faith."
7. Was Sartre a hedonist? Explain your answer.
8. Explain Wolf's objection to Sartre's position.
9. Explain the following terms used by Susan Wolf: "active engagement" and "projects of worth."
10. Is Susan Wolf a hedonist? Explain your answer.

Discussion Questions

1. Jeremy Bentham, a hedonist, famously claimed that, "prejudice aside," pushpin is as good as poetry. (Pushpin was a simple children's board game, like Chutes and Ladders.) Why might Bentham have said this? Would Susan Wolf agree?
2. Are there pains that are not directly bad?
3. Have you ever had to choose between doing something meaningful and doing something pleasurable and chosen the former? Does this suggest that there is something wrong with hedonism?

4. You're at a party, and someone says:

    > It was inevitable that I would become a musician. It's just very deeply embedded in who I am. Music is in my blood, and my bones. Ever since I was very small, I've written songs and I've been a performer. And I've always known that music was my destiny.

    Sartre would no doubt say that this person is living in bad faith. Do you agree?

5. Do you agree with Wolf that collecting rubber bands is not a "project of worth"? What do you think about competing on the uneven bars? What about watching movies? What methods do we have for answering questions like these?

What to Look at Next

- Chapter 2 of Alain de Botton's *The Consolations of Philosophy* contains an amusing discussion of Epicurus.
- Richard Layard's book *Happiness: Lessons from a New Science* is a hedonistic discussion of some questions of public policy.
- Sartre's "Existentialism Is a Humanism" is easy to find online. If you want a paper copy, we suggest the translation in Walter Kaufmann's anthology *Existentialism from Dostoevsky to Sartre*. This book also contains works from Dostoevsky, Kierkegaard, Nietzsche, Rilke, Kafka, Jaspers (pronounced "Yaspers"), Heidegger, and Camus.
- To learn more about Sartre's views on value, David Detmer's *Freedom as a Value: A Critique of the Ethical Theory of Jean-Paul Sartre* is a good place to start.
- To learn more about existentialism generally, start with Sarah Bakewell's *At the Existentialist Cafe: Freedom, Being and Apricot Cocktails*.
- We've discussed Susan Wolf's paper "Happiness and Meaning: Two Aspects of the Good Life." She expands on this paper in her book *Meaning in Life and Why It Matters*. The book includes responses from John Koethe, Robert M. Adams, Nomy Arpaly, and Jonathan Haidt.
- For a discussion of meaningfulness, you might want to look at Julian Baggini's *What's It All About?: Philosophy and the Meaning of Life*.

- As we said in section 14.1, the word "hedonist" is sometimes applied to people who devote themselves to sex, drinking, parties, and so on. Federico Fellini's movie *La Dolce Vita* is a fascinating exploration of hedonism in this sense.
- Jean-Paul Sartre wrote some very dense philosophical nonfiction. He also wrote some wonderful novels and plays. We suggest that you start with *Nausea*.
- John Barth's witty novel *The End of the Road* touches on many of the questions raised in this chapter.

Notes

1. We assume that neither movie is likely to cause them pain—so we disregard pain in this case. For simplicity, we also assume that Dev and Otávio are the only people affected by the decision.
2. Tiziano Dorandi, ed. *Diogenes Laertius: Lives of Eminent Philosophers* (Cambridge: Cambridge University Press, 2013), vol. 2, 667.
3. Richard Layard, *Happiness: Lessons from a New Science* (New York: Penguin, 2005), 182.
4. This lecture has been reprinted many times and is easy to find online. Our quotations are taken from Walter Kaufmann's anthology *Existentialism from Dostoevsky to Sartre* (New York: Meridian, 1956). However, Kauffman translates *mauvaise foi* as "self-deception"; we decided to use the more conventional translation "bad faith."
5. Kauffman, *Existentialism*, 309.
6. Kaufmann, *Existentialism*, 295–296.
7. The example is taken from the second chapter of *Being and Nothingness*; quote from the translation by Hazel Barnes (New York: Washington Square Press: 1956).
8. Kaufman, *Existentialism*, 59.
9. This response is not to be found in "Existentialism Is a Humanism," but rather in *Being and Nothingness*. For discussion, see chapter 2 of David Detmer's *Freedom as a Value: A Critique of the Ethical Theory of Jean-Paul Sartre* (La Salle, Il: Open Court, 1988).
10. The example is taken from Susan Wolf's paper "Happiness and Meaning: Two Aspects of the Good Life," *Social Philosophy and Policy* 14, no. 1 (1997): 207–225.
11. The discussion in this section is based on her paper "Happiness and Meaning."

12. Wolf, "Happiness and Meaning," 209.
13. Wolf, "Happiness and Meaning," 211.
14. Wolf, "Happiness and Meaning," 209.
15. Wolf, "Happiness and Meaning," 211.
16. Wolf, "Happiness and Meaning," 212.
17. Wolf, "Happiness and Meaning," 212.
18. Wolf, "Happiness and Meaning," 212.

CHAPTER 15

What Should We Do? (Part I)

15.1 Act Consequentialism and Act Utilitarianism

You've bought a concert ticket for tonight, but now you can't make it to the performance because you have to stay at home to work. You don't have time to organize the sale of the ticket, so you decide that either you'll just let the ticket go to waste or you'll give it as a gift to your friend Andi, or to your friend Jada. So you have three options:

Option 1: Let the ticket go to waste.
Option 2: Give the ticket to Andi.
Option 3: Give the ticket to Jada.

You realize that the first option is the best from a self-interested point of view: getting the ticket to Andi or Jada would be an irritation and an inconvenience. However, you also realize that the bother to you of passing on the ticket would be small compared to the benefit to Andi or Jada of going to the concert. So you rule out option 1. It then occurs to you that Jada would get much more out of the concert than Andi. So you figure that option 3 is preferable to option 2. So you choose option 3.

This process of weighing up costs (i.e., bad consequences) and benefits (i.e., good consequences) can be presented mathematically. We measure the benefits using positive numbers and the costs using negative numbers. For each option, the **aggregate good** is the sum of the numbers that measure the costs and the benefits that would result from your choosing that option.

	1: Let the ticket go to waste	2: Give the ticket to Andi	3: Give the ticket to Jada
You	0	−1	−1
Andi	0	10	0
Jada	0	0	20
Aggregate good	0	9	19

Option 3 has the highest score overall, so it looks to be the best choice.

Of course, in this simple case, the use of numbers is hardly necessary, but in more complicated cases, the mathematics may be helpful. (In practice, the costs and benefits are usually measured in dollars—in which case the decision-making process is called **cost-benefit analysis**.) Suppose, for example, that a committee is deciding whether a highway should be built between Somewheresville and Anyborough—two towns that are currently connected only by a dangerous, narrow, winding mountain road. The benefits in this case might include:

- Residents of the two towns will be able to travel about more quickly.
- Some businesses in the two towns will enjoy profit increases (e.g., Anyborough's hotels will get more visitors).
- There will be fewer road deaths.

The costs might include:

- The highway will cost $100,000,000 to build, and $250,000 each year to maintain.
- There will be some environmental damage; for example, many acres of wilderness will be covered with concrete.
- The ugly, noisy road will reduce the number of tourists traveling to the scenic, mountainous area between Somewheresville and Anyborough.

To make this decision using cost-benefit analysis, a figure in dollars is assigned to each of the costs and each of the benefits, and the project is approved if the net benefit is sufficiently large.

This method of decision-making—weighing up costs and benefits—is widely used and seems appropriate in many cases. And this is the motivation for the ethical theory known as **act consequentialism**:

Act consequentialism
The best thing to do, in any circumstance, is the action that will maximize the aggregate good.

There's an obvious objection, however, to this proposal: in many cases, it will be *very difficult* to figure out which action will maximize the aggregate good. Suppose, for example, that you're deciding which career to pursue. It's hard enough to assess the costs and benefits to you—let alone to predict the costs and benefits to other people.

The act consequentialist has two responses to this concern. First, one shouldn't expect an ethical theory to make all difficult decisions easy. Choosing a career, or deciding whether to build a highway, is inevitably a hugely complicated business. Any ethicist who promises an easy-to-follow recipe for making such big decisions is to be regarded with suspicion, just as we would be suspicious of a doctor who claimed to have a pill that cures all diseases.

Second, the act consequentialist's view is *not* that, whenever one makes a decision, one should do so by carrying out a mathematical calculation of costs and benefits: that would surely take too much time in most cases. Usually, the act consequentialist must rely on rough-and-ready generalizations, such as *typically one should brush one's teeth after breakfast* and *typically it is wrong to lie to strangers*. Act consequentialists do not carry out a complex calculation every morning before finally deciding to clean their teeth. Rather, after breakfast, they brush because they remember that, as a general rule, the costs of neglecting dental care far exceed the benefits.

Here's a second objection to act consequentialism. In many cases, it is not clear how to assign numerical values to the various costs and benefits—indeed, in some cases, it's not clear that it even makes sense to compare costs and benefits of very different kinds on a single numerical scale. For example, when the planners are thinking about whether to build the highway from Somewheresville to Anyborough, how can they assign a numerical value to the cost that is the environmental damage of the projected road-building? The planners will end up asking themselves questions like "How much damage is done, in dollars, when an acre of wilderness is covered in concrete?" It's not clear how to answer this question. It's not even clear that the question makes sense: perhaps trying to measure the badness of environmental damage in dollars is like trying to measure the height of the Eiffel Tower in degrees Fahrenheit.

Different act consequentialists have dealt with this issue in different ways: there are many varieties of act consequentialism. However, one form of act consequentialism has been more influential than the others: this is **act utilitarianism**, which incorporates a **hedonist** theory of value:[1]

> *Hedonism*
>
> Pleasure is always directly good, and pleasure is the only direct good. Pain is always directly bad, and pain is the only direct bad. Other things are good or bad indirectly only insofar as they bring about pleasure and/or pain.

If you've ever been asked by a doctor, "How much does it hurt, on a scale of zero to ten?" you'll be familiar with the idea that pains can be numerically measured. Act utilitarians believe that pleasures can also be numerically measured ("How good does that feel, on a scale of zero to ten?"). Typically, they use positive numbers to measure pleasures and negative numbers to measure pains. These numbers are called **utilities**. The **aggregate utility** of an action is the sum of all the utilities of the pleasures and pains that the action brings about. Act utilitarians believe that the best thing to do, in any circumstance, is the action that will maximize the aggregate utility.

The act utilitarian thus has a method—in principle, anyway—of measuring all costs and benefits on a single scale. In practice, of course, it can be tremendously hard to determine how much pleasure or pain will result from a given decision, but as we've said, you shouldn't expect an ethical theory to make all hard decisions easy.

Jeremy Bentham (1748–1832) was an English philosopher and early act utilitarian, and to this day, he is probably the most famous proponent of the doctrine. Bentham expressed his act utilitarianism like this:

> It is the greatest happiness of the greatest number that is the measure of right and wrong.[2]

Bentham drew many then-radical conclusions from this claim. He called for the abolition of slavery, on the grounds that the suffering endured by slaves far exceeded the benefits of slavery to the slave-owners and those who traded with them. In Bentham's time, to have homosexual sex in England was to commit a capital crime. However, Bentham contended that homosexual sex should be legal. He argued that it's typically pleasurable for the participants and causes no pain to third parties. Defenders of the status quo argued that homosexual

Jeremy Bentham (1748–1832) was the founder of modern utilitarianism.

sex is unnatural—but for the act utilitarian, this is irrelevant. What matters is pleasure and pain; naturalness has nothing to do with it. This tradition of act utilitarian radicalism persists. For example, Peter Singer—one of the founders of the animal liberation movement—is a utilitarian. Singer argues, to put it very briefly, that we should stop eating meat because the suffering of the farmed animals greatly exceeds the pleasures of eating meat.[3]

15.2 Objections to Act Utilitarianism

In this section, we will discuss two objections to act utilitarianism. The first objection, to put it crudely, is that act utilitarians cannot account for the duties that we have to people who are close to us: relatives, friends, compatriots, and so on. The second objection is that act utilitarians fail to recognize the rights of individual people.[4]

We'll illustrate the first of these two objections with a story. Suppose that Dominique lives 300 miles from her elderly, ailing uncle. She is his only relative. Every Saturday, she drives to his house, has lunch with him, helps him with his chores, and then drives home. The drive takes five hours each way, and so she only manages to spend five hours or so with her uncle.

A friend suggests to Dominique that, instead of visiting her uncle, she should visit the residents of her local nursing home—people who are currently strangers to her. Since she wouldn't have to spend ten hours each Saturday in her car, she could manage three five-hour visits in her Saturday, rather than just one. Dominique is puzzled. She insists that she has an obligation to help out her ailing uncle, precisely because he is *her* uncle. She has no such obligation to help out the people in her local nursing home.

What would an act utilitarian say about this? Well, Dominique's relevant options are these:

Option 1: Visit the uncle.
Option 2: Visit three residents of the local nursing home.

Now plausibly, Dominique will produce more utility if she chooses the second option: perhaps she will produce as much as three times as much utility if she goes for option2. So act utilitarianism seems to imply that Dominique should go for option 2. But critics of act utilitarianism— siding with Dominique against her friend—may say that Dominique has an obligation to her uncle *in particular*, precisely because he is her uncle. She has no such obligation to the residents of her local nursing home. Act utilitarianism, the critic will say, errs because it fails to recognize this familial obligation. In much the same way, it can be argued that act utilitarians neglect the obligations that we have to friends, neighbors, or compatriots. Such obligations are often called **special obligations**, and so we can summarize this complaint about act utilitarianism by saying that act utilitarians fail to recognize special obligations.

The act utilitarian has two responses available. The first, and more concessive, response goes like this. Act utilitarians may say that they *can* explain why it is that you should in many cases show special concern to your relatives, friends, neighbors, and compatriots: in many cases, you're better placed to help people close to you because you're more familiar with their characters and circumstances. It is easy to help out your sister or the guy next door; it is much harder to help out a stranger in a distant and unknown country. The second response is more forthright: act utilitarians often argue that many "commonsense" views about one's obligations to help others are radically mistaken; in particular, they argue that people in wealthy countries radically underestimate their obligations to aid distant strangers. We'll look at this point in more detail in chapter 16.

Now let's turn to the second objection to act utilitarianism. The second objection, in brief, is that act utilitarians fail to recognize the rights of individual people. Here is a story to illustrate the point. Suppose that a hacker has broken into the private cloud storage of a famous movie actor and has found embarrassing emails written by the actor. It would be tremendously upsetting to the actor if the emails were to be released online, and it would damage his career. However, many people—let's say, 20 million—would greatly enjoy the gossip about the actor's private life.

It seems it would be wrong for the hacker to circulate the emails without the actor's permission: to do so would be a gross violation of his privacy. However, act utilitarianism seems to imply that the hacker *should* release the emails: the number of people who would derive pleasure from reading them is *enormous*, and so releasing the emails, it seems, would maximize aggregate utility. It may help to think about this numerically. Suppose that each person who looks at the emails derives one unit of pleasure from the experience, and suppose that the actor will experience 1 million units of pain if the emails are released. Then, the aggregate utility of releasing the emails is 19 million. In this case, act utilitarianism seems to imply, wrongly, that the hacker should circulate the emails on the Internet.

Here is another story in the same genre:[5]

> At the end of a criminal trial, the magistrate has to decide whether to find the defendant guilty (in which case he will be executed) or innocent (in which case he will be released). The magistrate believes that the defendant did not commit the crime. However, a mob has gathered outside the courtroom. The members of the mob strongly believe that the man is guilty, and if he is found innocent, they will riot. They will destroy property and burn buildings. Many people will be killed in the ensuing tumult.

Many people who look at this story decide that it would be wrong for the magistrate to convict the defendant. It is just wrong, many people think, to punish someone for a crime that he didn't commit. With such cases in mind, Elizabeth Anscombe (1919–2001) was forthright about this (she was not given to understatement):

> But if someone really thinks, in advance, that it is open to question whether such an action as procuring the judicial execution of the innocent should be quite excluded from consideration—I do not want to argue with him; he shows a corrupt mind.[6]

However, act utilitarianism seems to imply that the magistrate *should* convict the defendant—because the suffering that would be caused by the rioting presumably exceeds the loss of utility to the defendant if he is convicted.

Our two stories have a common structure. In both cases, act utilitarianism seems to imply that one should inflict some horrible abuse on one person, on the grounds that the individual's interests are outweighed by the interests of a larger number of third parties. In both cases, the act utilitarian's conclusion is arguably counterintuitive. The objection can be put this way: its critics urge that act utilitarianism is mistaken because it neglects individual rights. In the story about the actor's private emails, the actor has a right to privacy. In the story of the magistrate and the mob, the defendant has a right to a fair trial. These individual rights should trump calculations of costs and benefits—or so say the critics of act utilitarianism.

How should the act utilitarian respond to stories of this kind?

In each case, the act utilitarian can respond bluntly by claiming that—whatever the critics say—the interests of the many really do outweigh the needs of the individual. Perhaps the magistrate *should* convict the innocent man; perhaps the hacker *should* release the emails. Alternatively, the act utilitarian may say that, when we think through these cases more carefully, we'll see that act utilitarianism does not in fact have the alleged counterintuitive consequences. For example, it could be argued that in fact the hacker would *not* maximize aggregate utility by circulating the actor's private emails. If the hacker circulates the emails (the act utilitarian may argue), this will encourage further privacy violations, and this will cause further suffering—so in the long run, it does not maximize aggregate utility to release the emails.

15.3 Rule Consequentialism and Rule Utilitarianism

Here's another way of thinking about the objection to act utilitarianism that we discussed at the end of the last section. What the act utilitarian fails to recognize—so the complaint goes—is that there are *general moral rules*, which should not be broken even when doing so maximizes aggregate utility. For example:

> *The privacy rule*
>
> It is wrong to circulate a person's private data (e.g., photographs, bank statements, diaries, emails, medical records, messages) without that person's permission.

The hacker may be able to maximize aggregate utility by releasing the actor's private emails on the Internet, but to do so would violate the privacy rule and would consequently be wrong. No doubt our statement of the privacy rule could do with some refinement—but the force of the complaint about act utilitarianism should be clear even so.

Similarly, it may be said that the magistrate should not convict the innocent defendant because to do so would violate this rule (or some more refined version of it):

> *The fair trial rule*
>
> You should convict a person of a crime only if you have seen evidence that establishes beyond reasonable doubt that the defendant is guilty.

But how are we to identify these supposed "general moral rules"? To see the force of this question, consider these putative moral rules:

> One must not charge interest on loans.
> One must not eat meat.
> One should not consume intoxicating drugs for pleasure.

How are we to evaluate supposed rules like these? How are we to decide which rules to accept and which rules to reject? Here's one approach: perhaps we should evaluate a putative moral rule by looking at how good or bad the effects of its being generally accepted would be. As an example, let's take a look at what the British Medical Association (BMA) has to say about confidentiality. According to the BMA, doctors should not share a patient's medical information without the patient's permission (except in certain exceptional cases). Their justification for imposing this rule is that "there is . . . a strong public interest in maintaining confidentiality so that individuals will be encouraged to seek appropriate treatment and share information relevant to it."[7] That is, if patients fear their medical records are not kept private, they might refuse to seek treatment or withhold information from a doctor. The BMA justifies their rule about confidentiality by arguing that if doctors follow the rule, the consequences of their doing so are desirable.

We might attempt to justify the privacy rule in the same way. When a person's private data is circulated without their permission, this is often very unpleasant for them. What's more, the *fear* of a violation of privacy can itself be highly disagreeable, even if one's privacy is not in fact violated. The fear of privacy violations can have indirect undesirable effects too. For example, as the BMA points out, if your private medical data was not secure, you might refrain from communicating with your doctor about an embarrassing medical condition for fear that the communications might be made public. In light of these points, we could argue that the general acceptance of the privacy rule has highly desirable consequences.

This brings us to **rule consequentialism**:

Rule consequentialism

The "*optimific moral code*" is that system of rules that—if generally accepted and followed—would produce the best consequences.
Under all circumstances, one ought to obey the optimific moral code.

For example, a rule consequentialist might say that the privacy rule is a component of the optimific moral code, and so we should all obey this rule. When rule consequentialism is combined with a hedonism, the result is **rule utilitarianism**:

Rule utilitarianism
The optimific moral code is that system of rules that—if generally accepted and followed—would maximize aggregate utility.
Under all circumstances, one ought to obey the optimific moral code.

Some philosophers believe that rule utilitarianism is an improvement over act utilitarianism. To see why, let's return to the story about the hacker and the actor. Recall from section 15.2 that the hacker has broken into the cloud storage of a famous actor, and that there are several embarrassing, personal emails that the actor once wrote. The hacker is considering circulating the emails on the Internet. As we saw in the last section, the act utilitarian may be stuck with the conclusion that the hacker *should* circulate the emails—a conclusion that many people find objectionable. The rule utilitarian may deal with this case by saying that the privacy rule appears in the optimific moral code. It is therefore wrong to break the privacy rule, and in particular, it would be wrong for the hacker to circulate the personal emails. We'll leave you to think about whether the rule utilitarian can respond to the story of the magistrate and the mob in a similar way.

Act utilitarians sometimes allege that rule utilitarians promote an overly rigid attitude to moral rules—an attitude sometimes derisively called "rule worship."[8] To see the objection, consider a different story. Michael and Ranajoy work in the same office and are close friends. Michael innocently stumbles across a private, goofy photograph of Ranajoy on holiday wearing a silly hat. Michael puts the photograph up on the office noticeboard. The picture amuses him, and he knows that the other people in the office will find it funny too. He also knows that Ranajoy will enjoy the attention.

Having argued that it is always wrong to violate the privacy rule, the rule utilitarian is apparently stuck with the conclusion that it is wrong for Michael to put the photograph on the office noticeboard. The act utilitarian may protest that this conclusion is absurdly inflexible. After all, the *point* of the privacy rule is to protect people from the harms caused by invasions, or potential invasions, of privacy. But in this case,

Ranajoy doesn't need any such protection: there's no prospect of his being harmed in any way. And so it seems that Michael has no reason to apply the privacy rule in this case.

The rule utilitarian might respond by insisting that it is wrong for Michael to post the picture on the noticeboard, even if Ranajoy happens to enjoy the attention. It is important not to violate a person's privacy, even in cases where no harm is likely to result. Alternatively, the rule utilitarian may reply that the privacy rule has not been properly formulated—it requires modification to accommodate cases like that of Michael and Ranajoy. Perhaps the rule should be put like this:

> *The privacy rule (new version)*
>
> Do not circulate a person's private data (e.g., photographs, bank statements, diaries, emails, medical records, messages) without that person's permission, unless you know that the person won't mind your doing so.

Of course, the act utilitarian may then attempt to undermine *this* version of the rule with another story. And so the argument goes on . . .

15.4 Kant's Universalization Test

We'll now leave the act utilitarian and the rule utilitarian to their dispute and turn to an entirely different way of thinking about moral rules. In this section and the next, we'll consider the moral philosophy of Immanuel Kant (1724–1804). As you'll quickly discover if you take one of his books off the shelf, Kant's writing is hard to digest; even now, two centuries later, there's a great deal of disagreement about what his views really were. Still, it's worth the trouble because Kant articulated, systematically and in great detail, a moral philosophy that has a radically different starting point to the consequentialist theories we've discussed so far. We don't have space to discuss more than a small part of Kant's vast system, so we'll focus on two of Kant's ideas that have been particularly influential: in this section, we discuss his universalization test; in the next section, we will discuss his humanity formula.[9]

Kant noted that, when we morally evaluate a person's actions, we're often interested not only in *what* they did but also in *why* they did it—that is, we're interested in their motivation. Consider, for example, a son who diligently and lovingly cared for his father in his old age—but only because he wanted to secure for himself the biggest possible share of the inheritance. The caring son, we suppose, did the right thing, but his motives were hardly admirable. In Kant's terminology, an action that is performed with praiseworthy motives is a **morally worthy** action.

Let's look at this point in more detail. Kant supposed that all rational actions are based on "maxims." For example, someone who brushes their teeth before bed might be following this maxim:

> To prevent cavities from forming, I brush my teeth before I go to bed each evening.

Note that the maxim specifies a kind of action (brushing), a purpose for that action (preventing cavities), and the circumstances in which that action is to be performed (before bed). Here are three more examples:

> To avoid accidents, I never drive when I'm tired.
> To improve my health, I eat an apple every day with dinner.
> So I don't get too cold, I wear a waterproof jacket when it rains.

For Kant, it is your maxim that describes *why* you're doing the action—your motivation. Hence, whether your action has moral worth depends on its maxim. So Kant asked, *what kind of maxim must an action have, if that action is to have moral worth?*

To put it very briefly for now, Kant's answer was that the morally worthy person attempts to follow *universal* moral rules—that is, rules that apply to everyone. What the morally worthy person does *not* do is expect other people to follow rules that the morally worthy person ignores. We think that this is a commonsense idea: think about how you would feel about a roommate who refused to do chores while expecting everyone else in the house to do their share.

Let's look at a different example in more detail. Consider a woman who is a moocher. The moocher has a money-making strategy. She takes out informal loans frequently; whenever she can get away with it, she refuses to repay the loan. The moocher's maxim is this:

> In order to maximize my personal wealth, I take out loans whenever I have the chance, and then I refuse to repay them.

Now it's not possible for everyone to use this money-making strategy successfully. If everyone adopted the moocher's maxim, nobody would be willing to make a loan, and so it would be impossible to profit from the strategy. The moocher's strategy works only because not everybody uses it. If we put this point to the moocher, she is likely to reply:

> I agree that my strategy wouldn't work if everybody used it. But that doesn't bother me because I know that most other people do repay their debts. Because other people pay their debts, I am able to make money using my strategy.

Kant would say that the moocher's actions do not have moral worth. Kant's thought was that if one's actions are to be morally worthy, one must deliberately follow rules that apply *universally*. But the moocher reneges on her debts while expecting other people to honor theirs. The moocher has one rule for herself and another rule for other people: she makes an exception for herself.

Here is another example. The callous man has resolved never to help out a stranger because he thinks that, when one helps a stranger, one rarely gets any benefit in return. His maxim is:

> In order to maximize my own well-being, I never help out a stranger.

Sometimes, the callous man receives help from strangers—and he knows that he benefits from their help. But he sees no reason to "pay it forward." Now we can imagine a situation in which everyone has this callous policy. But we think that no rational person would choose that situation: to achieve one's ends, whatever they are, one sometimes needs help from a stranger. Therefore, the callous man follows a maxim that, if he is rational, he will not want all other people to follow. So like the moocher, the callous man is not deliberately following *universal* moral rules. Like the moocher, the callous man has one rule for himself and a different rule for everybody else. And so, Kant would say, his actions do not have moral worth.

These two examples illustrate Kant's **universalization test**, which we now state in general terms:

> Given a maxim, consider whether it is possible for everyone to successfully adopt the maxim. If not, then actions performed on the basis of that maxim do not have moral worth. If it is possible for everyone to successfully adopt the maxim, consider whether it is possible rationally to choose that everyone adopts the maxim. If it is not possible, then actions performed on the basis of that maxim do not have moral worth.

Stated in this abstract way, Kant's test may seem strange. However, we think that Kant's idea has a basis in common sense. It is not unusual, when attempting to convince someone that some action is morally wrong, to ask, "But what if everyone did that?" The assumption behind this question is that if you wouldn't want *everyone* to do something, you shouldn't do it yourself. Kant's universalization test is a careful statement of this commonsense idea.

Nevertheless, there are important objections to Kant's position. We finish by describing one of them.[10] This is not an objection to Kant's universalization test. Rather, it is an objection to one of the premises that Kant uses when making his case for the test. Specifically, it is an objection to the claim a person's action has moral worth only when they act on the basis of a maxim they take to apply to everyone.

Imagine a compassionate man who, while out walking, comes across a child who has fallen out of a tree; the child is injured and unconscious on the ground. The compassionate man feels an immediate, unreasoned rush of sympathy and a desire to help the child. He responds to these feelings by taking off his coat and putting it on the child for warmth, calling an ambulance, and performing some basic first aid. The compassionate man doesn't think about his moral duties, and he certainly doesn't think about universal moral laws—his actions are entirely caused by feelings of empathy for this particular injured child. Kant was clear that actions of this kind do not have moral worth:

> Many people are so sympathetically constituted that without any motive of vanity or selfishness they find an inner satisfaction in spreading joy and take delight in the contentment of others if they have made it possible. But I maintain that such behaviour, done in that spirit, has no true moral worth, however amiable it may be and however much it accords with duty.[11]

Many of his readers find this claim objectionable: they say that the compassionate man's actions *are* morally worthy. If the critics are right about this, Kant's argument for his universalization test is not convincing.

15.5 Kant's Humanity Formula

Kant drew a distinction between "things" and "human beings." A **human being** is something that can choose goals and then take rational steps in the pursuit of those goals. For example, a human being might choose as a goal *running a marathon in less than four hours*, and then pursue that goal by training twice weekly. Kant calls this capacity for choosing goals and rationally pursuing them **humanity**. (So, human beings are the things that have humanity.) A "thing" is something that is not capable of choosing goals and pursuing them. A pebble is a "thing" in this sense, because it has no goals. A sieve is also a "thing." Perhaps the sieve does have a goal—getting lumps out of flour—but it has this goal only because it has been *assigned* this goal by human beings: the sieve is not capable of choosing its own goals. This use of the term "human being" is perhaps rather unusual: an intelligent alien could be a human being in Kant's sense, even though the alien would not be human in the biological sense.

The basic idea behind Kant's humanity formula is this: human beings, unlike things, are owed a certain kind of respect. When you're interacting with a human being, you must recognize that the person has the right to exercise their humanity—that is, the right to choose goals and pursue them. As Kant puts it, you have to treat the person's humanity "as an end." Kant wrote:

> A human being ... is not a thing and hence not something that can be used merely as a means.

The word "means" in this statement is a synonym of "tool." Think of a plumber who has an assistant and a box of tools. As they work, the plumber owes the assistant a certain kind of respect—the plumber must recognize that the assistant has a right to make their own decisions. The plumber does not need to respect a basin wrench in the same way. For example, the assistant has a right to choose to quit and pursue a different career; the basin wrench has no such right.

Now we're ready to look at Kant's **humanity formula**:

> So act that you use humanity, whether in your own person or in the person of any other, always at the same time as an end, never merely as a means.

This is rather abstract, so let's take a look at some examples.

Kant thought that his humanity formula implies that coercion is wrong. For example, imagine a slave-owner who forces slaves to work on a farm. The slaves would choose a different kind of life if they could, but the slave-owner prevents the slaves from making their own choices. In this way, the slave-owner violates the slaves' right to set their own goals and pursue them, treating them as though they were merely farm machinery—that is, the slave-owner treats them "merely as means."

Notice that Kant says you must treat humanity as an end "in your own person." To see what he meant by this, consider a lazy man who devotes all of his time to "idleness, amusement, [and] procreation" and lets his talents "rust." Kant thinks that the lazy man violates the humanity formula: he does not exercise his capacity to set goals and pursue them; that is, he fails to exercise her humanity.

Our last example is less straightforward but more interesting. Kant meant his humanity formula to imply that lying is wrong. Here is an example.

Arturo was an adult, and he'd been with his partner, Selena, for about six months. The two of them were captivated by each other, but they weren't happy together. They argued constantly, they couldn't stand each other's friends, and they had no shared interests. Arturo's father was convinced that his son would be better off without Selena and that Selena would be better off without his son. So he decided to step in. He made up a lurid story of infidelity by Selena and told it to his son. Just as he planned, Arturo broke of all contact with Selena—even though no part of his father's story was true. It turned out that Arturo's father was right in his prediction that Arturo and Selena would be better off apart. Soon after they split, Arturo and Selena each found new partners, and both were much happier in their new relationships.

Was Arturo's father right to interfere?

A Kantian is likely to say that Arturo's father was *not* right to interfere—even though his intervention in the end benefited both his son and Selena. From a Kantian point of view, Arturo had a right to make his own decision about whether to stay with Selena. Arturo's father in effect made this decision on Arturo's behalf—so he prevented his son from making the decision for himself. So Arturo's father prevented his son from exercising his humanity; he violated his son's right to make his own decisions.

15.6 Comparing Kantianism and Consequentialism

We spent the first three sections of this chapter discussing several versions of **consequentialism**. The next two sections were about **Kantianism**. We'd now like to say something about how these two views are related.

Traditionally, Kantianism and consequentialism have been thought of as opposing moral theories. We can see why by looking at a couple of examples. Consider slavery first. The Kantian and the consequentialist agree that it is wrong to keep slaves (of course!), but they give rather different accounts of *why* it is wrong. Roughly speaking, consequentialists think that slavery is wrong because the harm done to the slaves massively outweighs the benefits of slavery to the slave-owners and those who trade with them. Kantians thinks that slavery is wrong because the slave-owner fails to respect the slaves' right to make their own decisions. These two explanations don't directly contradict one another, but you can see that the consequentialist and the Kantian have rather different ways of thinking about the issue.

In some cases, Kantians and consequentialists may reach different conclusions about what a person should do. Think of the story of Arturo and Selena. As we've said, the Kantian position is that Arturo's father was wrong to lie to his son—he violated his son's right to make his own decisions. By contrast, an act utilitarian may well say that Arturo's father was right to lie because his lie produced, on balance, more pleasure than pain. We'll leave you to think about which position is correct.

So to repeat, Kantianism and consequentialism have traditionally been regarded as opposing positions. We've also seen, however, that there are many versions of consequentialism. It's also true that Kantianism comes in many varieties. Derek Parfit has recently argued that, as the two positions are refined, consequentialism and Kantianism converge.[12] He has said that Kantians and consequentialists are like two groups of mountain climbers approaching the summit of a mountain from different sides. On the summit of the mountain is "the supreme principle of morality." This is an inspiring thought; we're not sure whether it's true.

In this chapter, we've been talking in a very abstract, theoretical way about morality. In chapter 16, we'll look at some more concrete issues. As you consider the topics raised in the next chapter, you should ask, "What would an act utilitarian say about this? What about a rule utilitarian? What about a Kantian?"

Glossary

act consequentialism: The act consequentialist believes that the best thing to do, in any circumstance, is the action that will maximize the aggregate good. See section 15.1 for discussion.

act utilitarianism: The act consequentialist believes that the best thing to do, in any circumstance, is the action that will maximize the aggregate utility. Act utilitarianism is a version of act consequentialism. See section 15.1 for discussion.

aggregate good: Suppose we sum all the good and bad consequences of an action to find whether—on balance and overall—the consequences of the action are good or bad. The resulting sum is the aggregate good.

aggregate utility: When different utilities are added up, the result is an aggregate utility.

consequentialism: Consequentialism is a family of ethical theories. As the term suggests, consequentialists emphasize the consequences of actions and rules.

cost-benefit analysis: Sometimes one evaluates an action by assigning dollar values to all the consequences of the action. Good consequences are assigned positive dollar values; bad outcomes are assigned negative dollar values. The action will be taken if the total dollar value of its consequences is sufficiently large. This process of decision-making is called cost-benefit analysis.

hedonist: A hedonist believes that pleasure is always directly good, and that pleasure is the only direct good. Pain is directly bad, and pain is the only direct bad. Other things are good or bad indirectly only insofar as they bring about pleasure and/or pain. See chapter 14 for a more detailed discussion.

human being, humanity: In this chapter, we use the terms "humanity" and "human being" in a rather unusual way. Humanity is our capacity to choose our own goals and to take rational steps in pursuit of those goals. For example, one might choose as a goal running a marathon is less than four hours, and then pursue that goal by training twice weekly. A human being is a creature that has this capacity.

humanity formula: The humanity formula is one of the most influential components of Kant's grand system of ethics. We discuss it section 15.5. Part of what the humanity formula says is that one must respect the right of other human beings to make their own decisions.

Kantianism: Immanuel Kant (1724–1804) devised a vast ethical system. In this chapter, we look at only two components of the system: the universalization test (section 15.4) and the humanity formula (section 15.5).

morally worthy: Kant noted that when we morally evaluate a person's actions, we're often interested not only in *what* they did, but also in *why* they did it—that is, we're interested in their motivation. In Kant's terminology, an action that is performed with praiseworthy motives is a "morally worthy" action. See section 15.4.

optimific: The word "optimific" means *producing the best consequences overall.*

rule consequentialism: Rule consequentialists believe that one ought to obey the optimific moral code under all circumstances. The optimific moral code is a system of rules that—if generally accepted and followed—would produce the best consequences. See section 15.3 for more details.

rule utilitarianism: Rule utilitarians accept both hedonism and rule consequentialism.

special obligations: Special obligations are obligations that we have only to those who are "close" to us in some important way. For example, many people believe that parents have a special duty to care for their own children—and that they don't have a similar duty to care for the children of others. It has been argued that we have special obligations to family members, friends, colleagues, and compatriots.

universalization test: The universalization test is one of the most influential components of Kant's grand system of ethics. The test is motivated by the idea that a person's action is morally worthy only if the person follows *universal* moral rules—that is, rules that apply to everybody.

utility: We can measure pleasures and pains numerically. For example, eating an ice cream might have a score of +5, while a headache might have a score of −10, and a really bad headache might have a score of −20. These numbers are called "utilities."

worthy: See morally worthy.

Comprehension Questions

1. Give an example of the process of cost-benefit analysis. (Do not repeat an example from the chapter.)
2. What is act consequentialism? What is act utilitarianism?

3. List the objections to act utilitarianism that we consider in this chapter.
4. What is rule consequentialism? What is rule utilitarianism?
5. Give an example to illustrate the suggestion that the rule utilitarian and the act utilitarian will disagree about how to act in some cases. (Do not repeat an example from the chapter.)
6. Explain Kant's argument for his universalization test.
7. At the end of section 15.4, we present an objection to Kant's argument for his universalization test. Explain this objection.
8. Give an example to illustrate Kant's universalization test. (Do not repeat an example from the chapter.)
9. What is a human being (in the sense relevant in this chapter)?
10. Give an example to illustrate Kant's humanity formula. (Do not repeat an example from the chapter.)
11. Give an example to illustrate the suggestion that Kant and the act utilitarian will disagree in some cases about how to act. (Do not repeat an example from the chapter.)

Discussion Questions

1. Do some research on the ethical theory of the Mohist school of philosophy. How do their views relate to the ethical theories that we have looked at in this chapter?
2. What is the act utilitarian's best response to the allegation that act utilitarianism fails to recognize our "special obligations"?
3. To whom do we have special obligations? Relatives? Neighbors? Friends? Compatriots? Co-religionists? Explain your answer.
4. What is the act utilitarian's best response to the allegation that act utilitarianism fails to recognize the rights of individuals?
5. In section 15.2, we looked at two different objections to act utilitarianism. Do you find these objections persuasive? If so, do you think that these objections are effective against other forms of act consequentialism as well?
6. In section 15.3, we stressed that it is not easy to correctly formulate the privacy rule. What do you think is the best formulation? Can your version of the privacy rule be given a rule utilitarian justification?

7. In section 15.4, we illustrated Kant's universalization test using two examples: the moocher and the callous man. Think of another example.

8. Suppose that John wants to become a baker because he enjoys baking, he's good at it, and he sees a gap in the market. Inspired by Kant, one might say:

    > Suppose that everyone chose to become a baker. Then there would be nobody to grow the cereal crops, and nobody to grind the flour. Thus, baking would become impossible. So John's plan to become a baker fails the universalization test. So John shouldn't become a baker.

    What's wrong with this reasoning? Answer from a Kantian perspective.

9. What should a rule utilitarian say about Kant's humanity formula?

What to Look at Next

- Russ Shafer-Landau's *The Fundamentals of Ethics* and Simon Blackburn's *Being Good: A Short Introduction to Ethics* are excellent introductory works on ethics.
- Unusual among classics of nineteenth-century philosophy, John Stuart Mill's *Utilitarianism* is short and easy to read.
- Peter Singer is perhaps the most prominent active utilitarian writing today. You might like to start with his *Practical Ethics*, which addresses a wide variety of questions in applied ethics from an act utilitarian point of view.
- Brad Hooker develops a version of rule consequentialism in his book *Ideal Code, Real World: A Rule-Consequentialist Theory of Morality*.
- *Utilitarianism: For and Against* features essays by J. J. C. Smart (who writes "for" utilitarianism) and Bernard Williams (who writes "against" utilitarianism).
- If you want to read Kant's work on ethics, we suggest you should start with the *Groundwork for the Metaphysics of Morals*. We recommend Jonathan Bennett's translation, available at www.earlymoderntexts.com. While you're reading the *Groundwork,* you might find helpful Sally Sedgwick's *Kant's Groundwork of the Metaphysics of Morals: An Introduction*.
- Christine Korsgaard's "What's Wrong with Lying?" contains a fascinating and helpful discussion of the differences between consequentialist and Kantian thought about lying. It is published in

Philosophical Inquiry: Classic and Contemporary Readings, edited by Jonathan Adler and Catherine Elgin.
- It is common in fiction for a character to have to choose (as we might loosely put it) between the greater good and the rights of an individual. Ursula K. Le Guin's short, haunting story "The Ones Who Walk Away from Omelas" is an example. It is easy to find online. Alternatively, it is in Le Guin's collection *The Wind's Twelve Quarters*.

Notes

1. We discuss hedonism in section 14.1 of chapter 14.
2. From *A Fragment on Government* (Cambridge, UK: Cambridge University Press, 1988).
3. See Peter Singer, "Utilitarianism and Vegetarianism," *Philosophy & Public Affairs* 9, no. 4 (1980): 325–337.
4. As we've said, hedonism is one component of act utilitarianism. Therefore, any objection to hedonism will also be an objection to act utilitarianism. See section 14.1 of chapter 14 for some objections to hedonism.
5. The story is based on J. J. C. Smart's contribution to *Utilitarianism: For and Against* (Cambridge, UK: Cambridge University Press, 1973).
6. From her "Modern Moral Philosophy," *Philosophy* 33, no. 124 (1958): 1–19.
7. From the beginning of chapter 5 of Med*ical Ethics Today: The BMA's Handbook of Ethics and Law* (Oxford: BMJ Books, 2012).
8. The expression comes from J. C. C. Smart; see his contribution to *Utilitarianism: For and Against*.
9. The ideas we discuss in this section are presented in Kant's *Groundwork for the Metaphysic of Morals* (Cambridge, UK: Cambridge University Press, 1998).
10. The classic presentation of this concern about Kant's moral psychology is Friedrich Schiller's (1759–1805) essay "On Grace and Dignity." (This essay is available online in translation at https://www.google.ca/books/edition/Aesthetical_and_Philosophical_Essays/eWdiAAAAMAAJ.) Our version of the complaint has none of the nuance and subtlety of Schiller's essay!
11. Kant, *Groundwork,* 8.
12. Derek Parfit, *On What Matters* (Oxford: Oxford University Press, 2011).

CHAPTER 16

What Should We Do? (Part II)

Introduction

In this chapter, we will consider three hotly debated moral issues. But before we begin, a pair of preliminary points are in order. People new to this part of philosophy often ask about the relation between the terms "**ethics**" and "ethical" on the one hand and the terms "**morality**" and "moral" on the other. Though some philosophers urge that these terms should be used to express different concepts, that is not how we will use the words here. Rather, as we use them, ethics/ethical and morality/moral are simply stylistic variants.

The second point is about the distinction between morality and the law. Clearly, not everything that is illegal is also immoral. Prior to the American Civil War, it was illegal to harbor a fugitive slave, but it was not morally wrong to help a slave escape. In contemporary America, it is illegal to smoke pot in many states, though many Americans think there is nothing morally problematic about an adult smoking pot. Of course, if you think that pot smoking is morally wrong, then the example illustrates the converse point: not everything that is immoral is also illegal. As we write this, smoking pot is legal in a growing number of US states. Cheating on one's spouse is another example. Many people think it is morally wrong, but in most jurisdictions, adultery is not illegal.

As we discuss contemporary moral issues, it is important to keep the distinction between what is legal and what is moral in mind. The questions that will be center stage in our discussion will be whether certain actions—like performing an abortion or eating meat—are morally wrong. Some of the actions we will consider are clearly illegal, while others are clearly legal. Typically, however, this will have little bearing on the moral issue.

16.1 Is It Morally Wrong to Go to the Opera While People Are Starving?

Economists' evaluations of the work of aid agencies differ widely. The optimists point out that at least some aid programs have been spectacularly successful.[1] The World Health Organization's smallpox eradication program in the 1970s and the late 1960s, for example, rid the world of smallpox and cost only about $300 million.[2]

The pessimists say that—despite the odd success story—on average aid programs do little good and can even be harmful. Dambisa Moyo writes:

> The notion that aid can alleviate systemic poverty, and has done so, is a myth. Millions in Africa are poorer today because of aid; misery and poverty have not ended but increased. Aid has been, and continues to be, an unmitigated political, economic, and humanitarian disaster for most parts of the developing world.[3]

We are in no place to offer opinions on this issue. We do suggest, however, that *some* identifiable charities operating today do a lot of good per dollar.[4] For example, at the time of this writing, the charity evaluators at GiveWell estimate that the Against Malaria Foundation can prevent, approximately and on average, one additional death for each additional $5,500 that it receives in donations.[5]

It is perhaps surprising that saving a life costs so little. If GiveWell's estimate is approximately right, you don't have to be a multimillionaire to save a life by donating to charity. In fact, $5,500 is about the cost of a week-long family vacation to Walt Disney World in Florida. This isn't cheap, but it's not only the superrich who goes to Disney World.

And this raises a troubling question. If GiveWell's estimate is about right, anyone who takes their family on a week-long vacation to Disney

World may well be missing the chance to save a life. In view of this, *is it okay to go to Disney World?*

Peter Singer thinks that the answer to this question is no. He writes:

> I can see no escape from the conclusion that each one of us with wealth surplus to his or her essential needs should be giving most of it to help people suffering from poverty so dire as to be life-threatening. That's right: I'm saying that you shouldn't buy that new car, take that cruise, redecorate the house or get that pricey new suit. . . . The formula is simple: whatever money you're spending on luxuries, not necessities, should be given away.[6]

This is a dramatic claim, to say the least. Singer is not just saying that it's good to give money to effective charities. Rather, he's saying that anyone who spends money on luxuries (e.g., a holiday to Disney World) is "failing to lead a morally decent life." In this section, we'll look at Singer's argument, and we'll also consider a response by Kwame Anthony Appiah.

The first premise of Singer's argument requires little comment:[7]

> Premise 1: Suffering and death from lack of food, shelter, and medical care are very bad.

Singer's second premise is more contentious:

> Premise 2: By donating to aid agencies, the typical citizen of a wealthy country can prevent suffering and death from lack of food, shelter, and medical care without sacrificing anything nearly as important.

The "disposable" income (i.e., the income after taxes and other mandatory charges) of the median person in the US is about $40,000 per year.[8] So if the median person in the US were to give, say, 5 percent of their disposable income to an effective charity, they would give about $6,000 every three years. As we've said, it is estimated that the Against Malaria Foundation saves an additional life with each additional $5,500 that they receive. This provides, we think, strong support to Singer's second premise.

Note that the second premise concerns the *typical* citizen of a wealthy country. It is consistent with the observation that—even in the wealthiest countries—there are very many people who cannot give money to charities without great personal sacrifice.

Most controversial is Singer's third premise:

> Premise 3: If it is in a person's power to prevent something very bad from happening without sacrificing anything nearly as important, it is wrong for this person not to do so.

Singer supports this third premise with a story. Suppose that you are walking home through a park after a party. You pass a dank, muddy pond. It's shallow: you could cross the pond without ever being more than waist-deep in water. In the middle of the pond, there is a small toddler who was evidently trying to retrieve a lost ball. The toddler is now struggling to keep his mouth and nose above water. You could easily wade into the pond and save the toddler from drowning. The only catch is that you're still wearing your best party clothes, and you realize that you don't have time to remove your expensive shoes and clothes: If you rescue the toddler, your glamorous outfit will be ruined. Singer claims—and it is surely hard to disagree—that it would be very wrong for you not to rescue the toddler. It is in your power to prevent something very bad from happening (the death of a toddler) by sacrificing something much less important (a nice outfit); in such cases, Singer says, it is wrong not to take the opportunity to prevent the very bad thing from happening.

Now we can look at the argument as a whole:

> Premise 1: Suffering and death from lack of food, shelter, and medical care are very bad.
>
> Premise 2: By donating to aid agencies, the typical citizen of a wealthy country can prevent suffering and death from lack of food, shelter, and medical care without sacrificing anything nearly as important.
>
> Premise 3: If it is in a person's power to prevent something very bad from happening without sacrificing anything nearly as important, it is wrong for this person not to do so.
>
> Conclusion: If the typical citizen of a wealthy country does not donate to aid agencies, the person is doing something wrong.

We should again stress that Singer's claim is not just that it's praiseworthy to give money to effective charities. Rather, Singer's claim is that the typical citizen of a rich country, if that person fails to give money to effective charities, leads an immoral life.

In fact, Singer's conclusions are still more radical. Suppose that Sam has no dependents and that his disposable income is $60,000 per year.

By donating $6,000 each year to effective charities, Sam can prevent something very bad from happening each year without sacrificing anything nearly as important. So, according to Singer, Sam must donate $6,000 each year. But this is not enough, because by choosing to donate *another* $6,000 each year, Sam could *again* prevent something very bad from happening without sacrificing anything nearly as important. So for Singer, Sam must donate a *second* $6,000 each year. But this is still not enough, because by choosing to donate *yet another* $6,000 each year, Sam could once more prevent something very bad from happening without sacrificing anything nearly as important. And the argument can be repeated still further. Singer's conclusion is that Sam must live an austere life, donating a large proportion of his income to the most effective charities. "The formula is simple," he writes, "whatever money you're spending on luxuries, not necessities, should be given away."[9]

Among Singer's critics is Kwame Anthony Appiah, who discusses Singer's views in the final chapter of his book *Cosmopolitanism*. Appiah agrees with Singer that the world's richest inhabitants are duty bound to aid its poorest inhabitants. However, he believes that this duty is collective: the world's richest people have a shared duty to aid its poorest.

Peter Singer (*left*) and Kwame Anthony Appiah (*right*) have both written about the obligations that come with wealth.

Each wealthy individual, Appiah claims, is obliged to do only that individual's fair share. Now Appiah admits that it's tremendously hard to figure out what a person's "fair share" is, but he does provide a quick, back-of-the-envelope calculation. The economist Jeffrey Sachs has estimated that "extreme poverty" could be eliminated in twenty years, at a cost of $150 billion dollars per year.[10] Appiah says that this is about forty-five cents per day for each citizen of the United States, Canada, the European Union, and Japan. Thus, according to Appiah, the typical resident of a rich country is obliged to give not thousands, but only about $160 per year.

Appiah writes: "If so many people in the world are not doing their share—and they clearly are not—it seems to me that I cannot be required to derail my life to take up the slack." There is nothing wrong, Appiah writes, with "going to the opera when children are dying."

It seems to us that Appiah assumes here something like the following "fair share principle":

The fair share principle
Suppose that you realize that some tragedy will or may befall some other people. You can help, but there are other people who are also in a position to help. Then you are obliged to do no more than your fair share.

To be clear, this is not a quotation from Appiah. This is, rather, our attempt to make explicit the general principle that seems to be driving Appiah's thinking.

This, then, is Appiah's alternative position. But where does he find fault with Singer's argument? Appiah rejects the third premise of Singer's argument, which he calls **Singer's principle**:

Singer's principle
If it is in a person's power to prevent something very bad from happening without sacrificing anything nearly as important, it is wrong for this person not to do so.

Appiah rejects Singer's principle because it conflicts with his fair share principle. If you have donated your "fair share" to effective charities, he thinks, then it is not wrong for you to spend the remainder of your money on luxury items for yourself—even if, by giving more, you could "prevent something very bad from happening without sacrificing anything nearly as important."

So Singer's principle and **Appiah's fair share principle** are in conflict. You should think about which of the two principles is to be rejected. Here's a story that might help you think this question through:

> You live in a mountainous and sparsely populated area, many miles from the nearest hospital, and you work from home. As you are working, you learn that there has been a horrific road accident near your house, involving two buses. Forty people have life-threatening injuries and require urgent medical care. The emergency services have been summoned, but resources are limited and the authorities have announced that there is a need for members of the public to help drive the injured people to a hospital. You have at least forty neighbors within a few miles who have their own cars and are able to help. It is tough for you to help out: you have an enormous amount of work to do and your boss is pressuring you to stay at your desk. But you decide to do your bit: you drive an injured woman and her daughter to hospital, which takes several hours. At this point, you have done your share, or more than your share. However, you learn that none of your neighbors are helping—they say, "These people are strangers to me—it's not my business." And so there are still injured people lying by the road in need of a ride to the hospital.

The fair share principle seems to imply that, in this case, you have already discharged your moral obligation by driving two people to the hospital: you have already done your fair share. On this view, while it would be good for you to do more, you will have done nothing wrong if you choose to return to your desk. Singer's principle implies, on the contrary, that you are obliged to provide still more help: you should drive another injured person to the hospital. You may have done your fair share, but it remains the case that it is in your power to prevent something very bad from happening without sacrificing anything nearly as important. And so, according to Singer's principle, it would be wrong for you not to do more to help. You should think about whether Singer's principle or Appiah's fair share principle is most plausible in this case.

16.2 Vegetarianism

Vegetarians sometimes argue that it is wrong to eat meat because meat-eaters involve themselves in the infliction of suffering on animals. We call this the "argument from pain." In this section, we look at one version of this argument.

In this passage, the historian Norman Davies describes a regular attraction at the Midsummer's Fair in sixteenth-century Paris:

> A special stage was built so that a large net containing several dozen cats could be lowered onto the bonfire beneath. The spectators, including kings and queens, shrieked with laughter as the animals, howling with pain, were singed, roasted, and finally carbonized.[11]

Almost everyone now agrees that this brutal practice was wrong. Anyone organizing a similar cat-burning today would be given a hefty fine at least—and might even be imprisoned for animal cruelty.

In today's meat industry, however, horrible suffering is inflicted on animals routinely. We'll give you an example.[12] In some cases, the meat from an adult male pig has a particular smell called "boar taint," which a majority of consumers find unpleasant. There are several ways of preventing boar taint. One method is to slaughter the male pigs before they reach puberty, before the boar taint has developed. Another method is to administer injections to the male pigs that inhibit the production of testosterone and other steroids in the pig's testicles. However, in the United States, the most commonly used method is castration. The procedure is typically carried out when the pig is very young because a small piglet is easier to restrain than an older, stronger pig. It's a two-person job. The first holds the piglet still, exposing the scrotum to the second person. The second person makes a cut in the scrotum and squeezes one of the testicles out through the incision, then pulls the testicle away from the cut and separates it by cutting or tearing the spermatic cord. Next, a second incision is made in the scrotum, and the second testicle is removed. The whole procedure is typically carried out without anesthetic or analgesic. If you're interested, you can easily find videos of the procedure online—complete with recordings of tortured porcine screams.

As far as we know, there are no good data on the number of pigs who are castrated in this way, but we can make a back-of-the-envelope estimate. According to the US Department of Agriculture, more than 100 million pigs are now sold for meat in the United States each year.[13] About half of these are male. According to the American Veterinary Medical Association, "the vast majority of male piglets in the United States are castrated," and "castration is typically performed without anesthesia or analgesia."[14] We infer that 30 million is a reasonable, low-end estimate of the number of piglets that are castrated without pain relief each year.

The vegetarian argues that once we've understood that cat-burning in sixteenth-century Paris was wrong, we ought also to agree that today's meat production is morally wrong. In both cases, excruciating suffering is inflicted upon an animal for no good reason.

The vegetarian should concede that there are cases in which it's excusable to inflict pain on an animal. A person might inflict pain on a predator while defending livestock. A horse might experience pain while undergoing an important veterinary procedure. But, the vegetarian will insist, these are special cases—in typical cases, it is wrong to inflict horrible suffering on an animal. So far, the vegetarian's argument looks like this:

> Premise 1: It is morally wrong to inflict horrible suffering on an animal, except in self-defense or when it is necessary to prevent some greater harm.
>
> Premise 2: In today's meat industry, horrible suffering is inflicted on animals. This is not done in self-defense, and it is not necessary to prevent a greater harm.
>
> Conclusion: Contemporary meat-production methods are morally wrong.

The meat-eater may reply that meat production is necessary to prevent disaster: if we didn't eat meat, there would be widespread suffering from malnutrition. On this question, we philosophers must defer to dieticians. The conclusion of a recent review of the evidence on this subject is as follows:

> Both vegetarian diets and prudent diets allowing small amounts of red meat are associated with reduced risk of diseases, particularly [coronary heart disease] and type 2 diabetes. There is limited evidence of an association between vegetarian diets and cancer prevention. Evidence linking red meat intake, particularly processed meat, and increased risk of [coronary heart disease], cancer and type 2 diabetes is convincing and provides indirect support for consumption of a plant-based diet. . . .
>
> While vegetarian diets have not shown any adverse effects on health, restrictive and monotonous vegetarian diets may result in nutrient deficiencies with deleterious effects on health. For this reason,

appropriate advice is important to ensure a vegetarian diet is nutritionally adequate especially for vulnerable groups.[15]

So we don't think that meat production is necessary to prevent malnutrition.

Here is a more convincing response to the argument. The meat-eater may insist that, even if the argument shows that practices in the meat industry are immoral, it doesn't follow that buying a pork chop is wrong. By the time the meat-eater gets to the meat, the pig is already dead. And the meat-eater is not the person who cuts open the pig's scrotum and pulls the testicles out.

The vegetarian may respond as follows. The person who lowers the bag of cats onto the flames acts immorally, but so does anyone who pays for the cat-burning spectacle. This illustrates a more general point: if it is wrong to do something, it is also wrong to pay someone else to do it on your behalf. It is true that meat-eaters don't themselves inflict pain on animals, but they do pay for the infliction of pain on animals. And this, the vegetarian will insist, is immoral.

The meat-eater may reply that this argument, at most, shows that it is wrong to *buy* meat, not that it is wrong to *eat* meat. Suppose you come across a deer that has been accidentally killed by a car. If you eat the venison, you will not be inflicting pain on any animal or paying for someone to inflict pain on an animal. The argument from pain, then, does not establish that it is wrong to eat road kill. We think that the vegetarian should concede this point. The proper conclusion of the argument from pain is not that it is wrong to eat meat; rather, it is that it is wrong to buy meat:

> Premise 1: Contemporary meat-production methods are morally wrong.
>
> Premise 2: It is morally wrong to pay other people to act immorally on your behalf.
>
> Premise 3: People who buy meat pay for meat production.
>
> Conclusion: People who buy meat act wrongly.

The meat-buyer may respond that their own spending on meat is such a small proportion of the total that it doesn't make any difference. If the meat-buyer stopped buying meat, pig farms wouldn't scale back their operations, and no abattoirs would close.

Is this a convincing defense of meat-buying? Here is an analogy. Suppose that a team of fraudsters steals money from a string of vulnerable people and share the spoils among themselves. When challenged, one of the fraudsters says, "The team would have stolen all of that money even if I hadn't participated—I didn't make a difference, and so I'm not guilty of any wrongdoing." Presumably, we would not accept this defense. Even if the team would have stolen all the money without them, the fraudster is still guilty of participating in an immoral activity. In the same way, the vegetarian may insist that the meat-buyer acts wrongly because the meat-buyer participates in an immoral activity—even if the individual meat-buyer makes no difference to the amount of meat that is produced.

We now come to a much more powerful objection to the argument from pain. The meat-buyer may concede that it is wrong to buy meat from producers who inflict horrible pain on animals, but insist that it is okay to buy meat from humane meat producers. Suppose that a farmer treats the animals well—gives them plenty of outdoor space, provides them with sufficient feed and whatever veterinary care is necessary, keeps them warm in winter, and so on. When the animals are ready to be eaten, the farmer transports them peacefully to an abattoir, where they are painlessly killed. The argument from pain doesn't seem to establish that it is wrong to buy meat from this farmer. People who don't think that it is wrong to buy and eat meat, but add that it is wrong to buy meat from producers who treat animals inhumanely, are sometimes called **conscientious omnivores**.[16]

The vegetarian may insist in reply that almost all meat producers inflict horrible suffering on their animals, and that it is very difficult to figure out which meat has been humanely produced. On this view, a conscientious omnivore who lives up to the label will, in practice, buy little to no meat. Perhaps this is right. However, even if there are very few humane meat producers, it is reasonable to ask whether it is okay to buy meat from them.

We think that the argument from pain doesn't establish that it is wrong to buy meat that has been humanely produced. The vegetarian who wants to show that this is wrong will need a new argument. How might this new argument go?

We'll leave it to you to think about this, but here's a suggestion. We began by suggesting that, special cases aside, it is morally wrong to inflict horrible suffering on an animal. The vegetarian may now say that this is just a special case of a more general principle: it is wrong to *harm* an animal. The vegetarian may go on to insist that to kill an animal harms it—even if the death is entirely painless. If this is right, the vegetarian has the beginnings of an argument against the conscientious omnivore.[17]

16.3 Is Abortion Morally Wrong?

This section is about abortion, but before we get to that topic, we'd like to dwell on vegetarianism a moment longer. Some people think it's wrong to buy meat from mammals (e.g., pork) but add that it's okay to eat oysters. It seems fair to challenge such people to explain what the difference is between the two cases. It might be replied:

> The difference is that pigs have moral rights, but oysters do not.

This answer, on its own, doesn't seem satisfactory. It just leaves us with the question: *Why is it that pigs have moral rights and oysters do not?* If one insists that pigs have moral rights while oysters don't, one should describe—ideally, in scientific terms—the difference between pigs and oysters that explains their different moral statuses.

One might reply:

> The crucial difference between pigs and oysters is that pigs have noses and oysters do not.

This, again, doesn't seem to be a satisfactory answer. It is, of course, true that pigs have noses and oysters don't. But so what? This seems to be morally irrelevant. Here is a much more promising answer:

> The critical difference is that pigs can feel pain but oysters can't.

We're not sure whether it's true that oysters can't feel pain. But if they can't, this really does seem to be a morally relevant difference between pigs and oysters. The fact that pigs feel pain was an important assumption in the "argument from pain" in the last section; if oysters do not feel pain, an analogous argument will not establish that it is wrong to buy oysters to eat.

In philosophical jargon, a **naturalistic property** is any property that can be described in the language of science—including physics, chemistry, biology, and psychology. What we've just been suggesting is that if it's okay to buy oysters to eat but wrong to buy pork, then pigs and oysters must differ in their morally relevant naturalistic properties. More generally, we suggest:

> (1) If two actions or situations are morally different, then they must differ in their *morally relevant, naturalistic* properties.

This principle has played an important role in debates about abortion, as we shall see. Strangely, proponents of *both* positions in the abortion debate have made use of this principle. We'll begin with an argument in favor of the extreme **pro-life** position that claims all abortions are horribly morally wrong.

From time to time, news outlets report on cases of infanticide in which a mother kills her young child. Though the details are always gruesome, the facts about the mother's motives and her mental health are often unclear. So rather than focus on an actual case, let's consider a hypothetical case. Suppose that a woman, we'll call her Anne, gives birth to a normal baby girl and names her Beth. When Beth is seven years old, though she has always been a normal, well-behaved child, Anne decides that she no longer wants to have a child. So she gives Beth a tasty dessert laced with a large dose of a powerful barbiturate sleeping medicine. Beth quickly becomes unconscious and stops breathing. Within a few minutes, Beth is dead. What is your reaction to what Anne did? Most people are horrified by cases like this. They think that Anne's action is *very* morally wrong. If asked why, many people would offer a principle something like the following:

> (2) It is always morally wrong to kill an innocent person.

Now let's start our morally relevant difference argument. First, let's suppose that instead of killing Beth when she is seven, Anne does it when Beth is only two years old. There are lots of naturalistic properties that Beth at seven does not share with Beth at two. Beth at seven is older, taller, and heavier, and she has a much larger vocabulary. But do you think any of the naturalistic differences between Beth at seven and Beth at two are morally relevant? Most people think that the answer is no; they think it is very morally wrong for Anne to kill two-year-old Beth.

The next step in the argument is to push the age of the killing even earlier. Suppose that Anne decides she does not want to have a child just a few minutes after Beth is born, and so she gives Beth the barbiturates the first time she is alone with the baby, when Beth is only twenty minutes old. Here, again, there are many naturalistic differences between Beth at age two years and Beth at age twenty minutes. But are any of those differences morally relevant to whether it is wrong to kill Beth? If your answer is no, then you should think it is very wrong for Anne to kill newborn Beth, and indeed, most people do.

The third step in the argument—you probably see where this is going—is to move the time of the killing to *before* Beth is born. Suppose that, while Anne is already in labor, she decides that she does not want to be a parent. It would be more difficult to administer the barbiturates then, but with a bit of ingenuity or help from a willing doctor, it could be done. And there definitely are naturalistic differences between killing Beth when she is twenty minutes old and killing her ten minutes before she is born. In that half-hour period, Beth has traveled down the birth canal and has started breathing on her own. But do you think those differences are morally relevant? If it is seriously morally wrong to kill Beth when she is twenty minutes old, is it morally permissible to kill Beth before she has traveled down the birth canal and started breathing on her own? Here, again, most people answer with a resounding "no." But if that's right, then we've reached the first milestone in this pro-life argument: At least some abortions—those that are performed very, very late in pregnancy—are seriously morally wrong.

In the next part of our morally relevant difference argument, the proponent of the argument moves the time of the abortion earlier and earlier. At each earlier time, there are, of course, some naturalistic differences between Beth at that earlier stage in development and Beth at a later stage in development. To make the case, the pro-life advocate must argue that these naturalistic differences are not morally relevant—they do not mark the boundary between something it is morally permissible to kill and something it is morally wrong to kill. To do that, the advocate's strategy is to focus on other cases where the naturalistic feature in question is the only salient difference, and to argue that, since the absence of the naturalistic feature does not make it morally permissible to kill in those cases, it does not make it morally permissible to kill in the case of a human fetus either. There are, of course, lots of developmental milestones that might be proposed as marking the morally relevant boundary between something it is morally permissible to kill and something it is not morally permissible to kill. We can't consider all of them here. What we will do instead is to consider one of the naturalistic properties that is most often invoked in debates over abortion. We'll leave it to you to try to construct parallel arguments for other naturalistic properties that emerge as a fertilized egg develops into a baby.

The naturalistic property we'll focus on is *consciousness*. A fertilized egg can't feel pain, or pleasure, or other conscious states. A newborn baby clearly can. So at some point, as development unfolds, a fetus begins to be able to experience pain. There is considerable scientific debate about when, exactly, consciousness emerges. But it is agreed on all sides that newborns are certainly capable of feeling pain, and that, before the brain begins to develop, human embryos are not capable of feeling pain. So an advocate of the moral permissibility of some abortions might argue as follows:

> Consciousness marks a morally important boundary. After consciousness emerges, it is morally wrong to kill a developing child, but before consciousness emerges, killing the embryo or fetus is morally unproblematic. Since we are not sure exactly when consciousness emerges, it is good to be cautious. But since we know that there can be no consciousness before the brain circuits responsible for feeling pain develop, there is nothing morally problematic about abortions performed very early in pregnancy.

The pro-lifer whose argument we are developing will not deny that there is a time early in development when the fetus is not capable of consciousness. But the pro-lifer will insist this is of no moral importance, since the ability to feel pain and other conscious states is not morally relevant in cases like this: it does not mark a boundary between something that is morally permissible to kill and something that is not morally permissible to kill.

To make the point, the pro-lifer asks us to consider another pair of cases. Suppose that Charles, a twenty-year-old college student, has been involved in an automobile accident that resulted in a quite serious brain injury. Charles is now in the hospital, deeply unconscious and incapable of feeling any pain. But the news is not all bad. The neurologists treating Charles are administering a new drug that has been very successful in treating similar cases. It is slow acting, and the neurologists tell Charles's family that he will remain unconscious for several months. However, they assure the family that, in about eight months, Charles will have completely recovered and will be able to return to college the following semester. In this case, the pro-life argument observes, it would clearly be morally reprehensible if, after he has recovered and returned to school, someone who wanted Charles dead (let's call her Doris) were to kill him. But, the pro-life argument continues, surely it would be equally reprehensible if Doris killed Charles in his hospital bed while he was still deeply unconscious. Since the only salient naturalistic difference between Charles shortly after his accident and Charles after he recovers is that he is not capable of consciousness at the earlier time and is capable of consciousness at the later time, the pro-life advocate concludes that the capacity for consciousness is not a morally relevant naturalistic property. From the fact that a human is not capable of consciousness at one time and is capable of consciousness at a later time, it does not follow that it is morally acceptable to kill the human at the earlier time. Thus, we should not use the capacity of consciousness as a developmental milestone before which abortion is morally permissible.

This is certainly not the end of the argument. Someone who thinks some abortions are morally unproblematic can respond by arguing that there are morally relevant differences between the case of early abortion and the case involving Charles. Or this person can grant that the capacity for consciousness is not a morally important boundary and focus on some other naturalistic property that emerges in development. We'll leave it to you to explore those options and to consider whether pro-life arguments similar to the one proposed about Charles can be constructed for all the plausible developmental milestones.

Before leaving the topic of morally relevant difference arguments, we want to explain why arguments like the one we have sketched are two-edged swords, since they can also be used to argue for an extremely permissive **pro-choice** view on which not only abortion but also infanticide is morally permissible. To see this, let's assume that the pro-life advocate has been very successful in arguing that there are no morally relevant differences to be found as we move backward in time from the newborn to the just-fertilized human egg. So, the pro-life advocate concludes, if it is morally wrong to kill a newborn, it is also morally wrong to kill a newly fertilized egg. At this point, the extreme pro-choice advocate asks that we focus on the sperm and egg before fertilization. Imagine, this advocate argues, that a new kind of contraceptive pill has been developed. When a woman is taking the pill, her eggs secrete minute amounts of a chemical that will kill both sperm and egg when a sperm comes very close to an egg. If a sperm comes within 0.005 millimeter of an egg, both the sperm and the egg die instantly. Let's also assume that the drug is 100 percent successful, and that the pill has no other significant effects. This sounds like a terrific contraceptive pill—much better than the pills that are currently available. Moreover, the pro-choice argument continues, surely this safe and effective contraceptive is morally unproblematic. Surely there is nothing morally problematic about a drug that kills free-swimming sperm and unfertilized eggs.

Now the extreme pro-choice advocate launches a morally relevant difference argument for this side of the debate. The contraceptive drug we have imagined kills sperm and eggs when they are 0.005 millimeter apart. But suppose another drug is developed that does not kill the sperm and the egg until they are 0.001 millimeter apart. Is there a morally relevant difference between using the first drug and using the second? No one would think that the tiny difference in the distance at which the drugs are effective makes a moral difference. Next, imagine a third drug. This one kills the sperm and the egg at the very moment when the sperm and the egg come into contact. Does *that* make a serious moral difference? Here, again, it is very implausible to think that it does. Now suppose a fourth drug acts only after the egg's cell membrane has opened, but before any genetic material from the sperm enters the egg, a fifth drug acts only after part of the sperm's genetic material has entered the egg, and a sixth acts only after all the sperm's genetic material has entered the egg. Are there any morally relevant differences between these drugs? It would be very odd, the extreme pro-choice advocate urges, to say that using the first drug is morally unproblematic while using the sixth drug is morally prohibited. But if that's right, and if the pro-life advocate has successfully argued that there are no morally relevant differences to be found as we move backward in time from the newborn to the just-fertilized human egg, then it seems to follow that there are no morally relevant differences between what we might call "late contraception"—the use of the first or second drug—and early infanticide. So, our pro-choice advocate concludes, if you see nothing morally problematic about late contraception, you should agree that there is nothing morally problematic with abortion at *any* stage of pregnancy, and you should also agree that there is nothing morally problematic about early infanticide!

Confronted with this argument, many people are inclined to think more systematically about the process of embryonic and fetal development in the hope of finding a naturalistic feature that emerges in development that does mark a morally relevant boundary and that can't be challenged by analogies like our example of the unconscious college student. We leave it to you to decide whether this can be done.

While our focus thus far has been on morally relevant difference arguments, these are not the only arguments that have played an important role in philosophical discussions of abortion. An influential argument of a different sort challenges principle (2)—the claim that it is always morally wrong to kill an innocent person. Those who pursue this line of argument agree that, while it is usually morally wrong to kill an innocent person, there are important exceptions. Suppose that you are standing near the edge of a cliff, and a young child approaches asking for help. When the child is quite close to you, you see that terrorists have strapped remote-controlled guns to the poor child, and that these will start firing in all directions in just a few seconds. There is no time for you to run and nowhere to hide. The only way to prevent being killed is to push the child off the edge of the cliff, though it is clear that the fall will kill the child. Though the child is entirely innocent, many people think that you would be morally justified in pushing the child off the cliff since you are acting in self-defense. It's the child's life or yours. And if that's right, then principle (2) must be replaced with something more nuanced. Of course, self-defense is an issue that rarely arises in the context of abortion because it is rarely the case that a mother is presented with the stark choice between her own life and the life of her fetus. But such cases do occasionally arise. And many staunch opponents of abortion are willing to make an exception in such cases.

The self-defense case makes it plausible that there are exceptions to principle (2). Are there other exceptions that don't involve a trade-off of one life for another? An argument proposed by the philosopher Judith Jarvis Thomson (1929–2020) suggests that there are.[18] Thomson asks you to imagine that one morning you wake up in a hospital and find that your body is attached to the body of a complete stranger via a system of tubes through which blood and other fluids are flowing. You are, of course, quite startled. But a senior hospital official soon arrives to explain what is going on. The man you are attached to is a world-famous violinist who has a kidney disease that would lead to his death very quickly, unless he is attached to a person with a compatible body. Members of the Society of Music Lovers discovered that you are the only person with a compatible body. So late last night, they broke into your bedroom, drugged you, and attached your body to the body of the famous violinist. The official expresses great regret that this was done to you and assures you that the hospital had nothing to do with it. But now that you are hooked up to the violinist, his life is completely dependent on yours. If you disconnect the tubes, the violinist will die. Fortunately, the violinist will only need to be attached to your body for about eight or nine months. After that, he will have sufficiently recovered to survive on his own.

At this point, Thomson makes two further points. The first is that, while it would be very generous of you to remain attached to the violinist for the next eight or nine months, you have no moral obligation to do that. It would not be morally wrong for you to detach the tubes, even though this would result in the violinist's death. The second point is that this case is, in important respects, analogous to the case of a woman who finds herself unintentionally pregnant. In both cases, the only way to avoid being attached to another person for an extended period—with all the inconvenience that entails—is to take an action that results in the death of the other person. So if it is morally permissible for you to detach yourself from the violinist, then it is also morally permissible for a pregnant woman to have an abortion. Do you agree? If not, then presumably you think that the analogy is not a good one because there are morally relevant differences between the cases. What are they?

Glossary

Appiah's fair share principle: This is a moral principle that we attribute to Kwame Anthony Appiah:

> Suppose that you realize that some tragedy will or may befall some other people. You can help, but there are other people who are also in a position to help. Then you are obliged to do no more than your fair share.

To be clear, this isn't a quotation from Appiah; rather, it is our attempt to put into words what seems to us to be a premise of his argument.

conscientious omnivore: The conscientious omnivore thinks that it is wrong to buy meat that has been produced by inhumane farms or abattoirs, but does not think that it is otherwise wrong to buy meat.

ethics/moral theory: Ethics, or moral, theory is the study of how we should live, what we should care about, and what we should be like. (Some philosophers draw subtle distinctions between morality and ethics—we don't distinguish these things.)

naturalistic property: A naturalistic property is a feature of an object, action, or situation that can be described in the language of physics, chemistry, biology, or psychology. Some naturalistic properties a person might have include:

- Having mass of 80 kg
- Being angry
- Having a blood pressure of 120/70

Many philosophers believe that two things that differ morally must also differ in some naturalistic respect. On this point, see the beginning of section 16.3.

pro-life/pro-choice: In our terminology, the "extreme pro-life position" is that abortion is always morally wrong, and the "extreme pro-choice position" is that abortion is never morally wrong. In calling these positions extreme, we do not imply that they are in error. There are many intermediate views, according to which abortion is sometimes but not always morally wrong.

Singer's principle: Singer's principle is an important premise in Singer's argument, discussed in section 16.1. It is this: "If it is in a person's power to prevent something very bad from happening without sacrificing anything nearly as important, it is wrong for that person not to do so."

Comprehension Questions

1. What is Singer's principle? How does Singer argue for his principle?
2. "If the typical citizen of a wealthy country does not donate to aid agencies, that person is doing something wrong." How does Singer justify this claim?
3. Summarize Peter Singer's case for his claim that "whatever money you're spending on luxuries, not necessities, should be given away."

4. Explain why Singer's principle conflicts with Appiah's fair share principle.
5. Summarize the argument from pain.
6. We suggested that the argument from pain cannot establish that it is wrong to *eat* meat, only that it is wrong to *buy* meat. Explain this point.
7. Someone insists that buying meat is morally OK because that person's consumption is such a small portion of the total that it makes no difference. How might a vegetarian reply?
8. Explain what a conscientious omnivore is.
9. What is a naturalistic property?
10. Use an example to illustrate this claim: "If two actions or situations are morally different, then they must also differ in their *morally relevant, naturalistic* properties." (Don't repeat an example from the chapter.)
11. "If two actions or situations are morally different, then they must also differ in their *morally relevant, naturalistic* properties." Explain how a pro-life philosopher might use this principle to argue that late-stage abortions are immoral. What about abortions earlier in pregnancy?
12. "If two actions or situations are morally different, then they must also differ in their *morally relevant, naturalistic* properties." Explain how a pro-choice philosopher might use this principle to argue that abortion is permissible early in pregnancy. What about late-stage abortion?
13. Explain Judith Jarvis Thomson's story about the violinist. What is its relevance to the abortion debate?

Discussion Questions

1. Can you think of actions to go into each of the four boxes in this table?

	Legal	Illegal
Morally wrong		
Not morally wrong		

We'll do the top-right box for you: murder is both illegal and morally wrong. (Don't reuse examples from the chapter.)

2. Evaluate the second premise of Peter Singer's argument:

   Premise 2: By donating to aid agencies, the typical citizen of a wealthy country can prevent suffering and death from lack of food, shelter, and medical care without sacrificing anything nearly as important.

   When thinking about this topic, you might want to look at:

   - www.givewell.org.
   - Leif Wenar, "Poverty Is No Pond: Challenges for the Affluent," in *Giving Well: The Ethics of Philanthropy* ,ed. by P. Illingworth, T. Pogge, L. Wenar (Oxford: Oxford University Press, 2010), 104–132.

3. Consider Singer's principle:

   If it is in a person's power to prevent something very bad from happening without sacrificing anything nearly as important, it is wrong for that person not to do so.

   Do you think that Singer's story about the drowning toddler in the pond adequately motivates this claim? Given that Singer's principle conflicts with Appiah's fair share principle, which do you think we should accept, if either?

4. The conclusion of our version of the argument from pain is that people who buy meat act wrongly. When presenting this argument, we neglected to distinguish between different kinds of meat. Do you think that the argument from pain establishes that it is wrong to buy oysters? What about salmon? What about pork? What about dog or cat meat? What about meat from chimpanzees?

5. Put yourself in the position of a vegetarian who wishes to establish that it is wrong to buy meat even from humane farms and abattoirs. How would your argument go? How might a conscientious omnivore reply?

6. Put yourself in the position of a meat-eater who wishes to argue that it is okay to buy meat, regardless of whether the meat was humanely produced. How would you rebut the argument from pain?

7. Consider the following position:

   In my view, a newborn baby has a right to life, and so does a late-term fetus. This is why infanticide is wrong, and this is why late-term abortions are wrong. I also think that there is nothing wrong with destroying a newly fertilized egg—a newly fertilized egg doesn't have a right to life. The crucial question, then, is *when does the fetus acquire the right to life?* My proposal is that the fetus acquires a right to life when its weight reaches one pound.

Is this position consistent with principle (1) on page 353. Why or why not?

8. In classical antiquity, it was common for parents to abandon an unwanted newborn child to die. This practice was not regarded as immoral. Do you think that there is a morally important difference between this practice and the practice of late-term abortion?

9. A fetus is said to be "viable" when it is capable of surviving outside the uterus. Some people think that abortion is morally okay when, but only when, the fetus is not viable. Evaluate this position.

10. This is a question about Judith Jarvis Thomson's story about the violinist. Do you think that it would be okay to detach the violinist? If so, does this show that it is okay to have an abortion?

What to Look at Next

Is it morally wrong to go to the opera while people are starving?
- Peter Singer first presented his argument in his paper "Famine, Affluence, and Morality," *Philosophy and Public Affairs* 1, no. 1 (1972): 229–243. The paper is easy to find online.
- More recently, Singer has written a book defending his position: *The Life You Can Save.*
- Another writer who is sympathetic with Singer's position is William MacAskill. See his book *Doing Good Better.*
- Kwame Anthony Appiah presents his position in the final chapter of his book *Cosmopolitanism.*
- In his paper "Poverty Is No Pond: Challenges for the Affluent" (see the Discussion Questions), Leif Wenar challenges some of Singer's empirical assumptions.
- Some further criticisms of Singer's views can be found in section 3 of Jeffrey A. Schaler's *Peter Singer Under Fire: The Moral Iconoclast Faces His Critics.*

- Jeffrey Sachs is an "optimist" about aid programs; see his *The End of Poverty: Economic Possibilities for Our Time*. For a more pessimistic take, see Dambisa Moyo, *Dead Aid*; William Easterly, *The White Man's Burden*; or Angus Deaton, *The Great Escape*.

Vegetarianism

- The novelist Jonathan Safran Foer's book *Eating Animals* is a powerful discussion of vegetarianism.
- *Philosophy Comes to Dinner*, edited by Andrew Chignell, Terence Cuneo, and Matthew Halteman, contains many interesting articles. We suggest you start with Tristram McPherson's "Why I Am a Vegan (And You Should Be One Too)."
- In his "Eating Our Friends," Roger Scruton defends the conscientious omnivore. The article is printed in his book *A Political Philosophy*.
- Elizabeth Harman criticizes the conscientious omnivore in her paper "The Moral Significance of Animal Pain and Animal Death." (See endnote 18.)
- In "To Serve Man," an episode of *The Twilight Zone,* the members of an alien species, the Kanamits, farm people for their meat. The Kanamits are more intelligent and more technologically advanced than human beings. The Kanamits' attitude toward people is very like our attitude towards pigs. Do you think it's wrong for the Kanamits to eat people? If so, do you think that it's wrong for people to eat pigs?

Abortion

- Judith Jarvis Thomson's "A Defense of Abortion" (see endnote 19) contains her famous "violinist" story, which we presented at the end of this chapter.
- Don Marquis, "Why Abortion is Immoral," The Journal of Philosophy, vol. 86, no. 4 (April, 1989): 183–202
- Robert M. Baird and Stuart E. Rosenbaum's book *The Ethics of Abortion: Pro-Life vs. Pro-Choice* is a useful and varied anthology of articles.

Notes

1. Jeffrey Sachs is a leading optimist. See his *The End of Poverty: Economic Possibilities for Our Time* (New York: Penguin Books, 2006).
2. Frank Fenner et al., *Smallpox and Its Eradication* (Geneva: World Health Organization, 1988), 1366.

3. Dambisa Moyo, *Dead Aid: Why Aid Is Not Working and How There Is a Better Way for Africa* (Farrar, Straus, and Giroux, 2009) xix. Other aid pessimists include William Easterly's, *The White Man's Burden: Why the West's Efforts to Aid the Rest Have Done So Much Ill and So Little Good* (The Penguin's Press, 2006), and Angus Deaton's, *The Great Escape: Health, Wealth, and the Origins of Inequality* (Princeton University Press, 2013).
4. Note that Moyo stresses that her concern is government aid, not private charity, *Dead Aid*, 7. It is the latter which is our concern in this section. For more on this topic, see Holden Karnofsky, "The Lack of Controversy over Well-targeted Aid," GiveWell blog, November 6, 2015. See https://blog.givewell.org/2015/11/06/the-lack-of-controversy-over-well-targeted-aid/.
5. Of course, it is hard to make such estimates accurately: we encourage you to look at the GiveWell website to scrutinize their methods. See https://www.givewell.org/impact-estimates.
6. From "The Singer Solution to World Poverty," *New York Times*, September 5, 1999.
7. This version of the argument is taken from P. Singer, *The Life You Can Save* (New York: Random House, 2009), 15–16. We have made several trifling changes to the wording and we've re-ordered the premises.
8. For up to date statistics, look at the OECD website, https://stats.oecd.org/.
9. From "The Singer Solution to World Poverty."
10. Jeffrey Sachs, *The End of Poverty: Economic Possibilities for Our Time* (New York: Penguin, 2005). It should be stressed that Sachs's views are far from uncontroversial. If you wish to learn more, we recommend that you listen to the episodes of the EconTalk podcast featuring Easterly and Sachs. Episodes are available for download at http://www.econtalk.org/. We should add that, because *Cosmopolitanism* came out in 2006, and *The End of Poverty* came out in 2005, the figures in these books are out of date. We doubt that updating the figures would make a significant change to the philosophical issues, however. Note that $160 in 2005 is equivalent to about $250 today.
11. Norman Davies, *Europe: A History* (Oxford: Oxford University Press, 1996), 543.
12. For more information about the treatment of animals in modern farms and abattoirs, we recommend Jonathan Safran Foer's book *Eating Animals* (New York: Little, Brown, 2010).
13. The reader will be able to find up-to-date data through the US Department of Agriculture's Economics, Statistics, and Market Information System. See https://usda.library.cornell.edu/.
14. These quotations come from the American Veterinary Medical Association's "Literature Review on the Welfare Implications of Swine Castration,"

May 29, 2013. See https://www.avma.org/sites/default/files/resources/swine_castration_bgnd.pdf.
15. Claire T. McEvoy, Norman Temple, and Jayne V. Woodside, "Vegetarian Diets, Low-Meat Diets and Health: A Review," *Public Health Nutrition* 15, no. 12 (2012): 2287–2294.
16. The term comes from Peter Singer and Jim Mason's book *The Ethics of What We Eat: Why Our Food Choices Matter* (New York: Holtzbrinck, 2007).
17. For discussion of the debate between conscientious omnivores and vegetarians, see Roger Scruton, "Eating Our Friends," in his *A Political Philosophy: Arguments for Conservatism* (New York: Continuum, 2006); and Elizabeth Harman, "The Moral Significance of Animal Pain and Animal Death," in *The Oxford Handbook of Animal Ethics*, ed. Tom L. Beauchamp and R. G. Frey (Oxford: Oxford University Press, 2011).
18. Judith Jarvis Thomson, "A Defense of Abortion," *Philosophy and Public Affairs* 1, no. 1 (1971): 47–66. Our account of Thomson's argument departs from hers in a number of ways.

CHAPTER 17
....

Why Democracy?

Introduction

In several English-speaking countries across the world, there is increasing dissatisfaction with democracy, as shown in figure 17.1.[1]

We don't know what has caused these shifts in opinion. Perhaps it has something to do with the financial crisis of 2007–2008. Perhaps it has something to do with the rise of social media. We will leave these questions to the social scientists, take a step back from the particular concerns of today's politics, and ask in a more general way, *Why democracy?*

A thought experiment may help. Let's pretend that, in 2030, a volcanic eruption creates a new island in the Pacific. Under international law, the island is not under the control of any existing state, and so a struggle for power ensues. By an astonishing display of skill and charisma, you succeed in establishing your position as monarch. The island attracts tourists from across the world; it is also ideally located for fishing. Under your wise leadership, other industries are soon established on the island too. The economy flourishes, and immigrants arrive in large numbers. After five decades, the population is about 100,000. At this point, pleased with your achievements, you decide to retire.

But who should rule after you? You would like to put in place some system of government that will ensure the island continues to flourish

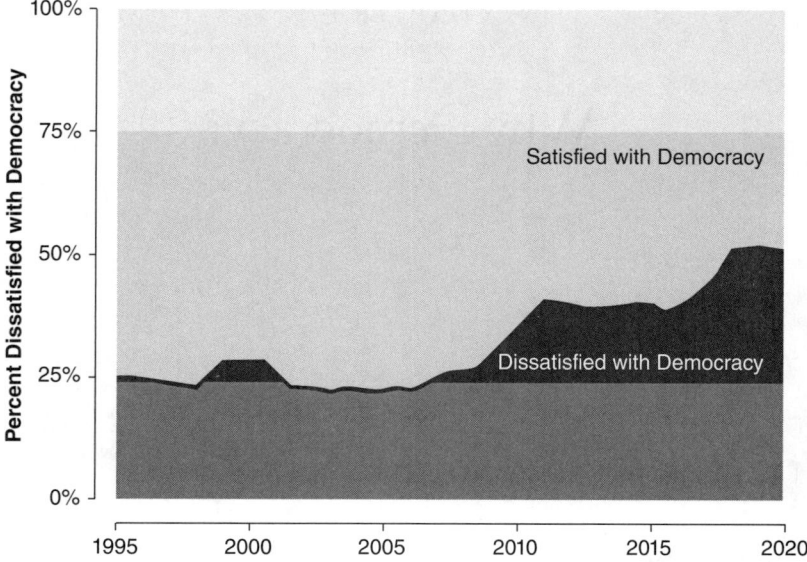

FIGURE 17.1 Growing dissatisfaction with democracy in the United States, the United Kingdom, Canada, Australia, and New Zealand

without your guidance. You invite social scientists, historians, and philosophers from around the world to advise you as you write the constitution of the new state.

Many of these experts recommend a democratic system of one kind or another. Perhaps the island should be ruled by a parliament, whose members are chosen by public vote. But there are alternatives.

Some suggest a **hereditary monarchy**. They say that you should pass the crown to your oldest child, who on retirement should pass the crown to *their* oldest child, and so on. This proposal appeals to your sense of family pride, but it has obvious shortcomings. For one thing, while you know your oldest child to be a wise and principled person, you can't be sure that your great-great-great-grandchildren will be similarly virtuous. And then there's the danger that one of your descendants will fail to produce an heir, which could cause chaos.

Some tell you that it would be a mistake to give *all* the people of the island the vote, insisting that many of them are too ignorant to use their vote wisely. They suggest a system in which only those who pass a certain exam are allowed to vote. A system like this—designed to put political power in the hands of the knowledgeable and the wise—is said to be an **epistocracy**.

Some say that the island's leaders should not be chosen by public vote at all. They suggest a system in which the island's rulers are arranged in a hierarchy, with a president at the top and leaders with very modest powers at the bottom (e.g., head of stationery procurement). Leaders who perform well are promoted by their superiors to the next level of the hierarchy. The president, in this system, will be an experienced public servant with a long track record of success at every level of government. Or so it is claimed.

Some propose a system in which a new parliament is formed every ten years, and each time, the members of parliament are chosen *at random* from the population. This is called **sortition**. The system might sound bizarre at first, but its proponents point out that, in many countries, *jurors* are chosen at random. Moreover, sortition has one important advantage. A parliament chosen at random in this way is very likely to be *representative* of the population as a whole: if 20 percent of the islanders are English-speaking, about 20 percent of the parliament will be English-speaking; if 10 percent of the islanders are Muslims, about 10 percent of the parliament will be Muslim; and so on. In this system, therefore, there will likely be no under-represented minorities.

At the end of the chapter, we'll ask you whether you will choose a democratic system. Before that, let's look at some of the arguments.

17.1 What Is Democracy?

Before we talk about the pros and cons of democratic government, let's talk about what we mean by the word "democracy." We don't have a complete answer to this question, but we can make a start. It's important first to distinguish between **direct democracy** and **representative democracy**. In *direct* democracy, policy questions are settled by public vote. For example, in 2016, there was a referendum on the question of whether the United Kingdom should leave the European Union. The majority said that the United Kingdom *should* exit the European Union, and in 2020, the United Kingdom did, indeed, leave. In *representative* democracy, voters choose leaders—presidents, congress people, members of parliament, and so on—who make policy decisions on their behalf. In this chapter, we will largely restrict our attention to representative democracy.

In a totally democratic system, every adult has an equal vote. However, most democratic countries are not totally democratic in this sense. In some countries, people found guilty of certain crimes are penalized by losing the vote, temporarily or permanently. In others, active members of the military are not able to vote. And in some countries, the voting system in effect gives some members of the electorate a more powerful vote, while others are given a less powerful vote. For example, in the United States, each state has two senators, but the states vary enormously in population: California is more than sixty times more populous than Wyoming.

In a totally democratic country, the governing party will not be able to use its powers to give itself an unfair advantage in elections. This means that opposition parties will be able to operate freely; for example, opponents of the government will not be imprisoned or otherwise silenced. It is important, too, that opponents of the government be able to make their case to the electorate, which requires a certain level of freedom of speech and freedom to protest. Moreover, in a fully functioning democracy, voters will not be bribed or bullied; one way to ensure this is to have people to vote in secret.

In some democratic countries, though not all, democratic forces are limited by mechanisms designed to protect individual rights. The ability of the US Supreme Court to limit the powers of Congress and the president is a prominent example, or so many would claim. Proponents of such mechanisms argue that, in a democracy, there is a danger that a majority of voters will use their voting power to inflict injustices on members of minority groups—a situation sometimes called the **tyranny of the majority**. To prevent this, they argue, there should be mechanisms that protect the rights of minority groups. Others will reply that these mechanisms can be abused, and that democracy itself is the best mechanism we have for the defense of individual rights. We won't pursue this question.

For sure, there is a lot more to be said about what democracy is. We don't have all the answers. If you want to think more about this topic, we recommend looking at the "democracy index" produced by *The Economist* magazine—which attempts to measure numerically how democratic the different countries are. We don't mean to endorse all *The Economist*'s views, though there is one thing we think the magazine gets right: democracy comes in degrees. Some countries (e.g., Taiwan) are highly democratic; others (e.g., North Korea) are not at all democratic. There are also many countries that are distributed between these two extremes.

17.2 The Basic Argument Against Democracy

Plato (c. 428–348 BCE) made his case against democracy in *The Republic*, which was written in about 375 BCE. In his discussion, he memorably compared ruling a country with being at the helm of a ship. In this section, we present an updated version of this analogy.

Let us suppose that you arrive at the airport to fly to a distant city. When you collect your boarding pass, you are offered a seat on an experimental, democratic flight. This flight will not have a traditional pilot. Instead, the decisions that would normally be made by a pilot will be made by a majority vote among the passengers—who are ordinary members of the public with no special knowledge of navigation, aerodynamics, and so on. You decide to decline this offer. Flying a plane requires much knowledge and skill, and many years of practice. Bad decisions can lead to disaster. It would be crazy to board a flight piloted by a bunch of know-nothings.

Critics of democracy argue that direct democracy is problematic in much the same way. Political decision-making, like flying a plane, requires much knowledge and skill, and years of experience. In both cases, bad decisions can have terrible consequences. In both cases—or so it is argued—experts should be in charge, not the ignorant public.

Back at the airport, the check-in agent offers you a seat on another, rather different experimental flight. On this second flight, just before take-off, the passengers will choose the pilot by a democratic vote. Again, the passengers are ordinary members of the public with no special knowledge of aeronautics, navigation, and so on. Again, you decline the offer. The passengers, having little knowledge of the business of piloting planes, might not make a wise choice of pilot. They might choose someone who is charismatic and articulate, but a terrible pilot. They might choose someone with impressive but irrelevant qualifications, or someone whose experience is with a totally different kind of plane.

Critics of democracy argue that representative democracy is problematic in much the same way. It is *difficult* to choose a good pilot, or a good political leader. In both cases, one needs much knowledge to make a sound choice. In both cases, a bad choice could have terrible consequences. And in both cases, the choice should be made by the knowledgeable, not by the ignorant public. (We'll leave it to you to illustrate this point with examples of terrible leaders who have been democratically elected.)

Back at the airport, you choose to board a flight with an expert pilot, who has many years of relevant experience. On this flight, the opinions of the passengers about who should be the pilot, or how the plane should be piloted, will be ignored. Critics of democracy argue that a country should be run in much the same way. Experts should make the decisions. These expert leaders will sometimes choose to do what the general public wants, but sometimes they won't, and often they shouldn't, because the general public is ignorant.

An important premise of this argument is that most voters are ignorant about political issues. We think that (whatever may be said about the rest of the argument) there is something to this premise. In 2013, a polling company asked British adults to estimate some percentages that were relevant to political debates of the time.[2] The table here shows the *average* answer for each question among the survey participants and compares it to the best available estimate of the true percentage. The *Independent* newspaper's article on the survey carried the memorable headline "British public wrong about nearly everything, survey shows."[3]

	Average Answer Among Survey Participants	Best Available Estimate
What proportion of the UK population are single parents?	28%	3%
What proportion of the UK population is not UK born?	31%	13%
What proportion of the UK welfare budget is claimed fraudulently?	24%	0.7%
What proportion of British girls aged 13–15 become pregnant each year?	15%	0.6%

And it's not just the British. In the United States, only about a half of adults know that each state has two senators, and 75 percent don't know the length of each senator's term.[4] At any given time, a majority of Americans cannot name the member of congress for their district.[5]

We could go on like this all day, but we suspect the statistics are not necessary. Be honest: How many European heads of state can you name? What about members of your country's cabinet? What is your country's total national debt? How many people in total currently serve in your country's armed services? If you can answer these questions well, you are very unusual!

We should emphasize here that we're not accusing you—or anyone—of *stupidity*. The point, rather, is that voters have little incentive to inform themselves. The American economist Anthony Downs pointed out that each voter has only a *tiny* chance of affecting the outcome of an election.[6] This means that each voter has very little incentive to inform themself about political issues. If your vote will almost certainly not make a difference, why bother researching the issues, when you could instead get some work done, or do some volunteering, or go to the beach? It is therefore entirely unsurprising that most voters know rather little about the big political questions of the day. Social scientists sometimes express this point by saying that voters are **rationally uninformed**.

We might summarize the argument like this:

> A majority of voters are not well informed on political issues.
>
> Political decisions (including decisions about who should rule) should be made by people who are well informed on the topic.
>
> *Therefore:*
>
> Political decisions (including decisions about who should rule) should not be made democratically.

We will spend most of the rest of this chapter, in effect, exploring answers to this challenge. In the next three sections, we'll consider some defenses of democracy—defenses that can be combined in various ways.

17.3 A Modest Defense of Democracy

Voters are unlikely to favor politicians who very conspicuously fail to serve them well. Politicians in a democracy who wish to stay in office, therefore, are incentivized to be responsive to the needs of voters, at least to some minimal extent. We can illustrate this point looking at the economist Amartya Sen's study of famines.

Sen was born in 1933 in Bengal, India—then part of the British Empire. As a child, he witnessed one of the great tragedies of the twentieth century: the Bengal famine of 1943, in which roughly 3 million Bengalis died. He later devoted much of his career as an economist to the study of famines—that is, to disasters in which a large proportion of people in a region are unable to access sufficient food, resulting in mass severe undernutrition and death.

Sen observed that famines like this were not uncommon in India under British rule. Once India became an independent democracy in 1947, the famines stopped. Indeed, Sen argued that famines *never* occur in democratic countries: "No famine has ever taken place in the history of the world in a functioning democracy."[7]

Sen's explanation of this point begins with the observation that famines are "easy to prevent."[8] You don't need to be an expert in social or medical science to understand that one can prevent a famine by transporting food to the affected area and distributing it. The food doesn't have to be expensive. Cheap staples, such as rice or potatoes, are enough. This means that, even in low-income countries, famines can be prevented, if the threat of famine is identified early enough. Sen adds that democratically elected rulers have a very strong incentive to prevent famines—few will vote for candidates who have allowed famines to occur. India's imperial rulers had no such incentive. During the Second World War, the British government went to great lengths to protect Britain's food supply. There was an effort to increase agricultural production in Britain, and the Royal Navy was tasked with defending ships bringing food from elsewhere. A system of rationing was introduced to prevent hoarding and to ensure an equitable distribution of basic foods. By contrast, the British government's response to news of the Bengal famine was half-hearted at best. Requests for shipments of foodstuffs were repeatedly denied, or fulfilled only in part. Lord Archibald Wavell, who became Viceroy of India in 1943, said that "the vital problems of India are being treated by His Majesty's Government with neglect, even sometimes with hostility and contempt."[9] The historian Yasmine Khan explains that the British government "prioritiz[ed] White lives and European lives over South Asian lives";[10] we might equally say that it prioritized the lives of voters over those unable to vote.

Sen also argues that "a free press and an active political opposition constitute the best early-warning system a country threatened by famines can have."[11] In a democracy, opposition parties are always keen to advertise the failings of the governing party. This means that, when a famine begins to occur, opposition parties will seek to advertise this fact. If there is a free press, news of the incipient famine will spread quickly. Undemocratic countries lack this "early-warning system."[12]

This is not to deny that democratically elected leaders will sometimes be incompetent, or corrupt, or worse. One proponent of democracy who was nevertheless vividly aware of the failings of some democratically elected leaders was Karl Popper (1902–1994), an Austrian who was born in Vienna. Popper saw the success of the Nazi party in the German elections of 1933, and the rise of fascism in Austria under Engelbert Dollfuss at about the same time. Popper fled Austria in 1937, shortly before the Anschluss (the political union of Austria with Germany). Popper had Jewish ancestry; had he stayed in Austria, he might well have been killed in the Holocaust. During the Second World War, he wrote *The Open Society and Its Enemies,* in which he explained his justification of democracy. For Popper, the great strength of democracy is *not* that elected leaders will always be good leaders; rather, it is that, in a democracy, the worst leaders can be removed from office without violence:

> [T]he fundamental problem of a rational political theory . . . can be formulated as follows: how is the state to be constituted so that bad rulers can be got rid of without bloodshed, without violence? . . . [T]he modern so-called democracies are all good examples of practical solutions to this problem . . . [F]or they all adopt what is the simplest solution to the new problem—that is, the principle that the government can be dismissed by a majority vote.[13]

It is perhaps worth separating two points here. The first is that, according to Popper, democratic countries are less prone to political violence—because those unhappy with the governing party can oppose it with political campaigns rather than with guns and bombs. The second is that, according to Popper, in a democracy the very worst rulers are unlikely to stay in their positions for long.

Let's put all of this together:

- Democratically elected leaders may often be incompetent, corrupt, or worse.
- However, in a democratic country, leaders are strongly incentivized to be responsive to the needs of their citizens, at least to some minimal extent.
- What's more, the very worst leaders can quickly be removed from office, without violence.

We call this a "modest" justification for democracy because there is no attempt here to argue that democratic countries are competently run. In the next section, we present a more ambitious case for democracy.

17.4 Are Democratic Countries Well Run?

Some proponents of democracy argue, more ambitiously, that democratic countries are—not always, but generally—comparatively well run. Some argue, for example, that democratic countries have higher rates of economic growth.[14] Others argue that democracies have better human rights records.[15] Still others argue that democratic countries outperform undemocratic countries in human development—for example, in infant mortality.[16]

Discussions of this issue in social science are complex and difficult, but a simple exercise suffices to make the point. Take a look at *The Economist*'s list of the most democratic countries, and compare it to the United Nation's list of countries with the highest scores on the "Human Development Index." You'll notice that there is a lot of overlap! This observation hardly settles the question, of course, but it does suggest that the story about the airplanes in section 17.2 is somewhat misleading. But how can this be? If the voters are so ignorant, how is it that so many democratic countries are "still flying," so to speak?

Some proponents of democracy will answer this question by claiming that, in some cases, a group of people can be wiser or more knowledgeable than the individual members of the group. One of your authors illustrated the point in one of his seminars with a multiple-choice general knowledge quiz. The quiz contained ten questions. For each question, four possible answers were presented, only one of which was correct. Students completed the quiz independently of each other. (The questions are at the end of this chapter.) The *average* score in the quiz was

5.7 out of 10—which is not very impressive when you realize that someone choosing answers at random could be expected to get 2 or 3 points just by chance. The highest score of any individual student was 8 out of 10. However, we might say that the students "collectively" answered a question correctly if the correct answer was chosen more often than any one of the incorrect answers. In this sense, the students *collectively* got a score of 9 out of 10. So the students as a group outperformed every individual student, and far outperformed the average student.

How does this happen? We think it works rather like this. Suppose that there are 100 students, and that 20 of them know the answer to a certain question. The remaining 80 students vote at random, so about 20 of them choose each of the four answers. Then, the correct answer will receive about 40 "votes," and each incorrect answer will receive about 20 "votes." In consequence, the students *collectively* choose the right answer even though a majority of them don't know the answer.

This is sometimes called the **wisdom of crowds**. Some proponents of democracy argue that a similar phenomenon is at work in democratic elections: individual voters may be very ill-informed, but as a group, the electorate is likely to make good choices much of the time. It is not claimed, of course, that the electorate is never wrong in its choices; in the quiz, the group didn't get *every* question right. The claim is rather that the electorate as a whole will often make wise choices even if the individual voters lack knowledge.

When making the case against democracy in section 17.2, we noted that many policy decisions require a great deal of specialist knowledge—knowledge that most voters lack. In some cases, democratic countries work around this problem by *delegating* decision-making power on technical questions to experts, who are appointed by politicians and not elected.

For example, most voters, and most elected politicians, do not have the necessary knowledge to write food safety regulations, such as what the maximum permitted level of lead in drinking water should be. In many democratic countries, in consequence, food safety rules are written by regulatory bodies that are staffed by experts, and not by elected politicians—at least, that's the goal.

For a rather more controversial example, consider the fact that, in many democratic countries, the decisionmakers in the central bank are *not* elected even though they have an enormous amount of political power; consider the Federal Reserve in the United States, for example. The proponents of this system say that managing the central bank requires an enormous amount of technical knowledge—technical knowledge that most elected politicians lack. Moreover, it is argued that the central bank should aim for long-term economic stability, which often involves making decisions that are unpopular in the short term. Elected politicians (especially when elections are approaching) are often afraid of making these unpopular decisions.

17.5 Noninstrumental Defenses of Democracy

Our last defense of democracy is perhaps more subtle, so we will introduce it with an analogy.

The members of Sofía's extended family are considering the living arrangements of an elderly member of the family, with dementia, who is no longer capable of making his own decisions or living independently. To settle the issue, the adults in the family meet for a discussion—but they don't invite Sofía. Together, they reach a decision: the elderly relative will live with Sofía and her spouse.

Sofía is aggrieved about her exclusion from the conversation. Her complaint is *not* that the wrong decision was made. She agrees that it's best for the elderly relative to live with her, and she is content to do the work this entails. Had she attended the meeting, she would have argued for this very arrangement. Sofía's complaint is that she should have been invited to the family meeting, and that she should have had the chance to contribute to the decision-making process.

Sofía explains her complaint in different ways. She says that the other members of the family did not accord her the *respect* that she deserves as an adult: they treated her like a child by making decisions without consulting her. She also complains about the *inequality* of the situation: Why should some members of the family have had a say while she did not? She also complains that she was put in a subordinate position relative to her siblings and cousins; they were taking control of aspects of her life without her participation.

That's the end of our story; let's get back to politics. Consider an epistocratic political system, in which only those who pass a certain exam are permitted to vote. It is a good bet that some of those who do not pass the exam will resent this system. But what, exactly, will be their complaint? Perhaps some will say that the system produces objectionable policies; they might, for example, say that those who pass the exam are able to secure unfair privileges for themselves. But they might also say that the fact that they are unable to vote is *itself* unjust—independently of the policy outcomes produced by the system. This complaint could be developed in several ways. They might say that the system does not afford them the *respect* they deserve as adults: the system treats them like children by imposing decisions on them without allowing them to participate in the decision-making process. They might complain about the *inequality* of this system: it is unfair that some people have the vote while others do not. Or they might complain that the system puts them in a subordinate position relative to those who pass the exam.

We have presented these ideas as an objection to epistocracy, but they can also be presented more positively as a justification of democracy. In a democracy, it has been argued, the citizens are *respected*. They are—in one way, anyway—treated as *equals* because they have equal votes. They are not *subordinated* to other citizens, which gives them liberty of a certain kind.

Philosophers distinguish between instrumental and noninstrumental arguments for democracy. To give an **instrumental argument for democracy** is to justify democracy by saying that the democratic process produces good outcomes—for example, the absence of famine, or a reduction in political violence. To give a **noninstrumental argument for democracy** is to justify democracy by saying that undemocratic systems are unjust *in themselves,* independently of the outcomes they produce. Some philosophers give *both* instrumental and noninstrumental arguments for democracy.

Conclusion

Let's return to the example we opened the chapter with. After listening to the arguments on one side and the other, you must make a decision about your island's constitution. Some have advised you against a democratic system, saying that the people on your island are too uninformed to make wise choices. Others have replied that a democratic system incentivizes leaders to care for their citizens, at least to some minimal extent. They add that, in a democratic system, the worst leaders can be removed from power without violence. Others, more ambitiously, argue that democratic countries are—not always, but in many cases—comparatively well run. Still others argue that a democratic system is preferable because it gives the citizens respect, equality, or liberty. Which of these arguments, if any, persuades you? What constitution will you choose?

Glossary

direct democracy: In a direct democracy, policy questions are settled by public vote. For example, in 2016, there was a referendum about whether the United Kingdom should leave the European Union. See section 17.2 for a longer discussion of the meaning of the word "democracy."

epistocracy: An epistocracy is a political system designed to put political power in the hands on the knowledgeable. This would include, for example, a system in which only those who pass a certain exam are permitted to vote, or a system in which more educated people are given extra votes.

hereditary monarchy: In a hereditary monarchy, when one monarch dies or otherwise leaves office, the crown passes to another member of the same family—perhaps the oldest son.

instrumental argument vs. noninstrumental argument for democracy: To give an *instrumental* argument for democracy is to argue that a democratic system will produce comparatively good laws and policies. To give a *noninstrumental* argument for democracy is to argue that undemocratic systems are unjust *in themselves,* independently of the laws and policies they produce. For more discussion, see section 17.5.

rationally uninformed: In a typical election, each voter has only a *tiny* chance of affecting the outcome. Thus, individual voters have very little incentive to inform themselves about the issues. Economists say that voters are "rationally uninformed."

representative democracy: In a representative democracy, the country's leaders (the president, members of parliament, senators, or whatever) are elected by a public vote. See section 17.2 for a longer discussion of the meaning of the word "democracy."

sortition: Sortition is the choosing of political officials *at random*.

tyranny of the majority: Some have argued that a weakness of democratic systems is that they sometimes allow a majority of voters to use their voting power to inflict injustices on members of minority groups. This is called the "tyranny of the majority." To prevent this, some democratic countries have in place mechanisms that are designed to limit democratic forces in order to protect individual rights.

wisdom of crowds: In some cases, a group of people can be wiser or more knowledgeable than the individual members of the group. This phenomenon is sometimes called the "wisdom of crowds." Philosophical discussions of this phenomenon often emphasize a mathematical result known as "Condorcet's Jury Theorem."

Comprehension Questions

1. Define the following terms: (a) hereditary monarchy, (b) epistocracy, and (c) sortition.
2. Describe some of the features of a democratic system of government. What is the difference between direct and representative democracy?
3. What do social scientists mean when they say that voters "rationally uninformed"?
4. In section 17.2, when presenting the "basic argument against democracy," we used an analogy involving airplanes. Come up with your own analogy to make the same point.
5. Summarize Amartya Sen's views about democracy and famine.
6. What is the "wisdom of crowds"? Suggest an example. (Don't repeat an example from the chapter).
7. What is the standard justification for central bank independence?
8. What is the difference between an instrumental argument and a noninstrumental argument for democracy?
9. In section 17.5, to explain some noninstrumental arguments for democracy, we told a story about a family making a decision about an elderly relative. Devise your own story that makes the same point.

Discussion Questions

1. In section 17.1, we described some characteristics of democratic systems of government. Do you agree with the points we make in this section? Are there *other* characteristics to add to the list? Suppose you were tasked with designing a "democracy index"—that is, a way of numerically measuring the degree to which a country is democratic. How would you go about it?
2. In the chapter's Introduction, we gave a list of different ways of choosing leaders (representative democracy, hereditary monarchy, sortition, etc.). Are there any other systems that should be considered alongside these? What do you see as the main advantages and disadvantages of each of these systems?
3. Is there a good case to be made for restricting voting rights to more knowledgeable people?
4. In most cases, each individual citizen in a democracy has only a miniscule chance of making a difference to the outcome of the vote. Does this mean that, for the typical citizen, educating oneself about politics is a waste of time?
5. The story in section 17.4 about the quiz strongly suggests that, *in some cases,* a group can outperform the individual members. But is it plausible that this happens in democratic elections? What similarities and differences are there between the quiz and a democratic election?
6. In section 17.5, we discussed noninstrumental arguments for democracy, mentioning respect, equality, and liberty. Someone might object:

> It's ridiculous to defend democracy by saying that it produces respect, or equality, or liberty. Many democratic countries have huge inequalities of wealth and power. In many democratic countries, many citizens are not respected. Democratic government are very capable of authoritarian laws.

Do you agree or disagree with this objection?

What to Look at Next

- Each year, *The Economist* magazine's "intelligence unit" produces a report on its democracy index. This report explains the unit's methodology, reports its findings, and comments on them.

- Alexander Guerrero argues that democracy divides us in "Democracy Divides Us," available at https://iai.tv/articles/democracy-divides-us-auid-1862?_auid=2020, and in "Against Elections: The Lottocratic Alternative," *Philosophy & Public Affairs* 42, no. 2 (2014): 135–178. His preferred alternative is a form of sortition.
- If you want to learn more about Plato's political views, we recommend "Plato's Politics," by Christopher Bobonich, in *The Oxford Handbook of Plato,* 2nd ed., edited by Gail Fine. There are many good translations of Plato's *Republic*; Desmond Lee's translation is one of them (Penguin Classics, with an introduction by Melissa Lane).
- For a more modern critique of democracy, see Jason Brennan's book *Against Democracy.* For a shorter version, see his "In Defense of Epistocracy: Enlightened Preference Voting," in *The Routledge Handbook of Political Epistemology.*
- Amartya Sen explains his views on democracy and famine in *Development as Freedom.* See chapter 6 of that book in particular.
- For an instrumental defense of democracy, see Thomas Christiano, "An Instrumental Argument for a Human Right to Democracy," Philosophy and Public Affairs, vol. 39, no. 2 (2011): 142–176.
- In his talk "How Do You Know if You're Truly Free?", Philip Pettit gives his take on political freedom and his justification of democracy. You can watch it on YouTube at https://www.youtube.com/watch?v=1rTEOU67zCo.
- For objections to some noninstrumental arguments for democracy, see Richard Arneson's essay "Democracy Is not Intrinsically Just," in *Political Philosophy in the Twenty-First Century,* edited by Stephen Cain and Robert Talisse.

Appendix: A General Knowledge Quiz

1. In which year did the Bolsheviks execute the tsar?

    (a) 1878
    (b) 1905
    (c) 1918
    (d) 1933

2. Which of these has the greatest atomic number?

   (a) Sodium
   (b) Oxygen
   (c) Magnesium
   (d) Tin

3. Which of the following animals lays eggs?

   (a) Echidna
   (b) Tasmanian Devil
   (c) Bandicoot
   (d) Wombat

4. Who played Xu Shang-Chi in *Shang-Chi and the Legend of the Ten Rings*?

   (a) Simu Liu
   (b) Meng'er Zhang
   (c) Benedict Wong
   (d) Tony Leung

5. Who plays Claire Dunphy in the sitcom *Modern Family*?

   (a) Sarah Hyland
   (b) Julie Bowen
   (c) Ariel Winter
   (d) Aubrey Anderson-Emmons

6. According to Wikipedia's "List of African countries by population," which of these countries is the largest by population?

   (a) Nigeria
   (b) Ethiopia
   (c) Democratic Republic of the Congo
   (d) Egypt

7. Which of the following would you find in a traditional French *moules marinière*?

   (a) Mussels
   (b) Oysters
   (c) Lobster
   (d) Scallops

8. Who was the Canadian prime minister in 1900?

   (a) Sir Charles Tupper
   (b) Sir Wilfred Laurier
   (c) Sir Robert Borden
   (d) Arthur Meighen

9. Who wrote the *Meditations on First Philosophy*?

   (a) Descartes
   (b) Spinoza
   (c) Locke
   (d) Hume

10. Who wrote *A Tale of Two Cities*?

    (a) Charles Dickens
    (b) Charlotte Brontë
    (c) George Eliot
    (d) Anthony Trollope

Notes

1. From "Global Satisfaction with Democracy 2020," from the Bennett Institute for Public Policy's Centre for the Future of Democracy. It's important to stress that the graph shows an average of opinion in the five countries, weighted by population, and that there is considerable variation among them. The level of dissatisfaction with democracy actually decreased in New Zealand. The increase in dissatisfaction was largest in the United States, which is also the by far largest of the five countries and so had a very large effect on the average. See https://www.cam.ac.uk/system/files/report2020_003.pdf.
2. Ipsos, "Perceptions Are not Reality," July 9, 2013, https://www.ipsos.com/en-uk/perceptions-are-not-reality.
3. Johnathan Paige, "British Public Wrong About Nearly Everything, Survey Shows," *Independent*, July 9, 2013.
4. Michael X. Delli Carpini and Scott Keeter, *What Americans Know About Politics and Why It Matters* (New Haven, CT: Yale University Press, 1996), 117.
5. Thomas R. Dye and Harmon Zeigler, *The Irony of Democracy: An Uncommon Introduction to American Politics*, 7th ed. (Pacific Grove, CA; Brooks/Cole Publishing, 1992), 206.

6. For example, Andrew Gelman and his co-authors studied the 2008 presidential election in the United States. They concluded that the state in which an individual's vote was most likely to matter were New Mexico, Virginia, New Hampshire, and Colorado. They estimate that, in these states, each person's vote had a 1 in 10 million chance of determining the national election outcome. See Andrew Gelman, Nate Silver, and Aaron Edlin, "What Is the Probability Your Vote Will Make a Difference?", *Economic Inquiry* 50, No. 2 (2012): 321–326.
7. Amartya Sen, *Development as Freedom* (New York; Alfred A. Knopf, 1999), 16. For dissent, see Olivier Rubin's "The Merits of Democracy in Famine Protection — Fact or Fallacy?", *European Journal of Development Research* 21, no 3. (2009): 699–717. Ourworldindata.org has an elegant chart depicting famines since 1850, categorized by the political system of the country in which they occurred.
8. Sen, Development as Freedom, 180.
9. Quoted in Yasmin Khan, India at War: The Subcontinent and the Second World War (Oxford; Oxford University Press, 2015), pg. 213.
10. "Churchill's Legacy Still Painful for Indians," *BBC News*, July 21, 2020.
11. Sen, *Development and Freedom*, 181.
12. Sen illustrates this point by considering the Great Chinese Famine of 1959–1961, in which some 30 million people died. Sen claims that this tragedy occurred in large part because there was no "early warning system."
13. Karl Popper, "The Open Society and Its Enemies Revisited," *The Economist*, April 23, 1988.
14. Daron Acemoglu et al. "Democracy Does Cause Growth," *Journal of Political Economy* 127, no. 1 (2019): 47–100.
15. Thomas Christiano, "An Instrumental Argument for a Human Right to Democracy," *Philosophy & Public Affairs*. 39, no. 2 (2011): 142–176.
16. See, for example, John Gerring et al., "Democracy and Human Development," *The Journal of Politics* 74, no. 1 (2012): 1–17.

APPENDIX A

Reading and Writing Tips

Seven Tips on Reading Philosophy

1. Read it (at least) twice

When reading a work of philosophy, start by reading it through quickly. On this first reading, skip over the finer details, trying to see the broad outlines of the piece. When you finish your first reading, try to summarize the work in a paragraph, and make a list of things that you don't yet understand. Underline or list words that are difficult or particularly important. Once you've done this, read through the work again, more slowly this time. As you go, attempt to fill in the gaps in your understanding. Try to explain the meanings of the words you identified as difficult or important. Once you've finished your second reading, have another go at summarizing the work in a paragraph.

2. One source is never enough

There is an enormous amount of disagreement in philosophy. This means that if you rely on just one source of information—no matter how good it is—you are likely to end up with an incomplete understanding of the issues. (Yes, we include our book in this!) If you want to understand a philosophical issue deeply, use several different sources.

Bear in mind that philosophical jargon is far from standardized. For example, if one writer claims that "liberalism" emerged in the nineteenth century and another writer traces "liberalism" back to the seventeenth century, it may well be because the two writers are using the term "liberalism" in different senses.

3. Use the secondary literature

If you're reading some great classic of philosophy, don't hesitate to look to the secondary literature for help. (Indeed, it's often helpful to look at the secondary literature *before* you read the original text.) It is usually easy to find good secondary sources with a quick web search.

4. When evaluating a work of philosophy, be precise

Once you've finished reading a philosophical work, you should think about whether you agree with the author's claims. If you disagree with the writer, try to be precise about where your disagreement arises. It is often helpful to analyze the argument, using the techniques described in chapter 2. Do you reject one of the premises of the argument? If so, which one? Is there a step in the argument that you take to be fallacious? Which? You might find it helpful to think about points of agreement as well as points of disagreement.

5. To search for books and articles use Google, Google Books, and Amazon

If you're looking for things to read, search using Google, Google Books, and Amazon. Most academic articles these days are made available in pdf format, so it is often helpful to add "filetype:pdf" to your Google search. Websites with the top-level domain ".edu" are often particularly helpful—these are university-based websites.

If you have access to JSTOR, try using its search feature. You should use the "Advanced Search" feature, restricting your search to "philosophy" (and perhaps other relevant disciplines).

If you're not sure whether the article you're looking at will be helpful, try reading just the first two pages and the last two pages. This should give you an idea of whether the article is worth reading more fully.

6. Use the right reference sources

The most authoritative reference work in philosophy is the *Stanford Encyclopedia of Philosophy*. This is free and easy to find online, though it is sometimes prolix. The *Internet Encyclopedia of Philosophy* is also very good, and it is also free. The *Routledge Encyclopedia of Philosophy* is excellent, though only subscribers can access it. The philosophy articles in Wikipedia are of varied quality. Very often, the best part of a Wikipedia article is the list of references at the bottom, which may direct you to more authoritative sources.

The *Oxford Dictionary of Philosophy* may help you with philosophical jargon. You can buy a paper copy of this, or you can access it online if you have a subscription.

7. Explain things in your own words

If you want to make sure that you really understand something you've read, try explaining it in your own words. Better still, try explaining it, in your own words, in several different ways. If you struggle to do this, it's a good indication that you don't really understand it.

Eighteen Tips for Writing Philosophy Papers

Of course, different instructors ask for different things when they assign work. We think that the advice below will be applicable in most cases—but pay close attention to your instructor's guidelines.

1. Your paper must have a thesis

Somewhere within the first paragraph or two of your paper, state the thesis that you will defend. Your thesis statement might look a bit like one of these:

- I will show that Smith's version of the "first cause" argument for theism is unsound.
- I will use a series of examples to show that Anthony Appiah's fair share principle is true.
- I will present counterexamples to the claim that every event has a cause.

Your paper shouldn't be a mere "book report" in which various different views are summarized. You need a thesis of your own.

2. You must have an argument for your thesis

It's not enough to present your own opinions: you need an argument. Your argument should be presented in some detail. You should explain your premises carefully and discuss how they support your conclusion.

You may find it helpful to imagine a reader who doesn't already accept your conclusions. How might you convince this reader?

It's okay to present more than one argument for your thesis, but don't bombard the reader with one argument after another after another. One carefully explained argument is far superior to a dozen bad ones.

Check out chapter 2 for some discussion of how arguments are structured.

3. Your conclusion should not be trivial, but at the same time, it's important not to be too ambitious

If it's obvious to everybody that your conclusion is true, there's no point in writing a paper to defend it. You don't want the reader to look at your thesis and think, "Well, duh!" Your thesis shouldn't be trivial.

At the same time, it's important not to overreach. It would be a mistake to critique *every* argument for theism in a single paper—this would take a whole book, or even a series of books.

Too trivial	Too ambitious
It is sometimes virtuous to give money to charity.	All of the arguments for the existence of God are fallacious.
There is controversy about whether hedonism is true.	All existing theories about the relation between mind and body are inadequate.
Some philosophers are dualists.	There is no good objection to hedonism.
Descartes was an important philosopher.	Every part of Kant's moral philosophy is correct.

4. Anticipate and respond to objections

Think about your argument from the point of view of someone who rejects its conclusion. What objections might this person have to your argument? Include replies to these objections in your paper.

5. Cut out irrelevant material

Your goal is to defend your thesis. Anything irrelevant to this goal should be taken out. For example, if you're writing about Kant's moral philosophy, you probably shouldn't tell your readers about his work in astronomy or explain that he lived in Königsberg.

6. Avoid flowery introductions

It's a running joke among philosophy professors that bad undergraduate papers begin, "Since the beginning of time, Man has looked up to the heavens and contemplated the meaning of life and his place in the universe." Concision is important; get to the point quickly.

7. Write simply and clearly

Don't think that complex, intricate writing is a sign of intelligence. Don't aim for literary flair or emotional impact. Keep it simple. It might help to pretend that your reader is a smart twelve-year-old. Never use an obscure word when you could use a familiar one.

It is a sad fact that many of the greatest philosophers have been terrible writers. Don't make the mistake of emulating them.

8. Be consistent in your vocabulary

You might think that it's clumsy to keep using the word "god" and choose to avoid this by sporadically replacing the word with near-synonyms like "deity," "supreme being," or "divine being." Don't do this: it may confuse your reader.

9. Look out for ambiguities; clarify your terms

Terminological confusion is a constant danger in philosophy; clarify your terms. Look at our discussion of the word "God" at the beginning of chapter 3 to see how this is done.

Ambiguous terms are especially dangerous. Consider as an example the word "human." As we explain in chapter 15, in Kantian philosophy a "human" is a being able to choose its own goals and take rational steps in pursuit of those goals. In other contexts, a "human" is any organism of the species *Homo sapiens*. If you use the word "human" in an ethics paper without explaining what you mean by the term, your reader may well be confused. Sadly, jargon terms in philosophy are often highly ambiguous.

10. Use examples

Philosophical arguments are often highly abstract and therefore hard to follow. It is often helpful to give concrete examples to help your reader follow along.

11. Your paper should have a clear structure

Let's suppose that you're writing a paper in which you attempt to use examples to undermine W. K. Clifford's claim that "it is wrong always, everywhere, and for anyone, to believe anything upon insufficient evidence." Your paper might have something like this structure:

> Section 1: Briefly explain the goals of the paper.
> Section 2: Explain Clifford's thesis. Illustrate the thesis with examples.
> Section 3: Present your examples to undermine Clifford's thesis.
> Section 4: Discuss objections to your argument.
> Section 5: Briefly summarize your conclusions.

This structure should be very clear to the reader from the start. Twist endings are great in movies, but they are terrible in philosophy papers. On the contrary, it is often a good idea in a philosophy paper to explicitly describe the structure of your paper in the introduction. ("I will begin by explaining Clifford's thesis, using examples. Then I will . . . ") Section headings can be helpful too.

12. If in doubt, cite!

Students are often unsure about whether they need to cite something they've used when preparing a paper. There's a simple rule you can apply here: if it crosses your mind that you should cite something, you should cite it!

Your instructor might give you specific instructions about how you should format your citations. However, what's most important is that you should give enough information about the cited work that your readers can find it themselves:

- If you cite a book, give the title of the book and the name of the author. You might also need to specify which edition of the book you're citing. A page number might be helpful too.
- If you cite an article from a journal, give the name of the author, the title of the paper, and the year of publication.
- If you cite something from the Web, give the title of the piece, the name of the author, and the URL.
- If the work you're citing has been translated, remember to give the name of the translator.

13. Don't plagiarize
Never use another writer's words without indicating very clearly that they are quoted. If you paraphrase another writer, you need to make it very clear that this is what you're doing.

14. No, seriously: Don't plagiarize
Many universities now use powerful software to detect plagiarism, and the penalties for plagiarism are often severe.

15. Write an outline
It's very hard to write a paper if you don't know what you're trying to say—and so most people find it very helpful to produce an outline before they sit down to write the paper. At the very least, you should have a list of the sections in your paper before you start; often it is helpful to have a much more thorough outline in which you describe what will happen within each section.

16. Start early
To write your philosophy paper, you have to:

- Find a thesis and an argument for the thesis.
- Think of objections to your thesis and argument, and responses to the objections.
- Figure out a structure for the paper.
- Write the paper.
- Edit the paper.

This all takes a lot of time, so get started early!

17. Read your paper aloud
Once you've completed a draft of your paper, read it aloud. This will help you find stylistic mistakes.

18. When proofreading, be pedantic
When you proofread your paper, make sure that what you say is *exactly* what you mean. Don't say that eating meat is murder when what you mean is that killing animals for food is a form of murder; don't claim to have refuted compatibilism when you have only refuted *Hume's version*

of compatibilism; don't say that God created everything when what you mean is that God created everything *except himself.* Pedantry may be a vice, but sloppiness is far worse.

For more information on writing philosophy, check out:

- A.P. Martinich, *Philosophical Writing: An Introduction*
- Anthony Graybosch, Gregory Scott, and Stephen Garrison, *The Philosophy Student Writer's Manual*
- Diedre McCloskey's *Economical Writing* is aimed at economists, but the book is excellent and almost all of her advice applies to philosophy.
- Another excellent book is Steven Pinker's *The Sense of Style: The Thinking Person's Guide to Writing in the 21st Century.*

APPENDIX B

The Truth About Philosophy Majors

Here's the inaccurate, old-school way of thinking:
- Philosophy majors have no marketable skills; they are unemployable.
- They are unprepared for professional careers in anything but teaching philosophy.
- They are useless in an economy built on exploding tech, speed-of-light innovation, and market-wrenching globalization.
- They are destined to earn low salaries.

Here's the new reality: all these assumptions are FALSE.

Careers

A wide range of data suggest that philosophy majors are not just highly employable; they are thriving in many careers that used to be considered unsuitable for those holding "impractical" philosophy degrees. The unemployment rate for recent graduates with a BA in philosophy graduates is 4.3 percent, lower than the national average and lower than that for majors in biology, chemical engineering, graphic design, mathematics, and economics.[1]

Nowadays, most philosophy majors don't get PhDs in philosophy; they instead land jobs in many fields outside academia. They work in business consulting firms, guide investors on Wall Street, lead teams of innovators in Silicon Valley, do humanitarian work for nongovernmental organizations, go into politics, and cover the world as journalists. They teach, write, design, publish, create. They go to medical school, law school, and graduate school in everything from art and architecture to education, business, and computer science. (Of course, besides majoring in philosophy, students can also minor in it, combining a philosophy BA with other BA programs, or take philosophy courses to round out other majors or minors.)

Many successful companies—especially those in the tech world—don't see a philosophy degree as impractical at all. To be competitive,

Photo 1: Carly Fiorina, businessperson and political figure
Photo 2: Stewart Butterfield, cofounder of Flickr and Slack
Photo 3: Sheila Bair, Nineteenth Chair of the FDIC

they want more than just engineers, scientists, and mathematicians. They also want people with broader, big-picture skills—people who can think critically, question assumptions, formulate and defend ideas, develop unique perspectives, devise and evaluate arguments, write effectively, and analyze and simplify complicated problems. And these competences are abundant in people with a philosophy background.

Plenty of successful business and tech leaders say so. Speaking of her undergraduate studies, philosophy major and eventual chief executive of Hewlett-Packard Carly Fiorina says, "I learned how to separate the wheat from the chaff, essential from just interesting, and I think that's a particularly critical skill now when there is a ton of interesting but ultimately irrelevant information floating around."[2]

Flickr co-founder Stewart Butterfield, who has both bachelor's and master's degrees in philosophy, says, "I think if you have a good background in what it is to be human, an understanding of life, culture and society, it gives you a good perspective on starting a business, instead of an education purely in business. You can always pick up how to read a balance sheet and how to figure out profit and loss, but it's harder to pick up the other stuff on the fly."[3]

Sheila Bair got her philosophy degree from the University of Kansas and went on to become chair of the Federal Deposit Insurance Corporation (FDIC) from 2006 to 2011. She says that philosophy "helps you break things down to their simplest elements. My philosophy training really helps me with that intellectual rigor of simplifying things and finding out what's important."[4]

> **PHILOSOPHY: A NATURAL SEGUE TO LAW AND MEDICINE**
> Law schools will tell you that a major in philosophy provides excellent preparation for law school and a career in law. Philosophy excels as a pre-law major because it teaches you the very proficiencies that law schools require: developing and evaluating arguments, writing carefully and clearly, applying principles and rules to specific cases, sorting out evidence, and understanding ethical and political norms. Philosophy majors

do very well on the LSAT (Law School Admission Test), typically scoring higher than the vast majority of other majors.

Philosophy has also proven itself to be good preparation for medical school. Critical reasoning is as important in medicine as it is in law, but the study and practice of medicine require something else—expertise in grappling with the vast array of moral questions that now confront doctors, nurses, medical scientists, administrators, and government officials. These are, at their core, philosophy questions.

David Silbersweig, a Harvard Medical School professor, makes a good case for philosophy (and all the liberal arts) as an essential part of a well-rounded medical education. As he says,

> If you can get through a one-sentence paragraph of Kant, holding all of its ideas and clauses in juxtaposition in your mind, you can think through most anything. . . . I discovered that a philosophical stance and approach could identify and inform core issues associated with everything from scientific advances to healing and biomedical ethics.[5]

Philosophy major and MSNBC journalist Katy Tur says, "I would argue that for the vast majority of people, an education of teaching you to think critically about the world you are in and what you know and what you don't know is useful for absolutely everything that you could possibly do in the future."[6]

It's little wonder then that the top ranks of leaders and innovators in business and technology have their share of philosophy majors, a fair number of whom credit their success to their philosophy background. The list is long, and it includes:[7]

Patrick Byrne, entrepreneur, e-commerce pioneer, founder and CEO of Overstock.com
Damon Horowitz, entrepreneur, in-house philosopher at Google
Carl Icahn, businessman, investor, philanthropist. . . .
Larry Sanger, Internet project developer, co-founder of Wikipedia
George Soros, investor, business magnate

Photo 4: Katy Tur, author and broadcast journalist for MSNBC
Photo 5: Damon Horowitz, entrepreneur and in-house philosopher at Google
Photo 6: Larry Sanger, Internet project developer, co-founder of Wikipedia

Peter Thiel, entrepreneur, venture capitalist, co-founder of PayPal
Jeff Weiner, CEO of LinkedIn

Of course, there are also many with a philosophy background who are famous for their achievements outside the business world. This list is even longer and includes:

Wes Anderson, filmmaker, screenwriter (*The Royal Tenenbaums*)
Stephen Breyer, Supreme Court justice
Mary Higgins Clark, novelist (*All By Myself, Alone*)
Ethan Coen, filmmaker, director
Stephen Colbert, comedian, TV host
Angela Davis, social activist
Lana Del Rey, singer, songwriter
Dessa, rapper, singer, poet
Ken Follett, author (*Eye of the Needle*)
Harrison Ford, actor
Ricky Gervais, comedian, creator of *The Office*
Philip Glass, composer
Rebecca Newberger Goldstein, author (*Plato at the Googleplex*)
Matt Groening, creator of *The Simpsons* and *Futurama*
Chris Hayes, MSNBC host
Kazuo Ishiguro, Nobel Prize-winning author (*The Remains of the Day*)
Phil Jackson, NBA coach
Thomas Jefferson, US president
Charles R. Johnson, novelist (*Middle Passage*)
Rashida Jones, actor
Martin Luther King Jr., civil rights leader
John Lewis, civil rights activist, US House of Representatives
Terrence Malick, filmmaker, director
Yann Martel, author (*Life of Pi*)

Photo 7: Stephen Breyer, US Supreme Court justice
Photo 8: Stephen Colbert, comedian, TV host
Photo 9: Angela Davis, social activist
Photo 10: Lana Del Rey, singer and songwriter
Photo 11: Chris Hayes, MSNBC host
Photo 12: Rashida Jones, actor
Photo 13: Martin Luther King Jr., civil rights leader
Photo 14: John Lewis, civil rights activist, US House of Representatives
Photo 15: Terrence Malick, filmmaker, director
Photo 16: Yann Martel, author (*Life of Pi*)

PHILOSOPHY MAJORS AND THE GRE

Philosophy majors score higher than *all other majors on the verbal reasoning and analytic writing sections of the GRE.*

	Verbal Reasoning	Quantitative Reasoning	Analytic Reasoning
Philosophy	160	154	4.3
Average	149.97	152.57	3.48

Educational Testing Service, 2017 GRE Scores, between July 1, 2013 and June 30, 2016.

Salaries

According to recent surveys by PayScale, a major source of college salary information, philosophy majors can expect to earn a median starting salary of $44,800 and a median mid-career salary of $85,100. As you might expect, most of the higher salaries go to STEM graduates (those with degrees in science, technology, engineering, and mathematics). But in a surprising number of cases, salaries for philosophy majors are comparable to those of STEM graduates. For example, while the philosophy graduate earns $85,100 at mid-career, the mid-career salary for biotechnology is $82,500; for civil engineering, $83,700; for chemistry, $88,000; for industrial technology, $86,600; and for applied computer science, $88,800. Median end-of-career salaries for philosophy majors (10 to 19 years' experience) is $92,665—not the highest pay among college graduates, but far higher than many philosophy-is-useless critics would expect.[8]

Another factor to consider is the increase in salaries over time. On this score, philosophy majors rank in the top 10 of all majors with the highest salary increase from start to mid-career. Philosophy's increase is pegged at 101 percent. The major with the highest increase: government at 118 percent. Molecular biology is the fifth highest at 105 percent.[9]

SALARY POTENTIAL FOR BACHELOR DEGREES

Major	Median Early Pay (0 to 5 yrs. work experience)	Median Mid-Career Pay (10+ yrs. work experience)
Mechanical Engineering	$58,000	$90,000
Applied Computer Science	$53,100	$88,800
Information Technology	$52,300	$86,300
Civil Engineering	$51,300	$83,700
Business and Finance	$48,800	$91,100
Biotechnology	$46,100	$82,500
Business Marketing	$45,700	$78,700
Philosophy	**$44,800**	**$85,100**
History	$42,200	$75,700
Advertising	$41,800	$84,200
General Science	$41,600	$75,200
Telecommunications	$41,500	$83,700
English Literature	$41,400	$76,300
Marine Biology	$37,200	$76,000

PayScale, "Highest Paying Bachelor Degrees by Salary Potential," *College Salary Report: 2017-2018,* https://www.payscale.com/college-salary-report/majors-that-pay-you-back/bachelors

Among liberal arts majors, philosophy salaries are near the top of the list. All liberal arts majors except economics earn lower starting and mid-career pay than philosophy does.

SALARY POTENTIAL FOR BACHELOR DEGREES

Major	Median Early Pay (0 to 5 yrs. work experience)	Median Mid-Career Pay (10+ yrs. work experience)
Economics	$54,100	$103,200
Philosophy	**$44,800**	**$85,100**
Political Science	$44,600	$82,000
Modern Languages	$43,900	$77,400
Geography	$43,600	$72,700
History	$42,200	$75,700
English Literature	$41,400	$76,300
Anthropology	$40,500	$63,200

Major	Median Early Pay (0 to 5 yrs. work experience)	Median Mid-Career Pay (10+ yrs. work experience)
Creative Writing	$40,200	$68,500
Theatre	$39,700	$63,500
Psychology	$38,700	$65,300
Fine Art	$38,200	$62,200

PayScale, "Highest Paying Bachelor Degrees by Salary Potential," *College Salary Report: 2017-2018*, https://www.payscale.com/college-salary-report/majors-that-pay-you-back/bachelors

Meaning

In all this talk about careers, salaries, and superior test scores, we should not forget that for many students, the most important reason for majoring in philosophy is the meaning it can add to their lives. They know that philosophy, after two-and-one-half millennia, is still alive and relevant and influential. It is not only for studying but also for living—that is, for guiding our lives toward what's true and real and valuable. They would insist that philosophy, even with its ancient lineage and seemingly remote concerns, applies to your life and your times and your world. The world is full of students and teachers who can attest to these claims. Perhaps you will eventually decide to join them.

Notes

1. Federal Reserve Bank of New York, "The Labor Market for Recent College Graduates," 11 January 2017, https://www.newyorkfed.org/research/college-labor-market/college-labor-market_compare-majors.html.
2. T. Rees Shapiro, "For Philosophy Majors, the Question After Graduation Is: What Next?" *Washington Post*, 20 June 2017. https://www.washingtonpost.com/local/education/for-philosophy-majors-the-question-after-graduation-is-what-next/2017/06/20/aa7fae2a-46f0-11e7-98cd-af64b4fe2dfc_story.html.
3. Carolyn Gregoire, "The Unexpected Way Philosophy Majors Are Changing the World of Business," *HuffPost*, 3 January 2017, https://www.huffingtonpost.com/2014/03/05/why-philosophy-majors-rule_n_4891404.html.
4. Shapiro, "For Philosophy Majors."
5. David Silbersweig, "A Harvard Medical School Professor Makes a Case for the Liberal Arts and Philosophy," *Washington Post*, 24 December 2015.
6. Shapiro, "For Philosophy Majors."

7. American Philosophical Association, "Who Studies Philosophy?" (accessed 14 November 2017), http://www.apaonline.org/?whostudiesphilosophy.
8. PayScale, "Highest Paying Bachelor Degrees by Salary Potential," *College Salary Report: 2017–2018*, https://www.payscale.com/college-salary-report/majors-that-pay-you-back/bachelors.
9. PayScale; reported by Rachel Gillett and Jacquelyn Smith, "People with These College Majors Get the Biggest Raises," *Business Insider*, 6 January 2016, http://www.businessinsider.com/college-majors-that-lead-to-the-biggest-pay-raises-2016-1/#20-physics-1.

Resources

American Philosophical Association, "Who Studies Philosophy?" http://www.apaonline.org/?whostudiesphilosophy.

BestColleges.com, "Best Careers for Philosophy Majors," 2017, http://www.bestcolleges.com/careers/philosophy-majors/.

Forbes, "That 'Useless' Liberal Arts Degree Has Become Tech's Hottest Ticket," 29 July 2015, https://www.forbes.com/sites/georgeanders/2015/07/29/liberal-arts-degree-tech/#5fb6d740745d.

Philosophy is a Great Major, "Choose your career. Get a job. Be prepared for the unexpected." https://philosophyisagreatmajor.com/.

University of Maryland, Department of Philosophy, "Careers for Philosophy Majors," http://www.philosophy.umd.edu/undergraduate/careers.

University of North Carolina at Chapel Hill, Department of Philosophy, "Why Major in Philosophy?" http://philosophy.unc.edu/undergraduate/the-major/why-major-in-philosophy/.

GLOSSARY

a priori/a posteriori: To understand these terms, contrast the design argument for theism with the ontological argument. The design argument relies on observations—more specifically, it relies on observations of plants and animals. To make these observations, we rely on sense perception—on sight, hearing, smell, touch, and taste. The ontological argument doesn't rely on sense perception in this way. The design argument is therefore an a posteriori argument, while the ontological argument is an a priori argument. More generally, an a priori argument is one that doesn't rely on observation. An a posteriori argument does involve observation.

abduction: In an abductive argument, one begins with a number of observations, and one suggests an explanation for those various observations. If one judges that the proffered explanation is a good explanation and better than any available alternatives, one cautiously infers that the explanation is correct. Also called "inference to the best explanation."

act consequentialism: The act consequentialist believes that the best thing to do, in any circumstance, is the action that will maximize the aggregate good.

act utilitarianism: The act consequentialist believes that the best thing to do, in any circumstance, is the action that will maximize the aggregate utility. Act utilitarianism is a version of act consequentialism.

active engagement: Susan Wolf says that, to lead a meaningful life, one must be "actively engaged" in "projects of worth." She writes, "A person is actively engaged by something if she is gripped, excited, involved by it."

agent relativism: Agent relativism consists of the following two claims:

- When it's said that a person's action is morally wrong, what's meant is that the action is condemned by the ethical code of that person's culture.
- When it's said that a person's action is morally okay, what's meant is that the action is not condemned by the ethical code of that person's culture.

aggregate good: Suppose we sum all the good and bad consequences of an action to find whether—on balance and overall—the consequences of the action are good or bad.

aggregate utility: When different utilities are added up, the result is an aggregate utility.

analytic functionalism: See functionalism.

anguish and bad faith: Sartre claimed that "it is we who give [life] meaning, and value is nothing more than the meaning we give it." He also claimed that it can be frightening to recognize this truth, especially when we face big decisions. He called this particular fear "anguish"—that is, anguish is the pain we experience when forced to make difficult decisions about what to value. Sartre went on to claim that sometimes people respond to anguish with self-deception: they pretend that they are not free to choose what to value. He called this particular sort of self-deception "bad faith."

animalism: Animalism is a theory of personal identity which holds that people are biological organisms, and that the criteria for numerical identity of people are the same as the criteria for numerical identity of biological organisms. Animalists maintain that a person after a kidney transplant is numerically identical to the person who receives the kidney transplant. They hold that the same is true for a person who has a brain transplant. The person after the transplant is numerically identical to the person who receives the transplant.

apparent memories: See real and apparent memories.

Appiah's fair share principle: This is a moral principle that we attribute to Kwame Anthony Appiah:

> Suppose that you realize some tragedy will or may befall some other people. You can help, but other people are also in a position to help. Then, you are obliged to do no more than your fair share.

To be clear, this isn't a quotation from Appiah; rather, it is our attempt to put into words what seems to us to be a premise of his argument.

argument: An argument is an attempt to rationally justify some assertion—which is called the "conclusion" of the argument. Typically, when you make an argument, you take certain things for granted (these are your "premises"), and you attempt to show that if one accepts the premises, one should accept the conclusion too.

atheism: Atheism is the claim that God does not exist. Atheists are people who think that theism is false. (See theism).

behavioral dispositions: We'll start by explaining what a disposition is, in general. Then we'll look at *behavioral* dispositions in particular. Consider *fragility, solubility in water,* and *elasticity*. These are dispositions. When an object has a disposition, it has a propensity to respond in a particular way to events of particular kinds:

- Barring special circumstances, a fragile object will break if it is struck.
- Barring special circumstances, an object that is soluble in water will dissolve when put in water.
- Barring special circumstances, an elastic object will return to its original shape after it has been deformed.

Now a behavioral disposition is a special kind of disposition—a disposition where the response is a particular sort of behavior. Here are some examples:

- Mortimer will close his eyes when he is sitting.
- Li breaks into song when she is in the shower.
- Shanee sighs when someone mentions money.

Boo! Hurrah! theory: Expressivism is sometimes referred to as the "Boo! Hurrah! theory" because, according to expressivists, saying that X is morally bad is a bit like saying "Boo!" to X, and saying that X is morally good is a bit like saying "Hurrah!" to X.

Cartesian: "Cartesian" is an adjective derived from the Latin form of Descartes's name: Cartesius. It is used to describe things that are in some way associated with Descartes. For example, Descartes invented coordinate geometry, and so coordinate geometry is sometimes called "Cartesian geometry." Cartesian is always spelled with a capital C.

Cartesian circle: Some philosophers believe that Descartes's "proof" of the existence of God is circular. The circle in Descartes's argument is called the "Cartesian circle."

Cartesian mind: Descartes held that the mind is a nonmaterial thing that is capable of consciousness, intentionality, and rationality.

clear and distinct perception: Descartes claimed that when he considered the claim *I exist*, he felt compelled to believe. He couldn't help believing that he existed. He referred to this inner compulsion as clear and distinct perception. It is important not to confuse clear and distinct perception with sense perception.

coherentism: Coherentists believe that a system of beliefs is justified to the extent that it is *coherent*—that is, to the extent that the beliefs fit together in the right kind of way. (Explaining in detail what "coherence" consists of is, of course, an important task for coherentists.)

compatibilism: Compatibilists believe that determinism is compatible with the claim that we have free will.

conclusion: When one makes an argument, one attempts to rationally justify some assertion. This assertion is the conclusion.

conscientious omnivore: The conscientious omnivore thinks that it is wrong to buy meat that has been produced by inhumane farms or abattoirs, but does not think however that it is otherwise wrong to buy meat.

conscious: "Conscious" is a difficult and contested term in philosophy. In chapter 11, we used the term in the following way: a person's mental state is conscious when the person can detect the state by introspection. For example, *being hungry* is a conscious state because you can find out whether you are hungry by introspection (at least in typical cases).

consequentialism: Consequentialism is a family of ethical theories. As the term suggests, consequentialists emphasize the consequences of actions and rules.

contingent beings and necessary beings: A contingent being is a thing that could have not existed. For example, you are a contingent being because your parents could have never met, in which case you would not exist. A necessary being is any being that is not contingent.

cosmological argument: Proponents of cosmological arguments think that there must be some explanation of the existence of contingent things or the existence of the universe as a whole or the occurrence of contingent events. They argue that the best or only explanation is that God created the universe and initiated all causal chains.

cosmology: The study of the history and future of the universe as a whole. Currently, it is usually regarded as a branch of physics.

cost-benefit analysis: Sometimes one evaluates an action by assigning dollar values to all the consequences of the action. Good consequences are assigned positive dollar values; bad outcomes are assigned negative dollar values. The action will be taken if the total dollar value of its consequences is sufficiently large. This process of decision-making is called "cost-benefit analysis."

declarative sentence: Contrast these sentences:

Declarative	Not declarative
Alba is tall.	Is Alba tall?
It is summer.	If only it were summer!
The door is closed.	Close the door!

The sentences on the left are declarative; the sentences on the right are not. "Is Alba tall?" is interrogative, "If only it were summer!" is optative, and

"Close the door!" is imperative. Note that only declarative sentences are capable of being true or false. For example, the sentence "Is Alba tall?" is not true, and it is not false. Note also that a sentence of the form "S knows that p" is grammatical only when "p" is replaced by a declarative sentence:

Grammatical	Not grammatical
Ella knows that Alba is tall.	Ella knows that is Alba tall?
Shanice knows that it is summer.	Shanice knows that if only it were summer.
Raul knows that the door is closed.	Raul knows that close the door.

deductively valid: An argument is deductively valid when it is guaranteed that if the premises are true, the conclusion must also be true.

descriptive cultural relativism: Descriptive cultural relativism maintains that different cultures around the world have different ethical codes, and that in many cases what is considered wrong in one culture is not considered wrong in another culture.

design argument: Proponents of design arguments (or teleological arguments) argue that many parts of the biological world appear to be exceptionally well designed; they argue that God must be the designer.

determinism: According to determinists, given the state of the universe at any one time, the laws of physics fix the whole of the rest of history. So if you could "rewind" history and run it again from exactly the same starting point, history would be exactly repeated.

direct democracy: In a direct democracy, policy questions are settled by public vote. For example, in 2016, there was a referendum about whether the United Kingdom should leave the European Union. See section 17.2 of chapter 17 for a longer discussion of the meaning of the word "democracy."

direct realism: See realism.

direct value vs. indirect value: Something is *indirectly* valuable if it is valuable as a means to something else. For example, a concert ticket is valuable because you can use it to gain access to a concert. Something is *directly* valuable if it is valuable not as a means to something else, but in its own right. It is plausible that pleasure is directly valuable. Philosophers use a number of synonyms for "direct" and "indirect":

Synonyms for "directly valuable"	Synonyms for "indirectly valuable"
intrinsically valuable	extrinsically valuable
noninstrumentally valuable	instrumentally valuable
inherently valuable	
valuable for its own sake	
valuable in its own right	

divine command theory: Divine command theorists make the following two claims:

- When an action is morally wrong, it is morally wrong because it is forbidden by God.
- When an action is morally okay, it is morally okay because it has not been forbidden by God.

Most theists believe that something is morally bad *if and only if* God disapproves of it, since they think that God is omniscient and perfectly morally good. But the divine command theory makes a much stronger claim. It says that things are bad *because* God disapproves; it is God's disapproval that *makes* it wrong. Many theists disagree with this much stronger claim.

dualism: Beware! "Dualism" is a word that is used in many different ways in philosophy. In chapter 4, we use "dualism" as a label for the claim that (a) God is very powerful, but (b) there is another very powerful agent, an evil agent, who is responsible for creating suffering, and (c) God is incapable for the time being of preventing the evil agent from creating suffering. For another meaning of "dualism," see substance dualism.

eliminativists: Eliminativists think that folk psychology is a false theory and that the mental states posited by folk psychology (e.g., beliefs) don't really exist.

emotive meaningfulness: See literal meaningfulness and emotive meaningfulness.

empirical evidence: Empirical evidence is evidence acquired by sense perception—that is, by sight, touch, smell, hearing, or taste.

empiricist: Empiricist philosophers emphasize the importance of empirical evidence (i.e., the evidence of sense experience) and stress the limitations of a priori reasoning. Some empiricists believe that there can be no a priori knowledge at all. More moderate empiricists make an exception for logic and mathematics. Empiricism is usually contrasted with rationalism.

enumerative induction: In an inductive argument, one starts by identifying some pattern in cases that have been studied; then, one suggests on this basis that the pattern will extend to other cases as well. For example, if you buy a few cakes from Tina's Café and they are all stale, you might infer that most or all the cakes that Tina sells are stale.

epistemic cultural relativism: Epistemic cultural relativism in its simplest form asserts that a person is justified in using a method of forming beliefs if but only if the method is generally approved of in his or her culture.

epistemically basic belief: An epistemically basic belief is a belief that is justified, but not because it is has been inferred from some other justified belief.

epistocracy: An epistocracy is a political system designed to put political power in the hands on the knowledgeable. This would include, for example, a system in which only those who pass a certain exam are permitted to vote, or a system in which more educated people are given extra votes.

equivalence relation: An equivalence relation is a relation that is reflexive, symmetric, and transitive. See these terms also. Most philosophers think that personal identity is an equivalence relation.

essence: The term "essence" is used in many different ways in philosophy. In chapter 14, essence means *purpose*. For example, we might describe the essence of a sieve by saying that it is for getting lumps out of flour.

ethics/morality: Ethical, or moral, questions are about how we should live, what we should care about, and what we should be like. (Some philosophers draw subtle distinctions between morality and ethics—we don't distinguish these things.)

evidential reasons and pragmatic reasons: When you have evidence that a belief is true, that's an *evidential reason* for the belief. When you have evidence that a belief is likely to be beneficial, that's a *pragmatic reason* for the belief.

evil demon: In the first chapter of his *Meditations on First Philosophy*, Descartes imagined that he is psychologically manipulated by an evil demon. Descartes's evil demon has become a stock character in modern Western philosophy.

expressing or evincing a feeling or emotion vs. asserting that one has a feeling or emotion: This distinction is best explained by example. If you accidentally hit your thumb with a hammer, you might shout "Ouch!" (or perhaps something more colorful and unprintable). If you did that, you would be expressing or evincing your pain. You might also say, "My thumb really hurts!" If you did that, you would be asserting that you are in pain. Note that when a person asserts having a feeling or emotion, what the person says is typically either true or false. But when a person expresses or evinces a feeling or emotion, what the person does is neither true nor false.

expressivism: Expressivists maintain that moral claims are expressions of emotion, or commands. For example, the expressivist might say that "stealing is wrong" expresses disapproval of stealing, or is equivalent to the command *Don't Steal!*

externalist and internalist: An internalist believes that whether or not a person's belief is justified depends only on how that belief is related to the person's other mental states. An externalist denies this. Reliabilism is an example of an externalist position.

fallibilism: Fallibilists think that a belief can be justified even when the belief is justified in a way that does not *guarantee* the truth of the belief. For example, our memories are not 100 percent reliable. Nevertheless, the fallibilist may insist, a belief may be justified on the basis of memory.

first cause argument: Proponents of the first cause argument claim that God is the "first cause" or "unmoved mover"—that he initiated all the causal processes in the universe.

folk psychology: Here are some banal, everyday claims about our psychology:

- A toothache is a kind of pain.
- Disgust often causes retching.
- Prolonged exposure of the skin to very cold or very hot objects causes pain.
- Sufficient eating causes the cessation of hunger.

All banal psychological claims of this kind, together, constitute "folk psychology." Folk psychology is often contrasted with scientific psychology.

foundationalism: Foundationalists think that, to be justified, a belief must either be epistemically basic or be inferred (using good inferences) from epistemically basic beliefs.

functionalism: Functionalists believe that a mental state can be entirely characterized by describing (a) its characteristic causes, (b) what effects it has on other mental states, and (c) what behaviors it can produce on its own or when combined with other mental states. For example, perhaps we can characterize pain by collecting observations such as these:

- Pain is caused by bodily damage (e.g., burns on the skin).
- When someone is pain, they typically desire that the pain stops.
- Pain often causes people to scream or yell.

Functionalists come in at least two varieties: analytic functionalists and psychofunctionalists.

happiness: "Happiness" is a contested term in philosophy. Some people use the term "happiness" as a synonym for "pleasure." Other people use the term as a near synonym of "well-being" or "welfare."

hedonists: Hedonists think that pleasure is always directly good, and that pleasure is the *only* direct good; they think that pain is directly bad, and that pain is the *only* direct bad. Finally, hedonists think that other things are good or bad indirectly only insofar as they bring about pleasure and/or pain. For the hedonist, something that brings about a good deal of pleasure but little or no pain is very good; something that brings about a good deal of pain but little or no pleasure is very bad; something that brings about pain and pleasure in equal amounts is neither good nor bad.

hereditary monarchy: In a hereditary monarchy, when one monarch dies or otherwise leaves office, the crown passes to another member of the same family—perhaps the oldest son.

human being, humanity: In chapter 15, we use the terms "humanity" and "human being" in a rather unusual way. Humanity is our capacity to choose our own goals and to take rational steps in pursuit of those goals. For example, one might choose as a goal running a marathon is less than four hours, and then pursue that goal by training twice weekly. A human being is a creature that has this capacity.

humanity formula: The humanity formula is one of the most influential components of Kant's grand system of ethics. Part of what the humanity formula says is that one must respect the right of other human beings to make their own decisions.

idea: An idea (as the term was used by Locke, and by us in chapter 6) is an object that exists in a mind. For example, mental images are ideas. Sensations (e.g., sensations of pain) are also ideas.

ideal conditions: The qualified attitude theory explains the meaning of "morally good" and "morally bad" in terms of the attitudes people would have under ideal conditions. Under ideal conditions, a person

- is fully informed about the relevant facts;
- has thought through the issue carefully;
- is psychologically normal, not drunk, not under the influence of psychoactive drugs, and not suffering from a psychological disorder that affects moral feelings or reasoning; and
- is not biased by self-interest.

idealism: Idealists deny that material objects exist. Typically, they endorse some variant of Berkeley's slogan "to be is to be perceived." Berkeley was an idealist.

incompatibilists: Incompatibilists think that if determinism is true, it follows that we do not have free will.

indirect realism: See realism.

indirect value: See direct value vs. indirect value.

inductive argument: The term "inductive argument" is annoyingly ambiguous in philosophy. Some philosophers use the term "induction" to cover enumerative induction only. Some philosophers use the term "induction" more broadly, so that it covers *all* nondeductive arguments.

inference to the best explanation: See abduction.

instrumental argument vs. noninstrumental argument for democracy: To give an *instrumental* argument for democracy is to argue that a democratic system will produce comparatively good laws and policies. To give a *noninstrumental* argument for democracy is to argue that undemocratic systems are unjust *in themselves,* independently of the laws and policies they produce. For more discussion, see section 17.5 of chapter 17.

intentional: An intentional state is a mental state that is "about" something—something which may or may not be real. Here are some examples:

- Thinking about New York City
- Admiring the president
- Wanting a pet unicorn

internalist: See externalist and internalist.

introspection: The process of "looking inward" to investigate one's own mental state. For example, if you are asked "How are you feeling today?" you might introspect to find out that you are feeling happy but slightly stressed.

Kantianism: Immanuel Kant (1724–1804) devised a vast ethical system. In this book, we look at only two components of the system: the universalization test and the humanity formula.

libertarianism: Libertarians think that *if* determinism is true, we lack free will. But they also think that we have free will. So they conclude that determinism is false.

literal meaningfulness and emotive meaningfulness: A declarative sentence is literally meaningful if it succeeds in expressing a proposition that is either true or false. (Sometimes the term "cognitively meaningful" is used instead of "literally meaningful.") A declarative sentence that is not literally meaningful might nevertheless evoke some emotional or imaginative response in a reader. Think, for example, of sentences in nonsense poetry. Such sentences have emotive meaning, but not literal meaning.

material object: A material object is an object that is not a mind and which exists outside of any mind. It is plausible that trees, apples, mountains, moons, and ice cubes are material objects—though Berkeley would have denied this.

materialism: Materialism was Berkeley's name for the claim that material objects do exist.

meaningfulness: We won't attempt a succinct characterization of meaningfulness in the glossary. See sections 14.1 and 14.3 of chapter 14.

metaethical cultural relativism: According to metaethical ethical relativism, claims about the ethical rightness or wrongness of an action are actually claims about whether that action is condoned or condemned by the ethical code of a culture. There are two versions of metaethical relativism: agent relativism and speaker relativism. They differ on which culture's ethical code is relevant, the code of the speaker's culture or the code of the "agent"—that is, the person whose action is being assessed.

mind-brain identity theory: Mind-brain identity theorists claim that mental states are brain states. For example, a mind-brain identity theorist might say that *pain* is a certain pattern of neural activity in the brain. The mind-brain identity theory is often just called "identity theory" for short.

moral evil vs. natural evil: When a bad state of affairs arises because of human wrongdoing, it is moral evil. Other bad states of affairs are natural evils.

moral skepticism: Moral skeptics claim that we have no way of knowing whether moral claims are true or false.

morally worthy: Kant noted that when we morally evaluate a person's actions, we're often interested not only in *what* they did, but also in *why* they did it—that is, we're interested in their motivation. In Kant's terminology, an action that is performed with praiseworthy motives is a "morally worthy" action.

naïve realism: This is another name for direct realism. See realism.

naïve representationalism: This is our name for the claim that (setting aside the odd case of illusion) material objects closely resemble our ideas of them. This is not a standard term in philosophy.

natural evil: See moral evil vs. natural evil.

natural kind: A category of things that share attributes because they share underlying mechanisms, processes, and properties. Biological species and chemical elements and compounds are widely viewed as being natural kinds.

naturalistic property: A naturalistic property is a feature of an object, action, or situation that can be described in the language of physics, chemistry, biology, or psychology. Some naturalistic properties that a person might have include:

- Having mass of 80kg
- Being angry
- Having a blood pressure of 120/70

Many philosophers believe that two things that differ morally must also differ in some naturalistic respect.

necessary and sufficient condition: A is a necessary and sufficient condition for B if and only if A is a necessary condition for B and A is a sufficient condition for B. Being a number that is only divisible by itself and by 1 is a necessary and sufficient condition for being a prime number, for example.

necessary being: See contingent beings and necessary beings.

necessary condition: A is a necessary condition for B if and only if everything that is B must also be A. For example, being male is a necessary condition for being an uncle.

necessary truth: Compare these two statements:

- The Philadelphia Eagles won the 2017 Super Bowl.
- Either some team won the 2017 Super Bowl, or no team did.

Both of these statements are true, but only the second is a *necessary* truth. The Philadelphia Eagles *did in fact* win the 2017 Super Bowl, but they could have lost—the New England Patriots could have beaten them. By contrast, it is *impossible* for the second statement to be false.

no-branching constraint: The no-branching constraint is a condition that some philosophers impose on theories of personal identity. The constraint specifies that, at any given time, there can only be one person who is numerically identical to a person at an earlier time. If at a later time there are two people who, according to the theory, are numerically identical with a person at an earlier time, then *neither* of these are the same person as the person at the earlier time.

nonmaterial: In this book, we use the term "nonmaterial" for things that are not made of matter.

nonphysical: In this book, we use the term "nonphysical" for things that cannot be detected or studied by physics or any of the other natural sciences.

numerical identity and qualitative identity: Objects A and B are qualitatively identical if and only if they are very similar to each other. Two cell phones with the same model number are usually qualitatively identical. When a retailer says that all the cell phones in a display are identical, this mean means that they are qualitatively identical. If you buy a cell phone and use it for several years, it will typically not be qualitatively identical to the cell phone you bought, since you will have added apps, scratched the surface and made other sorts of changes.

Objects A and B are numerically identical if and only if they are the very same thing, even if they have significantly different properties. If you have broken the screen on your cell phone, it is not qualitatively identical to the phone you bought. But it is numerically identical.

The job for a philosophical theory of personal identity is to explain what is required for a person at one time and a person at another time to be numerically identical.

objective: Beware! The term "objective" is used in many ways in philosophy. In chapter 13, we define "objective" as follows: A claim is objective if and only if (i) it is either true or false and (ii) the truth or falsity of the claim does not depend on who makes the claim, where the claim is made, or when the claim is made.

omnipotent: Many theists believe that God is all-powerful. To use the philosophical jargon, the claim is that God is "omnipotent." Often, this is understood to mean that God is capable of doing *anything*. However, see section 4.1 of chapter 4 for discussion of this point.

omniscient: Many theists believe that God is "omniscient"—that is, that he knows everything.

one drop of blood rule: A rule for classifying people as Negro that specified if a person had one Negro ancestor, that person would be classified as Negro. Also known as the "hypodescent rule."

ontological argument: In chapter 3, we discuss Anselm's argument for the existence of God. Anselm's argument and other arguments similar to it are called "ontological arguments."

ontology: The study of which things exist. For example, "Do souls exist?" is an ontological question.

optimific: The word "optimific" means *producing the best consequences overall.*

pain and pleasure: Roughly, pleasures are positive sensations. This includes:

- The taste of chocolate
- The thrill a skier feels when going down a mountainside
- The satisfaction one takes in finishing a crossword
- The awe a mountaineer feels when admiring the view from the summit

Pains are negative sensations. This includes:

- The heartache of the person whose love is unrequited
- The feeling of humiliation a bullied child experiences when he's mocked in public
- The sensation of being too cold when you are not properly dressed for the snow

panpsychism: Panpsychists claim that some form of consciousness is present in all matter—even in trees, even in pebbles.

person stage: A person stage is a short temporal segment of the life of a person. We arbitrarily assumed that a person stage is a ten-second segment. Thus, you pass through 360 person stages every hour. Theories of personal identity try to specify the conditions under which two person stages are stages of the same person.

phenomenalists: The phenomenalists were a group of philosophers in the mid- to late-nineteenth century and the first half of the twentieth century. Their views were Berkeleyan. Some of them, however, weakened Berkeley's doctrine from "to be is to be perceived" to "to be is to be perceivable."

philosophical behaviorism: Philosophical behaviorists make the following two claims:

1. The meaning of a sentence attributing mental states to an individual can be analyzed into a set of sentences about how the individual would behave under a variety of circumstances.
2. Mental states and processes are behavioral dispositions.

philosophical zombies: Philosophical zombies are exactly like ordinary people in every physical, biological, and behavioral respect. They move and talk and interact just like ordinary people. What makes them philosophical zombies is that, unlike ordinary people, they have no conscious experiences. We usually drop the "philosophical" and just call them "zombies."

physicalism: Physicalism is the view that physics can ultimately explain everything that occurs in the universe, and that if two objects are physically identical, then they are identical in every respect.

potentially infinite process: A potentially infinite process is a process which could in principle be continued indefinitely. For example, the process of counting (1, 2, 3, 4, . . .) is potentially infinite. Some philosophers have claimed that it is impossible for an infinite sequence of events ever to be completed.

pragmatic reasons: See evidential reasons and pragmatic reasons.

premises: When you make an argument, typically you have to take certain things for granted. These are your premises.

primary qualities and secondary qualities: Locke distinguished two sorts of quality: primary qualities and secondary qualities. Here are some examples:

Primary Qualities	Secondary Qualities
Shapes (round, square, etc.)	Colors
Solidity	Tastes
Motion and rest	Heat

According to Locke, in the case of primary qualities, one's idea of the quality resembles the quality itself, but in the case of secondary qualities, one's idea of the quality does not resemble the quality itself.

principle of sufficient reason: There are different versions of the principle of sufficient reason. The simplest version is this: "Every 'Why?' question has an answer."

principle of the uniformity of nature: The claim that objects observed in the future will typically conform to patterns observed in the past.

projects of worth: Susan Wolf says that, to lead a meaningful life, one must be "actively engaged" in "projects of worth." She gives the following as examples of projects of worth: scientific research, political activism, building relationships with friends and family members, and creating and appreciating works of art. She gives the following as examples of activities that are not projects of worth collecting rubber bands, riding rollercoasters, and meeting movie stars.

pro-life/pro-choice: In our terminology, the "extreme pro-life position" is that abortion is always morally wrong, and the "extreme pro-choice position" is that abortion is never morally wrong. In calling these positions "extreme," we do not wish to imply that they are in error. There are many intermediate views, according to which abortion is sometimes but not always morally wrong.

proof by contradiction: This is another term for arguments by *reductio ad absurdum*.

proposition: A proposition is the *meaning* of a declarative sentence. Arguably, these three different sentences express the same proposition:

"Cats are mammals."
"Chats sont des mammifères."
"Los gatos son mamíferos."

Some propositions are true; some are false. Many philosophers think that when a person knows something, the thing that is known is always a true proposition.

psychofunctionalism: See functionalism.

qualified attitude theory: According to the qualified attitude theory:

- When a person says that an action is morally wrong, this means that the person would disapprove of it, given ideal conditions.
- When a person says that something is morally okay, this means that the person would not disapprove of it, given ideal conditions.

qualitative identity: See numerical identity and qualitative identity.

quality: A quality is an observable characteristic of an object. For example, redness, squareness, sourness, and moistness are qualities. This is a slight simplification of Locke's own definition: Locke said that a quality is "the power to produce an idea in our mind."

racial essence: Prior to the emergence of modern genetics, racialism maintained that racial essences were underlying natural properties of people that are inherited from their parents and that are causally responsible for the unique physical, moral, intellectual, and cultural characteristics that members a race were thought to have.

racialism: The theory that human beings can be divided into a small number of groups, called "races," in such a way that the members of these groups share a number of fundamental, heritable, physical, moral, intellectual, and cultural characteristics with one another that they do not share with members of any other race.

racism: There's some controversy about what racism is, but roughly, we might say it is the belief that some races are inferior to others, or we might say that racism is a system of oppression, in which some racial groups are subordinated to others.

radical libertarianism: Radical libertarians think that our actions are not governed by physical law. (This is not a standard term.)

rationalist: Rationalist philosophers emphasize the value of a priori methods of reasoning, and they stress the limitations of empirical methods. Rationalism is usually contrasted with empiricism.

rationally uninformed: In a typical election, each voter has only a *tiny* chance of affecting the outcome. Thus, individual voters have very little incentive to inform themselves about the issues. Economists say that voters are "rationally uninformed."

real memories and apparent memories: A real memory is a mental state representing an experience that the person having the memory actually experienced. An apparent memory is a mental state representing an experience that the person having the memory did not experience, though it seems to the person that it did. People cannot distinguish real memories from apparent memories by introspection.

realism: The term "realism" is highly ambiguous in philosophy. In the sense that is important in this book, a realist believes that material objects exist. Realists come in two varieties: direct realists and indirect realists. The indirect realists (e.g., Locke) believe that we can't perceive material objects; we can only perceive mental representations of material objects. The direct realists believe that we can perceive material objects.

***reductio ad absurdum*:** In a proof by *reductio ad absurdum* (*reductio* for short), one shows that a claim is false by deducing a contradiction from it. Sometimes *reductio* arguments are called "proofs by contradiction."

reflexive relation: A relation is reflexive if and only if everything stands in that relation to itself. *Having the same birthday* is a reflexive relation; everyone stands in the relation to herself.

reliabilism: According to reliabilists, a belief is epistemically justified just in case it was produced by a reliable process—that is, a process that produces true beliefs most of the time.

representative democracy: In a representative democracy, the country's leaders (the president, members of parliament, senators, or whatever) are elected by a public vote. See section 17.2 of chapter 17 for a longer discussion of the meaning of the word "democracy."

rule consequentialism: Rule consequentialists believe that one ought to obey the optimific moral code under all circumstances. The optimific moral code is a system of rules that—if generally accepted and followed—would produce the best consequences.

rule utilitarianism: Rule utilitarians accept both hedonism and rule consequentialism.

s-memory: In this book, we use the term "s-memory" as a label for an experience that is either a real memory or an apparent memory.

scientific libertarianism: Scientific libertarians think that we can have free will because our neural processes are not deterministic. There is some kind of randomness in our brain processes, and in consequence, we have free will. (This is not a standard term.)

seat of consciousness: The seat of consciousness is the part of a person that has conscious experiences. Descartes and soul theorists think that the seat of consciousness is a nonmaterial, nonphysical thing—the soul or the Cartesian mind. Many contemporary philosophers and scientists think that the seat of consciousness is the brain.

secondary qualities: See primary qualities and secondary qualities.

simple subjectivism: According to simple subjectivism:

- When someone says that an action is morally wrong, what this means is that the person disapproves of it personally.
- When someone says that an action is morally okay, what this means is that the person does not disapprove of it personally.

Singer's principle: Singer's principle is an important premise in Singer's argument, discussed in chapter 16. It is this: "If it is in a person's power to prevent something very bad from happening without sacrificing anything nearly as important, it is wrong for that person not to do so."

skeptical theism: Skeptical theists believe that God has reasons for permitting suffering, reasons that we cannot understand.

skepticism: In ordinary English, a skeptic is someone who doubts. When philosophers talk about skepticism, they usually have in mind extreme forms of doubt. The philosophical skeptic might doubt that their body exists, or that other people are conscious, or that the universe has existed for more than five minutes.

socially constructed group: A group whose members do not constitute a natural kind. The members of a socially constructed group are included in the group only because they have a cluster of properties that some people found of interest.

sortition: Sortition is the choosing of political officials *at random*.

soul: Soul theorists maintain that the soul is a nonphysical, nonmaterial part of a person that is the seat of consciousness and the part of a person that engages in thought. Soul theorists believe that a person at time t_1 and a person at time t_2 are numerically identical if and only if they have the same soul.

speaker relativism: Speaker relativism is a version of metaethical cultural relativism. According to speaker relativism:

- When it is said that a person's action is morally wrong, what's meant is that the action is condemned by the ethical code of *the speaker's* culture.
- When it is said that a person's action is morally okay, what's meant is that the action is not condemned by the ethical code of *the speaker's* culture.

If speaker relativism is correct, then most moral claims are not objective, since they are claims about the moral code of the person making the claim. If two speakers, S_1 and S_2, both say that P's action is wrong, and if S_1 and S_2 come from different cultures with different ethical codes, then it is possible for S_1's statement to be true and S_2's statement to be false.

special obligations: Special obligations are obligations that we have only to those who are "close" to us in some important way. For example, many people believe that parents have a special duty to care for their own children—and that they don't have a similar duty to care for the children of others. It has been argued that we have special obligations to family members, friends, colleagues, and compatriots.

strong social constructionism: The view that a group should not be counted as a race unless it is culturally, economically or politically distinct from other groups. Strong social constructionism entails that if the political, economic, and cultural differences between groups that we now call races were to disappear, races would disappear.

substance: The term "substance" has a complicated history and is used differently by different philosophers. For the purposes of this book, all you need to know is that if a dualist claims that the mind and the body are distinct "substances," this means that a human being is not an entirely physical system. On the contrary, the dualist thinks that a human being has two parts: a physical part (the body) and a mental part (the mind).

substance dualism: Substance dualists believe that each human being is composed of two fundamentally different parts: a mind and a body. These two parts may interact, but they are fundamentally different. Cartesian dualism is the version of substance dualism espoused by the French philosopher René Descartes.

sufficient condition: A is a sufficient condition for B if and only if everything that is A must also be B. For example, being an uncle is a sufficient condition for being male.

symmetric relation: A relation is symmetric if and only if for any objects a and b, if a stands in the relation to b, then b stands in the relation to a. *Being married to* is a symmetric relation; if a is married to b, then b is married to a.

teleological argument: See design argument.

theism: Theism is the claim that God exists. Theists are people who believe that God exists. We assume that if God exists at all, the following things are true of him:

1. God created the universe.
2. God is omnipotent.
3. God is perfectly good.
4. God is omniscient.
5. God deserves our unqualified love and complete obedience.

theodicy: To give a theodicy is to explain why an omnipotent, omniscient, and perfectly good God might permit suffering. (Note that the term "theodicy" is used in several different ways by different philosophers.)

thinking: In chapter 5, we use "thinking" to refer to all kinds of conscious mental activity—including such things as wanting to eat a muffin, wondering whether it is snowing, and feeling cold.

transitive relation: A relation is transitive if and only if for any objects a, b, and c, if a stands in the relation to b and b stands in the relation to c, then a stands in the relation to c. *Being taller than* is a transitive relation; if a is taller than b and b is taller than c, then a is taller than c.

tyranny of the majority: Some have argued that a weakness of democratic systems is that they sometimes allow a majority of voters to use their voting power to inflict injustices on members of minority groups. This is called the "tyranny of the majority." To prevent this, some democratic countries have in place mechanisms that are designed to limit democratic forces in order to protect individual rights.

universalization test: The universalization test is one of the most influential components of Kant's grand system of ethics. The test is motivated by the idea that a person's action is morally worthy only if the person follows universal moral rules—that is, rules that apply to everybody.

utility: We can measure pleasures and pains numerically. For example, eating an ice cream might have a score of +5, while a headache might have a score of –10, and a really bad headache might have a score of –20. These numbers are called "utilities."

verificationism: Verificationists think that all literally meaningful declarative sentences fall into one of three categories:

- Sentences that are true in virtue of the meanings of the words they contain (e.g., "All vixens are foxes").
- Sentences that are false in virtue of the meanings of the words they contain (e.g., "Veronica is a vixen but not a fox").
- Sentences that can be verified or falsified empirically (e.g., "It will rain sometime today in Times Square").

Verificationists sometimes claim that an obscure philosophical claim is not literally meaningful because it doesn't fall into one of these three categories. For example, the philosopher A. J. Ayer argued in this way that Heidegger's claim that "The Nothing itself nothings" is not literally meaningful.

wisdom of crowds: In some cases, a group of people can be wiser or more knowledgeable than the individual members of the group. This phenomenon is sometimes called the "wisdom of crowds." Philosophical discussions of this phenomenon often emphasize a mathematical result known as "Condorcet's Jury Theorem."

CREDITS

Page xxs: GL Archive/Alamy Stock Photo
Page 14: Mohamed Osama/Alamy Stock Photo
Page 34: Science History Images/Alamy Stock Photo
Page 42: Boscorelli/Alamy Stock Photo
Page 45: Ian Dagnall/Alamy Stock Photo
Page 66: Pictorial Press Ltd/Alamy Stock Photo; Lebrecht Music and Arts Photo Library/Alamy
Page 82: Georgios Kollidas/Alamy Stock Photo
Page 111: 19th era/Alamy Stock Photo
Page 132: duncan1890/iStock.com; History collection 2016/Alamy Stock Photo
Page 177: GeorgiosArt/iStock.com
Page 207: INTERFOTO/Alamy Stock Photo
Page 249: GL Archive/Alamy Stock Photo
Pages 250, 251, 254, and 258: © macrovector/Shutterstock.com
Page 278: Library of Congress Prints and Photographs Division Washington, LC-USZ62-114649
Page 306: Kristin Chavez/UNC-Chapel Hill
Page 321: Granger Historical Picture Archive/Alamy Stock Photo
Page 345: David Shakbone; Alletta Vaandering

INDEX

Figures and tables are indicated by "f" and "t" following page numbers. Illustrations are indicated by italicized page numbers.

abduction, 17, 29, 43, 45, 138–40
abolition of slavery, 321
abortion, 269, 353–59, 363
abstract reasoning, 102
act consequentialism, 319–20, 334
actions, morally worthy, 329–31, 336
active engagement, 305–8, 310
act utilitarianism, 320–25
   Bentham and, 320–21, *321*
   cost-benefit analysis and, 320, 324
   definition of, 335
   hedonism and, 320, 339n4
   individual rights and, 322–24
   objections to, 322–25
   obligations and, 322–23, 336
   pain and, 320–22, 324, 334
   pleasure and, 320–23, 334
   rule utilitarianism vs., 327
   suffering and, 322, 324, 325
adultery, 341
Against Malaria Foundation, 342, 343
agent relativism, 277–79, 286
aggregate good, 317–19, 335
aggregate utility, 320, 323–25, 327, 335

agnosticism, 4
aid agencies, 342–46, 362
air, Boyle's experiments with, 126
alienation, 305
Amazon, 388
American Veterinary Medical Association, 348
analytical skills, development of, 28
analytic functionalism, 219–20, 223, 224
anguish, 302, 310
animalism, 260, 262
animal liberation movement, 322
animals
   artificial selection and, 46
   design argument and, 41–42
   mental states of, 208
   pain of, 1, 5, 236n6, 349–52
   suffering of, 322, 347–49, 351, 352
   vision of, 105–6, *106f*
Anscombe, Elizabeth, 324
Anselm of Canterbury, 48–53, 57, 91
Anton-Babinski syndrome, 98
apparent memories, 250–52, 263
appeals to authority, 4–5, 9

Appiah, Kwame Anthony, 183–85, 187, 193, 343, *345*, 345–47, 359
applied science, 133–34
a priori/a posteriori, 86, 95, 101–2, 118, 123n2
Aquinas, Thomas, 34, 61n2, 64–65, 71
arguments, 9–24
   abductive, 17, 29, 43, 45, 138–40
   conceivability, 204, 215
   conclusions of, 10–16, 18–19, 22
   cosmological, 38–40, *40f*, 56, 59, 137–38
   criticism of, 20
   deductively valid, 14–16, 29
   definition of, 9, 29
   for democracy, 373–80, 382
   design, 41–48, *42f*, 56, 61n6
   evaluation of, 13, 14, 20–24, 28, 388
   extraneous comments in, 11
   fine-tuning, 60
   first cause, 33–38, *34*, *35–37f*, 56, 61n2
   inductive, 16–17, 29

425

arguments (*continued*)
inferences in, 17, 21–23
multistep, 18–23
objections to, 390
ontological, 48–53, 57, 59, 91, 93
from pain, 347, 350–52, 362
parodies of, 52–53
from perspectival variation, 104, 116–17
persuasive, 15, 16, 139
in philosophy papers, 389–90
premises of, 10–15, 18–22
presentation of, 10
pro-choice, 356–60
pro-life, 353–56, 360
reductio, 49, 51–52, 57
Aristotle, *14*, 38, 150, 151
Arnauld, Antoine, 98
Artane, 85
artificial selection, 46
The Assayer (Galileo), 121
astronomy, 81–83, 107, 132–33
atheism
agnosticism vs., 4
arguments for, 63, 67–68
definition of, 33, 56, 76
on history of the universe, 33–34, 38–39
problem of evil and, 63, 67–68
Sartre and, 300
atomists, 37, 38
Augustine of Hippo, 69
Australia, dissatisfaction with democracy in, 368*f*
authority, appeals to, 4–5, 9
Ayer, A. J., 230, 236n8, 281–82

Back to the Future: Part II (film), 126
Bacon, Francis, 130–31, 143n3
bad faith, 302–4, 310
Bair, Sheila, 396, *396*
bees, vision of, 105, 106*f*
behavior
control of, 173
mental states and, 211, 220
patterns of, 236n7
predictions of, 166–67

behavioral dispositions, 211, 214, 227–28
behaviorism, 209–15, 219–20, 229, 236n7
Being and Nothingness (Sartre), 302
beings, necessary vs. contingent, 40, 56
beliefs
certainty of, 92
chain of, 150–51
clear and distinct perception and, 89–92
coherentism and, 152–54
deduction and, 155
delusions and, 153, 162
epistemically basic, 136–38, 140, 151, 160, 162
evidential reasons for, 31–32, 56
experience and, 154, 157
fallibilism and, 158
foundationalism and, 149–52
induction and, 155, 163
inferences and, 155
justification of, 31–32, 54, 148–59, 163
mathematical, 157
mental states and, 157, 220, 221, 223
perception and, 151, 155, 157
personal identity and, 245–47
pragmatic reasons for, 31–32, 56
predictions and, 163
propositional knowledge and, 147, 148
race and, 187–88
religious, 31, 54, 55
skepticism and, 157
superstition and, 147–48
truth and, 154–59
Benedict, Ruth, 276–79, *278*
Bengal famine (1943), 374
Bennett, Jonathan, 99–100nn 2–3, 235n1
Bentham, Jeremy, 312, 320–21, *321*

Berkeley, George, 102, 109, *111*, 111–17, 121, 235n4
Bible, 2, 3, 65
Big Bang theory, 38, 39
biology, design argument and, 41–48
birds, vision of, 106
birth control, 356–57
black holes, perception and, 116
blind spots, 48, 62n9
The Blind Watchmaker (Dawkins), 61n8
Block, Ned, 224–25
BMA (British Medical Association), 326
body. *See* mind-body problem
Boo! Hurrah! theory, 281–82, 286
boredom, 305
Boswell, James, 121
Boyle, Robert, 126
brain. *See also* mind
computers connected by, 153–54
consciousness and, 245, 355
mind-brain identity theory, 215–19, 221, 229
neurons in, 224–25, 245
personal identity and, 259–61
brain continuity, 261
brain-in-the-vat thought experiment, 153–54, 162
Breyer, Stephen, 398, *398*
British Medical Association (BMA), 326
The Brothers Karamazov (Dostoevsky), 290
Butler, Joseph, 250, 255
Butterfield, Stewart, 396, *396*

Calvin, John, 275
Canada, dissatisfaction with democracy in, 368*f*
Candide (Voltaire), 66, 75–76
capital punishment, 269
careers for philosophy majors, 395–97
Carroll, Lewis, 236n8

Cartesian, defined, 95, 100n6
Cartesian circle, 93, 93f, 96, 98
Cartesian dualism, 204–9
Cartesian mind, 243, 245, 262
causal chains, 35–37f, 35–38
causation, 13, 220–21, 221f
certainty
  achieving, 87–89
  of beliefs, 92
  Descartes on, 81, 83–89, 95
  difficulty finding, 83–87
  in mathematics, 86
  perception and, 85–87, 89–90
  senses and, 84–85
chain of beliefs, 150–51
Chalmers, David, 204, 226
chance events, 166, 167, 174–76
charities, 305, 342–46
chauvinism, 219, 221, 222, 224
China
  famine in (1959–1961), 386n12
  flooding in (1931), 68, 75
Christianity. *See also* God
  Bible and, 2, 3, 65
  dualism and, 71
  on meat-eating, 2
  principles of, 3
  theism and, 33, 44
Churchland, Paul, 223
circular reasoning, 136, 150–51
citations, 392
clear and distinct perception, 89–93, 96, 235n1
Clifford, W. K., 54–55
codes of ethics, 276–77, 279–80
coercion, 332
cogito, ergo sum (I think, therefore I exist), 87, 157
coherentism, 152–54, 159
Colbert, Stephen, 398, *398*
cold, as property of ideas, 113
color
  Berkeley on, 112–13
  inverted color spectrum, 208–9, 212, 216
  lighting and, 112
  Locke on, 107–8
  mind and, 112–13
  of objects, 107–8
  perception of, 106, 108, 112, 117, 155
  of sky, 108, 124n10
  of water, 124n10
compassion, 331
compatibilism, 23, 29, 170–74, 178
compulsions, 172
computers. *See also* robots
  blind spot on screen, 62n9
  brains connected to, 153–54
  consciousness and, 5
  mathematics and, 207
  reductio arguments and, 49
  simulations, 87
conceivability argument, 204, 215
conclusions
  of arguments, 10–16, 18–19, 22
  definition of, 29
  giveaway words and phrases as markers of, 11
  to philosophy papers, 390
confidentiality. *See* privacy issues
conscientious omnivores, 351, 352, 360
consciousness. *See also* unconsciousness
  brain and, 245, 355
  computers and, 5
  definition of, 228
  experiences and, 204, 205, 208, 227, 243
  of matter, 227
  naturalistic properties and, 356
  pain and, 355
  seat of, 243, 245, 263
consequentialism
  act, 319–20, 334
  as basic belief, 138
  definition of, 335
  Kantianism compared to, 333–34
  rule, 326–27, 336
contingent beings, 40, 56
contraceptives, 356–57
contradictions, 49, 51–53, 64, 65, 226
control, 168, 169, 172–73, 175–76 *See also* free will
Copernicus, Nicolaus, 82
Copleston, Frederick, 4, 7n3, 60

correlation and causation, 13
corruption, 3, 324, 375, 376
cosmological argument, 38–40, 40f, 56, 59, 137–38
cosmology, defined, 56, 61n3
Cosmopolitanism (Appiah), 345, 365n10
cost-benefit analysis, 317–20, 324, 335
Craig, William Lane, 290–91
critical attitude, 133
critical reasoning, 397
criticism of arguments, 20
cube experiment, 102–4, 103f, 110, 116–17
cultural relativism, 163, 276–80, 286, 288–89

Darwin, Charles, 41, *45*, 46–48, 59
David, Jacques-Louis: *Death of Socrates*, xx
Davidson, Donald, 100n7
Davies, Norman, 348
Davis, Angela, 398, *398*
Dawkins, Richard, 61n8, 65
death, numerical identity and, 242–43
Death of Socrates (David), xx
deception, 84, 87, 92, 105, 126, 302–3
decision-making
  cost-benefit analysis for, 317–19
  in democracy, 369–73, 377–78
  in epistocracy, 379
  free will and, 5, 72, 168, 171, 175–76
  humanity formula and, 333
  physical laws and, 177
  Sartre on, 301–3
  scientific libertarianism and, 175–76
declarative sentences, 146, 159, 164n2, 209, 236n8
deduction and beliefs, 155
deductive validity, 14–16, 29
Del Ray, Lana, 398, *398*
delusions, 153, 162, 302
Demjanjuk, John (Ivan the Terrible), 239–41, 244, 258, 268n1

democracy, 367–82
  argument against, 371–73, 379
  decision-making in, 369–73, 377–78
  defense of, 373–80, 382
  direct, 369, 371, 380
  dissatisfaction with, 367, 368f, 385n1
  instrumental argument for, 379, 380
  justification of, 375, 376, 379
  noninstrumental argument for, 378–80, 382
  representative, 369–72, 380–81
  thought experiment on, 367–69
  voting in, 9–10, 19–22, 368–79, 386n6
democracy index (*The Economist*), 370–71, 376, 382
Democritus, 37
Dennett, Daniel, 212–13
Descartes, René
  Cartesian circle and, 93, 93f, 96, 98
  on certainty, 81, 83–89, 95
  on clear and distinct perception, 89–93, 96, 235n1
  cogito, ergo sum and, 87, 157
  conceivability argument and, 204, 215
  criticisms of, 98
  dualism and, 205–7
  evil demon thought experiment, 86–88, 91–92, 95, 96, 98
  foundationalism and, 151
  on God, 59, 90–93
  legacy of, 93–94
  Meditations on First Philosophy, 81, 83, 93–95, 99n2, 100n10, 204
  on mental states, 88, 89
  mind-body problem and, 204
  ontological argument of, 59, 91, 93, 96
  portrait of, *82*
  rationalism of, 102
  skepticism of, 87
  theism and, 90–93
descriptive cultural relativism, 276–77, 286

design argument, 41–48, 42f, 56, 61n6
desire, 171–73, 220
determinism
  compatibilism and, 171–74
  definition of, 29, 165, 178
  free will and, 23, 167, 169, 172
  hard, 178, 181n2
  incompatibilism and, 169–70, 172, 174
  libertarianism and, 174–77
  neuroscience and, 170
  predictions and, 166–67
  responsibility and, 168–70
  soft, 181n2
d'Holbach, Baron, 170, 181n2
direct democracy, 369, 371, 380
direct realism, 116–17, 118f
direct value, 296–97, 310
disposable income, 343–45
divine command theory, 272–76, 287
divine vs. human goodness, 69–70
dogmatism, 138
Dollfuss, Engelbert, 375
Dostoevsky, Fyodor, 290
Downs, Anthony, 373
dreams, 87, 88, 110
dualism
  Cartesian, 204–9
  challenges to, 206
  definition of, 76, 80n8, 228
  on problem of evil, 71
  substance, 205, 230
Du Bois, W. E. B., 191, 193, 199n10
duplication, 256–57

earthquakes, 67–75
The Economist democracy index, 370–71, 376, 382
Eichmann, Adolf, 258–59
eliminativism, 223–24, 228
Elisabeth of Bohemia, 206, *207*
emotions. *See* feelings
emotive meaningfulness, 229, 236n8
empathy, 72, 331
empirical evidence, 101–2, 119, 133

empiricism, 102, 119
engagement, active, 305–8, 310
entomology, 269
enumerative induction, 16–17, 29, 126, 140, 163
Epicurus, 80n6, 298
epistemically basic beliefs, 136–38, 140, 151, 160, 162
entomology, 269
epistemic cultural relativism, 163
epistemic justification, 148–49, 152–55, 162
epistemology, 145, 155, 159, 160, 203
epistocracy, 369, 378–80
equivalence relation, 240, 253, 256, 262
essence, 300, 302, 311
ethics. *See also* morality
  animal pain and, 236n6
  codes of, 276–77, 279–80
  definition of, 360
  objective truths and, 271–72, 285
  science compared to, 269
  of sexuality, 276–78, 291–92
  use of term, 341
euthanasia, 269
Euthyphro (Plato), 293n3
evaluation of arguments, 13, 14, 20–24, 28, 388
evidence, empirical, 101–2, 119, 133
evidential reasons for beliefs, 31–32, 56
evil
  as absence of goodness, 69
  moral, 76, 80n10
  natural, 73, 76, 80n10
  problem of, 63, 66–73, 75, 78
evil demon thought experiment, 86–88, 91–92, 95, 96, 98
evolutionary theory, 41, *45*, 46–48, 59, 100
existence
  cause of, 143n15
  essence and, 300
  greatness and, 50–52
  of material objects, 110, *111*, 114
  in mind, 50–52

of race, 183, 187
in reality, 50–53
existence of God, 31–60
See also theism
as central principle of Christianity, 3
Copleston-Russell debate on, 4, 60
cosmological argument for, 38–40, 40*f*, 56, 59, 137–38
Descartes on, 59, 90–93
design argument for, 41–48, 42*f*, 56, 61n6
first cause argument for, 33–38, *34*, 35–37*f*, 56, 61n2
multistep argument for, 22–23
ontological argument for, 48–53, 57, 59, 91, 96
Pascal's Wager and, 60
practical vs. evidential arguments for, 32
pragmatic case for, 53–55
problem of evil and, 63, 66–68
super-heavy stone puzzle and, 64
"Existentialism Is a Humanism" (Sartre), 300
experience
beliefs and, 154, 157
consciousness and, 204, 205, 208, 227, 243
mind-brain identity theory and, 217
personal experience of God, 58
expressivism, 281–83, 287
externalism, 154–56, 160
extraneous comments in arguments, 11
extraterrestrials, 218–19, 222, 224
eyes, anatomy of, 41, 42*f*, 48
See also vision

fair share principle, 346–47, 359
fair trial rule, 325
fallibilism, 158, 160
famines, 71, 73, 374–75, 386n7, 386n12
feelings, 9, 281–82, 287, 299, 331
fine-tuning argument, 60
Fiorina, Carly, 396, *396*

first cause argument, 33–38, *34*, 35–37*f*, 56, 61n2
floods, 65, 68, 75
folk psychology, 223, 224, 228
foundationalism, 149–52, 160, 162
Frankfurt, Harry, 173
freedom
of press, 375
restrictions on, 168–69
Sartre on, 300–304, 309
of speech, 370
free will
compatibilism and, 171–74
decision-making and, 5, 72, 168, 171, 175–76
determinism and, 23, 167, 169, 172
Hume on, 171–73
incompatibilism and, 169–70, 172, 174
libertarianism and, 174–77
suffering and, 72–73
wrongdoing and, 73, 78
Freudians, 133
Fry, Stephen, 63
functionalism, 219–26, 228–29

Galileo Galilei, 83, 121, 132
Gaunilo of Marmoutiers, 52–53
Gelman, Andrew, 386n6
generality problem, 156
general knowledge quiz, 376–77, 383–85
Genesis (biblical book), 2, 65
genetic mutations, 47, 48
Gettier, Edmund and Gettier cases, 158–59
GiveWell, 342, 365n5
Glasgow, Joshua, 188–93, 196
God. *See also* existence of God; theism
Bible as source of information on, 3
definition of, 4, 33, 49–51, 59
Descartes on, 59, 90–93
divine command theory, 272–76, 287
goodness of, 7n3, 33, 38, 40, 44, 58, 65, 67–70
ideas and, 116

as intelligent designer, 43
laws of logic and, 1
masculine pronouns and, 61n1
morality and, 65, 273–76, 286
as necessary being, 40
omnipotence of, 33, 38, 40, 44, 49, 58, 64–71, 180, 274
omniscience of, 22–23, 33, 38, 40, 44, 49, 58, 65–70, 180, 276
perception of, 115
perfection of, 59, 66
personal experience of, 58
purpose for human beings, 300
resurrection and, 242–44
rethinking the nature of, 70–71
super-heavy stone puzzle and, 64–65
will of, 75, 78, 275
wrongdoing by, 65
The God Delusion (Dawkins), 61n8, 65
"God Is Able" (King), 53–54
good, aggregate, 317–19, 335
goodness
evil as absence of, 69
of God, 7n3, 33, 38, 40, 44, 58, 65, 67–70
human vs. divine, 69–70
Google and Google Books, 388
gravitation, theory of, 17, 139, 167
Great Chinese Famine (1959–1961), 386n12
greatness and existence, 50–52
Guerrero, Alexander, 383

Haidt, Jonathan, 291–92
hallucinations, 85–88, 91, 92, 94, 97, 110, 116
happiness, 298, 307, 311, 320
See also pleasure
Happiness: Lessons from a New Science (Layard), 298
hard determinism, 178, 181n2
Hardimon, Michael, 188, 189, 192, 193
Harvey, William, 83
Hawking, Stephen, 5
Hayes, Chris, 398, *398*
heat, 107, 113, 124n7

hedonism
  act utilitarianism and, 320, 339n4
  criticisms of, 298–99
  definition of, 295–96, 311, 335
  meaningfulness and, 299, 309
  pain and, 296, 297, 299, 320
  pleasure and, 296–99, 320
  rule utilitarianism and, 327
Heidegger, Martin, 210, 230
height comparisons, 186, 186–87f
Hemings, Sally, 196
hereditary monarchy, 368, 380
Hinduism, 33, 245
Holocaust, 68–71, 75, 153, 162, 259, 291, 375
homosexuality, 321–22
Horowitz, Damon, 397, 397
human beings, defined, 331–32, 335
Human Development Index (United Nations), 376
humanity, defined, 332, 335
humanity formula, 331–33, 335
human thought processes, 166–67
human vs. divine goodness, 69–70
Hume, David
  on design argument, 44–45
  empiricism of, 102
  on free will, 171–73
  induction and, 128–31
  on material objects, 110
  portrait of, 132
  on predictions, 126, 127, 138, 139
  on reasoning, 125, 135
  skepticism of, 45, 130, 131
hypodescent rule. See one drop of blood rule

ideal conditions, 284–85, 287
idealism, 111, 112, 115–19, 118f
ideas
  Berkeley on, 111–16
  definition of, 119
  God and, 116
  Locke on, 105, 114
  mental images, 104–6, 109, 110

identity. See also numerical identity; personal identity
  equivalence relation and, 207, 240, 256, 262
  mind-brain identity theory, 215–19, 221, 229
  qualitative, 240, 262–63
ignorance
  of cause-and-effect patterns, 74
  of God's will, 75, 78
  of voters, 368, 371–73, 376
illusions, 87–88, 92, 105, 167, 183–84, 197
immunizations, 71, 74
imperative sentences, 164n2
impossibility
  of infinity, 34, 36
  of mystery boxes, 77
  of predictions, 129
  of super-heavy stones, 64–65
  of zombies, 225–27
income, disposable, 343–45
incompatibilism, 169–70, 172, 174, 178
indeterministic processes, 61n5
indirect realism, 102–6, 103f, 109–10, 116–17, 118f, 123n4
indirect value, 296–97, 310
individual rights, 174, 322–24
induction
  beliefs and, 155, 163
  enumerative, 16–17, 29, 126, 140, 163
  Hume and, 128–31
  predictions and, 17, 126–28, 138, 139
  reasonableness of, 136
  reliability of, 136
  scientific methodology and, 130–31
inductive arguments, 16–17, 29
inequality, 378–79, 382
inevitability, 6, 174, 261, 276, 279, 302, 313
infanticide, 353, 356, 357, 362
inferences
  in arguments, 17, 21–23
  beliefs and, 155
  reasonable, 135

inference to the best explanation. See abduction
infinity, 33–34, 36, 37
informal logic, 28
instrumental argument for democracy, 379, 380
intentional mental states, 204, 229
internalism, 154, 156, 160
interrogative sentences, 164n2
interventions, humanity formula and, 333
introductions of philosophy papers, 391, 392
introspection, 202, 229
intuition, 214, 260, 286
inverted color spectrum, 208–9, 212, 216
Islam and Muslims, 33, 44
isolation objection, 154

"Jabberwocky" (Carroll), 236n8
James, William, 116, 174
Jefferson, Thomas, 196
Jews. See Judaism and Jews
Jones, Rashida, 398, 398
JSTOR digital library, 388
Judaism and Jews
  Holocaust and, 68–71, 75, 153, 162, 259, 291, 375
  on meat-eating, 2
  Nazi death camps for, 239–40, 244, 258, 268n1
  theism and, 33, 44
justification
  of beliefs, 31–32, 54, 148–59, 163
  of democracy, 375, 376, 379
  epistemic, 148–49, 152–55, 162
  of knowledge, 157, 158
  of predictions, 127, 138
  of privacy rules, 326
  of propositional knowledge, 148
  of suffering, 71–73, 78

Kalām cosmological argument, 59
Kant, Immanuel, and Kantianism
  consequentialism compared to, 333–34
  definition of, 335–36
  humanity formula, 331–33, 335

maxims and, 329–31
radical libertarianism, 176–77, *177*
transcendental self, 176–77
universalization test, 328–31, 336, 338
Kepler, Johannes, 107, 132
Khan, Yasmine, 374
killing, 353–56, 358
King, Martin Luther, Jr., 53–54, 78, 398, *398*
knowledge, 145–59 *See also* omniscience
coherentism and, 152–54
externalism and, 154–56
foundationalism and, 149–52
fourth condition of, 159
general knowledge quiz, 376–77, 383–85
internalism and, 154, 156
justification of, 157, 158
limitations of, 6
of mental states, 88, 89
propositional, 146–48
types of, 145–46, 162

Laplace, Pierre-Simon, 166, 167, 175
Lavoisier, Antoine, 127
laws
of logic, 1
moral, 273–75, 286, 331, 341
physical, 71, 166, 167, 169, 175–77, 205
law school, 396–97
Layard, Richard, 298
laziness, 333
Leibniz, Gottfried Wilhelm, 39–40, *66*, 66–67
Leopold II (Belgium), 68, 75
Leucippus, 37
Lewis, John, 398, *398*
Lewontin, Richard, 185–86
libertarianism, 174–79
The Life of Samuel Johnson (Boswell), 121
lighting conditions, 112, 123n5
Lisbon earthquake (1755), 67–75
"The Lisbon Earthquake" (Voltaire), *66*

literal meaningfulness, 209, 229, 236n8
Locke, John
Berkeley and, 109, 111, 112, 114
cobbler and prince thought experiment, 248
on color, 107–8
empiricism of, 102
foundationalism and, 151
on heat, 107
on ideas, 105
indirect realism and, 104, 110, 117, 123n4
inverted color spectrum thought experiment, 208
memories theory and, 247–49, *249*
on objects, 105–8, 110, 114
on qualities, 108–9, 112, 114, 121, 124n11
science and, 106–7
logic, 1, *14*, 28, 128, 139, 151
luxuries, 343, 345, 346
lying, 333, 334

Mach, Ernst, 116
Machery, Edouard, 186
Mackie, J. L., 73
Malick, Terrence, 398, *398*
malnutrition, 349–50
Malthus, Thomas, 46
Manichaeanism, 71
marijuana use, 341
Martel, Yann, 398, *398*
Marxists, 133
materialism, 111–15, 117, 119
material objects, 105, 107, 109–11, *111*, 114–17, 119
mathematics
abstract reasoning and, 102
a priori methods and, 101, 123n2
beliefs and, 157
certainty in, 86
clear and distinct perception in, 89
computers and, 207
cost-benefit analysis and, 317–19
deductively valid arguments in, 15

in evil demon thought experiment, 86, 87, 91
logic and, 139
reductio arguments in, 49
The Matrix (film), 87, 153
matter, 205–6, 227
maxims, of Kant, 329–31
McGinn, Colin, 236n11
meaningfulness
emotive, 229, 236n8
happiness and, 307
hedonism and, 299, 309
literal, 209, 229, 236n8
Sartre and, 309
Wolf on, 305–9
meat-eating, 1–2, 269, 279–80, 322, 347, 349–51, 362
meat industry practices, 348–51
medical school, 397
Meditations on First Philosophy (Descartes), 81–100, 204
"Memorial" (Pascal), 58
memory
apparent, 250–52, 263
in evil demon thought experiment, 86, 91
fallibility of, 94
personal identity and, 247–59, 251*f*, 254*f*
real, 250–52, 263
s-memory, 252, 253, 255, 263
teletransporter experiment and, 255–57, 258*f*, 261
memory theory of personal identity, 247–59, 251*f*, 254*f*
mental images, 104–6, 109, 110, 116, 123n5
mental objects, 105, 110
mental states
of animals, 208
behavior and, 211, 220
beliefs and, 157, 220, 221, 223
brain and, 215–19
eliminativism and, 223–24
intentional, 204, 229
introspection and, 202
intuition and, 214
knowledge of, 88, 89
matter and, 205
verificationism and, 210–11

metaethical cultural relativism, 277–79, 288
metaphysics, 203, 205, 211, 215, 220
Mill, John Stuart, 116, 127
mind. *See also* ideas
  Cartesian, 243, 245, 262
  color and, 112–13
  existence in, 50–52
  introspection and, 202
  location of, 206
  matter and, 205–6
  metaphysics and, 205
mind-body problem, 203–4, 208, 211, 215, 220
mind-brain identity theory, 215–19, 221, 229
Mlodinow, Leonard, 5
monarchy. *See* hereditary monarchy
monotheism, 44, 70
Moore, G. E., 2, 138
moral claims, 278, 281–82, 284, 286
moral codes, 326–27
moral duties, 331
moral evil, 76, 80n10
morality. *See also* ethics
  of abortion, 353–59, 363
  cultural relativism and, 276–80
  debates regarding, 269
  definition of, 360
  God and, 65, 273–76, 286
  simple subjectivism and, 280–84
  truth and, 285
  use of term, 341
moral judgments, 282–84
moral laws, 273–75, 331, 341
morally worthy actions, 329–31, 336
moral paralysis, 75, 78, 80n12
moral questions, 274, 397
moral responsibility, 168, 175, 176, 257
moral rules, 276, 325–30
moral skepticism, 270, 273, 274, 278, 285, 288
Morning, Ann, 188
Moyo, Dambisa, 342, 365n4
multiracial populations, 196

multistep arguments, 18–23
murder, 353–56, 358
Muslims and Islam, 33, 44
mutations, genetic, 47, 48
mysterianism, 218, 236n11
mystery box puzzle, 77

naïve realism. *See* direct realism
naïve representationalism, 105, 106, 112, 119
natural evil, 73, 76, 80n10
naturalistic properties, 352–56, 358, 360
natural kinds, 190, 194
natural selection, 41, *45*, 46–48, 59
nature, principle of uniformity of, 128–30, 136–37, 139, 140
Nazi death camps, 239–40, 244, 258, 268n1
necessary beings, 40, 56
necessary conditions, 241, 261, 262
necessary truth, 127–29, 140
neuroscience, 170, 215, 217–18, 224
Newton, Isaac, 17, 102, 106, 124n7, 131, 133, 139, 167
New Zealand, dissatisfaction with democracy in, 368*f*, 385n1
nihilism, 300
no-branching constraint, 256–58, 262
noninstrumental argument for democracy, 378–80, 382
nonmaterial, 243, 262
nonphysical, 243, 262
nonsense poetry, 236n8
normative questions, 2, 6
Notre Dame Cathedral, 83–84, 86, 97
Novum Organum (Bacon), 130–31
numerical identity
  death and, 242–43
  definition of, 240, 262–63
  memory theory and, 253, 256–58
  necessary conditions and, 241
  soul theory and, 244–47

objections to arguments, 390
objective, defined, 288
objective truths, 270–73, 285
objects
  Berkeley on, *111*, 111–15
  color of, 107–8
  existence of, 110, *111*, 114
  heat and, 107
  Hume on, 110
  Locke on, 105–8, 110, 114
  material, 105, 107, 109–11, *111*, 114–17, 119
  mental, 105, 110
  qualities of, 108–9
obligations, 322–23, 336, *345*, 346–47
obsessive-compulsive disorder (OCD), 172
omnipotence
  definition of, 56–57, 64, 76
  of God, 33, 38, 40, 44, 49, 58, 64–71, 180, 274
  incompatibility with omniscience, 65
  mystery box puzzle and, 77
  perfection and, 59
omniscience
  definition of, 57, 76
  of God, 22–23, 33, 38, 40, 44, 49, 58, 65–70, 180, 276
  incompatibility with omnipotence, 65
  mystery box puzzle and, 77
  perfection and, 59
one drop of blood rule, 185, 194, 199n4
On the Revolutions of the Heavenly Spheres (Copernicus), 82
ontological arguments
  by Anselm of Canterbury, 48–53, 57, 91
  by Descartes, 59, 91, 93, 96
  for existence of God, 48–53, 57, 59, 91
ontology, defined, 48, 57
The Open Society and Its Enemies (Popper), 375
optimific moral code, 326–27, 336
The Origin of Species (Darwin), 46

Outlaw, Lucius, 183, 187
outlines, 393

pain. *See also* suffering
  act utilitarianism and, 320–22, 324, 334
  anguish, 302, 310
  of animals, 1, 5, 236n6, 349–52
  argument from, 347, 350–52, 362
  causal network and, 220–21, 221*f*
  consciousness and, 355
  definition of, 311
  functionalism and, 219–22
  hedonism and, 296, 297, 299, 320
  Sartre and, 304
  verification of, 210
Paley, William, 43–47, 61n8
panpsychism, 227, 229
Parfit, Derek, 334
parodies, 52–53
parrot principle, 129–30
Pascal, Blaise and Pascal's Wager, 58, 60
Patterns of Culture (Benedict), 276
perception
  beliefs and, 151, 155, 157
  black holes and, 116
  certainty and, 85–87, 89–90
  clear and distinct, 89–93, 96, 235n1
  of color, 106, 108, 112, 117, 155
  empirical evidence and, 101
  fallibility of, 94
  of God, 115
  of heat, 107
perfection of God, 59, 66
personal identity, 241–61
  brain and, 259–61
  importance of, 241–42
  memory theory of, 247–59, 251*f*, 254*f*
  soul theory of, 243–47
person stages, 248–52, 250*f*, 255, 263
perspectival variation, 104, 116–17

persuasive arguments, 15, 16, 139
phenomenalism, 116, 119
Philomena (film), 241
philosophical behaviorism, 209–15, 219–20, 229
philosophical method, 4–5
philosophical questions, 1–3, 5–6, 9
philosophical zombies, 225–27, 230
philosophy
  defined, 1–6
  disagreement in, 387
  evaluation of works, 388
  in everyday life, 1–2, 401
  goals of, 4–6
  reading, 387–89
  reference sources, 388–89
  religion and, 3, 5
  science and, 5–6, 152
  secondary sources, 388
  terminological confusion in, 387–88, 391
  writing papers on, 389–94
philosophy majors, 395–401
  assumptions regarding, 395
  careers for, 395–98
  GRE scores and, 399
  salaries of, 399–401
phosphenes, 109
physicalism, 225–27, 230
physical laws, 71, 166, 167, 169, 175–77, 205
plagiarism, 393
Plantinga, Alvin, 137
Plato, *xx*, 148, 164n3, 293n3, 371
pleasure. *See also* happiness
  act utilitarianism and, 320–23, 334
  definition of, 311
  hedonism and, 296–99, 320
  Sartre and, 304
  from suffering, 298–99
  trivial, 306
pluralism, 6
poetry, 236n8, 312
Popper, Karl, 131–34, *132*, 375
post hoc rationalizations, 292
posttraumatic stress disorder (PTSD), 72

potentially infinite processes, 36, 57
poverty, 342, 343, 346
pragmatic reasons for beliefs, 31–32, 56
predictions
  behavioral, 166–67
  beliefs and, 163
  induction and, 17, 126–28, 138, 139
  justification of, 127, 138
  making, 126–28
  parrot principle and, 129–30
  weather-related, 23, 83
premises
  of arguments, 10–15, 18–22
  definition of, 29
  giveaway words and phrases as markers of, 12
presentation of arguments, 10
press freedoms, 375
primary qualities, 108–9, 112, 114, 119–21
principle of sufficient reason, 39, 40, 57, 61n5
principle of uniformity of nature, 128–30, 136–37, 139, 140
privacy issues, 323–28
probability judgments, 134
problem of evil, 63, 66–73, 75, 78
pro-choice arguments, 356–60
programs, deterministic, 165–66
projects of worth, 306–12
pro-life arguments, 353–56, 360
proofreading, 393–94
proofs by contradiction. See *reductio ad absurdum*
propositional knowledge, 146–48
propositions, defined, 146, 160
psychofunctionalism, 219, 224, 225
psychological behaviorism, 236n7
PTSD (posttraumatic stress disorder), 72
punishment, 241, 257, 259
Putnam, Hilary, 212

qualified attitude theory, 283–85, 288, 294n12
qualitative identity, 240, 262–63

qualities, 108–9, 112–14, 119–21, 124n11
quantum revolution, 167
questions
  moral, 274, 397
  normative, 2, 6
  philosophical, 1–3, 5–6, 9
  yes/no, 129–30

race, 183–99
  beliefs and, 187–88
  biologically based theory of, 193, 198
  existence of, 183, 187
  genetic diversity and, 185–87
  as illusion, 183–84, 197
  multiracial populations, 196
  nonracialist meanings of, 187–93
  one drop of blood rule and, 185, 194, 199n4
  skin color and, 188, 189f
  as social construction, 190–92, 196
racial essences, 184, 194
racialism, 184–87, 193, 194, 196
racism, 184, 194, 196, 285
radical libertarianism, 174, 176–79, *177*
radioactive decay, 167, 174–75
random events. *See* chance events
rationalism, 102, 120
rationally uninformed voters, 373, 380
rational thought, 204–5
reading philosophy, 387–89
realism
  definition of, 120
  direct, 116–17, 118f
  indirect, 102–6, 103f, 109–10, 116–17, 118f, 123n4
reality, existence in, 50–53
real memories, 250–52, 263
reasonable inferences, 135
reasonableness of induction and, 136
reasoning
  abstract, 102
  a priori/a posteriori, 101, 102
  circular, 136, 150–51
  critical, 397

GRE scores and, 399
Hume on, 125, 135
mistakes in, 94
scientific, 125, 131, 138
reasons for beliefs, 31–32, 56
reductio ad absurdum, 49, 51–52, 57
reflexive relation, 240, 263
refraction, 107, 108
Reid, Thomas, 116, 143n15, 250, 255
reincarnation, 245
reliabilism, 154–56, 160, 163
religion. *See also specific religions*
  beliefs regarding, 31, 54, 55
  philosophy and, 3, 5
representative democracy, 369–72, 380–81
The Republic (Plato), 371
respect, 63, 275, 332, 334, 378–80, 382
responsibility
  determinism and, 168–70
  moral, 168, 175, 176, 257
  for suffering, 71
resurrection, 242–44
right and wrong. *See also* ethics; morality
  act utilitarianism on, 320
  cultural relativism and, 276–79
  determination of, 274, 275
  normative questions of, 2
  objective truths of, 273
Robbins, Lionel, 290
robots, 201–3, 207–8, 211–12, 219, 222, 224
Rorty, Richard, 94, 100n7
Rosenberg, Noah, 192
rule consequentialism, 326–27, 336
rule utilitarianism, 327–28, 336
Russell, Bertrand, 4, 7n3, 40, 60, 116
Ryle, Gilbert, 209

Sachs, Jeffrey, 346, 364n1, 364n10
Sacks, Oliver, 85
sacrifice, 291, 343–47, 362
Salmon, Wesley, 136

Sanger, Larry, 397, *397*
Sartre, Jean-Paul, 296, 300–304, 309
Satan, 71
sceptical theism. *See* skeptical theism scepticism. *See* skepticism
science
  applied, 133–34
  ethics compared to, 269
  Locke and, 106–7
  neuroscience, 170, 215, 217–18, 224
  philosophy and, 5–6, 152
  probability judgments in, 134
  trial and error in, 133
scientific libertarianism, 174–76, 178
scientific methodology, 5–6, 125, 130–31
scientific reasoning, 125, 131, 138
scientific theories
  abduction and, 17
  Descartes and, 83, 102
  truth of, 157
seat of consciousness, 243, 245, 263
secondary qualities, 108–9, 114, 119–21
self-deception, 302–3
self-defense, 358
self-interest, 285, 317
semantic claims, 211, 215
Sen, Amartya, 73, 374, 375, 386n12
senses
  certainty and, 84–85
  deception through, 84, 87, 92, 105
  empirical evidence and, 101
  mathematics and, 101
  smell and taste, 113
Seton, Elizabeth Ann, 75
sexuality
  ethics of, 276–78, 291–92
  homosexuality, 321–22
Shakespeare, William, 97
shape, as property of ideas, 114
Shoemaker, Sydney, 247
Silbersweig, David, 397
simple subjectivism, 280–84, 288

Singer, Peter, 322, 343–47, *345*, 360, 362
Singer's Principle, 346
size, as property of ideas, 113
skeptical theism, 74–76, 78
skepticism
  beliefs and, 157
  definition of, 96, 160–61
  of Descartes, 87
  of Hume, 45, 130, 131
  moral, 270, 273, 274, 278, 285, 288
Skinner, B. F., 236n7
sky, color of, 108, 124n10
slavery, 272, 285, 321, 332–34, 341
smallpox eradication program, 342
smell, sense of, 113
s-memories, 252, 253, 255, 263
socially constructed groups, 190–92, 194, 196
Socrates, *xx*, 3, 44
soft determinism, 181n2
solidity, 113, 114
sortition, 369, 381, 383
soul, defined, 243, 264
soul theory of personal identity, 243–47
speaker relativism, 279–80, 288–89
special obligations, 323, 336
speech, freedom of, 370
Spencer, Quayshawn, 192–93, 198
Star Trek television series, 255
Star Wars films, 201, 211
Strawson, Peter, 134–36
strong social constructionism, 191–92, 194
subjectivism, 280–84, 288
substance, defined, 230
substance dualism, 205, 230
suffering. *See also* pain
  act utilitarianism and, 322, 324, 325
  of animals, 322, 347–49, 351, 352
  free will and, 72–73
  justification of, 71–73, 78
  pleasure from, 298–99
  prevention of, 343, 344, 362
  problem of evil and, 68, 71–73

skeptical theists on, 74
slavery and, 321
sufficient conditions, 261, 262, 264
Summa Theologica (Aquinas), 61n2
super-heavy stone puzzle, 64–65
superstition, 147–48
surface texture, 108
symmetric relation, 240, 264

taste, sense of, 113
teleological argument. *See* design argument
telescopes, 132, 152
teletransporter experiment, 255–57, 258*f*, 261
texture of surfaces, 108
theism. *See also* existence of God
  Berkeley and, 116
  claims of, 33, 58
  contradictions of, 64, 65
  definition of, 33, 57, 76
  Descartes and, 90–93
  evidential arguments for, 32
  on history of the universe, 33–34
  logical puzzles for, 64–65
  monotheism, 44, 70
  pragmatic case for, 32, 53–55
  revisionary versions of, 23
  skeptical, 74–76, 78
theodicy, 71–73, 77
Theodicy (Leibniz), 66, 67
thesis statements, 389
things, defined, 332
thinking
  cogito, ergo sum, 87, 157
  definition of, 96
  examples of, 88
  human thought processes, 166–67
  rational, 204–5
  wishful, 54
Thomson, Judith Jarvis, 358–59
thought experiments
  brain-in-the-vat, 153–54, 162
  cobbler and prince, 248
  on democracy, 367–69
  evil demon, 86–88, 91–92, 95, 96, 98
  inverted color spectrum, 208

teletransporter malfunction, 256–57, 258*f*
world of only babies, 191–92
Three Dialogues between Hylas and Philonous (Berkeley), 121
tolerance, 276, 277
tough projects, 299, 305
transcendental self, 176–77
transitive relation, 240, 253, 264
Treblinka (Nazi death camp), 239–40, 244
trial and error, 133
truth
  beliefs and, 154–59
  clear and distinct perception and, 89
  morality and, 285
  necessary, 127–29, 140
  objective, 270–73, 285
  propositional knowledge and, 146–48
  of scientific theories, 157
Tur, Katy, 397, *397*
2001: A Space Odyssey (film), 126
tyranny of the majority, 370, 381

unconsciousness, 94, 213, 331, 353, 355–56, 358
United Kingdom
  Bengal famine and (1943), 374
  dissatisfaction with democracy, 368*f*
  exit from European Union, 369
  uninformed voters in, 372
United Nations Human Development Index, 376
United States
  2008 presidential election, 386n6
  disposable income in, 343
  dissatisfaction with democracy, 368*f*, 385n1
  Federal Reserve system, 378
  meat industry in, 348–49
  multiracial population in, 196
  uninformed voters in, 373
universalization test, 328–31, 336, 338
universal moral rules, 329, 330

universe
  atheists on history of, 33–34, 38–39
  atomist views of, 37, 38
  best possible, 66, 66–67, 75
  Big Bang theory, 38, 39
  cosmology and, 56, 61n3
  determinism and, 166, 169
  theists on history of, 33–34
unmoved movers, 38
utilitarianism. *See* act utilitarianism; rule utilitarianism
utilities, defined, 320, 336
Utopia argument, 52–53

vaccinations, 71, 74
validity, deductive, 14–16, 29
value
  direct vs. indirect, 296–97, 310
  of free will, 72
  hedonist theory of, 320
  Sartre on, 301–4

vegetarians, 1, 2, 269, 279–80, 283, 347–52, 362
verificationism, 209–11, 230
vision
  Anton-Babinski syndrome and, 98
  of bees, 105, 106*f*
  of birds, 106
  blind spots and, 48, 62n9
  certainty and, 84–85
  color perception and, 106, 112
  eye anatomy and, 41, 42*f*, 48
Voltaire, 66, 67, 72, 75–76, 80n6
voting, 9–10, 19–22, 368–79, 386n6

Wachowski, Lilly and Lana, 87
water, color of, 124n10
Watson, J. B., 236n7
Wavell, Archibald, 374
wealth, 193, 329, 343–46, *345*, 382
weather prediction, 23, 83
Wikipedia, 389

will, free. *See* free will
will of God, 75, 78, 275
wisdom of crowds, 377, 381
wishful thinking, 54
Wolf, Susan, 296, 305–10, *306*
World Health Organization, 342
worthwhile activities, 306–12
writing philosophy papers, 389–94
wrongdoing. *See also* right and wrong
  belief with insufficient evidence and, 54–55
  free will and, 73, 78
  by God, 65
  moral evil and, 80n10
  suffering and, 71

Xenophon, 44

yes/no questions, 129–30

Zagzebski, Linda, 273
zombies, 225–27, 230
Zoroastrianism, 71